Case Studies in
Interdisciplinary
Research

Case Studies in
Interdisciplinary Research

Allen F. Repko
The University of Texas at Arlington

William H. Newell
Miami University of Ohio

Rick Szostak
University of Alberta

Los Angeles | London | New Delhi
Singapore | Washington DC

For information:

SAGE Publications, Inc.
2455 Teller Road
Thousand Oaks,
    California 91320
E-mail: order@sagepub.com

SAGE Publications India Pvt. Ltd.
B 1/I 1 Mohan Cooperative
    Industrial Area
Mathura Road, New Delhi 110 044
India

SAGE Publications Ltd.
1 Oliver's Yard
55 City Road
London EC1Y 1SP
United Kingdom

SAGE Publications
    Asia-Pacific Pte. Ltd.
33 Pekin Street #02-01
Far East Square
Singapore 048763

Printed in the United States of America

Library of Congress Cataloging-in-Publication Data

Case studies in interdisciplinary research / Editors: Allen F. Repko, William H. Newell, Rick Szostak.
        p. cm.
Includes bibliographical references and index.
ISBN 978-1-4129-8248-1 (pbk.)

    1. Interdisciplinary research—Case studies. I. Repko, Allen F. II. Newell, William H. III. Szostak, Rick, 1959-

Q180.55.I48C37 2012
001.4—dc22   2010035403

This book is printed on acid-free paper.

11   12   13   14   15   10   9   8   7   6   5   4   3   2   1

Acquisitions Editor:	Vicki Knight
Associate Editor:	Lauren Habib
Editorial Assistant:	Kalie Koscielak
Production Editor:	Catherine M. Chilton
Copy Editor:	Diana Breti
Typesetter:	C&M Digitals (P) Ltd.
Proofreader:	Eleni Georgiou
Indexer:	Molly Hall
Cover Designer:	Candice Harman
Permissions:	Adele Hutchinson

Brief Contents _____

Detailed Contents_____

Preface _____

As disciplines have generated increased understanding over the last century, it has become widely recognized that the complex problems facing humanity require new approaches for organizing, synthesizing, and applying this knowledge. Developing a comprehensive understanding of complex societal problems, and especially resolving them, requires interdisciplinary thinking and research.

The recent publication of several books on interdisciplinary research, including Julie Thompson Klein's (1990) *Interdisciplinarity: History, Theory, and Practice* and (2010) *Creating Interdisciplinary Campus Cultures: A Model for Strength and Sustainability;* William H. Newell's (Ed.) (1998) *Interdisciplinarity: Essays From the Literature;* Peter Weingart and Nico Stehr's (Eds.) (2000) *Practicing Interdisciplinarity;* Carol S. Palmer's (2001) *Work at the Boundaries of Science;* Rick Szostak's (2004) *Classifying Science: Phenomena, Data, Theory, Method, Practice;* The National Academies' (2005) *Facilitating Interdisciplinary Research;* Tress et al.'s (2005) *From Landscape Research to Landscape Planning: Aspects of Integration, Education, and Application;* Sharon J. Derry, Christian D. Schunn, and Morton Ann Gernsbacher's (Eds.) (2005) *Interdisciplinary Collaboration: An Emerging Cognitive Science;* John Atkinson and Malcolm Crowe's (Eds.) (2006) *Interdisciplinary Research: Diverse Approaches in Science, Technology, Health, and Society;* Allen Repko's (2008) *Interdisciplinary Research: Process and Theory;* and Rick Szostak's (2009) *The Causes of Economic Growth: Interdisciplinary Perspectives,* shows that the growing and diverse field of interdisciplinary studies has come of age. These works offer a variety of insights into interdisciplinary research, share a common conception of interdisciplinarity, and appreciate that integration is the best way to address complex problems.

In particular, Repko's (2008) book stresses the need for students and scholars alike to be self-consciously interdisciplinary and approach the research process in a way that is explicitly interdisciplinary. The book invites students and academics to think about, and hopefully practice, interdisciplinarity in a more systematic and methodologically self-conscious way. It also demonstrates how to use the disciplines in interdisciplinary work, critically evaluate disciplinary insights, create common ground among conflicting insights, perform integration, and produce *a more comprehensive and nuanced*

CASE STUDIES IN INTERDISCIPLINARY RESEARCH

understanding of a problem. Now that an integrated model of the interdisciplinary research process exists, it needs to be applied to a variety of complex problems in language that is comprehensible to students and non-specialists.

The purpose of this book is to apply the model of the interdisciplinary research process that Repko (2008) delineates to a variety of research questions appropriate to interdisciplinary inquiry. Producing interdisciplinary understandings of these questions calls for drawing on insights from multiple disciplines in the natural sciences, the social sciences, the humanities, some applied disciplines such as law, and interdisciplinary fields such as American studies and cultural analysis. Each writer creatively applies the model of the research process as appropriate to the problem at hand and the disciplines involved. The strategy of this book differs from the publications listed above in at least four ways: (1) the contributors, to varying degrees, are explicitly interdisciplinary and comprehensive in their approaches; (2) they adhere, to varying degrees, to the notion of an overall interdisciplinary research process that subsumes the research method(s) of their respective disciplinary orientations; (3) their reflections on and critiques of the model yield new insights that advance our understanding of interdisciplinary research in general; and (4) they exemplify the defining qualities that characterize high quality interdisciplinary work. These case studies thus serve (1) to establish the feasibility of applying the interdisciplinary research process, (2) to show by example how the theory that undergirds the field informs the interdisciplinary research process, (3) to demonstrate how this process draws on the disciplines relevant to the problem or focus question, (4) to distinguish this research process from disciplinary methods, (5) to show how to integrate scholarly insights into a complex problem, and (6) to show how to produce an interdisciplinary understanding of a problem and express this new understanding in ways that are meaningful, practical, and purposeful.

Audience

The primary audience for this book is students and faculty at colleges and universities in the U.S., Canada, Europe, and elsewhere that offer courses and programs that are interdisciplinary. These courses and programs typically require advanced undergraduate and graduate students to conduct research on a broad range of problems, topics, and issues involving two or more disciplines. The book will help students become familiar with the interdisciplinary research process and how to apply it to a wide range of problems. This book can be used as a supplement to Repko (2008). Because the case studies are self-contained, the book can be used on its own, as well. Given the range of case studies in this book, it should be of interest to any course or program with an interdisciplinary focus.

Both students and faculty can benefit from it in several ways. A major problem that instructors experience in teaching upper level undergraduate and graduate interdisciplinary courses is not being able to show students examples of professional integrative work that are explicitly interdisciplinary. The Repko (2008) book contains many examples of interdisciplinary research, but these are, of necessity, discussed only briefly. Students need to consult detailed examples of professional work that is explicitly and self-consciously interdisciplinary and that focuses on topics that span the natural sciences, the social sciences, the humanities, and the applied fields. By reading and analyzing article-length integrative essays on problems that are similar to the course problem, topic, or theme, students will be able to see how professional interdisciplinarians approach similar problems, use the steps in the research model, and apply particular best practice strategies or techniques.

Second, students and instructors will appreciate that these case studies demonstrate a shared conception of interdisciplinarity that reflects an emerging and broad-based consensus. Critics of interdisciplinary studies still frequently charge that it has no widely accepted definition. One critic writing in the *Chronicle of Higher Education* complains, for example, that interdisciplinarity has become "so fuzzy that a university's commitment to it is close to meaningless" (Wasserstrom, 2006, p. B5). For many in the Academy, interdisciplinarity is whatever someone says it is. However, a broad-based consensus has emerged about what interdisciplinary studies is. This consensus is reflected in no less than four definitions advanced by prominent institutions and scholars. The National Academy of Sciences, National Academy of Engineering, and the Institute of Medicine (National Academies) in *Facilitating Interdisciplinary Research* (2005) defines interdisciplinary research as

> a mode of research by teams or individuals that integrates information, data, techniques, tools, perspectives, concepts, and/or theories from two or more disciplines or bodies of specialized knowledge to advance fundamental understanding or to solve problems whose solutions are beyond the scope of a single discipline or area of research practice. (p. 26)

Research, says the National Academies (2005), "is truly interdisciplinary when it is not just pasting two disciplines together to create one product but rather an integration or synthesis of ideas and methods" (p. 27).

A second definition is offered by Rhoten, Boix-Mansilla, Chun, and Klein (2006). They define interdisciplinary education as

> a mode of curriculum design and instruction in which individual faculty or teams identify, evaluate, and integrate information, data, techniques, tools, perspectives, concepts, or theories from two or more disciplines or bodies of knowledge to advance students' capacity to understand issues, address problems, and create new approaches and solutions that extend beyond the scope of a single discipline or area of instruction. (p. 3)

A third definition is put forth by Veronica Boix-Mansilla (2005). She is particularly concerned with the product of interdisciplinary work: the "interdisciplinary understanding." Interdisciplinarity, she says, is

> the capacity to integrate knowledge and modes of thinking drawn from two or more disciplines to produce a *cognitive advancement* [emphasis added]—for example, explaining a phenomenon, solving a problem, creating a product, or raising a new question—in ways that would have been unlikely through single disciplinary means. (p. 16)

More recently, the National Science Foundation (2009) has stated its own definition of interdisciplinarity, which synthesizes these definitions:

> A *mode* [emphasis added] of research by teams or individuals that *integrates* [emphasis added] information, data, techniques, tools, perspectives, concepts, and/or theories from two or more disciplines or bodies of specialized knowledge to advance fundamental understanding or to solve problems whose solutions are beyond the scope of a single discipline or area of research practice.

These definitions share the following core features:

- Interdisciplinary research has a particular substantive focus.
- The focus of interdisciplinary research extends beyond a single disciplinary perspective.
- A distinctive characteristic of interdisciplinary research is that it focuses on a problem or question that is complex.
- Interdisciplinary research is characterized by an identifiable process or mode of inquiry.
- Interdisciplinary research draws explicitly on the disciplines.
- The disciplines provide insights into the specific substantive focus of interdisciplinary research.
- Interdisciplinary research involves integration.
- The objective of integration is pragmatic: to produce a cognitive advancement in the form of a new understanding, a new product, or a new meaning (Note: The term *meaning* is important in the humanities, where it is often equated with the intent of the author or artist [Bal, 2002, p. 27]).

These core features are reflected in the case studies in this book. Developing a consistent conception of what interdisciplinarity is, says Newell (2007), will enable faculty and students "to show the ways in which they are rigorously following through on the implications of that definition" (p. 2).

Third, students and instructors will find the many examples of *how* integration is achieved particularly helpful. The feasibility of integration is the focus of debate between generalist interdisciplinarians and integrationist interdisciplinarians. Generalist interdisciplinarians understand interdisciplinarity loosely to mean "any form of dialog or interaction between two or more disciplines" while minimizing, obscuring, or rejecting altogether the role of integration (Moran, 2002, p. 16). Integrationist interdisciplinarians, on the other hand, stress the priority of integration and are concerned with developing a distinctively interdisciplinary theory-based research process and describing how it operates (Newell, 2007, p. 245; Vess & Linkon, 2002, p. 89). Integrationists point to a growing body of literature that explicitly connects integration with interdisciplinary research. The case studies in this book reflect and operationalize the integrationist understanding. They show how integration both can and should lie at the heart of interdisciplinary analysis.

Fourth, these case studies demonstrate best interdisciplinary research practice across the Academy. Although the interdisciplinary research process can be applied to any field, the best strategies and the form of the final interdisciplinary understanding tend to vary across the natural sciences, social sciences, humanities, and applied fields. Natural scientists may seek a comprehensive model, humanists an insightful metaphor, and applied scholars a useful technology or public policy. The interdisciplinary research process and these exemplary applications of it serve to establish standards by which quality interdisciplinary analysis (by scholars or students) may be distinguished from superficial interdisciplinarity. As Szostak (2007) comments, "Any scholar who wishes to teach and/or do research in an interdisciplinary manner should have some interest and expertise regarding . . . how interdisciplinary research might best be performed" (p. 4). These case studies employ diverse, flexible, and critical approaches to applying the research model while adhering to best practices that continue to evolve.

Finally, these case studies make the argument that interdisciplinarity is, in fact, contributing something distinctive and valuable to the Academy and to society at large. Developing a distinctive research process grounded in theory and applying it to a wide range of topics that span the sciences and the humanities will help to solidify the field in the Academy. Though the case studies draw upon disciplinary methods and insights, they clearly distinguish these from the interdisciplinary research process, showing that it is as rigorous as disciplinary methodologies. Because the field of interdisciplinary studies has only just reached the point at which there is sufficient potential for scholarly consensus on the principles of the field, these case studies serve simultaneously to establish the feasibility of the interdisciplinary research process and provide guidance on how this is best applied.

The Research Model

The case studies in this book are each self-contained. That is, they each explain how they draw upon the interdisciplinary research process as delineated in Repko (2008) and apply the model in creative ways. The steps in the process are as follows:

- State the problem or focus question (Step 1)
- Justify using an interdisciplinary approach (Step 2)
- Identify relevant disciplines (Step 3)
- Conduct the literature search (Step 4)
- Develop adequacy in each relevant discipline (Step 5)
- Analyze the problem and evaluate each insight into it (Step 6)
- Identify conflicts between insights and their sources (Step 7)
- Create or discover common ground (Step 8)
- Integrate insights (Step 9)
- Produce an interdisciplinary understanding and test it (Step 10)

Though the model may appear linear, it is not. The order in which some steps are taken will vary depending on the character of the problem; some steps may be compressed. For most steps, the model calls for revisiting earlier steps and making appropriate revisions. Readers are encouraged to consult Repko (2008) for a detailed discussion of the steps in the research process and the recommended guidelines or strategies for performing each of them. The authors that follow all explain which of these (or which new ones) they are applying.

Outline of Chapters

This book is divided into three parts. Part I raises some broad questions regarding the very possibility of identifying superior strategies for performing interdisciplinary work. Part II presents case studies that focus primarily on how to draw on disciplinary insights and prepare for integration. Part III presents case studies that focus primarily on how to perform integration, revisits the questions posed in Part I, and discusses the centrality of integration.

Part I: Introduction

This part of the book asks whether there is a best way of doing interdisciplinary research and examines the evidential basis for arguments regarding process. It contains Chapter 1.

Chapter 1: The Interdisciplinary Research Process

Chapter 1 by Szostak addresses two broad questions. First, "Is there a best way of doing interdisciplinary research?" Some interdisciplinarians might worry that any such process must limit their freedom to pursue their curiosity. It is noted, though, that the interdisciplinary research process modeled and pursued here guides interdisciplinarians to consider any disciplinary insight, theory, method, or phenomenon of study that might be relevant to their research question. Moreover, the process itself is both flexible and iterative:

Researchers are guided to revisit earlier steps as their research proceeds and to choose from a broad (and growing) set of strategies for performing each step. The second question is "What would an interdisciplinary research process look like?" Explorations of both these questions provide the rationale for the case studies in this book and serve to illustrate the broad consensus that has emerged for the sort of research process advocated in Repko (2008).

Part II: Drawing on Disciplinary Insights

The primary focus of the case studies in Chapters 2 to 4 is to provide guidance on how to perform the earlier steps of the interdisciplinary research process.

Chapter 2: Jewish Marriage as an Expression of Israel's Conflicted Identity

In Chapter 2, Tayler explores the issue of marriage laws in Israel. These laws reflect the inherent conflict between the democratic and Jewish nature of Israel. There is no civil marriage in Israel, and Jewish marriage is entirely the province of orthodox rabbis. Non-orthodox Jews or people pursuing cross-religious marriages must therefore travel elsewhere to marry. Tayler carefully examines the conflicts that exist among various disciplinary analyses of marriage law in Israel. She concludes that a move toward civil marriage can be achieved and would strengthen the democratic character of the state while also serving the goal of respecting and strengthening Israel's unique cultural heritage. She argues that a similar integration across democratic and Jewish perspectives is possible beyond the particular issue of marriage.

Chapter 3: The Metropolitan Problem in Interdisciplinary Perspective

Connor examines the process of metropolitanization in 20th century America. The vast majority of Americans moved to cities and suburbs during that century. Connor first shows that the terms "city" and "suburb" have conflicting meanings across disciplines. He could hone his research question only as he came to appreciate the conflicts among disciplinary perspectives—a good example of the iterative nature of the research process. Connor stresses the strategies of theory extension and organization and shows how these can be powerfully applied in tandem. The inequality instantiated in modern urban landscapes reflects a complex historical process in which socially powerful groups were able to forge both institutions and ideas that benefitted them. He makes the much more provocative claim that theory shaped reality and that public choice theories not only justified but drove the process. He writes, "Public choice ideas have, in fact, been more important as shapers of public life than descriptors of it." Fully understanding this complex phenomenon requires that interdisciplinarians examine the feedback loop from theory to practice. Connor shows in detail how the process of identifying and superseding conflicts in insights is aided by appreciating how disciplinary perspectives have evolved over time. He illustrates how disciplinary theories tend to be investigated by methods that are complementary and how interdisciplinarians are guided to prefer methods that are not biased in favor of a particular disciplinary perspective.

Chapter 4: Mektoub: *When Art Meets History, Philosophy, and Linguistics*

Bal shows how interdisciplinary analysis is critical to the understanding of particular works of art. Importantly, she argues that the particular work will dictate the disciplines that should be consulted. *Mektoub*, the work addressed here, is grounded in the history of the Algerian war for independence. The essay explores psychological, sociological, and linguistic issues and integrates several different art forms and literary references. Bal shows how each of the relevant disciplines enriches our understanding of the work. In the first section of her chapter, Bal reflects on how the interdisciplinary research process can be applied in the humanities and how interdisciplinarians must let the work guide them to relevant disciplinary insights. She does not reflect as formally as other authors on how particular steps should be performed. Yet, the reader should readily appreciate how disciplinary insights are identified, conflicts explored, and integration achieved.

Part III: Approaches to Integration

The primary focus of the case studies in Chapters 5 to 10 is to show various ways integration can be achieved.

Chapter 5: *Integrating Theory-Based Insights on the Causes of Suicide Terrorism*

Repko applies the integrated model to the problem of the causes of suicide terrorism. He examines the theory-based insights into the problem by leading disciplinary experts from a variety of disciplinary orientations, as called for by the early steps of the research process. He finds that these approaches typically focus on only one or two possible causal factors. After examining these theory-based understandings and identifying the sources of conflict between these insights, he creates common ground between them, integrates these theoretical explanations, and produces a more inclusive and nuanced understanding of the problem than prevailing disciplinary analyses provide. Insights into the interdisciplinary research process are presented along the way.

Chapter 6: An Interdisciplinary Analysis of the Causes of Economic Growth

In this case study, Szostak reviews how different disciplines shed light on the question of why some countries experience more rapid growth than others. There is, of course, no simple answer to this question. Szostak analyzes different potential causes of growth in turn, while not losing sight of their interactions. Szostak thus stresses the importance for interdisciplinarians of mapping the various causal interactions that may be relevant to a particular interdisciplinary research question. One policy implication that flows fairly directly from this mapping exercise is that different causal factors will be of greatest importance in different times and places: Some countries may need better technology, while in others the primary need is better institutions. For several causal factors, Szostak shows how integrating insights from different disciplines leads to a more comprehensive and nuanced understanding. With respect to institutions, for example, the emphasis of sociologists on power relations provides a useful complement to the economists' stress on rational calculation in appreciating why some countries have more effective institutions than others.

Chapter 7: Why We Talk: An Interdisciplinary Approach to the Evolutionary Origin of Language

How did humans first develop the ability to speak? Why were we the only species to develop this ability? Why is human language so complex? Van der Lecq notes that this set of interconnected questions has already been explored in a more narrow interdisciplinary fashion. She reminds us that it is often useful to integrate partial interdisciplinary understandings into a more comprehensive interdisciplinary understanding. That is, interdisciplinary research—like disciplinary research—is an ongoing process in which one interdisciplinarian can build on the research of others. The interdisciplinary research process is as useful here as when directly integrating disciplinary insights. Van der Lecq finds that language emerged in humans primarily because human groups were too large to be able to achieve social cohesion through the alternative process of grooming. Yet, language does more than just establish social bonds; it simultaneously communicates meaning, and successful communication bestows prestige on the speaker. Language co-evolved with culture: Human language became more complex as human groups became more complex. Complexity theory shows how the complex form of modern language reflects this evolutionary process: Rules of grammar emerged as humans moved beyond one-word utterances. Van der Lecq notes that the word *evolution* is used both in a narrow sense of "evolution by natural selection" and in a broader sense of "any evolutionary process." She urges interdisciplinarians to recognize this common source of semantic confusion, and she notes that it calls for a different integrative strategy than simple redefinition.

Chapter 8: Understanding Human Action: Integrating Meanings, Mechanisms, Causes, and Contexts

How do humans understand the actions of others? Keestra breaks this important and complex process into three parts and then shows how each can, in turn, be understood as a set of components and operations. He thus urges interdisciplinarians to pursue a "mechanism-based explanation" of complex processes that nevertheless exhibit some regularity. Such an explanation will involve mapping the components (things in the world) and the operations that they perform (and thus the influences they exert on each other). He notes that mechanistic explanations are common in natural science and are increasingly advocated in the social sciences and the humanities. In such an explanation, the mechanism itself serves as common ground. The interdisciplinarian needs to first integrate competing insights regarding the components and operations that should be included in the mechanism; it may also be necessary to address competing insights regarding particular components or operations. In the particular case of human action understanding, the key components of the mechanism reside within the human brain. Keestra shows that insights from cognitive science are as critical to achieving a more comprehensive understanding of this problem as are insights from the social sciences and the humanities.

Chapter 9: Integrative Theory in Criminology Applied to the Complex Social Problem of School Violence

In this chapter, Henry and Bracy address the problem of school violence. They note that in recent decades, no fewer than 13 different disciplines or interdisciplinary fields have addressed the issue of crime prevention. Some criminologists have recognized the inadequacy of single-discipline perspectives in explaining violent criminal behavior and have grappled with how best to integrate different disciplinary insights in order to achieve superior public policies. With respect to school violence itself, Henry and Bracy urge an approach that embraces individual, institutional, and cultural variables. They also note that one sort of crime can encourage other sorts, and thus it is problematic to study them independently. School violence can only be understood within a very complex web of interactions; rare events such as rampage shootings, though perhaps unpredictable at a local level, reflect certain unfortunate combinations of causal interactions. Students of the interdisciplinary research process will benefit enormously from this review of debates within criminology regarding integration and, particularly, the strengths and weaknesses of different integrative strategies. Henry and Bracy show how these strategies, supplemented by insights from a variety of disciplines, can be tailored to the specific problem of school violence and integrated to provide a comprehensive understanding and then concrete policy recommendations.

Chapter 10: Research Integration: A Comparative Knowledge Base

Klein stresses the centrality of integration to the interdisciplinary research process. She traces the historical evolution of the concept of integration and the increasing recognition of its importance. She shows how the interdisciplinary research process as outlined by Repko (2008) draws upon and reinforces insights of other scholars regarding interdisciplinary research. Klein draws four main lessons for interdisciplinary research. First, the best strategies for performing the various steps in the interdisciplinary research process will vary across research questions. The case studies in this volume provide detailed support for this insight. Second, whether pursuing individual or team research, interdisciplinarians are guided to articulate carefully a research question and to appreciate relevant terminology before attempting integration. Third, they should be willing to revisit earlier steps in their research while performing later steps. Fourth, they must take care to communicate the results of interdisciplinary research to target audiences in a manner audiences can both appreciate and comprehend.

Conclusion

In the conclusion, Newell summarizes the lessons learned in this book. The case studies illustrate both the feasibility and desirability of the interdisciplinary research process across the Academy. Moreover, they show how that process supports cumulative scholarship: The case studies often build upon previous interdisciplinary scholarship and set the stage for further integrative efforts. Newell is gratified by the degree to which the case studies also clarify and extend the process outlined by Repko (2008). The bulk of the Conclusion is devoted to reviewing, step by step, new key insights into how best to perform interdisciplinary research that are generated by these case studies. Yet, these case studies also alert us to challenges in the performance of interdisciplinary research and thus invite further scholarship regarding the interdisciplinary research process.

Professor Allen F. Repko, PhD
Former Director
Interdisciplinary Studies Program
School of Urban and Public Affairs
University of Texas at Arlington

Professor Rick Szostak, PhD
Department of Economics
University of Alberta

Professor William H. Newell, PhD
Western College Program
Miami University

References

Bal, M. (2002). *Traveling concepts in the humanities: A rough guide.* Buffalo, NY: The University of Toronto Press.

Boix-Mansilla, V. (2005, January/February). Assessing student work at disciplinary crossroads. *Change, 37,* 14–21.

Moran, J. (2002). *Interdisciplinarity.* New York: Routledge.

National Academies of Sciences, National Academy of Engineering, & Institute of Medicine. (2005). *Facilitating interdisciplinary research.* Washington, DC: National Academies Press.

Newell, W. H. (2007, December). Six arguments for agreeing on a definition of interdisciplinary studies. *AIS Newsletter, 29*(4), 1–4.

Repko, A. (2008). *Interdisciplinary research: Process and theory.* Thousand Oaks, CA: Sage.

Rhoten, D., Boix-Mansilla, V., Chun, M., & Klein, J. (2006). *Interdisciplinary education at liberal arts institutions.* Teagle Foundation White Paper. Retrieved from http://www.teaglefoundation.org/learning/pdf/2006_ssrc_whitepaper.pdf

Szostak, R. (2007, October). How and why to teach interdisciplinary research practice. *Journal of Research Practice, 3*(2), Article M17.

Vess, D., & Linkon, S. (2002). Navigating the interdisciplinary archipelago: The scholarship of interdisciplinary teaching and learning. In M. Taylor Huber & S. P. Morreale (Eds.), *Disciplinary styles in the scholarship of teaching and learning: Exploring common ground* (pp. 87–106). Washington, DC: American Association for Higher Education and the Carnegie Foundation for the Advancement of Teaching.

Wasserstrom, J. N. (2006, January 20). Expanding on the I-word. *The Chronicle of Higher Education,* B5.

Acknowledgments _____

T he editors would foremost like to thank each of the authors for the care and patience with which they wrote their chapters. The editors had a very clear vision of what this book should look like and were pleased that the authors proved willing to shape their ideas in a way that allowed a truly coherent book to emerge. The editors also thank each author for the insights provided not only into their topics but also into the interdisciplinary research process.

The editors are particularly indebted to Vicki Knight, the Senior Acquisitions Editor, Research Methods, Statistics, and Evaluation at Sage, for her support of this project. Lauren Habib, Associate Editor, and the editorial staff at Sage have been a pleasure to work with throughout. They have provided support and sound advice from the moment we first approached them with the proposal for this book. We hope that Sage will continue to build upon its expertise in envisioning and marketing books about interdisciplinarity. We would also like to thank Sage's outside reviewers who read and commented on the initial proposal and on drafts of the various chapters: Angela Hunter, University of Arkansas at Little Rock; Steven McAlpine, University of Maryland, Baltimore County; Daniel J. Klenow, North Dakota State University; and Richard Castellana, Fairleigh Dickinson University.

The editors would also like to thank the many wonderful scholars they have interacted with over the years within the Association for Integrative Studies. It is not possible to list all the names. It is important, nevertheless, to emphasize that this book and the core ideas that shape it had their genesis in the rich intellectual landscape that is the AIS.

Each editor also extends thanks of a more personal nature. Allen Repko would like to thank his wife, Doris, for her inspiration and unflagging support. He would also like to thank Rick and Bill for their vision, enthusiasm, and hard work throughout the project. Rick Szostak would like to thank his children, Mireille, Julien, and Theo, for enriching his life with their life-affirming spirit. And he would like to thank Jennifer, his partner, for making his life much more wonderful than he had imagined was possible. Bill

Newell would like to thank his wife, Susan, for her remarkable patience while he focused on this volume and the seniors in the Western College Program for revealing to him through their capstone projects many of the insights into interdisciplinary process that have enriched his understanding and graced his subsequent contributions to the professional literature on interdisciplinarity.

About the Editors _____

Allen F. Repko is the former Director of the Interdisciplinary Studies Program, School of Urban and Public Affairs, University of Texas at Arlington, where he developed and taught the program's core curriculum. The program is one of the largest in the U.S. He has written extensively on all aspects of interdisciplinary studies and has twice served as co-editor of the interdisciplinary journal *Issues in Integrative Studies*. His research interests include strategies for conducting interdisciplinary research, administration, and program assessment. Though just "retired," he remains active writing, consulting, conducting workshops, and speaking at conferences. He is writing the second edition of *Interdisciplinary Research: Process and Theory* (2008), which is scheduled for release in 2011. He serves on the board of the Association for Integrative Studies (AIS). His e-mail address is allenrepko@att.net.

William H. Newell is Professor of Interdisciplinary Studies at Miami University, where he has been directing the two-semester 10-credit senior project workshop since 1995. He has edited two books, including the foundational *Interdisciplinarity: Essays from the Literature*, and two special issues of journals. He has published more than 30 articles and chapters on interdisciplinary studies, with seminal contributions to the theory and practice of interdisciplinarity recognized in his receipt of the Kenneth E. Boulding Award. Newell has served as consultant or external evaluator on interdisciplinary higher education more than 100 times. The founding president of the Association for Integrative Studies in 1979, he has served since 1983 first as its Secretary-Treasurer and then as Executive Director.

Rick Szostak is Professor of Economics (and Acting Director of the Science Technology and Society program) at the University of Alberta, where he has taught since earning his PhD from Northwestern University in 1985. He is the author of 9 books and 30 articles, all interdisciplinary in nature. Many of these publications address how to best perform interdisciplinary research, teaching, or administration. He created and teaches two courses about how to do interdisciplinary research. He also teaches courses on economic growth, economic history, and STS. During a term as Associate Dean, he created the Office of Interdisciplinary Studies (which administers eight programs and stand-alone courses about interdisciplinarity), the STS program, and an individualized major program. He has served on the Board of the Association for Integrative Studies for several years. His Web site is http://www.economics.ualberta.ca/faculty_rick_szostak.cfm

About the Contributors _

Mieke Bal, a cultural theorist and critic, is a Royal Netherlands Academy of Arts and Sciences (KNAW) professor. She is based at the Amsterdam School for Cultural Analysis (ASCA), University of Amsterdam. Her areas of interest range from biblical and classical antiquity to 17th-century and contemporary art and modern literature, feminism, and migratory culture. Her many books include *A Mieke Bal Reader* (2006), *Travelling Concepts in the Humanities* (2002), and *Narratology* (3rd ed., 2009). Mieke Bal is also a video artist; her internationally exhibited works include *Separations, State of Suspension, Becoming Vera,* and the installation *Nothing is Missing*. Her feature film, *Mère Folle*, a theoretical fiction about madness, premiered Fall, 2010. Occasionally she acts as an independent curator. Her Web site is www.miekebal.org.

Nicole L. Bracy is a research scientist and Adjunct Professor at San Diego State University. Her research interests include school policing, school disciplinary practices, and students' legal rights in schools. Her research has been published in *Youth and Society, Journal of Contemporary Criminal Justice,* and *Youth Violence and Juvenile Justice.* She is currently co-editing a book (with Muschert, Henry, and Peguero) titled *The Columbine Effect: Fear and the Expansion of School Antiviolence Policy.*

Michan Andrew Connor is an Assistant Professor of Interdisciplinary Studies in the School of Urban and Public Affairs at the University of Texas at Arlington. His research focuses on issues of race, political power, and the institutional and cultural politics of place in American metropolitan areas. Connor is particularly interested in connecting humanistic approaches to culture and institutional studies of politics to develop more integrated understanding of how laws, regulations, and institutions on the one hand and values, ideologies, and identities on the other mutually shape metropolitan regions. In his 2008 dissertation, *Creating Cities and Citizens* (Department of American Studies and Ethnicity, University of Southern California), Connor argued that changes to municipal boundaries in Los Angeles County during the 20th century have been an unrecognized influence on racial formation in the region because they affected both the spatial distribution of resources and the politicized definitions of community. His current work on Los Angeles County is focused on leveraging multiple disciplinary perspectives to develop a metropolitan framework that integrates the fields of urban and suburban history.

Stuart Henry is Professor and Director of the Interdisciplinary Studies Program at the University of Texas at Arlington. He was formerly Director of the School of Public Affairs at San Diego State University and served seven years as the Chair of the Department of Interdisciplinary Studies at Wayne State University. He is a member of the executive board of the Association for Integrative Studies and has served as co-chair of their annual conference (2003 and 2010). He is the author or editor of 25 books and more than 100 articles, mostly on criminology, social control, and deviant behavior. His most recent books are *Essential Criminology* (2010), *Social Deviance* (2009), and *The Politics of Interdisciplinary Studies: Interdisciplinary Transformation in Undergraduate American Higher Education* (co-edited with Tanya Augsburg, 2009).

Machiel Keestra studied philosophy and psychology in Amsterdam and Heidelberg. He was a staff member at the International School of Philosophy in the Netherlands and in the General Studies Department of the University of Amsterdam, where he now has a tenured assistant professorship at the Institute for Interdisciplinary Studies. He is involved with and teaches in the Interdisciplinary (Natural and Social Sciences) Bachelor, Brain and Cognitive Sciences Master, and Interdisciplinary Honours programs. His research ranges from the philosophy of tragedy to the cultural history of mathematics and currently focuses on the philosophy of the cognitive sciences, resulting in an interdisciplinary thesis: *Sculpting the Space of Actions: Mechanisms and Meanings, Causes and Contexts*. In addition, he is involved in building a European interdisciplinary network, and in 2008 he was appointed "International Liaison" by the Association for Integrative Studies.

Julie Thompson Klein is Professor of Humanities at Wayne State University and has held visiting posts in Japan, New Zealand, and Nepal. She received the Kenneth Boulding Award for outstanding scholarship on interdisciplinarity, the Ramamoorthy and Yeh Transdisciplinary Distinguished Achievement Award, and the Joseph Katz Award for Distinguished Contributions to the Practice and Discourse of General and Liberal Education. Her authored and edited books include *Interdisciplinarity: History, Theory, and Practice* (1990); *Interdisciplinary Studies Today* (1994); *Crossing Boundaries* (1996); *Mapping Interdisciplinary Studies* (1999); *Transdisciplinarity* (2001); *Interdisciplinary Education in K–12 and College* (2002); *Promoting Interdisciplinary Research* (2005); *Humanities, Culture, and Interdisciplinarity* (2005); and *Creating Interdisciplinary Campus Cultures* (2010). She is also co-editor of *The Oxford Handbook of Interdisciplinarity* (2010).

Marilyn R. Tayler is Professor in the Political Science and Law Department at Montclair State University. The holder of a JD and a PhD in Latin American Literature, she founded and coordinates the jurisprudence major, an interdisciplinary law in the liberal arts major. Her scholarship includes books, articles, and presentations in areas such as constructivist and interdisciplinary pedagogy, the right to a court interpreter, and existentialism in the work of several Latin American authors.

Ria van der Lecq is Associate Professor at Utrecht University, The Netherlands. Trained as a classical scholar at Leiden University, she researched and taught medieval philosophy and critical thinking in Utrecht. She has published various critical editions of the logical works of the 14th-century French philosopher John Buridan. In 2003, she set up a successful Liberal Arts and Sciences program with an interdisciplinary core curriculum in which undergraduates learn how to think integratively and how to do interdisciplinary research. Her areas of interest include interdisciplinary education, history of ancient and medieval philosophy (historical roots of the liberal arts), and critical thinking.

PART I

Introduction

1

The Interdisciplinary
Research Process

Rick Szostak

Introduction

This book provides case studies of the performance of interdisciplinary research. It is hoped that these case studies will prove instructive both to students and other scholars as they perform interdisciplinary research. This introductory chapter does not provide a detailed overview of these case studies: Brief descriptions of each chapter are provided in the Preface, and a discussion of lessons learned and questions raised is provided in the concluding chapter. Rather, this chapter engages some broad questions regarding the very possibility of identifying superior strategies for performing interdisciplinary research. In doing so, it provides the rationale for the case studies that follow: It is both feasible and desirable to identify interdisciplinary best practices.

Is there a best way of doing interdisciplinary research? If so, what is it? Do practicing interdisciplinarians across different fields seem to follow some set of universal practices or strategies? These broad questions drive this chapter. The first section addresses a set of epistemological and practical questions regarding the possibility and advisability of an "interdisciplinary research process." The second reviews efforts to develop such a process. In particular, it discusses the process outlined in Repko (2008)—in which the chapters in this book are grounded—and how this relates to other suggestions in the scholarly literature regarding an interdisciplinary research process. As various characteristics of the interdisciplinary research process are identified, later chapters that particularly exemplify them are noted.

Should Interdisciplinarians Identify Such a Process?

This section opens with a set of epistemological queries that have been raised regarding the feasibility and desirability of an interdisciplinary research process: Does the structure inherent in such a process interfere with the freedom of interdisciplinarians to follow their curiosity? Should interdisciplinarians mimic disciplinary research practice? And is interdisciplinary research inherently revolutionary? It then moves toward more practical concerns: Would an interdisciplinary research process improve the practice of interdisciplinarity (in teaching as well as research) and perhaps even enhance the pursuit of quality interdisciplinarity within the academy?

Structure Versus Freedom

One of the main attractions of interdisciplinary research is that it allows researchers freedom from disciplinary constraints. Disciplines take their strength from a shared perspective that includes many elements: a shared set of topics that are addressed, a shared but limited set of theories and methods that are applied to them (and often a shared set of assumptions about how they are to be applied), a shared set of epistemological assumptions regarding what can be known and how, often shared ethical assumptions about what is "good," and often shared ideological attitudes. It is these areas of agreement that allow specialized research to proceed so easily: Writers need not explain their theory or method or subject matter *unless they deviate in some way from what is expected.* These expectations are institutionalized in the discipline's publication, hiring, and promotion decisions. Interdisciplinarians may (or may not) respect the power of specialized research but are always conscious that it has powerful disadvantages. The strong incentive to obey disciplinary preferences regarding theory, method, and subject matter means that disciplinarians *necessarily* ignore competing theories or methods, and they also ignore related phenomena that might cast an important light on the issues addressed by the discipline. Likewise, the very set of issues that are addressed may be arbitrarily curtailed due to theoretical or methodological preferences—as when economists turned away from the study of economic growth for decades because they lacked a compelling mathematical model of growth.

Interdisciplinarity, then, must embrace a freedom to explore *any* theory or method or phenomenon that the researcher(s) think appropriate to the question being asked. This might be proclaimed to be the basic nonnegotiable principle of interdisciplinary research. Because the best-known research methodologies in the Academy are those disciplinary methodologies that succeed only by limiting freedom, some interdisciplinarians naturally fear that any proposed "interdisciplinary research process" would inevitably also limit the freedom of interdisciplinarians. If so, interdisciplinarity could not fulfill its function as the antidote to restrictive disciplinary perspectives.

In the second section, then, it is important to hold any proposed interdisciplinary process to very high standards of academic freedom. A process that would limit interdisciplinarians in the same way that disciplinary methodologies limit disciplinarians would defeat the very purpose of interdisciplinarity.

The Role of Shared Methodologies

The idea of an interdisciplinary research process naturally reminds one of disciplinary methodologies. It would be undesirable to discipline interdisciplinarity in this way. Yet it can, at the same time, be appreciated that much of the strength of disciplines comes from these shared methodologies (and much of the rest comes from the way these are instantiated in disciplinary reward structures).

Do shared methodologies enhance the productivity of research? As noted above, they enhance communication within disciplines (while unfortunately limiting communication across disciplines). Researchers can easily explain to another member of their discipline what minor novelty they are attempting to introduce into the shared research agenda. Many scholars will find it both comforting and straightforward to follow a recommended research trajectory. It may be thought that those attracted to the academic life will be those who are determined to chart their own path. However, the scholarly requirement to add something new to the body of human understanding is not easily achieved, and many scholars find it professionally rewarding to follow what others do.

Disciplinary standards are closely allied to disciplinary methodologies. Economists are expected to use mathematical models and/or statistical analysis. Naturally, economists are then judged on their mastery and application of sophisticated mathematical techniques (which is easier to evaluate than their understanding of the economy itself). Should interdisciplinarians aspire to interdisciplinary standards? One of the problems faced by interdisciplinary teaching programs is a claim that interdisciplinarity infuses the Academy, and thus special interdisciplinary programs are no longer needed (Augsburg & Henry, 2009). Interdisciplinary research programs could face a similar critique. The best rejoinder would be to claim that one is doing a better form of interdisciplinarity. It is all too easy, after all, to do superficial "interdisciplinarity": to read one book in sociology and repeat its insights with no understanding of how that book rests within the wider discipline. Disciplinarians, with their formalized (but disciplining) standards, can all too readily identify examples of superficial interdisciplinarity and then claim that interdisciplinarity is inherently inferior. Still, some interdisciplinarians may hesitate to proclaim standards precisely because they do not wish to limit freedom. A question to ask in the second section of this chapter is whether an interdisciplinary research process can support both standards and freedom.

Revolutionary Versus Normal Science

Thomas Kuhn famously argued in the 1960s that scientific understanding does not advance entirely through a gradual process of accretion of new bits of understanding, but rather that the history of science is punctuated by occasional revolutions during which some of the previous understandings are replaced by quite novel understandings. The Kuhnian distinction between revolutionary and normal science was undoubtedly overdrawn and has now been supplanted in the study of science by more recent debates. These decades of discussion will not be reviewed here. However, the Kuhnian distinction has useful implications for the present discussion. Scholars closely following disciplinary methodologies would clearly fall within the "normal science" category. Interdisciplinarians are more likely to celebrate grand new syntheses that set scholars on entirely new research trajectories: These would qualify as "revolutionary science." And scholars of scientific discovery note that such revolutionary insights tend to come from connecting ideas from different disciplines (Root-Bernstein, 1989). Is interdisciplinary research inherently revolutionary (as suggested by Pohl, van Kerkhoff, Hirsch Hadorn, & Bammer, 2008, p. 413)? If so, then an interdisciplinary research process might be less useful. Of course, even revolutionary insights come only to the prepared mind, and thus there may well be strategies scholars can follow in order to increase their chances of achieving revolutionary insights. If, though, interdisciplinarity can proceed as normal science, then some sort of shared process may be much more important.

For Kuhn, revolutionary science was exceptional; the vast bulk of scholars produced normal science. Scholars in the humanities might imagine that revolution is more likely in their realm. Still, unless the phrase is stripped of its intended meaning, revolutionary scholarship—that which truly breaks free from preceding theories and methodologies—must be rare. To identify interdisciplinarity with revolution is then to suggest that only a very small minority of scholars can be interdisciplinarians. If interdisciplinary scholarship is to be established within the Academy, then it is necessary either to identify some third form of scholarship between normal and revolutionary or to identify how interdisciplinarians can slowly and gradually build upon the work of other interdisciplinarians.

Disciplines concur in having a guiding methodology but differ in the precise nature of that guiding methodology. Perhaps the answer for interdisciplinarity is likewise for different groups of interdisciplinarians to coalesce around quite different research agendas. There need be no common elements among these. Yet, it is noteworthy that there are common elements of disciplinary methodologies: Disciplines (among other things) accept only a minority of the theories and methods they might embrace and apply these to a subset of the (relationships among) phenomena that they might study. Should there also be common elements among interdisciplinary methodologies? And should these, then, be quite different from the common elements of disciplinary methodologies? In particular, should interdisciplinary methodologies be more open in terms of theory, method, and phenomena than are disciplinary methodologies? If so, is it possible to structure normal science around such openness? Many interdisciplinarians, especially in natural science, have argued that this is possible. This set of related questions should inform much of what is done in the second section of this chapter.

The case studies performed in this book can be seen as normal science. Authors follow a logical research strategy. Yet, this process does not at all restrain them from displaying creativity, nor from reaching novel conclusions. As Newell discusses in the concluding chapter, the authors of these case studies clearly saw themselves as contributing to an ongoing conversation.

Interdisciplinarity and Training

At this moment in the history of the Academy, most scholars who would define themselves as interdisciplinary simply "do" interdisciplinarity. They have not taken courses on how to do interdisciplinarity. They may not have ever read an article or book focused on how to do interdisciplinarity. Importantly, they may never have reflected very much on what it means to be interdisciplinary.

The analogy with university teaching is too tempting. Most scholars were never taught how to teach. They just go out and do it. And most do it very well. Or at least most appear to do it very well, given that the standards by which university teaching is judged have evolved in a world where university teachers are not expected to reflect much on the nature of their teaching. Even at that, most universities in the developed world have established some sort of bureaucracy designed to help scholars teach. Increasingly, scholars do take courses on how to teach. At many universities, graduate students are now expected, even required, to take such courses. The age of the untrained university teacher may thus be slowly drawing to a close. Should the age of the untrained interdisciplinarian be far behind?

Disciplinarians are not generally taught their disciplinary perspective explicitly. Yet, the fact that they are taught just one or two types of theory and one or two methods provides a solid introduction to that disciplinary perspective. Interdisciplinarians lack even this introduction. Most practicing interdisciplinarians received disciplinary PhDs. Even those with PhDs from interdisciplinary programs will rarely have experienced course material about interdisciplinarity: maybe about the nature of some interdisciplinary theme (such as environmental studies, gender studies, or cognitive science) but not about interdisciplinarity itself. As with university teaching, one can look at the glass half full and say "this works" or look at the glass half empty and wonder whether it might work much better if interdisciplinarians reflected on the nature and purpose of interdisciplinarity and asked how interdisciplinary analysis might best be performed.

Strategic Interdisciplinarity

The place of interdisciplinarity within the Academy is still contested. To be sure, almost every university president extols the value of interdisciplinarity—at least as long as granting agencies continue to do so. However, longstanding interdisciplinary programs have been cut at several institutions. As noted above, these cuts are often justified by claiming that interdisciplinarity now infuses the Academy. Among the many lessons drawn in Augsburg and Henry (2009) are that interdisciplinarians need to integrate their efforts with those of disciplinarians, and interdisciplinarians need to distinguish quality interdisciplinarity from superficial interdisciplinarity. An interdisciplinary research process might support quality interdisciplinarity within the Academy if it had two characteristics: standards such that superficial interdisciplinarity could be distinguished from quality interdisciplinarity, and a symbiotic relationship between interdisciplinary research and specialized research.

The last point—and the careful way it was worded—deserves further treatment. Interdisciplinarians differ in the way they view disciplines. Some see disciplines as the strong base from which interdisciplinary analysis proceeds. Others see disciplines as a problem to be overcome. Few, though, would doubt that specialized research—in which some group of scholars collectively applies a particular theory and method to a particular problem—will and should always have a place in the Academy. Interdisciplinarians can debate (or not) the ideal institutional structure for both specialized and interdisciplinary research. The point here is that a process for interdisciplinary research should specify how it draws upon (and, ideally, informs) specialized research.

It is sometimes suggested that students can only master interdisciplinarity after obtaining a solid grounding in one or two disciplines. The sense that interdisciplinarity is an optional add-on to a disciplinary education poses an obvious threat to at least undergraduate interdisciplinary programs. If it were accepted that there is an interdisciplinary research process, and that this is complementary to disciplinary methodologies, then it would make sense for students—perhaps disciplinary students as well as interdisciplinary students—to learn simultaneously about disciplines and interdisciplinarity. Interdisciplinary undergraduate programs (and general education courses) would have an obvious place alongside specialized (disciplinary) programs.

What Would an Interdisciplinary Research Process Look Like?

This section begins with a brief review of Repko (2008) and then discusses a few other recent efforts to identify interdisciplinary best practices. It will be argued that these efforts are complementary and point toward a consensus approach to interdisciplinary research.

Interdisciplinary Research: Process and Theory

Repko (2008) wrote the first book-length treatment of the interdisciplinary research process. Repko draws in turn on a variety of works by scholars of interdisciplinarity: Klein (especially 1990), Newell (especially 2007), Szostak (2002, 2004), and Bal (especially 2002). He also draws heavily on works in cognitive science and social psychology. Most important, for each step in his recommended research process, Repko provides examples of application from the humanities, social sciences, and natural sciences. And for each step, he suggests a handful of strategies or guidelines that might usefully be applied. Repko proposes 10 broad steps:

1. State the problem or focus question.

2. Justify using an interdisciplinary approach.

3. Identify relevant disciplines.

4. Conduct the literature search.

5. Develop adequacy in each relevant discipline.

6. Analyze the problem and evaluate each insight into it.

7. Identify conflicts between insights and their sources.

8. Create or discover common ground.

9. Integrate insights.

10. Produce an interdisciplinary understanding and test it.

This research process in particular is similar to those advocated by Szostak (2002) and Newell (2001). One can identify five common groups of steps in these three approaches. The first steps involve identifying an inter-disciplinary research question. The second set of steps guide the researcher to identify relevant phenomena, theories, methods, and disciplines. The third set of steps involve evaluating disciplinary insights. The fourth set of steps focus on finding common ground across disciplinary insights. The final steps require reflection, testing, and communication of results.

At the level of these broad steps, it would be hard to maintain that the process interferes with freedom: Scholars are still encouraged to employ *any* scholarly (or, indeed, nonscholarly) theory or method and draw connections across *any* set of phenomena. Indeed, Repko (2008) provides potentially exhaustive tables of phenomena, theory types, and methods that interdisci-plinary scholars might want to embrace. It might be objected that the linear nature of the process is restrictive: What if one wants to revisit Step 1 while performing Step 6? Repko and other advocates of such a process take pains to emphasize its iterative nature: Researchers are indeed encouraged to revisit earlier steps as they perform later steps, alter the question as new information is uncovered, embrace additional theories and methods as the limits of the first ones chosen become apparent, and so on. Seeing it in this iterative sense, one might worry not that the process is too restrictive but that it provides little structure. Yet, it does provide a checklist of tasks that the interdisciplinarian should ideally perform. The value of revisiting earlier steps is highlighted in many of the case studies that follow, notably that of Connor (Chapter 3).

Concerns with structure may reappear at lower levels of granularity. The Repko (2008) book contains a host of suggestions for how to best pursue each step. Again, though, the intent has been to survey all useful strategies. For example, Repko discusses a common interdisciplinary approach: From the guiding question, one first identifies relevant disciplines and then looks within these for relevant insights. Yet, he also highlights an alternative approach (pioneered in Szostak, 2004) whereby the interdisciplinarian first reflects on relevant theory types and methods and only then progresses to identify relevant disciplines. These approaches are quite distinct, yet both lead to an appreciation of different insights within their disciplinary contexts. Likewise, several distinct strategies for evaluating disciplinary insights, integrating them, and then identifying a common ground are provided. With respect to evaluation, Repko discusses how to evaluate the theories applied, methods used, phenomena considered, data employed, epistemological assumptions engaged, relationship between insight and perspective, and potential biases of researchers; he also urges researchers to use insights generated by one community as a device to evaluate insights generated by another. As for building common ground, Repko first surveys a variety of critical thinking strategies identified by cognitive scientists before suggesting several broad techniques for achieving common ground: redefinition (semantic adjustment of terms or assumptions); extension (of a theoretical idea to a new domain); organization (identifying hidden commonalities across fields and establishing how these are related); and transformation (seeing differences of kind as differences of degree instead). Each of these strategies might be useful in some circumstances but not others. If other interdisciplinarians wish to suggest further strategies, these could be added to the lists proffered by Repko. Of course, any suggestion that "you may want to try X" may divert attention from strategy "Y." Still, it would be unfortunate if the only way to avoid such a potential bias were to eschew giving interdisciplinarians any advice on how to proceed. Arguably, then, an interdisciplinary research process can provide a useful structure while remaining flexible enough to embrace all viable research strategies.

Of course, some interdisciplinarians might object to the outcome. They may find the idea of "common ground" disquieting, most likely if they wish to see some grand theory triumph over all alternative explanations. Yet, even here it is possible that common ground may take the form of one overarching theory. Most important, a scholarly methodology should be designed to encourage inquiry rather than to guarantee that a particular form of outcome is generated.

One may worry that no single researcher, and even most interdisciplinary teams, could adequately perform each of Repko's (2008) steps. Yet, the process can hardly require researchers to do the impossible. It can, however, guide them to reflect on what they have missed. If, for example, time constraints (coupled with the interdisciplinary-unfriendly nature of library catalogues) have forced a less-than-exhaustive literature survey, interdisciplinarians can usefully reflect on what might have been missed. In this way, the recommended process may serve as a support for a cumulative interdisciplinary scholarship. Subsequent researchers can fill in the gaps in previous research. The case studies in this book establish that one researcher can, indeed, do a very good job of performing most, if not all, steps in the Repko process; yet, most chapters also point to further research that other interdisciplinarians could perform that would further enhance our understanding of the question at hand.

The Ecology of Team Science

Though Repko (2008) provides the only textbook treatment of the interdisciplinary research process, a handful of other scholars have, in recent works, also shed important light on interdisciplinary research. These authors, representing a broad range of research fields and hailing from at least three continents, share insights broadly consistent with those of Repko.

Stokols, Misra, Moser, Hall, and Taylor (2008) focus on the particular needs of interdisciplinary teams. They note that the effectiveness of interdisciplinary teams varies a great deal. Team size matters (though the optimal size varies by project); homogeneity of team members along various social dimensions matters (homogeneity encourages conversation but limits novelty); personality of team leaders matters (though firm advice on what qualities are best is lacking at present); and personality of team members also matters (openness, methodological flexibility, and willingness to devote time to listening appear to be important). In terms of process, they emphasize the need to develop "shared conceptual frameworks that integrate and transcend the multiple disciplinary perspectives represented among team members" (p. S97). That is, the process of integration needs to start early: Whereas Repko (2008) stresses integration of insights to form a common ground understanding, Stokols et al. urge some integration of disciplinary perspectives in order to allow participants to work toward a later integration of insights. It may, though, prove more difficult in practice to integrate perspectives than to integrate insights. When interdisciplinary research extends beyond the Academy (which the authors appreciate is important for some types of research but not others), then some sort of educational function may also be critical: Scholars need to learn how to communicate to the public, and members of the public need to learn about scholarly research. Academy-community collaboration also requires careful identification of common goals, distribution of power and control, and organizational support.

Stokols et al. (2008) do not distinguish the social from cognitive aspects of interdisciplinary team research. Interdisciplinary teams work best when there are many informal opportunities for team members to interact. They also work best either when team members have strong personal incentives to pursue team goals or, alternatively, when team efforts are evaluated entirely at the team level; cases in which team members face a choice between pursuing individual versus team glory are generally problematic. Teams work best when there is both a high level of trust and a shared dream. Teams operating at a distance need not only to utilize the best communications technology but to appreciate that special steps are necessary to create a feeling of social cohesion at a distance. For team interdisciplinary research, then, one might want to encourage very early steps in the research process that set up the right incentive structure, select the right sorts of leaders and team members, create mechanisms for interaction, and establish the right physical and technological infrastructure.

The case studies in this book are each performed by one or two authors. The special challenges of team research were thus not confronted directly. Yet, as Klein points out in Chapter 10, the strategies for team building advocated by Stokols and others are generally complementary to the strategies for individual research advocated by scholars such as Repko. These case studies are thus useful, not just for the individual interdisciplinarian but also for the interdisciplinarian involved in some sort of team research project.

Integration and Implementation Sciences

Bammer (2005) suggests the creation of a new academic field focused on integrating the insights of specialized researchers and applying the holistic insights gained. Her main motivation is the recognition that interdisciplinarians too often "reinvent the wheel," discovering over and over good strategies for performing interdisciplinary research. She also speaks at some length to the strategic advantages of providing an institutional home for interdisciplinarity (see above), and she appreciates that such a home will only be provided and respected if there is some set of core strategies and skills associated with integration. She notes that both academics and policy makers interested in interdisciplinary analysis do not know where to turn for advice. This book—and Repko (2008)—can be considered a response to such a call for advice on how to perform interdisciplinary research.

Bammer (2005) suspects that interdisciplinarians will be called upon to deal with "complex" problems: those that involve not only interactions among many phenomena but significant nonlinearities in how some phenomena influence others. Newell (2001) had made a similar argument; those who responded to him in that volume of *Issues in Integrative Studies* generally concluded that complexity was often, but not always, at play in the problems addressed by interdisciplinarians. Bammer herself notes that there is a big difference between how "complexity" is used by complexity theorists and how it is used in common parlance; it could be that the latter usage more closely captures the essence of interdisciplinary questions. Bammer's suggestion that interdisciplinarians cope with the emergent properties of complex systems could thus be treated not as a mandatory practice but as a mandatory question to be asked: Are there emergent properties to be addressed in the system of causal links being investigated? Notably, the Repko-like process pursued in Szostak (2009) and in his chapter on economic growth (Chapter 6) has exactly such a step. Bammer worries that there are several competing approaches to complexity analysis. She argues convincingly that these might well be integrated into a coherent set of strategies. Integration is, in part, possible because different approaches deal with different kinds of complexity: Some emphasize equilibria, others stress cycles, still others focus on change in some direction, and many speak of stochastic outcomes (these are, notably, the different sorts of time-path that every theory should specify, as identified in Szostak, 2004). It should thus be possible to develop a menu of complexity theories and methods that are applied to different situations. Yet, integration is also possible because many similar elements appear in quite different approaches to complexity: concerns with hierarchy of phenomena, boundaries between phenomena, networks and flows, and feedback loops among phenomena. Note that several case studies, but most explicitly those of Szostak (Chapter 6) and Keestra (Chapter 8), show how mapping the relationships between variables can be invaluable; those two chapters also address issues of hierarchy.

Bammer (2005) argues that interdisciplinarity will also involve both academic teams and interaction with nonacademics. But as Stokols et al. (2008) have stated, the size of teams and degree of community interaction vary widely depending on the question being addressed. As noted above, strategies for organizing teams and interacting with the public should be developed by interdisciplinarians, but some interdisciplinary projects may not require one or both of these. Bammer discusses how interaction with nonacademics can be useful at various stages of the research process: identifying research questions, identifying relevant theories and methods, identifying problems with these, identifying practices that seem to work, and testing policies and procedures. Bammer devotes particular attention to the last of these. If interdisciplinarians will investigate complicated systems of relations among diverse sets of phenomena, then there is likely to be a great deal of uncertainty surrounding any policy recommendations that might result from interdisciplinary research (indeed, Bammer identifies uncertainty as one of the hallmarks of interdisciplinary research). These recommendations must thus be explained carefully to policy makers and the public, and they must be carefully tested in practice. The idea that academics can simply produce ideas to be taken "off the shelf" by policy makers will be especially inappropriate for interdisciplinary research. Rather, academics, policy makers, and the public should work together in testing policy recommendations (Funtowicz & Ravetz, 2008 make a similar point). Although several chapters address the policy implications of the analysis performed, Henry and Bracy (Chapter 9) discuss most fully how testing might proceed. Connor (Chapter 3) is notable for showing how policy implications can influence scholarly discourse itself.

Bammer (2005) also usefully extends her gaze beyond the confines of an individual research project in two important respects. First, she cites Klein (1990) on the value of encouraging specialized researchers to pursue questions identified by interdisciplinary researchers. Within a team of researchers, it may be possible to encourage specialized research of this sort. More often, though, one key aspect of interdisciplinary research is to identify questions or research strategies that are understudied by specialized researchers (this is also a step performed in Szostak, 2009). This sort of symbiotic relationship between integrative and specialized research deserves emphasis: Integrative research not only builds on specialized research but also informs it (and not just about questions but about relevant phenomena, theories, and methods). Second, Bammer urges interdisciplinarians to engage seriously with information scientists in developing better systems for organizing human understanding. One of the main barriers to interdisciplinarity is that scholars simply do not know where to look for relevant information. In a particular project, this means, most obviously, that greater care must be taken with the literature search than is generally the case for specialized research. Yet, interdisciplinarians should not lose sight of the wider goal of suggesting how information could be better organized to serve further research (Szostak, 2008).

Types of Interdisciplinarity

Julie Thompson Klein has, in a variety of publications, developed typologies of different types of interdisciplinarity. Given the vast array of different types of interdisciplinarity identified, does it make sense to speak of one interdisciplinary process? As with the analysis of Stokols et al. (2008) above, one possibility is that different types of interdisciplinarity can be seen as representing different choices within an overarching research process. If so, then an understanding of the overall process would help researchers and others evaluate whether the choices made in a particular research project were appropriate.

Klein describes a spectrum of types of integration. Partial integration involves an ad hoc and temporary borrowing of tools and approaches from one discipline for use by researchers based in another. If this borrowing becomes more sophisticated and enduring, one can speak of supplementary integration. Full integration (or better yet, unifying integration) occurs when the ideas from one discipline are so absorbed into the other that some new synthesis emerges. Although Klein's focus in these comparisons is on the emergence (or not) of interdisciplinary research fields rather than the structure of individual research projects, it is nevertheless true that individual researchers face a choice regarding the degree of integration to be pursued in a particular project. The analysis above has generally stressed relatively full sorts of integration. One of the earliest steps in the Repko (2008) process is an evaluation of whether the research question is appropriately interdisciplinary. If the answer is affirmative, then partial integration, while better than nothing, will likely not yield as useful an understanding as will full integration.

If, however, a research question is largely disciplinary, then partial integration may be all that is required. Van der Lecq (Chapter 7) and Henry and Bracy (Chapter 9) explore how partial integrations can be further integrated to generate a more holistic understanding.

One can also speak of different means of integration. Sometimes, integration is primarily semantic: The meanings of concepts are adjusted to carry a similar meaning across communities (Klein [Chapter 10] notes that there are a handful of strategies for achieving semantic consensus). Van der Lecq (Chapter 7) and Tayler (Chapter 2) pay particular attention to this strategy. Sometimes integration occurs by adjusting the assumptions of theories so that they are complementary. Repko (Chapter 5) is particularly notable in this regard. Sometimes integration involves placing competing theories within an overarching framework. Connor (Chapter 3), Szostak (Chapter 6), and Keestra (Chapter 8) do this in quite different ways. As should be clear by now, these different integrative strategies can be seen as complements.

As with Stokols et al. (2008) above, Klein (1990) appreciates that research groups operate in quite different ways (see also Pohl et al., 2008, p. 415). Sometimes the group engages in cooperative learning, with all group members involved in regular conversations about how to proceed. At other times, group tasks are divided among members on the basis of expertise, with members working largely independently for long periods. In still other cases, group leaders take on much of the responsibility for integrating ideas produced by group members. The suitability of these different approaches to different circumstances can be judged in terms of how well they generate particular results: Do they identify relevant disciplines, theories, methods, and phenomena? Do they evaluate these different theories? Do they integrate them?

Transdisciplinary Perspectives

While the *Handbook of Transdisciplinary Research* edited by Hirsch Hadorn et al. (2008) has no chapter devoted to the articulation of an interdisciplinary research process, there is support for the idea in many chapters. "Transdisciplinary research needs concrete paradigms to help researchers understand problems in context and to structure the research accordingly" (Hoffman-Riem et al., 2008, p. 7). Pohl et al. (2008) suggest, "A paradigm is critical for integration to improve its scientific profile" (p. 413). They are confident that a broad research process can be identified by comparing successful research programs: "We can start to identify a number of forms of collaboration and integration that appear more or less consistently in transdisciplinary research" (p. 415). They note, in particular, that it is difficult to assess interdisciplinary research projects in the absence of some sense of how these should proceed. Messerli and Messerli (2008, p. 60) argue that transdisciplinary projects may have difficulty gaining research funding in the absence of well-defined research practices that lend themselves to peer review. Bergmann and Jahn (2008, p. 98) provide a more practical rationale:

Integration must occur throughout the entire project, and this is best achieved with some guiding model that allows planning and regular evaluation. This process must be general enough to be universal but differentiated enough to identify key questions that research planners must grapple with in particular cases.

Wiesmann et al. (2008, pp. 436–437), among many others, emphasize that any interdisciplinary research process must be iterative. Because the guiding question is chosen interactively, it will inevitably be refined as research is undertaken and even as policy recommendations are devised. Decisions about what disciplines to engage are inevitably revisited as research proceeds. Teamwork increases the need for an iterative approach because the development of shared theories, models, or outputs is inherently a circular process. As noted above, several of the case studies in this book speak to the value of revisiting earlier steps.

Teamwork is emphasized by all authors in the *Handbook*. Successful teamwork processes "require carefully structured, sequenced, and selected negotiations and interactions" (Wiesmann et al., 2008, p. 437). This takes time, requires mutual acceptance of team goals, and depends on encouraging mutual respect. If independent specialized research is undertaken within the broader project, this must be carefully planned so that it is known in advance when and how this will ideally be integrated into the broader project. As with Stokols et al. (2008), teamwork implies additional steps at the start of the research process.

Bergmann and Jahn (2008) argue that research questions must themselves emerge from a team effort: The team is motivated by some shared societal concern or problem but must then identify well-defined research questions that can be pursued by scholars. Developing the question and creating the team may themselves be symbiotic processes. Messerli and Messerli (2008, pp. 53–54) observe that environmental (and social) problems often occur in clusters or syndromes, and thus guiding questions must often be multifaceted. The next task involves identifying the key disciplines and the key differences in their approach to the research question (this step may lead to a revision of the team and/or question). Després, Fortin, Joerin, Vachon, Gatti, and Moretti (2008, p. 329) identify four broad types of knowledge that must be gathered together: "scientific" knowledge about how the world works, "practical" knowledge about what is possible, "ethical" knowledge about desirable goals, and (for some projects) "aesthetic" knowledge of what is beautiful. The case studies in this book all address "scientific knowledge"; those with a significant policy component also address "practical" insights; ethical issues are addressed most clearly in Tayler (Chapter 2), Repko (Chapter 5), and Szostak (Chapter 6); Bal (Chapter 4) investigates aesthetic knowledge to the greatest extent.

Several authors speak of identifying subquestions for disciplinary research. Wiesmann et al. (2008, p. 436) stress the symbiotic relationship between specialized and integrative research. Bergmann and Jahn (2008) alternatively celebrate the advantages of having interdisciplinary subgroups pursue sub-questions: It is then much easier to achieve integration at the level of the project as a whole. In either case, it is essential that the relationship between the guiding question and subquestions be carefully specified at the outset, though of course the relationship may change as research proceeds. It is also essential that there be regular interactions between subgroups: Integration cannot just be left until the end (p. 94). Several chapters in this book show how even individual researchers can benefit from identifying and addressing subquestions.

The focus on integration will vary by project: Sometimes developing shared understandings of concepts is critical, in other cases it is theories that must be integrated, in other cases models, in still other cases policy developments (Pohl et al., 2008, p. 416). As noted above, some of the cases in this book focus on concepts while others stress theories; a handful of chapters, including Tayler (Chapter 2) and Henry and Bracy (Chapter 9), address how policies might be integrated.

Wiesmann et al. (2008) speak to the difficulty of evaluating interdisciplinary research projects. They cannot be evaluated fairly against the standards of any one discipline. As noted above, this is one major advantage of developing a shared understanding of the ideal interdisciplinary research process within the community of interdisciplinarians. The exemplary research projects included in this book provide a standard against which similar projects might be compared.

Because interdisciplinary research is motivated in general by social problems, researchers will usually want to generate both scholarly contributions and practical policy advice. These are two quite different sorts of output. Bergmann and Jahn (2008, p. 96) argue that they require different types of integration. Scholarly audiences may be most interested in integration at the level of theories and methods. Policy makers will seek integration of diverse policy proposals. Ideally, of course, the first sort of integration should support the second. Bergmann and Jahn feel that very few interdisciplinary research projects succeed on both counts. The chapters in this book by Tayler (Chapter 2), Connor (Chapter 3), Szostak (Chapter 6), and Henry and Bracy (Chapter 9) each strive in their own way to address the concerns of both scholars/students and policy makers.

Conclusion

In this brief overview, there has been little time to comment at length on the evidential basis for these various arguments regarding process. Briefly, though, it might be noted that the works cited reflect a balance between a deductive approach (looking at scholarship on interdisciplinarity, cognitive thinking, social psychology, and organization, and deducing what should work best) and an inductive approach (looking at interdisciplinary research projects and seeing what works and what does not). In good interdisciplinary fashion, research from a variety of fields and a variety of theories and methods have been drawn upon in each of the works cited above. The inductive and deductive approaches are increasingly being combined as researchers apply recommended processes in their research; they can then reflect on how well these worked. As noted at several points above, the case studies in this book serve both to highlight the value of the interdisciplinary research process and to clarify its nature.

It would be straightforward to integrate the processes reviewed above. The team-building steps advocated by Stokols et al. (2008) or contributors to Hirsch Hadorn et al. (2008) could be added to a Repko-like process. So too could Bammer's (2005) stresses on emergent properties, discussions beyond the Academy, and implementation. Likewise, the development of subquestions and reintegration of these into the overall project can be seen as a further option available to interdisciplinary researchers. Several chapters in this book pursue such a strategy. Moreover, these various amendments could be treated iteratively: Although one wants a cohesive team from the start, one may revisit teambuilding strategies as the research process unfolds. The different approaches to interdisciplinarity identified by Klein (1990), Pohl et al. (2008), and others can be seen as choices within this iterative process; the appropriateness of particular choices can be judged in terms of how well the research process achieves its goals.

Potentially, at least, this integrated research process meets the objections raised in the first section: It provides structure without interfering with freedom, it facilitates normal research by interdisciplinarians, it encourages use of the widest range of theories and methods and phenomena, it encourages standards grounded in this sort of flexible structure, and it strengthens the case for a role for interdisciplinarity within the Academy that is clearly symbiotic with specialized research. Teams of interdisciplinarians, including nonacademic participants, should thus be able to achieve success employing the interdisciplinary research process, just as have the researchers pursuing case studies in this book.

References

Augsburg, T., & Henry, S. (Eds.). (2009). *The politics of interdisciplinary studies: Interdisciplinary transformation in undergraduate American higher education.* Jefferson, NC: McFarland.

Bal, M. (2002). *Traveling concepts in the humanities: A rough guide.* Toronto: University of Toronto Press.

Bammer, G. (2005). Integration and implementation sciences: Building a new specialization. *Ecology and Society, 10*(2), 6. Retrieved from http://www.ecology andsociety.org/vol10/iss2/art6/

Bergmann, M., & Jahn, T. (2008). CITY: Mobil: A model for integration in sustainability research. In G. Hirsch Hadorn, H. Hoffmann-Riem, S. Biber-Klemm, W. Grossenbacher-Mansuy, D. Joye, C. Pohl . . . E. Zemp (Eds.), *Handbook of transdisciplinary research* (pp. 89–102). Dordrecht: Springer.

Després, C., Fortin, A., Joerin, F., Vachon, G., Gatti, E., & Moretti, G. (2008). Retrofitting postwar suburbs: A collaborative design process. In G. Hirsch Hadorn, H. Hoffmann-Riem, S. Biber-Klemm, W. Grossenbacher-Mansuy, D. Joye, C. Pohl . . . E. Zemp (Eds.), *Handbook of transdisciplinary research* (pp. 327–344). Dordrecht: Springer.

Funtowicz, S., & Ravetz, J. (2008). Values and uncertainty. In G. Hirsch Hadorn, H. Hoffmann-Riem, S. Biber-Klemm, W. Grossenbacher-Mansuy, D. Joye, C. Pohl . . . E. Zemp (Eds.), *Handbook of transdisciplinary research* (pp. 361–368). Dordrecht: Springer.

Hirsch Hadorn, G., Hoffmann-Riem, H., Biber-Klemm, S., Grossenbacher-Mansuy, W., Joye, D., Pohl, C. . . . Zemp, E. (Eds.). (2008). *Handbook of transdisciplinary research*. Dordrecht: Springer.

Hoffmann-Riem, H., Biber-Klemm, S., Grossenbacher-Mansuy, W., Hirsch Hadorn, G., Joye, D., Pohl, C. . . . Zemp, E. (2008). Idea of the handbook. In G. Hirsch Hadorn, et al. (Eds.), *Handbook of transdisciplinary research* (pp. 3–18). Dordrecht: Springer.

Klein, J. T. (1990). *Interdisciplinarity: History, theory and practice*. Detroit: Wayne State University Press.

Messerli, B., & Messerli, P. (2008). From local projects in the Alps to global change programmes in the mountains of the world: Milestones in transdisciplinary research. In G. Hirsch Hadorn, et al. (Eds.), *Handbook of transdisciplinary research* (pp. 43–62). Dordrecht: Springer.

Newell, W. H. (2001). A theory of interdisciplinary studies. *Issues in Integrative Studies, 19,* 1–26.

Newell, W. H. (2007). Decision-making in interdisciplinary studies. In G. Morcol (Ed.), *Handbook of decision making* (pp. 245–264). New York: Marcel Dekker.

Pohl, C., van Kerkhoff, L., Hirsch Hadorn, G., & Bammer, G. (2008). Integration. In G. Hirsch Hadorn, et al. (Eds.), *Handbook of transdisciplinary research* (pp. 411–426). Dordrecht: Springer.

Repko, A. (2008). *Interdisciplinary research: Process and theory*. Thousand Oaks: Sage.

Root-Bernstein, R. (1989). *Discovery*. Cambridge: Harvard University Press.

Stokols, D., Misra, S., Moser, R. P., Hall, K. L., Taylor, B. K. (2008). The ecology of team science: Understanding contextual influences on transdisciplinary collaboration. *American Journal of Preventive Medicine, 35,*(2S), 96–115.

Szostak, R. (2002). How to do interdisciplinarity: Integrating the debate. *Issues in Integrative Studies, 20,* 103–122.

Szostak, R. (2004). *Classifying science: Phenomena, data, theory, method, practice*. Dordrecht: Springer.

Szostak, R. (2008). Classification, interdisciplinarity, and the study of science. *Journal of Documentation, 64*(3), 319–332.

Szostak, R. (2009). *The causes of economic growth: Interdisciplinary perspectives*. Berlin: Springer.

Wiesmann, U., Biber-Klemm, S., Grossenbacher-Mansuy, W., Hirsch Hadorn, G., Hoffmann-Riem, H., Joye, D. . . . Zemp, E. (2008). Enhancing transdisciplinary research: A synthesis in fifteen propositions. In G. Hirsch Hadorn, et al. (Eds.), *Handbook of transdisciplinary research* (pp. 433–442). Dordrecht: Springer.

PART II

Drawing on Disciplinary Insights

2 Jewish Marriage as an Expression of Israel's Conflicted Identity

Marilyn R. Tayler

Introduction

Marriage, according to the laws of Israel, is an exclusively religious institution; there is no civil marriage. There are Jewish, Muslim, Christian, Baha'i, and Druze institutions designated to administer marriage laws for their own religious groups.[1] Although Israel is a secular democracy, it does not maintain full separation of religion and state. Israel largely identifies itself as a Jewish *and* secular democratic state. For reasons to be explored later, however, Israel has accepted the Orthodox Rabbinate's exclusive control of Jewish marriage. The question is whether such a connection between religion and state is compatible with a democracy in the area of marriage law. For example, a couple consisting of one partner who is Jewish and the other non-Jewish may not marry in Israel (religious law endorsed by state law); they may, however, marry abroad and have their marriage registered in Israel (state law). The non-Jewish spouse may immigrate and be granted automatic Israeli citizenship under Israel's "Law of Return" (state law), but would not be entitled to status as a Jew (religious law).[2] The Israeli legal system is considered to be "unique among modern legal systems" in its delegation of marriage to religious courts (Zamir & Zysblat, 1996, pp. 12–13).

A study of the institution of Jewish marriage and its place in Israel's conflicted identity may generate insights that can be applied to broader issues of inequality, such as the situation of Israeli Arabs, a sizable minority who face issues in some ways analogous to those of non-Orthodox Jews and

---

[1]There are 14 religious communities in Israel: Jewish, Muslim, Druze, Baha'i and 10 Christian denominations (Freudenheim, 1967, pp. 86–87).

[2]The Law of Return, approved on July 5, 1950, "gave all Jews everywhere the legal right to immigrate to Israel and receive Israeli citizenship" (Isaac, 1981, p. 73). The law did not define the word *Jew*. As a result of the 1970 Shalit Supreme Court case, the meaning of *Jew* in the Law of Return follows the Orthodox definition for both religious and national identification (p. 75).

other non-Jews in Israel. An interdisciplinary approach to the institution of Jewish marriage is necessary because no single discipline is able to provide a comprehensive understanding of its complex and emblematic role in Israeli democracy. The interdisciplinary research process offers the most effective way to consider each contributing discipline's perspective, find common ground between conflicting insights, integrate these insights, and apply the resulting understanding to broader issues in Israel as a Jewish and democratic state.

Drawing On Disciplinary Insights

Step 1: State the Focus Question[3]

The overall question of how Israel can be both a Jewish and a democratic state at the same time is one of the most actively debated by Israel Studies scholars. Former Israeli Supreme Court Justice Barak (2002), for example, notes the "duality" of a state that characterizes itself as both Jewish and democratic. Mazie (2006) points out that most commentators tend to regard "'Jewish' as a code word for limitation and 'democratic' as an indicator of freedom" (p. 94). The meanings of *Jewish, democratic*, and *Jewish and democratic* are unclear because the terms have multiple definitions, depending on their context. The tension between the terms creates problems for the institution of Jewish marriage in Israel and, more broadly, for Israel's conflicted identity.

The categorization of Israel as a Jewish state is rooted in religion, ethnicity, and national identity. The religious meaning of Judaism has its origins in the Bible and includes Jews professing religious beliefs from ultra-Orthodox to atheist (Sharkansky, 1999, p. 61). Jewish ethnicity was forged in the historical isolation and marginalization of Jewish communities over many centuries, as a byproduct of anti-Semitism, especially in Europe (Berlin, 1978). Zionism, a primarily secular movement, effectively made Judaism a national identity, in addition to a religious and ethnic identity. Despite being a "Jewish State," Israel is not a theocracy, nor is Judaism the official state religion (Edelman, 1994, pp. 50–51). The institution of Jewish marriage exemplifies the complex relationship between religion and the state in Israel.

The roots of democracy in Israel predate the establishment of the state. They are found in the European-based Zionist movement and the *Yishuv*, the

---

[3]Each of the steps refers to the research process model presented in Repko (2008). Because the approach is iterative and nonlinear, the division of a fluid process into steps may give the misleading impression of a unidirectional sequence. The steps are sequenced by Repko to describe the overall progression of the process. In this chapter, all future subtitles enumerating the 10 steps in the two parts of the interdisciplinary research process will not be separately footnoted. See Repko, p. 142, for an integral model of the process that includes an enumeration of the two parts with the 10 constituent steps.

term used to describe the pre-1948 Jewish society of Palestine (Sheffer, 1996, p. 21). Israel meets the broad criteria for a democratic state: providing opportunities for effective participation, equality of voting, gaining enlightened understanding, exercising final control over the public agenda, and including adults in its governmental institutions (Dahl, 1998, pp. 38, 85). Democracy may also be viewed as an ideal and, as such, not fully attainable in practice (Gavison, 2007, p. 98). Democracy requires a sense of shared purpose or identity, as does religion.

An important consideration in the protection of civil rights, such as the right to marry, is constitutional protections. Israel does not have a formal written constitution. Rather, over the years, the Knesset—the Israeli Parliament—has developed a series of Basic Laws that provide the equivalent of constitutional guidance in particular areas. In 1992, the Knesset passed two Basic Laws, Freedom of Occupation and Human Dignity and Liberty. These laws are particularly important for several reasons:

- the phrase "Jewish and democratic state" is first formally used explicitly,
- the laws constitute the beginning of a formal Israeli Bill of Rights, and
- there is implicit authority for judicial review.

Judicial review, the power of the Supreme Court to declare legislation unconstitutional, is viewed by many as a "constitutional revolution" under the leadership of former Chief Justice Barak (Barak, in Arian, 2005, pp. 310–311). Judicial review empowers the Court to intervene in marriage laws and resulting civil rights violations, where previously the ultimate authority would have rested with the legislature.

Thus, Israel's identity as a secular yet Jewish democratic state is clearly conflicted. The topic may be stated as a focus question: How does the institution of Jewish marriage express Israel's conflicted identity as a Jewish and democratic state? The broader ramifications of this question for Israel as a Jewish and democratic state, extrapolated from exploration of Jewish marriage through the interdisciplinary research process, will, in Step 10 of the process, be applied to the situation of Israeli Arabs.

Step 2: Justify Using an Interdisciplinary Approach

There are several justifications for using an interdisciplinary approach in the present study. One justification flows from the complexity of the question posed. Klein and Newell's (Newell, 1998) classic definition states,

Interdisciplinary studies may be defined as a process of answering a question, solving a problem or addressing a topic that is too broad or complex to be dealt with adequately by a single discipline or profession. . . . IDS draws on disciplinary perspectives and integrates their insights through construction of a more comprehensive perspective. (p. 245)

This definition highlights the two parts of the interdisciplinary process: disciplinary insights and integration. To be truly interdisciplinary, research "is not just pasting two disciplines together to create one product but rather is an integration and a synthesis of ideas and methods" (National Academy of Sciences, 2005, p. 27).

A second justification typically used for an interdisciplinary approach occurs when essential phenomena, which are part of the research problem, are examined by more than one discipline. The two main approaches to interdisciplinary research are perspectival and classification (Repko, 2008, p. 84). The perspectival approach begins by identifying the relevant disciplines. The classification approach, developed by Rick Szostak (2000), begins with a schema that organizes phenomena in the human world, moving from broad, general, more abstract categories to the more specific in levels of phenomena; the phenomena are then linked to particular disciplines. Szostak defines phenomena as "any identifiable entities, concrete or abstract, individual or collective. . . . ongoing, indeed eternal, characteristics of human society" (p. 118). Although the present study essentially follows the perspectival approach, Szostak's classification of phenomena is also utilized because more possible linkages are discovered than by relying solely on the perspectival approach.

A third justification for an interdisciplinary approach occurs when the problem requires the researcher to draw upon an interdisciplinary field. An analysis of the institution of Jewish marriage falls within the field of Israel Studies, whose signal journal, *Israel Studies*, presents scholarship in fields such as the history, politics, society, and culture of Israel. The present integrative study, then, falls broadly within the emergent interdisciplinary field of Israel Studies.

Steps 3 and 4: Identify Relevant Disciplines and Conduct a Literature Search

The term *discipline*, in the context of interdisciplinary research, encompasses subdisciplines, schools of thought, and interdisciplinary fields (Repko, 2008, pp. 52, 101). What they all have in common is that each is characterized by its own perspective or worldview (Newell, 2006, p. 251). The potentially relevant fields for this study include religion, religious studies, political science, law, history, sociology, and cultural studies.

In several cases, there is an overlapping of different disciplinary perspectives. Klein (1996) says that disciplinary boundary crossing most frequently occurs at the level of subdisciplines, rather than entire disciplines (p. 42), and that the interactions among these disciplinary "neighbors" may result in boundary blurring (p. 70). These effects must be taken into account in determining which disciplines and their insights are essential to a focused analysis of the topic.

Through an in-depth literature search, the list of selected possible disciplines is reduced to the *most* relevant disciplines. There are several criteria that interdisciplinarians typically apply to this selection process:

- to narrow the topic, sharply focus the research question, and state the problem clearly;
- to understand the background of the problem;
- to situate or contextualize the problem;
- to identify the concepts, assumptions, theories, methods, and data used by each discipline's experts in their writing on the problem. (Repko, 2008, pp. 176–177)

In the present study, several disciplines are eliminated through the literature search. Cultural studies, an interdiscipline, is eliminated because its insights are encompassed within some of its constituent disciplines, which are among the other disciplines selected. Sociology is eliminated because its contribution through research on Israeli society would de-focus the research question due to its emphasis upon groups within the society rather than governing structures. History is eliminated because it essentially provides background to contextualize other disciplines' perspectives. To be included as a discipline, history would have to be considered in terms of patterns, contexts, and causal links, which are not the primary focus of the present study. Religious studies is eliminated because it is the academic study of religion from external perspectives. In contrast, religion, which is one of the essential disciplines for this study, refers to the theological belief system internal to Judaism; in Israel, this is generally equated with the Orthodox denomination of Judaism.

The essential disciplines for this study, then, are religion, political science, and law. The literature search is particularly challenging because of the diverse nature of the disciplines. Due in part to the multiple meanings of the terms *Jewish* and *democratic* as well as the way in which an aspect of one discipline becomes embedded in a perspective of another, the literature search reveals some problems of boundary blurring, as defined by Klein (1996, p. 70). For example, as a discipline, law deals with the application of case, statutory, and regulatory law by courts, the political branches of government, and the private sector. Law within political science refers to the politics of lawmaking and legal decision making. Further, the fact that "Israel Studies" is itself an interdisciplinary field complicates the process of attributing particular insights, theories, concepts, and assumptions to constituent disciplines.

During the literature search, a useful approach is to develop a data management table, an important organizing tool that prevents the accumulation of masses of unprocessed information and facilitates easy access to critical pieces of information later in the research process (Repko, 2008, pp. 281–282). Several examples are found in Step 6, below.

Step 5: Develop Adequacy in Each Relevant Discipline

Newell (1998) confirms the emerging consensus "that interdisciplinary study should build explicitly and directly upon the work of the disciplines" (p. 542). He terms the required adequacy in each discipline as "quite modest," consisting of a basic understanding of how the discipline approaches a question such as the one under consideration together with the applicable insights, theories, concepts, and assumptions (Newell, 2006, p. 253). He observes that, in the interdisciplinary process, it is not the disciplines themselves but the insights provided by disciplinary perspectives that are compared (Newell, 1998, pp. 543–546).

The overall perspectives of the most relevant disciplines on Jewish marriage are stated below:

• Religion views the world in terms of transcendent beliefs whose source is divine revelation, usually expressed through organized forms of worship. Religion may include laws or guidance governing various aspects of human life, as there is no separation between what is valid for the religious life and for human conduct. Religion, as theology, views the world through the eyes of believers, while religious studies additionally draws upon other disciplines for understanding. The religious perspective, as applied to Jewish marriage, is theological and views halakhic law (Torah and subsequent Jewish religious law) interpreted by the Orthodox Rabbinate as the sole valid basis for marriage. This perspective finds the exclusive delegation of the institution of marriage by the state to religious authorities to be consistent with religious law.

• Political science views the world in terms of relationships of power. The perspective of political science provides motivations and explanations for choices made in developing law and policies for the Jewish and democratic State of Israel, whose founding and governing ideology is Secular Zionism. The political perspective views the exclusive delegation of Jewish marriage to religious authorities as consistent with Zionism, politically pragmatic, and important for the preservation of power.

• Law "refers to a set of rules and regulations *and* to the social institution that creates, implements, and enforces these rules and regulations" (Barkan, 2009, p. 21). Law is created by the judicial branch as well as by the political branches of government—executive and legislative. The state generally provides the mechanisms of enforcement for the legal system to function. The legal perspective views Jewish marriage as an institution whose function the democratic State of Israel has delegated exclusively to religious authorities. In this regard, the legal perspective must take into account the complex relationships between religious (Jewish) law and state (secular) law and, more broadly, between religion and state.

Overall, the disciplinary perspectives most relevant to an analysis of the factors in Israel's conflicted identity that relate to Jewish marriage hew closer to the humanities than to the social sciences. In humanities disciplines, there is an emphasis on qualitative research methods. Religion is generally viewed as a humanities discipline. Law, here, hews closer to the humanities while in other instances it partakes of the social sciences as well as the humanities.[4] Although political science, as a social science, employs both quantitative and qualitative empirical research methods, most sources relevant to the present study rely upon the methodologies of qualitative research.

In humanities disciplines, the "data" are generally the literature of the discipline, which may include its primary source material but also rely heavily upon secondary authority, such as critical commentary and analysis. Research, then, consists primarily of an analysis of the literature rather than an analysis of empirical data. In political science, some qualitative studies are empirical while others, such as those dealing with institutions, often work with "data" in the humanistic sense. Because the disciplinary perspectives most relevant to this study are not as theory-laden as is typical in the social sciences, it will be important to analyze the phenomena, concepts, and assumptions as well as relevant theories of the disciplines in order to evaluate disciplinary insights.

Step 6: Analyze the Problem and Evaluate Each Insight Into It

There are two parts to Step 6: "analyze the problem from the perspective of each relevant discipline, and evaluate each relevant insight into the problem . . . identifying strengths and weaknesses" (Repko, 2008, p. 217). As the perspective of each discipline contributes only a part of the integrated whole, it is important to view the research question from each relevant discipline's perspective, as illustrated in Table 2.1.

The second part of Step 6 focuses on evaluating disciplinary insights. By focusing on each discipline's insights into the question through its phenomena, assumptions, concepts, and theories, strengths and weaknesses are revealed.

In evaluating disciplinary insights, it is essential to refine the data management tables developed in Step 4, the literature search. The most relevant insights of each discipline are identified, some theory-based and others not. Underlying disciplinary assumptions and key concepts are also included in the tables. More information is included in the table than may be necessary because it is not possible to know until the later steps of the process exactly which insights will prove essential to the process of integration. The discovery

---

[4]Law has been categorized as both a humanities discipline and a social science discipline. Donald (2002) categorizes law as an applied social science (p. 30). See generally Sarat (2004) for a discussion of law as a liberal arts discipline, both humanities and social science.

| Table 2.1 | Identification of Disciplinary Perspectives on the Problem |

Most Relevant Disciplines	Perspective on the Question Stated in General Terms
Religion	Sees Jewish marriage theologically, governed exclusively by Torah and other religious law and therefore validly delegated by the state and available only to those deemed to have the status of Jews according to Orthodox Judaism.
Political science	Sees marriage in Israel as delegated exclusively to religious authorities to accommodate the balance of power among Jewish groups in the state and to preserve the Jewish nature of the democratic state against threats from Arab minorities.
Law	Sees the legal question of the delegation of Jewish marriage to the Orthodox Rabbinate as consistent with a democratic society that is not characterized by the separation of religion and state. Finds pragmatic solutions to issues such as the absence of civil marriage without directly addressing civil rights violations.

of comparable elements among the insights of the different disciplines prepares for the second part of the process, integrating insights and producing an interdisciplinary understanding.

The Insights of Religion

Religion typically sees the ultimate source of laws governing human behavior as divine revelation. The discipline of "religion," as it refers to Judaism in Israel, is limited to the Orthodox denomination because it is the only one that enjoys any official recognition by the state.[5] Conservative and Reform Judaism never developed a strong following in Israel, where most non-Orthodox Jews consider themselves to be secular.[6]

The perspective of religion on Jewish marriage in Israel has its roots in the role of religion in European Jewish life over the centuries. The insight termed *halakhah governing human conduct* derives from the Orthodox Jewish notion that there is no distinction made between laws governing religious life and human conduct. Historically, Jewish law has both a religious and a national character: religious because its ultimate source is divine revelation, and national because it is an essential part of the life of the Jewish people throughout its history. *Halakhah* denotes Jewish law as derived from the

---

[5]In 1982, Reform rabbis were unsuccessful in petitioning the Supreme Court of Israel to recognize marriages performed by them (Rebhun & Waxman, 2004, p. 295).

[6]According to Shetreet (1997), the personal attitude of Israelis toward religion and tradition is 4% ultra-Orthodox, 12% religious, and almost 40% traditional (modern/moderate orthodox). This leaves more than 40% secular and less than 5% Reform or Conservative (p. 194).

Torah and ancient scholarly works as interpreted by modern Orthodox Jewish rabbinical authorities. Halakhah developed as a binding form of communal law that created ethnic cohesiveness among European Jews, prior to the rise of the Zionist movement at the end of the 19th century (Berlin, 1978, p. 16). As a living legal system, it has evolved through the work of scholars, whose duty it was and is to preserve its spirit and purpose while continuing its evolution (Elon, 1967a, pp. 517–518, 561).

How does the religious perspective allow for engagement in civic life? Elazar's (1998) *covenant theory* provides a theo-political rationale, emanating from the original covenant of biblical Israel:

> A covenant is a morally informed agreement or pact based upon voluntary consent and mutual oaths or promises, witnessed by the relevant higher authority. . . . Most are meant to be of unlimited duration, if not perpetual. (p. 8)

> The Bible describes how God sets Israel aside for His religio-political purposes through covenant. Covenant is not just a device but shapes the whole worldview of the Jewish people. (p. 375)

Elazar (1998) finds that the ancient biblical covenant could be disconnected from direct reliance upon God, thereby providing a foundation for civic obligations (p. 19). The biblical covenant tradition provided the earliest evidence of "a religion of ethical nationalism" (p. 33), which Elazar characterizes as not an "ancient traditional constitution" (p. 210) retained through the centuries "as part of the deep structure of Jewish life, both religious and political" (p. 318).

How, then, was the present system of Jewish marriage developed? The *religious communal continuity* insight provides a historical rationale for the institution. According to Elon (1967b), the Jews who lived in Palestine during the Ottoman Empire—until 1917—were ruled under the "millet system," in which each minority religious group had its own community and some autonomy and protection regarding marriage laws (p. 425). In the matter of Jewish marriage, exclusive authority was granted to the Rabbinical Courts. This system continued under the British Mandate, from 1920 to 1948, the period when the British ruled Palestine after the partition of the Ottoman Empire. Subsequent to Israeli independence in 1948, the millet system was carried over and remains to the present day with regard to marriage law. The religious communal continuity insight fails to account for the differences in the structure between a monolithic pre-state all-Jewish Orthodox minority community and the religiously and ethnically diverse populace of the sovereign State of Israel.

A complete understanding of the religious insights relating to Jewish marriage must consider the views of those who object to Orthodox monopoly of the institution. Batkay's (1989) *Orthodox hegemony theory* finds its basis in the political arena: the retention of power. The exclusivity of the Orthodox establishment justifies itself in the name of the values of "unity" and "authenticity" (p. 126). Batkay continues,

By refusing to legitimate the ritual acts of non-Orthodox religious authorities, the Orthodox rabbinate insures that *it* retains the power of approving the choice of marriage partners for Jews. From the perspective of the Orthodox leadership in Israel, the goal is to protect Jewish peoplehood; from the viewpoint of non-Orthodox movements, however, the main objective of the Orthodox leaders is the consolidation of their own power. (p. 126)

The same conclusions that Batkay (1989) draws with regard to the role of different Jewish denominations occur in the violation of the rights of the nonreligious and those desiring civil marriage.

The major religious insights are set forth in Table 2.2.

The Orthodox religious assumption that halakhic law governs both religious and human conduct is the underpinning of most religious insights. Religious insights may be grouped into sets of assumptions. Both the *halakhic law governing human conduct* and the *religious communal continuity* insights provide religious justification for the delegation of Jewish marriage to

Table 2.2 Religious Insights

General Insight	Insight Into the Question (Scholarly Opinion)	Assumption(s)	Concepts
Halakhah governing human conduct	Jewish marriage is determined according to the rules of Torah (Barak, 2002). Jewish law has both a religious and a national character (Elon, 1967a, pp. 517–518).	Jewish law (halakhah) governs both religious life and human conduct.	Halakhah (Elon, 1967a, pp. 517–518); Torah, values of Jewish tradition (Barak, 2002).
Covenant theory (theo-political)	The biblical covenant between God and the Jewish people provides the foundation for civic responsibility (Elazar, 1998, p. 19).	Covenant tradition binds the deep structure of Jewish religious and political life.	Covenant (Elazar, 1998, p. 8).
Religious communal continuity	The system of Jewish marriage, as continued by the State of Israel, has its roots in the Ottoman millet system (Elon, 1967b, p. 425).	Same.	Millet system (Elon, 1967b, p. 425).
Orthodox hegemony theory (theo-political)	Jewish marriage provides unlimited hegemony for the Orthodox in order to preserve power (Batkay, 1989, pp. 119, 126).	Jewish law (halakhah) binds religious and political life.	Reform Judaism, Conservative Judaism (Batkay, 1989, pp. 119, 126).

the Orthodox Rabbinate. In contrast, the assumptions of both *covenant theory* and *Orthodox hegemony theory* are theo-political. *Both theories explicitly extend halakhah governing human conduct to the political sphere.* All of the religious insights share the emphasis upon "Jewish" in the conflicted nature of Israel as a Jewish and democratic state.

The Insights of Political Science

Political science emphasizes relationships of power and the legitimacy of power. Traditional political science includes an analysis of regime types or forms of government as well as the influence of political principles in shaping these realms (Ceaser, 1990, pp. 42, 73). As applied to Israel, this includes debates over the classification of its democracy, its institutions of government, and the resulting laws and policies.

An exploration of the perspective of political science on Jewish marriage must begin with an understanding of the political circumstances leading to the current formulation of the institution. Its antecedents are found among the Jews in both Europe and pre-state Palestine. The insight termed *communal-based (non-state) politics* refers to the historical marginalization of European Jews in earlier centuries. This was a consequence of anti-Semitism, which bred a sense of Jewish alienation from politics (Berlin, 1978, p. 16). Berlin's theory is that the core of Jewish life, formed through continuity from European roots of prior centuries, is the Jewish religion (p. 10). In the Palestinian pre-state period, communal-based (non-state) politics was exercised through partial communal self-government under both the Ottoman Empire and the British Mandate. Thus, the essential political elements of a Jewish nation were honed during that time. The political system of the late 1940s has been described as a "Republican Democratic model . . . applied . . . to the Jewish sector" (Peled, cited in Sheffer, 1996, p. 33).

A complete history of the political dynamic must consider the political effects of statehood in 1948. Zionism,[7] according to Peretz and Doron (1999), was Israel's "propelling national ideology" (p. 2), whose essential elements are as follows:

1. Jews are a separate people, and their common religious and cultural characteristics qualify them to be perceived as a national entity;

2. Because of the prevailing anti-Semitism rooted in Gentile society, Jews cannot expect to be treated as equals by their European "host" nations; and

3. The only solution to Jews' aspirations to equality and normalcy is to establish . . . a national homeland. (p. 22)

---

[7]Isaac (1981) notes that of the three Zionist ideas—religious, socialist, and Zion as refuge—the secular socialist vision came to dominate (pp. 2–4). Secular Zionism has also been called Labor Zionism and Socialist Zionism.

The policies of David Ben-Gurion, Israel's first prime minister, epitomized secular Zionism's conciliation and accommodation, termed *mamlachtiut*. They were intended to reconcile the Jewish traditional past with the needs of a contemporary civic state (Dowty, 1998, p. 62). This is termed the *secular Zionist religious-political accommodation* insight. The position of Judaism in the state was defined by a series of political arrangements, with freedom of religion in the private sphere and traditional Judaism in the public sphere (Horowitz & Lissak, 1989, p. 228). One result was the retention of "the status quo in synagogue-state affairs (meaning arrangements in effect during the pre-state period regarding religion and religious practice would be extended into the state period), and by affording monopoly status to Orthodox Judaism . . . on matters . . . such as marriage" (Arian, 2005, pp. 10–11). For a Jewish marriage to take place, both parties must be recognized as Jewish by the Orthodox Rabbinate. The Orthodox definition of "Who is a Jew?" recognizes only maternal Jewish lineage and, further, only recognizes conversions to Judaism in Israel conducted by Orthodox rabbis.

Orthodox Jews had wanted to create a state founded upon Jewish law, halakhah. When that failed, they joined with secular Zionists to preserve and maximize the role of religious law within the State of Israel. This is termed the *halakhic politics* insight. The Orthodox, politically well-organized and well-represented, "regard the prevalence of religious law as a vested right and existing religious tribunals as strongholds of the faith" (Shiloh, 1970, p. 480). Religious primacy inherently creates political tensions in a democracy because adherents are loyal to a power that they believe is greater than any state.

To understand fully the political insights relating to Jewish marriage, consideration must be given to significant segments of Israeli society who are affected by the current status of the institution. This is termed the *religious-political coercion* insight. Since the Rabbinical Courts apply rules to the entire Jewish population that are subscribed to by only a minority, the result is animosity that deters the development of a common political culture even among the Jews of Israel (Arian, 2005, pp. 61, 72). The non-Orthodox Jewish majority has had its rights sacrificed in the name of accommodation and appeasement in halakhic politics. One explanation for this acquiescence is that, as a group, Israelis are less enthusiastic about individualism than about the maintenance of the Jewish State (Jacobsohn, 1993, p. 5).

The major political insights are set forth in Table 2.3.

Three of the political insights build upon an understanding of the role of Orthodox Judaism in the State of Israel. The *communal-based (non-state) politics* insight provides a historical basis for the non-state government in the pre-state Jewish community, many of whose practices were carried over when Jews became the majority population in the State of Israel. The *secular Zionist religious-political accommodation* insight attempts to reconcile the competing interests of the state and the Orthodox community, though

Table 2.3   Political Insights

General Insight	Insight Into the Question (Scholarly Opinion)	Assumption(s)	Concepts
Communal-based (non-state) politics	The marginalization of Jews in European politics prior to the 20th century (Berlin, 1978, p. 10) led to legitimacy without sovereignty in Palestine (Arian, 2005, p. 6).	Historical alienation produced an insular homogeneous religious-based Jewish political structure.	Anti-Semitism, pogroms (Berlin, 1978, p. 16); legitimacy, sovereignty (Arian, 2005, p. 6).
Secular Zionist religious-political accommodation	By preserving the status quo of pre-state arrangements, Zionists retained the monopoly of Orthodox Judaism in matters of Jewish marriage (Arian, 2005, pp. 10–11).	Politics is a struggle over whose values and interests will prevail (Repko, 2008, p. 60).	Political culture (Edelman, 1994, p. 55); *mamlachtiut* (Dowty, 1998, p. 62).
Halakhic politics	Halakhic politics are designed to maximize the role of religious law within the state (Horowitz & Lissak, 1989, pp. 142–143).	Same.	Accommodation (Dowty, 1998, p. 168).
Religious-political coercion	Conservative, Reform and secular Jews, as well as non-Jews, view the existing arrangements applying the religious laws of marriage as religious coercion (Dowty, 1998, p. 161).	Same.	Secular Israelis (Dowty, 1998, p. 161).

compromise sometimes comes at the expense of democratic practices. The *halakhic politics* insight demonstrates the Orthodox community's political agenda of furthering the role of halakhic law in the state. In contrast, the *religious-political coercion* insight is the political expression of the religious *Orthodox hegemony theory*, in which accommodation functions at the expense of democracy. While all of these insights share the emphasis upon the "democratic" elements in the insights regarding Israel as a Jewish and democratic state, some support and others conflict with the democratic vision of the state.

The Insights of Law

Law focuses upon rules of the state. Jurisprudence focuses upon the sources and functions of law within the social context. Laws originate in the political branches of government—the legislative and executive branches—and are interpreted by the judiciary. Edelman (1994) distinguishes law and politics: "In politics, values and principles are perceived as instrumental tools for achieving certain results. Law, on the other hand, is perceived as flowing from an impartial, objective analysis of rules and principles" (p. 33). Law, thus, represents the codification of policy shaped through politics.

An understanding of the legal perspective on Jewish marriage must begin with the precursors of Israel's present legal institutions in the Yishuv (pre-state Palestine). This is termed the *secular pre-state legal antecedents* insight. It refers to informal consensual non-halakhic-based court systems set up at several periods during the British Mandate, thereby creating the secular basis for the current Israeli court system.

During the same pre-state period in the Yishuv, the Orthodox Rabbinate attempted to sow the seeds of a dominant role for religious law. This insight is termed *halakhic pre-state legal antecedents*. Whatever the potential role for halakhic law as national law, Jewish religious law did not assume such a role in the State of Israel except in the area of personal status law, which includes Jewish marriage (Elon, 1967c, p.102; Elon, 1967b, pp. 442, 454).

With the advent of statehood, religious institutions were accorded special status to "exercise State functions according to their Religious Law, and their activities are recognized by, and are binding upon, the State, as if carried out by its own authorities and officials and in conformity with its laws" (Freudenheim, 1967, p. 87). In the case of the Orthodox Rabbinate's monopoly on Jewish marriage law, religious law was thereby converted into state law. The Rabbinical Court system became a public institution whose structure and jurisdiction were determined by state authority (Edelman, 1994, pp. 52–53, 61). This structure makes Israel "the only modern state in the world lacking a territorial law of marriage and divorce" (Shachar, in Shapira & DeWitt-Arar, 1995, p. 3). This is termed the *interrelationship of religion and state* insight.

The Israeli legal system, therefore, is basically secular but has adopted religious norms in particular arenas—such as Jewish marriage—in order to arrive at legal solutions without challenging the overall Jewishness of the state. This insight is termed *legal pragmatism theory*. Barak-Erez (2007) describes the model of legal accommodation, in which "many legal arrangements reflect pragmatic compromises rather than doctrinal decisions" (p. 118). For example, Sharkansky (1999) points out the incongruities between religious law and the rules followed by state authorities regarding Jewish marriage, in that couples who cannot or who choose not to be married by the Orthodox Rabbinate can marry overseas (p. 66). Mazie (2006) terms the option of civil marriage abroad the "exit option" (p. 165). Thus, legal pragmatism effectively erodes the exclusivity of the power of the Orthodox Rabbinate to dictate who can marry.

In maintaining the current marriage laws, the avoidance of conflicts with one group, the Orthodox Rabbinate, only sows the seeds of conflict with others, particularly in civil rights violations. The *freedom of religion and freedom from religion* insight has particular impact in the area of Jewish marriage. The effect of the current system, according to Mazie (2006), is that

> it makes citizens subject to a religious authority whether or not they accept its legitimacy or believe the religious truths it represents. Israel's delegation of authority to Jewish religious courts requires a large group of citizens (secular and other non-Orthodox Jews) to adhere to the comprehensive religious doctrine of a minority (ultra-Orthodox Jews) when participating in major life events such as marriage and divorce. (p. 183)

Mazie (2006) concludes that in the classification of relationships between religion and democracy, imposing religion—including the determination of what is or is not proper in Judaism—would not survive the legal test of "strict scrutiny" (pp. 258–259).

The major legal insights are set forth in Table 2.4.

Table 2.4   Legal Insights

General Insight	Insight Into the Question (Scholarly Opinion)	Assumption(s)	Concepts
Secular pre-state legal antecedents	Jewish legal institutions were developed during the pre-state period (Shamir, 2000, pp. 30–33; Shetreet, 1994, p. 30).	The rule of law in Israel has developed in the absence of separation between religion and state.	Hebrew Law of Peace; Hebrew Courts of Peace (Shamir, 2000, pp. 30–33).
Halakhic pre-state legal antecedents	Halakhic law scholars in Europe and Palestine in the early 20th century worked for the renewal of halakhic law as national law for the future state (Elon, 1967b, p. 419).	Same.	HaMishpat Ha'Ivri Society (Elon, 1967b, p. 419).

(Continued)

Table 2.4 (Continued)

General Insight	Insight Into the Question (Scholarly Opinion)	Assumption(s)	Concepts
Interrelationship of religion and state (contrast: separation of church and state)	In areas such as Jewish marriage, religious institutions exercise state functions according to religious law, and their activities are binding as if carried out by state authorities (Freudenheim, 1967, p. 87).	Same.	[Absence of] territorial law of marriage and divorce (Shachar, in Shapira & DeWitt-Arar, 1995, p. 3).
Legal pragmatism theory	According to the model of legal accommodation, "many legal arrangements reflect pragmatic compromises rather than doctrinal decisions" (Barak-Erez, 2007, p. 118).	Same.	Accommodation (Barak-Erez, 2007, p. 118).
Freedom of and from religion	The Rabbinical Courts, as the exclusive legal authority on marriage, subject the majority of Israelis to the religious doctrine of the Orthodox minority. Imposing religion does not survive strict scrutiny (Mazie, 2006, pp. 183, 259).	Same.	Human rights issue (Gavison, 2007, p. 137).

All the legal insights share a common assumption that the rule of law has developed in Israeli democracy in the absence of separation of religion and state. Although the *secular pre-state legal antecedents* insight and the *halakhic pre-state legal antecedents* insight are mutually exclusive, Jewish marriage under the millet system applied in both cases because the Ottoman law was both religious and communal. Even after statehood was achieved in 1948, the vestigial legal structure of Jewish marriage remained as it had previously been under the millet system.

According to the *interrelationship of religion and state* insight, the state delegates, designates, validates, and provides exclusive authority to the Orthodox Rabbinate in the matter of Jewish marriage. Legal pragmatism theory illustrates how the institution of Jewish marriage is able to function in Israel's heterogeneous society: It relies upon legal accommodation to meet the needs of the secular majority while maintaining the unity of the Jewish state.

The *freedom of and from religion* insight illustrates that the accommodation of the Orthodox community's interests violates the civil rights of the secular majority. This occurs particularly in the absence of civil marriage. All of these insights demonstrate the competing interests of "Jewish" and "democratic" in legal considerations of Israel's conflicted nature as a Jewish and democratic state.

Integrating Insights and Producing an Interdisciplinary Understanding

The first part of the interdisciplinary research process set forth the main disciplinary insights regarding Jewish marriage that express Israel's conflicted nature as a Jewish and democratic state. Each disciplinary perspective provided only a partial explanation.

The primary focus of the second part of the research process is to utilize the contributions of the disciplines to create common ground between these insights, integrate them, produce a new understanding, and test it. Newell (1998) describes integration as

> essentially holistic thinking, in which the different facets of a complex reality exposed through different disciplinary lenses are combined into a new whole that is larger than its constituent parts, that cannot be reduced to the separate disciplinary insights from which it emerged. . . . It requires an act of creative imagination, a leap from the simplified perspectives that give the disciplines their power to a more holistic perspective of a richer more complex whole. (p. 55)

In other words, "the interdisciplinarian needs to contextualize the contribution of each discipline within the overall complex system" (Newell, 2006, p. 250).

Step 7: Identify Conflicts Between Insights and Their Sources

Conflicts occur between insights within a discipline and between disciplines. Possible sources of conflict are the underlying assumptions, constituent concepts, and theories that are expressed as disciplinary insights (Repko, 2008, pp. 248–255). Because each discipline has its own worldview, insights of different disciplines may not simply be combined; rather, they must be evaluated first in the context of the specific question (Newell, 1998, p. 110). The differences in disciplinary assumptions provide greater likelihood for conflicts between, rather than within, disciplines. The scholarly insights of religion, political science, and law, as described earlier, are explored in Step 7 to highlight conflicts within each discipline and between them.

Sources of Conflict Within the Same Discipline

Some conflicts within the same discipline simply present alternative views, while others represent diametric opposition. The sources of conflict within each discipline—religion, political science, and law—are discussed in Step 6 above.

Sources of Conflict Between Disciplines

Having identified sources of conflict within the same discipline, it is now necessary to identify sources of conflict between the disciplines. This process is not clear cut because many of the disciplinary insights have embedded within them elements of other disciplines. One source of conflict between disciplines involves insights in support of the primacy of religion, religious politics, and laws favoring religion. These are termed *religious-based insights*. The other source of conflict involves insights that arise because of the effects of religious-based insights upon the civil rights of those affected by decisions made on a religious basis. These are termed *civil rights violation insights*. Once these sources of conflict are identified and clarified, the process of creating or discovering common ground can proceed.

Religious-Based Insights. A contrastive study of religious-based insights reveals conflicts between groups of insights across disciplines. The halakhah governing human conduct insight is viewed from the standpoint of Orthodox Judaism as the role of divine revelation in human affairs. The legal application of the religious insight is the halakhic pre-law legal antecedents insight, which represents the efforts of halakhic scholars in the pre-state era to develop halakhic law as the national law for the future state of Israel.

These insights conflict with the political reality of the creation of the pluralistic yet Jewish State of Israel. The secular Zionist religious-political accommodation insight demonstrates compromises to retain the status quo of the Orthodox Jewish pre-state monopoly in matters of Jewish marriage. In other words, a secular Zionist government adopted a purely religious solution to Jewish marriage for reasons of political accommodation. At the same time, the Orthodox Rabbinate joined with the secular Zionists to play halakhic politics in order to maximize the role of the Orthodox in the non-halakhic State of Israel.

Civil Rights Violation Insights. From the legal perspective, the interrelationship of religion and state insight demonstrates the embedded role of religion within the legal system. Yet, it is not the interrelationship itself that causes problems but the violations of civil rights that result from the impermissible imposition of religion.

Each of the disciplines deals with individuals and groups whose civil rights are denied due to the monopoly of the Orthodox Rabbinate in matters of Jewish marriage. Some of the insights are theory-based, while others are not. Religion's Orthodox hegemony theory attributes the motivations of the Orthodox to the preservation of power rather than to a desire for doctrinal purity. Political science's religious-political coercion insight recognizes that the Zionist accommodation of the Orthodox monopoly in matters of Jewish marriage results in religious coercion exercised against secular Jews, among others. Law's freedom of and from religion insight recognizes that the status quo results in a lack of equal protection for the majority, which must function under the religious dictates of a minority. Although most Israelis recognize the legitimate interest of maintaining a Jewish majority in Israel, they acknowledge that the present approach to Jewish marriage imperils the civil rights of citizens.

Religious-Based Insights and Civil Rights Violation Insights. Barak-Erez's (2007) legal pragmatism theory describes legal accommodation as a matter of "pragmatic compromises rather than doctrinal decisions" (p. 118). It is reflective of an effort to seek functional legal solutions that do not necessarily follow religious doctrine. In her book *Outlawed Pigs: Law, Religion and Culture in Israel* (2007), Barak-Erez recounts the story of the Israeli legislative prohibitions against pig breeding and pork sales, from the original religious prohibitions to the present situation, in which pork is available almost everywhere that a demand exists (p. 102). The death knell for pork-trading prohibitions came in the 2004 Israeli Supreme Court *Solodkin* case, when Chief Justice Barak wrote a unanimous decision for the court. The decision regulated the pork trade on the basis of the characteristics of each local community, its needs, and the availability of the product nearby. The compromise reflected a completely secular view, respectful of the wishes of the majority secular constituency in each community and without religious consideration of the Jewish character of the state (pp. 97–99). Barak-Erez applies legal pragmatism theory to Jewish marriage, describing the current situation that permits the registration in Israel of marriages performed abroad, thereby effectively providing a legal alternative for those who cannot or choose not to marry under the strictures of current law. However, this theory does not address questions of civil rights violations.

Barak-Erez (2007) indicates that the success of legal pragmatism theory has become more problematic. In the past, the secular and religious factions would each assume that their compromises and accommodations were temporary and that the other side would eventually cease to oppose them. Now positions are hardening as both sides realize that everyone is here to stay. Therefore, opponents are poised to launch frontal assaults on previously inviolable agreements such as religious marriage law and the absence of civil marriage in Israel (p. 120).

By fostering civic engagement from a religious basis, theo-political covenant theory provides an opening to take advantage of the situation created by the increasing difficulties in applying legal pragmatism theory. Because covenant theory binds the deep structure of Jewish religious and political life, it provides a justification for the Orthodox to build effective solutions grounded in a sound religious foundation.

Step 8: Create or Discover Common Ground

Step 8, the creation or discovery of common ground, is the essential pre-requisite to integration. Common ground is created by modifying the concepts, assumptions, or theories that produce disciplinary insights. It is not created by modifying the insights themselves or by modifying the overall disciplinary perspectives (Repko, 2008, pp. 279–280). Newell (2006) speaks of bringing out "latent" or "potential" commonalities (p. 257), an allusion to the intuitive, nonlinear, and challenging nature of this step. Both Repko (2008, p. 281) and Newell (2006, p. 258) describe the nature and extent of the conflicts that will, in turn, determine the techniques to be used in creating common ground. Below, the conflicts are grouped according to their nature and extent.

Nature and Extent of Conflicts

A. No actual conflict in insights but commonality is obscured by discipline-specific terminology or context.

- Religion, law—Halakhah governing human conduct insight and halakhic pre-state legal antecedents insight.
- Religion, political science, law—Orthodox hegemony theory; secular Zionist religious-political accommodation; halakhic politics; and interrelationship of religion and state.
- Religion, political science, law—Religious communal continuity insight; communal-based (non-state) politics insight; and secular pre-state legal antecedents insight.

B. Insights that are different, rather than opposing; they present alternatives.

- Religion, law—Halakhah governing human law; covenant theory; and halakhic pre-state legal antecedents vs. political science, law—secular Zionist religious-political accommodation; halakhic politics; and "interrelationship of religion and state.
- Religion, law—Religious communal continuity insight and halakhic pre-state legal antecedents insight.

- Law, political science, religion—Covenant theory lays a foundation for legal pragmatism. Legal pragmatism theory places more weight on compromise in seeking legal solutions than on doctrinal considerations and thereby demonstrates a willingness to de-emphasize the dictates of religious principles in order to achieve pragmatic ends.

C. Insights that are diametrically opposed.
   - Law—Secular pre-state legal antecedents insight and the halakhic pre-state legal antecedents insight present diametrically opposed visions of legal institutions for the future State of Israel.
   - Religion, political science, law—Orthodox hegemony theory; religious political coercion; freedom of and from religion. From different disciplinary perspectives, each of these insights demonstrates opposition to the insights of accommodation, whose effect is to ignore the rights of significant portions of the population. These are diametrically opposed to the insights of accommodation, political science, law—secular Zionist religious-political accommodation; halakhic politics; and interrelationship of religion and state.

The Discovery/Creation of Common Ground

Having examined the nature and extent of conflicts, the techniques described by Newell (2006) and Repko (2008) will be used to discover or create common ground. Four techniques are described by Newell (2006):

1. *Redefinition* "reveal[s] commonalities in concepts or assumptions that may be obscured by discipline-specific terminology."

2. *Extension* "extends the meaning of an idea beyond the domain of the discipline into the domain of another discipline."

3. *Organization* "identifies a latent commonality in meaning," redefines, and then "arrays the redefined insights or assumptions to bring out a relationship among them."

4. *Transformation* is used for dichotomous concepts, to change dualistic either/or thinking into both/and thinking. (pp. 258–260)

5. Repko (2008) adds a fifth technique, *theory expansion,* which is "used to modify a theory so that it can address all of the causation insights pertaining to a problem." (p. 281)

With regard to the term *Jewish,* only in the area of personal status laws such as Jewish marriage does the word have the same meaning in religion, politics, and law because, in this one area, the Knesset has by explicit legislative enactment delegated and validated the exclusive role of the Orthodox Rabbinate. Any *redefinition* of *Jewish* must take into account the preservation of the Jewish character of the State of Israel. Because integration involves change, the redefinition of *Jewish* would encompass cultural and national identity definitions, in order to take into account civil rights violation insights and religious-based insights.

Because the State of Israel is a democracy rather than a Jewish theocracy, it must be responsive to the needs of its pluralistic society. A *redefinition* of *democratic* in the context of *Jewish and democratic* requires recognition of the civil rights of all within a heterogeneous society. It requires distinguishing among the different types of religion-state connections and excluding those that are incompatible with a democracy.

Using the technique of *organization*, historical continuity provides political and legal justification for maintaining the status quo in the Orthodox Rabbinate's monopoly on the institution of Jewish marriage in the State of Israel. Ben-Gurion's secular Zionist religious-political accommodation insight resulted in the acceptance of the status quo regarding the institution of Jewish marriage in order to placate the Orthodox constituency and solidify a unified base against Arab threats. From the legal perspective, the politics of *mamlachtiut* are memorialized as the laws of accommodation and compromise in the interrelationship of religion and state insight.

The technique of *extension* relates the insights from religion, political science, and law that are grouped as religious-based insights. The underlying assumption of an unquestioned divine source does not negate the possibility of human action, but rather provides guidance through halakhah governing human conduct. Covenant theory encourages more active civic engagement by structuring civic responsibility as a part of religious covenant. The religious-based society envisioned in the pre-state Yishuv was homogeneous and Orthodox. Through halakhic politics, the Orthodox Rabbinate maximizes its influence within the present-day pluralistic sovereign state. The Rabbinate's interactions and compromises may be viewed as an Orthodox adaptation to a heterogeneous society. Thus, the original description of Orthodox hegemony theory as unlimited supremacy of the Orthodox Rabbinate to the detriment of all other Jewish denominations in order to preserve power must be extended beyond the theo-political to the legal sphere to encompass the best tool available to the Orthodox to maximize the presence and influence of halakhah in the state. Covenant theory serves as a rationale for this extension.

The technique of *extension* also explains the opposition to accommodation in civil rights violation insights. From a political perspective, the religious-political coercion insight, and from a legal perspective, the freedom of and from religion insight both underscore constitutional deficiencies in terms of the lack of civil liberties for non-Orthodox denominations, the Jewish secular majority, and Jews wishing to marry non-Jews. From a religious perspective, civil rights violations are a consequence of the Orthodox hegemony theory. From the historical evidence of the religious communal continuity insight in the pre-state Yishuv, it can be seen that the same regulations were applied to all designated minority religious groups under the millet system, with a designated religious body in charge of marriage laws for each group.

Thus, historically, there was not a model for civil marriage overseen by the state. In contrast to its historical antecedents, the State of Israel is a pluralistic democracy and, as such, has responsibility to protect the civil liberties of all its citizens. Due to the absence of separation between religion and state, theological issues are woven into the very framework of the legitimacy of the state (Lorberbaum, 2007, pp. 160–161).

The preceding two examples demonstrate the conflicts between religious-based insights and civil rights violation insights, as expressed through the insights of religion, political science, and law. The technique of extension helps us to understand these conflicts but does not move sufficiently toward integration. In order for these conflicts to be reconciled, the technique of *transformation* will be needed "to replace the either/or [dualistic] thinking, which is characteristic of the disciplines, with both/and [inclusive] thinking" (Newell, 2006, p. 260).

The technique of *theory expansion* provides the best method for creating common ground in preparation for integration. This technique is used to expand a theory's focus to include additional insights without distorting the theory (Repko, 2008, pp. 281–283). The theory of legal pragmatism prioritizes compromise in seeking legal solutions over doctrinal considerations. Religious-based insights and political insights are taken into account in the calculus of compromise, in order to arrive at legally pragmatic solutions. However, the recognition by each faction that the other side is not going away has hardened positions. Compromise between the factions has become more difficult because the right to marry civilly, outside a prescribed religious setting, is viewed by one faction as a civil right and by the other faction as antagonistic to the continuity of the Jewish identity of the state.

Legal pragmatism theory must be expanded to take into account the concerns of the Orthodox in order to make possible a more comprehensive vision. Covenant theory affords an opportunity to expand legal pragmatism theory by appealing to, and more actively engaging, the political interests of the Orthodox. Covenant theory accomplishes this expansion by incorporating the rationale that a theo-political covenant can be disconnected from direct reliance upon God to promote civic engagement in a political structure. It would enable the Orthodox to retain their own *religious* doctrinal purity while not violating the *civil rights* of citizens.

Step 9: Integrate Insights

Performing Step 8 makes it possible to create common ground. In Step 9, this common ground is used to integrate the various conflicting insights under discussion. Newell (2006) describes integration in the following way: "once common ground has been constructed, the modified insights can be integrated into a more comprehensive understanding of the complex problem . . . [which] should be responsive to each disciplinary perspective but beholden to none of them" (pp. 257, 261).

The process of integrating insights proceeds from our original question: How does the institution of Jewish marriage express Israel's conflicted identity as a Jewish and democratic state? The insights clearly cannot be viewed in disciplinary isolation, as each requires an understanding of the others for a complete picture.

Regarding religious-based insights, Newell's (2006) either/or to both/and transformation begins with the evolution of a homogeneous isolated Jewish community into a heterogeneous sovereign Jewish state. Integration can build upon the Orthodox Rabbinate's pragmatic impetus to compromise. Legal pragmatism theory, as applied to Jewish marriage, provides a sound basis to reconcile competing disciplinary insights and accomplish integration.

Covenant theory encompasses the respect for human rights. This may help to effectuate a mindset change among the Orthodox, through the realization that a monopoly over an unwilling populace in Jewish marriage is neither in their best interests nor necessarily representative of the fruits of their religious tradition. Rabbi Isaac Halevi Herzog, the first chief Rabbi of the State of Israel, maintained that "the State of Israel is not charged with the implementation of the Torah's vision of a political society but it is, however, obliged not to openly legislate against Torah law" (cited in Lorberbaum, 2007, p. 160). Legal pragmatism theory, supported by covenant theory, demonstrates the opportunity to go beyond the limitations of religious-based insights.

Legal pragmatism theory also integrates the essential elements that can lead to transformation of the civil rights violation insights. The increasing difficulty of compromise under the old ways is what will make change possible. The introduction of civil marriage would equalize the situation for all religious groups as well as the nonreligious and those wishing to intermarry. Theo-political covenant theory provides a platform for potential Orthodox receptivity to change. This would produce both/and, rather than either/or, results per Newell. In order to deal with civil rights violation insights, a viable law permitting some kind of marriage for all in Israel is required. Civil marriage would provide the legal and political answer. "For many years, marriage and divorce laws were considered the ultimate symbol of preserving the ideal of a single Jewish nation. This is now being contested, with a clear tendency to prioritize personal liberties over symbols" (Barak-Erez, 2007, p. 120).

The original reason for rigidity in matters of halakhah was the threat to the very identity of the Jews, a posture which can be replaced with "elasticity in the interpretation and application of Halachic principles . . . where the great majority of the Jewish population, though appreciative of Jewish tradition and anxious to retain Jewish institutions in the field of family law, is far removed from Orthodox thought" (Shiloh, 1970, p. 492).

Legal Pragmatism Theory Supported by Covenant Theory as the Basis for Integration

A comprehensive statement of legal pragmatism theory, as expanded through covenant theory, recognizes the following concerning Jewish marriage:

If the institution of Jewish marriage is to be responsive to the religious, political, and legal concerns of Israeli society and the State of Israel, it must take into account the civil rights of all the citizens of the state. The Orthodox Rabbinate's monopoly on Jewish marriage is inconsistent with the civil rights of groups constituting the majority of the population; nonetheless, the interests of the Orthodox must also be taken into account if the result is to be a win-win solution. Legal pragmatism theory demonstrates a willingness to go beyond political accommodation rooted in historical circumstances that date to the founding of the State of Israel. Covenant theory provides a theo-political basis for the Orthodox to move beyond traditional positions.

In its current form, Jewish marriage in Israel is a vestige of historical circumstance and religious symbolism. Orthodox Jews have pragmatically agreed to other compromises in the secular State of Israel. Because Israel is not and has never been a theocracy, civil marriage would not undermine its democratic underpinnings. Civil marriage would not change the nature of religious Jewish marriage, and therefore it finds support in covenant theory. The current exclusively religious marriage laws are no longer essential to the preservation of the Jewish state, as is proven in current practice by the "exit option" of marrying abroad and then having the marriage recorded in Israel.

To offer a win-win situation for the Orthodox in implementation of civil marriage, it is necessary to assure the preservation of religious principles. The alternative of a legally valid nonreligious ceremony need not eschew religious values. For example, one element of Orthodox Jewish marriage that can be incorporated into civil marriage is that the state can develop and make available to the Orthodox Rabbinate a registry of all those who marry civilly, in order to keep track of unions that may be forbidden under Jewish law (Mazie, 2006, p. 185). Orthodox Jewish marriage also requires premarital counseling, which is instruction on morality; civil marriage could encompass this dimension by including required moral counseling. Additionally, Mazie (2006) notes that many Jews want to retain a religious ceremony in addition to a civil ceremony (p. 168). The civil marriage option would also remove an important source of secular resentment. The Orthodox Rabbinate would no longer be required to perform marriage ceremonies for non-Orthodox couples, which dilutes the religious content and significance of the ceremony. The civil marriage option thus has benefits to the Orthodox community, which makes possible the transformation from either/or thinking to both/and thinking.

It is only through the process of constructing a more comprehensive understanding that the descriptive nature of the original question is transformed into one of policy: How *should* the institution of Jewish marriage express Israel's conflicted identity as a Jewish and democratic state? No single discipline could produce this understanding. It is only by integrating the insights of religion, political science, and law at the level of their theories, concepts, and assumptions that a more complete understanding of the question can be achieved.

Step 10: Produce an Interdisciplinary Understanding of the Problem and Test It

Through an interdisciplinary understanding of the insights in Jewish marriage, there is a cognitive advancement in the comprehension of Israel's conflicted identity as a Jewish and democratic state. The final step in the interdisciplinary process is testing the understanding gained with regard to Jewish marriage in a more general context. While a full exposition of such a test is beyond the scope of this chapter, possible directions for further study are noted.

One of the most prominent areas to which the religious, political, and legal insights may be expanded is the treatment of the Arab citizens of Israel. Israeli Arabs face issues of inclusiveness, civil rights, and religious equality that, in some ways, are analogous to the civil rights violations found in the institution of Jewish marriage. Cultural diversity and cultural conflicts provide challenges in a democracy, but they are manageable when other conditions for democracy are present (Dahl, 1998, pp. 149–151, 183–185). Rebhun and Waxman (2004) conclude that "in the treatment of its Arab citizens, Israel's democracy is flawed, just as racism is a blight on American democracy. . . . For many, Zionism has not yet fully achieved its mission and will not do so until Israel becomes a fully developed Jewish democracy" (p. 472).

In the debate over Israel as a democratic state, scholars have applied a variety of sometimes conflicting characterizations. Whatever the formal characterization of its democracy, Israel is a pluralistic society. Israeli Arab citizens generally do not consider themselves equal stakeholders with Israeli Jewish citizens in the society as it is presently structured. Gavison (2007) suggests that "Israeliness," the common citizenship and culture of Jews and non-Jews, holds the promise to express the kind of secular unity that can integrate the Arab population. This requires changes in the present conception of "Jewishness" in the national culture (p. 91).

Israeli Arabs are citizens of a country whose first language is Hebrew, whose flag is a Jewish star, and whose national anthem declares the hopes of the Jewish people. Just as the Orthodox Rabbinate fears the consequences if they lose their monopoly over Jewish marriage, so the broader Jewish population fears the consequences if Israel provides increased rights to its Arab minority. Yet, the respect for the civil rights of all that is inherent in civil marriage provides an instructive paradigm for the use of compromise in seeking solutions to the dilemma of the civil rights of Arab Israelis and their inclusion in the national culture. As with the issue of marriage discussed in this chapter, the issue of Israeli Arabs may be addressed in a win-win manner through recognition of the increasing difficulty of compromise under the old ways; the recognition that pragmatic elasticity in matters of halakhah balanced by preservation of underlying religious principles may lead to increased empathy for the Israeli Arab situation among non-Orthodox and secular Jews, respect for the civil rights and human rights of Arab Israelis, and greater equality between Arab Israelis and Jewish Israelis.

The flaws and conflicts in Israel as a Jewish and democratic state do not negate its characterization as such. Rather, democracy requires adherence to core values and ideals toward which the society moves but which may elude complete realization.

Conclusion

The integrative process provides a paradigm for producing an interdisciplinary understanding of the institution of Jewish marriage, reflecting Israel's conflicted identity as a Jewish and democratic state. The problem is complex and cannot be comprehended without taking into account the perspectives and insights of different disciplines. The unique contribution of the interdisciplinary approach is found in the second part of the process, through the achievement of integration. Here, conflicts were found between religious-based insights and civil rights violation insights. Because Israel does not have separation of religion and state, the situation is complex. Creating common ground bridges the perspectives of religion, politics, and law to achieve an understanding that no one discipline could produce. Integration builds upon the secular nature of the state, the need to ensure the civil liberties of all citizens, and the deference to be paid to religion in certain aspects of Israeli life. The possibility of fruitful compromise through the introduction of civil marriage does not impede religious marriage, but it does provide an alternative. The present study lays the foundation for the application of its process and findings to another great problem of civic inequality: the situation of Israeli Arabs. Thus, the institution of Jewish marriage provides a model for an interdisciplinary approach to other aspects of Israel's conflicted identity as a Jewish and democratic state.

References

Arian, A. (2005). *Politics in Israel: The second republic* (2nd ed.). Washington, DC: CQ Press.

Barak, A. (2002, August 23). *Jewish or democratic? Israel's top judge reflects on values.* Retrieved January 11, 2009, from http://www.myjewishlearning.com/history_community/Israel/Israeli_Politics/IsraeliSupremeCourt/DemocraticJewish .htm. (Reprinted from *The Forward*, August 23, 2002)

Barak-Erez, D. (2007). *Outlawed pigs: Law, religion and culture in Israel.* Madison, WI: University of Wisconsin Press.

Barkan, S. E. (2009). *Law and society: An introduction.* Upper Saddle River, NJ: Pearson.

Batkay, W. M. (1989). Jewish religions(s) and the Jewish state: The case of conservative and reform Judaism in Israel. In G. Benavides & M. W. Daly (Eds.), *Religion and political power* (pp. 119–132). Albany: State University of New York Press.

Berlin, W. S. (1978). *On the edge of politics: The roots of Jewish political thought in America.* Westport, CT: Greenwood Press.

Ceaser, J. W. (1990). *Liberal democracy and political science*. Baltimore, MD: Johns Hopkins University Press.

Dahl, R. (1998). *On democracy*. New Haven, CT: Yale University Press.

Donald, J. G. (2002). *Learning to think: Disciplinary perspectives*. San Francisco: Jossey-Bass.

Dowty, A. (1998). *The Jewish state a century later*. Berkeley: University of California Press.

Edelman, M. (1994). *Courts, politics and culture in Israel*. Charlottesville: University of Virginia Press.

Elazar, D. J. (1998). *Covenant and civil society*. New Brunswick, NJ: Transaction.

Elon, M. (1967a). The sources and nature of Jewish law and its application in the State of Israel. Part I. *Israel Law Review, 2*, 515–565.

Elon, M. (1967b). The sources and nature of Jewish law and its application in the State of Israel. Part III. *Israel Law Review, 3*, 416–457.

Elon, M. (1967c). The sources and nature of Jewish law and its application in the State of Israel. Part IV. *Israel Law Review, 4*, 80–140.

Freudenheim, Y. (1967). *Government in Israel* (M. Silverstone & C. I. Goldwater, Trans.). Dobbs Ferry, NY: Oceana.

Gavison, R. (2007). *Conditions for the prosperity of the State of Israel: "Where there is no vision, the people cast off restraint"—A meta-purpose for Israel and its implications* (R. Danieli & Y. Levy, Trans.). Haifa, Israel: Metzilah and the Samuel Neaman Institute, The Technion.

Horowitz, D., & Lissak, M. (1989). *Trouble in utopia: The overburdened polity of Israel*. Albany: State University of New York Press.

Isaac, R. J. (1981). *Party and politics in Israel: Three visions of a Jewish state*. New York: Longman.

Jacobsohn, G. J. (1993). *Apple of gold: Constitutionalism in Israel and the United States*. Princeton, NJ: Princeton University Press.

Klein, J. T. (1996). *Crossing boundaries: Knowledge, disciplinarities, and interdisciplinarities*. Charlottesville: University of Virginia Press.

Lorberbaum, M. (2007). Religion and state in Israel. In M. Halbertal & D. Hartman (Eds.), *Judaism and the challenges of modern life* (pp. 152–164). London: Continuum.

Mazie, S. V. (2006). *Israel's higher law: Religion and liberal democracy in the Jewish state*. Lanham, MD: Lexington Books.

National Academy of Sciences, National Academy of Engineering, and Institute of Medicine of the National Academies. (2005). *Facilitating interdisciplinary research*. Washington, DC: The National Academies Press.

Newell, W. (Ed.). (1998). *Interdisciplinarity: Essays from the literature*. New York: College Entrance Examination Board.

Newell, W. (2006). Decision making in interdisciplinary studies. In G. Morcol (Ed.), *Handbook of decision making* (pp. 245–264). London: CRC Press.

Peretz, D., & Doron, G. (1999). *The government and politics of Israel* (3rd ed.). Boulder, CO: Westview Press.

Rebhun, U., & Waxman, C. I. (Eds.). (2004). *Jews in Israel: Contemporary social and cultural patterns*. Lebanon, NH: Brandeis University Press.

Repko, A. (2008). *Interdisciplinary research: Process and theory*. Thousand Oaks, CA: Sage.

Sarat, A. (Ed.). (2004). *Law in the liberal arts*. Ithaca, NY: Cornell University Press.

Shamir, R. (2000). *The colonies of law: Colonialism, Zionism and law in early mandate Palestine.* Cambridge: Cambridge University Press.

Shapira, A., & DeWitt-Arar, K. C. (Eds.). (1995). *Introduction to the law of Israel.* The Hague: Kluwer Law International.

Sharkansky, I. (1999). *Ambiguity, coping and governance: Israeli experience in politics, religion, and policymaking.* Westport, CT: Praeger.

Sheffer, G. (1996). Has Israel really been a garrison democracy? Sources of change in Israel's democracy. *Israel Affairs, 3,* 13–38.

Shetreet, S. (1994). *Justice in Israel: A study of the Israeli judiciary.* Dordrecht: Martinus Nijhoff.

Shetreet, S. (1997). Reflections on Israel as a Jewish and democratic state. *Israel Studies, 2,* 190–197.

Shiloh, I. S. (1970). Marriage and divorce in Israel. *Israel Law Review, 5,* 479–498.

Szostak, R. (2000). Toward a unified human science. *Issues in Integrative Studies, 19,* 115–157.

Zamir, I., & Zysblat, A. (1996). *Public law in Israel.* Oxford, UK: Clarendon Press.

3

The Metropolitan Problem in Interdisciplinary Perspective

Michan Andrew Connor

Introduction

Over the course of the 20th century, the United States became a metropolitan nation. In 1910, only 28% of Americans lived in cities or their surrounding suburbs, but by 2000, 80% of Americans lived in metropolitan areas, and in 37 of 50 states, the majority of the population lived in metropolitan areas (Hobbs & Stoops, 2002, pp. 1, 7). Although metropolitan areas are commonly designated by the name of the largest city in the region, the political, cultural, and demographic preeminence of large cities has been steadily eroding. Suburban population (31% of Americans) had nearly reached parity with urban (32%) in 1960. By 2000, just over half of the U.S. population lived in suburbs, while only three in ten Americans lived in cities (Hobbs & Stoops, 2002, p. 33). This ongoing process of metropolitanization is important because social benefits and problems are not evenly distributed in space; residential location ties individuals and families to spatial patterns of distribution. Sections of metropolitan areas can be described as "communities of opportunity" (Reece, Rogers, Gambhir, & powell, 2007), and differences in opportunity organized spatially can have tremendous effects. Local living environments influence life chances; shape perceptions, political views, and values; and structure political, economic, social, and ecological conflicts. On one level, then, the problem of metropolitan formation is a deeply practical one that resonates with public policy and social justice issues.

But the metropolitan problem is also a scholarly problem, in the sense that efforts to understand metropolitan areas have been incompletely developed and inadequately integrated. Though there is evidence that "metropolitan studies" (as distinct from "urban" or "suburban" studies) is emerging as a multidisciplinary scholarly endeavor, its practitioners to date have not developed self-consciously integrative and interdisciplinary methods. More often, metropolitan scholars continue to address similar, though not wholly congruent, sets of problems and issues using characteristically disciplinary methods and theoretical approaches. In this chapter, adapted from a larger research project, the application of a purposefully interdisciplinary research process is considered as a demonstration of one possible interdisciplinary synthesis for metropolitan studies.

Scholars in interdisciplinary fields occasionally evaluate their methodologies relative to established disciplinary practices, though this reflection is episodic, ad hoc, and often contentious.[1] Repko (2008) provides a more purposefully interdisciplinary description of the process of research that proceeds in steps from problem definition to the communication of findings, with attention to the particular demands of interdisciplinary scholarship. Although Repko defines 10 steps within this process, they can be aggregated into three larger groups of steps: problem definition and the identification of disciplinary literatures that relate to it, the cultivation and analysis of scholarly knowledge and ideas that illuminate aspects of a problem, and the evaluation and resolution of conflicts inherent in disciplinary findings through integrative thought.

In this chapter, identifying and evaluating conflicts among disciplinary literatures is particularly important. Repko (2008) identifies this work with the latter steps of the process. However, in the research supporting this chapter, conflicts between disciplinary insights were, in fact, instrumental in the very definition of the research problem. I began with primary research related to metropolitanization in Los Angeles County. While searching for secondary literatures that could illuminate evidence found in archives, public documents, and newspapers, I became aware of significant conflicts. Different disciplinary literatures embedded different assumptions about political agency, the nature of social life, and the value or legitimacy of inequality in metropolitan areas. They reflected different theoretical explanations for political and social change. Most important, different disciplinary literatures contained radically different assumptions about the spatial scale of social change. Scholars in some disciplines were prone to organize inquiry in terms of "urban" or "suburban" problems, while scholars working from other perspectives attempted to explain phenomena within a metropolitan framework. Encountering conflicts of spatial framing in different disciplinary literatures forced me to proceed in a nonlinear

---

[1] For example, readers may refer to the 2008 American Studies Association Presidential Address by Philip Deloria, reprinted with commentary in the journal *American Quarterly*. Deloria and two interlocutors identify three possible models of American Studies practice that range from a pragmatic integrative interdisciplinarity (Deloria, 2009), to a guarded and selective adoption of disciplinary methodologies (Singh, 2009), to a pointed rejection of disciplinary structure as an obstacle to free intellectual inquiry (Halberstam, 2009).

fashion between phases of work in which the core problem was defined provisionally and redefined (Repko, 2008, pp. 142–143). Ultimately, I saw that the concept of metropolitan formation was a more appropriate descriptor of the research problem than the concepts of urbanization or suburbanization. Therefore, I redefined my research question to ask, "What metropolitan-scale processes have changed urban and suburban places in post-World War II Los Angeles County?"

The metropolitan formation studied here nominally began on April 16, 1954 with the incorporation of Lakewood, a large residential subdivision that became the first new city created in Los Angeles County since 1939. Lakewood differed from previously incorporated suburban cities in the county because its government purchased its municipal services from the county government through fee-for-service contracts negotiated annually between the two governments. Rather than operating police, fire, or street departments, Lakewood's founders planned for their city to purchase the services of a designated number of police car patrols, fire trucks, or pothole crews from the county's existing departments. This arrangement, which became known as the Lakewood Plan, was devised and publicized before the incorporation election, and voters who decided whether to form a new city understood this form of government as a way to operate a city at reduced cost by relying on the economies of scale that the county government provided. In the ensuing decades, the Lakewood Plan became a key vehicle for changing the metropolitan landscape as well as a subject of political controversy. These changes are discussed below, but for now it is most important to note that the Lakewood Plan spurred a sudden wave of suburban municipal incorporations. Between 1954 and 1970, 32 new "contract" or "Lakewood Plan" cities formed in Los Angeles County, with more than 700,000 residents (Hoch, 1981; G. J. Miller, 1981).

Suburbanization in Los Angeles County thus involved more than a simple redistribution of population. Each new municipal incorporation created new political boundaries that divided administrative responsibility, economic resources, and community allegiance, a process that has been referred to as "fragmentation" (Fogelson, 1993). Academic treatments of metropolitanization, both in Los Angeles and nationally, are fragmented by disciplinary and theoretical divisions much as metropolitan areas are fragmented by political and sociocultural boundaries. Scholarship remains fragmented because of the establishment, policing, and maintenance of disciplinary boundaries that often impede understanding. Scholars in some fields have adopted narrow spatial framings and analyzed either "cities" or "suburbs," often evaluating phenomena in terms of master narratives like the urban crisis or the rise of suburbia. Conversely, spatial framings that emphasize regional dynamics may miss the impact of local places on political, cultural, and community consciousness. In this chapter, interdisciplinary understanding (the ultimate goal of the research process) is defined as a "cognitive advancement" that leverages the valuable insights attained within different disciplinary perspectives (Mansilla, 2005; Repko, 2008) and is produced, in large part, by evaluating competing spatial and theoretical frameworks and identifying a more productive and appropriate research focus.

Cities and Suburbs: Spatial Framings of Metropolitan Issues

Grouping metropolitan places under the binary designations of cities and suburbs has important lineages in scholarly research, discussed below. These lineages account for some of the scholarly validation of the terms and their tenacity as analytical frameworks. But the binary categorization also has a significant normative impact that must be acknowledged. Scholars concerned with economic and social justice have used the binary of city and suburb so frequently to critique inequality that the word "suburb" often connotes racial homogeneity, affluence, a particular built landscape, or exclusionary practices that make the poor or minorities feel unwelcome (Harris & Lewis, 2001; Hayden, 2003; Kruse & Sugrue, 2006a). Within a set of normative assumptions expressed by spatial categories, the city/suburb distinction is a convenient shorthand for inequality, though much closer analysis is necessary in order to explain how the distinctions between cities and suburbs have contributed to inequality.

Other research challenges the usefulness of the terms "city" and "suburb" as analytical categories by subjecting them to critical scrutiny. Researchers with the Kirwan Institute for the Study of Race and Ethnicity at The Ohio State University have employed Geographical Information Systems (GIS) software to identify local areas as "communities of opportunity." This method maps the resources available to a typical resident of a given census tract and facilitates metropolitan-scale comparisons between neighborhoods of high and low opportunity. In many metropolitan areas, there are "inner city" and "suburban" areas of both high and low opportunity, showing the imprecision of these designations (Reece et al., 2007). This pattern has also been observed in Los Angeles County, where many older suburbs exhibit high levels of poverty, weak fiscal health, and compromised quality of life (Pastor, 2001).

Thus, the normative project reflected in these studies (exposing and critiquing how different packages of opportunity are organized by metropolitan places) also demands a taxonomical adjustment. Racial and economic inequality are organized through place in American metropolitan areas, but they do not conform to the binary form suggested by common terminology. Metropolitan distributions of resources and opportunity may create resource-rich central city communities and resource-poor or "at-risk" suburbs (Pastor, 2001; Scott & Soja, 1996; Teaford, 2006). The inadequacy of the city/suburb dichotomy is compounded by the multiplicity of terms that flow from different disciplinary perspectives. In legal terms, most metropolitan places in the United States are, in fact, "cities," with a common status as public corporations established by state law to govern local affairs (Briffault, 1990, p. 348). Yet, despite the fact that all cities are formally equal, some areas may derive a different utility from their legal powers. This example of conflicting terminology reflects a larger challenge inherent in interdisciplinary research. Differences in disciplinary terminology in this case cannot be resolved simply by identifying a common name for phenomena that cross disciplinary boundaries. An adequate redefinition of terms must necessarily address the multiple parallel descriptors of metropolitan places; recognize that they refer to legal, political, cultural, and geographic qualities of places; and seek to substitute inclusive and expansive concepts for exclusive and narrow ones.

The multiple and overlapping qualities of places mean that a full understanding of the relationship between different metropolitan places must include the historical agency that has constructed such relationships and the ways that places affect people's lives. Although the statement that all social activity unfolds in and requires place is undeniable, its seeming obviousness has caused many disciplinary scholars to avoid thinking through the meanings of space and place as essential, but often unacknowledged or partially examined, components of their core theoretical and analytical practices (Ethington, 2007; Soja, 1994). Integrative work is performed in this chapter to produce an analysis that is *spatially* integrated at the metropolitan (or regional) scale and *analytically* integrated through its attention to the legal, political, and cultural dimensions of relationships between metropolitan places. This chapter uses the integrative techniques of organization and extension to identify the explicit and implicit spatial content of diverse disciplinary theories and insights and square them with a more comprehensive theorization of the spatiality of social life (Repko, 2008, pp. 281–283, 289). This involves (1) identifying an integrative theory that potentially connects the domains of multiple disciplines and (2) organizing understanding of knowledge produced within those disciplines to illustrate points of connection with the integrative theory.

Though these operations are mutually supportive of and necessary to each other, I will discuss first the search for an integrative theory. Elements of the relationship between places, social life, and individual consciousness have been most comprehensively explored by the philosopher Henri Lefebvre (1991), who defines these interconnections as the *social production of space*. Most researchers who have adopted Lefebvre's (unfortunately rather idiosyncratic) ideas have been economic geographers evaluating the broad scope of spatial changes associated with world-historical shifts in the organization of capital and the state, in an attempt to describe the way that forms of space relate to capital accumulation (Harvey, 1989, 1990; Soja, 1994). But the production of space also facilitates and demands attention to the way that particular local places affect and are affected by social forces, political movements, and the application of ideas to the world (Malpas, 1998). To help us understand the importance of the local, Lefebvre's theorization is defined by three interconnected "spatial terms" representing facets of the relationship of space and social life: *spatial practices, spaces of representation,* and *representations of space.* Most immediately and personally, people's lives and consciousness are affected by places and their experiences in them (spaces of representation). These experiences in places may support the formation of ideas about how places might be rearranged or changed to conform to some ideal (representations of space). Action by individuals, groups, and institutions may work to implement or enforce those representations in the dominant spatial ordering (spatial practice) of society (Lefebvre, 1991, p. 33). Metropolitanization is arguably the dominant spatial practice of the United States in the 20th century, and it is supported by and has promoted particular ways of thinking, kinds of social experience, and kinds of political and ideological conflict.

This framework encompasses institutions, legal rules and doctrines, diverse forms of human agency, and ideas as factors in a process of producing particular places. Metropolitan researchers may catalogue phenomena under one term or another, but they should ideally recognize that the three terms are inherently interrelated in the production of places; ideas affect institutions, experiences affect ideas, and institutions enable or constrain experiences. Metropolitan Los Angeles, like other metropolitan areas, is a produced place. The core of this chapter presents primary research on Los Angeles as an empirical context for a critical assessment of disciplinary literatures, which illustrate some, but not all, aspects of the empirical findings. Implicit and explicit disciplinary assumptions about place and space are examined and contrasted, systematically organized, and subjected to the extension of spatial theory in order to produce an integrated understanding.

Historical Perspectives on Metropolitan Formation

The "metropolitan problem" is defined by gaps and contradictions between disciplinary understandings of metropolitan formation. This chapter, and the research from which it developed, began with the premise that metropolitan formation could be understood as a historical problem originating in past actions that laid the groundwork for later social possibilities while foreclosing others. Metropolitan formation, whether taken as a whole or in terms of its constituent parts of urbanization and suburbanization, is a spatial and temporal development. Common sense would suggest that historians might contribute valuable insight on these changes. Indeed, seeking to explain such change is central to the historical enterprise, both in terms of research and pedagogy (Grossman & Katz, 2008; Tilly, 1996). In a seminal essay, Charles Tilly (1996) argued for the importance of historical contingency, the recognition that "social action in a given time and place constrains what will happen next there and in adjacent places . . . through long strings of path-dependent processes" (p. 715). This notion of historical contingency is a principle that, I have argued elsewhere, should be applied to metropolitan formation (Connor, 2008).

Unfortunately, however, historians have not always organized their investigations of this contingency in the most productive ways, and disciplinary convention is a significant reason. In this sense, defining the core research problem works in a recursive or dialectical relationship to critiques of disciplinary approaches to it. Building competence or adequacy in the historical literature opens new sets of questions to an interdisciplinary researcher even as it resolves other questions. This is illustrated by comparison of the scholarly practices of different groups of historians, which reflect both agreement in terms of research methods and divergence in terms of assumptions about the most relevant sites of social change. Insights from historians in the established fields of urban and suburban history and from those in a still-developing field that might be called "metropolitan history" are particularly relevant to this inquiry.

Historians of American cities have long enjoyed relative certitude about the object of their study and its literal and figurative centrality. To be an urban historian was to study cities and the process of their development. Early professional historians (who were working during rapid American urbanization) took as self-evident that the most important social changes had happened in large cities. Urban historians in different eras have expanded their field of inquiry by identifying different, but still essentially urban, social processes to evaluate. Some have focused on the infrastructure that enabled the expansion of cities or their improvement as sanitary living environments (Keating, Moehring, & Tarr, 1985; Tarr, 1996; Warner, 1973). Others have devoted attention to the characteristic social conflicts found in large and complex urban communities. American demographic trends and the perceived phenomenon of "white flight" have led some historians to equate "the city" with the political and social fortunes (and activism) of racial minorities. Josh Sides (2003) has argued compellingly that "the history of urban America is inseparable from the history of race in America" (p. 8), a formulation reflected in both case studies and synthetic works that have refocused attention on the urban context of African American and other civil rights movements (Countryman, 2006; Sugrue, 2008). Urban cultural historians have also identified groups of urbanites and their communities with (occasionally overlapping or "intersectional") challenges to patriarchal gender norms, heteronormative sexual mores, and the claim of economic elites to privileged standing in the urban polity (Chauncey, 1994; Ryan, 1997; Sides, 2009; Stansell, 1987).

Methodological Patterns in Urban and Suburban History

Despite the thematic evolution of urban history, however, two core disciplinary patterns have remained relatively constant. First, the case study methodology has encouraged a process of "turfing," in which historians have been more willing to cultivate expertise in the history of a particular city than to discuss the process of urban historical change in abstract or conceptual terms (Mohl, 1998). Historians have resisted reducing the cities they studied to mere iterations of generic processes. This tendency has both creditable and suspect motives: creditable for defending the proposition that individual cities are complex social and institutional entities that cannot be perfectly compared, but suspect for resisting synthetic analysis, perhaps out of the fear of undermining the significance of their own work. This particularism has been abetted by historians' selective embrace of the social theory created by Chicago School sociologists. Although urban historians rarely internalized the sociologists' premise that the study of one city like Chicago could provide insight into the process of urbanization in *all* cities, they did adopt a focus on the local urban neighborhood as a spatial frame and interpreted the process of urbanization in terms of the individual's adjustment to urban society through neighborhood institutions (Mohl, 1998; Tilly, 1996). This orientation sustained the second major tendency in the field, a tendency to "take city limits as boundaries for the analysis of ostensibly self-contained urban processes" (Tilly, 1996, p. 710). History's characteristic limitations with respect to the metropolitan problem can, therefore, be characterized as partly methodological and partly analytical. Spatial assumptions structured the sources of data (city archives and municipal agency records) and the interpretations applied to the data.

The subfield of suburban history emerged from a sense that qualitatively different social processes drove the formation of American suburbs. Generally credited as a founding text of the field, Kenneth T. Jackson's *Crabgrass Frontier* (1985) was published at a moment when differences between archetypal suburbs and inner cities were severe. Jackson argued that suburbanization was driven by a broad-based national cultural and political bloc that fused social prejudices (against the poor, minorities, dense cities, and apartment housing) with public policy (particularly federal support for highway and housing construction and mortgage underwriting). This coalition expanded the suburban settlement that supported the formation of a white middle class, embedding both class and racial inequalities in the spatial form of the nation's metropolitan areas. Other early suburban historians expanded investigations of the technological innovations that facilitated "streetcar suburbs" and then highway-driven dispersal, as well as cultural tropes that valorized suburbs as retreats from the political corruption, racial and ethnic mixing, and industrial pollution of large cities (Fishman, 1987; Warner, 1973). Early suburban history thus presented a national synthesis of the historical convergence of motive, means, and opportunity. It also provided an explanation for the popularity of suburbanization: Both political and business elites and millions of moderate-income Americans had incentives to support and defend the pattern (Jackson, 1985; Lipsitz, 1995; Teaford, 1979).

Intradisciplinary Debate and the New Suburban History

This view resonated with popular understandings of the relationship between suburbs and cities. But it was unsustainable as a disciplinary consensus because historians kept finding evidence that contradicted received ideas about suburbs. As in other disciplinary debates, researchers who initially viewed their own findings as anomalous began to collectively question paradigms in their disciplines, challenging the synthesis established by early suburban historians and questioning the validity of sweeping generalizations about American suburbs (Kruse & Sugrue, 2006a). In one of the works inaugurating the New Suburban History (NSH) movement, Andrew Wiese (2004) documented African American suburban community development to demonstrate that "historians have done a better job excluding African Americans from the suburbs than even white suburbanites" (p. 5). Wiese didn't simply expose an overlooked historical phenomenon; he exposed limits in his discipline's guiding assumptions and ideas.

NSH expanded as other scholars began applying political, cultural, class, gender, and ethnic perspectives developed by urban historians to case studies of a wide variety of American suburbs. These scholars have demonstrated the historical presence in the United States of industrial and working-class residential suburbs (Nicolaides, 2001, 2002), suburbs peopled by racial minorities (Gonzalez, 2009; Wiese, 2004), and suburbs that have undergone rapid and disruptive racial transition (Sides, 2004). Other NSH scholars have considered typically white and affluent suburbs but have challenged the perception that these were cultural and civic wastelands (Nicolaides, 2006). NSH pays more critical attention to the influence of suburban places—of lifestyles and emergent political cultures organized around block, school, and consumption. Historians have disagreed about whether to characterize suburban politics in terms of racial segregation rationalized through the real estate market (Freund, 2007), hard-right anticommunism (McGirr, 2002), the reorganization of citizenship through the role of consumer (Cohen, 2003), or embryonic forms of "centrism" that guided Bill Clinton's electoral successes (Lassiter, 2004, 2006). Despite their disagreements, however, these accounts have punctured older views of suburbs as apolitical.

The explosion of attention to the suburbs is salutary, and the strength of the emergent field is well-reflected in the publication of an edited volume as a foundational statement of purpose for the NSH and in the organization of scholarly bodies like the National Center for Suburban Studies at Hofstra University, which hosted a 2009 conference dedicated to "the diverse suburb," where the NSH perspective was strongly represented (Kruse & Sugrue, 2006b; National Center for Suburban Studies, n.d.). Understanding metropolitan formation in Los Angeles County, like in other American regions, depends heavily on the insights of NSH because of the tremendous diversity of the new cities formed there between 1954 and 1970. As the core of this chapter will demonstrate, the process of metropolitan formation in Los Angeles linked many different kinds of places in complex political, social, and cultural or symbolic relationships. Yet, although the development of NSH has given historians greater insight into the diversity of suburbs, it is not in itself adequate as a disciplinary school of thought to explain metropolitan formation. This can be demonstrated by assessment of the theories and assumptions that urban and New Suburban historians still tend to hold in common.

Parallels Between the New Suburban History and Urban History

Methodological parallels between urban histories and NSH are evident. Unfortunately, methodology often separates analysis of cities and suburbs in metropolitan regions. The intensive treatment of local places using the characteristic case study method may undermine scholars' ability to understand relationships between different kinds of metropolitan places. To date, few synthetic efforts at metropolitan history exist. The most notable, by Teaford (1979, 2006), established and then revisited a typological narrative of metropolitan change in which "suburbs" superseded "cities" as the economic, demographic, and political centers of metropolitan regions; residents of those suburbs looked to their local communities to exercise a civic life more narrowly drawn around the single-family home and the roles of homeowner and taxpayer; and a "centrifugal" mode of metropolitan organization replaced the "centripetal" pattern of the pre-WWII city.

This synthetic approach presents a heuristic metaphor of "fragmentation," but it ultimately tells us little about the specific links between suburban ascendancy and urban decline and how such links may have operated. Many of the leading NSH scholars have articulated a sense of purpose for their field that includes generating metropolitan models of process and causation, lamenting the fact that "just as most urban histories left the suburbs out, few suburban histories discussed central cities at all, except through the rear-view mirror of those fleeing urban life" (Kruse & Sugrue, 2006a, p. 4). Yet, the practice of NSH remains largely defined by a narrowly local case study method, and historians consequently struggle to find theoretical and analytical tools to address metropolitan dynamics.

Alternate Spatial Framings in the Social Sciences _____

Some historians have begun the work of connecting metropolitan places by tracing the linkages between real estate credit; business development and industrial location; taxation; and racial, class, or gender ideologies that have affected metropolitan places in the immediately local and regional senses. Institutional or ideological constraints have influenced companies' choices of where to locate and whom to hire; the decisions of the affluent about where to live and buy homes; and the ability of different jurisdictions to maintain infrastructure, schools, and public services in ways that favored some (mostly suburban) places and populations. Such influences in combination shaped the opportunity structure of metropolitan regions and constrained the ability of urban communities to resist decline and disinvestment (Gordon, 2008; Self, 2003). Works addressing this sort of influence remain exceptional, however. Tilly's (1996) warning still applies: Historians, for all their successes in demonstrating the path-dependencies of social change within cities and within suburbs, have failed to look for social processes operating at the metropolitan scale.

Metropolitics: Fighting Fragmentation

This spatial framing by historians is particularly unfortunate because the transformations in historiography described above occurred alongside tremendous ferment in social science analysis of metropolitan areas. By the early 1960s, policy scholars were increasingly concerned that the proliferation of suburbs as centers of population, employment, and local government undermined the strength of urban centers and fostered dysfunctional relationships between places. Developing adequacy in the perspective of social scientists and awareness of paradigms like this helped me to comprehend the limits of historical analysis. At the same time, these social science ideas, many of which were oriented toward shaping public policy, should be evaluated with an eye to their historical context and influence as representations of space intended to alter spatial practices. Robert Wood's *1400 Governments* (1961), for example, indicted excessive administrative localism in greater New York, creating a paradigm for a national movement of reformist urban thought (O'Connor, 2008).

Other scholars found Southern California fertile ground for their analysis and proposed as a general rule that the proliferation of political jurisdictions there worked against the public interest (Bigger, 1961; Bigger & Kitchen, 1952; Crouch, 1961, 1963; Engelbert, 1961). This metropolitan orientation in California policy circles produced a 1961 report by the Commission on Metropolitan Area Problems convened by Democratic governor Edmund Brown. This report declared that the emerging political fragmentation of Los Angeles County, represented by the incorporation of so many new cities under the Lakewood Plan, created isolated and antagonistic local political publics incompatible with metropolitan labor markets and social dynamics, and even suggested that emergent home-rule sentiment without regard to a metropolitan interest was "undemocratic" and threatened to create metropolitan "apartheid" through political boundaries (Sherwood, 1961, p. 19).

Regional events lent some credence to these fears, as the reorganization of metropolitan political geography coincided nearly exactly with a dramatic redistribution of population, income, and municipal fiscal health. One of the most obvious patterns observers spotted was that the new cities created after Lakewood were overwhelmingly white. This amounted to a reversal of earlier patterns toward slightly greater residential racial integration in the region and connected racial resegregation with local government. Between 1950 and 1970, the percentage of the regional population living in racially exclusive cities (defined somewhat imperfectly as those with less than 1% black population) grew from 24% to 33% (Ethington, Frey, & Myers, 2001; G. J. Miller, 1981, p. 135). The new and largely owner-occupied housing stock in these areas was overwhelmingly financed through federally guaranteed loans that made home ownership cheaper than renting, in many cases. Because these loans were administered in a racially discriminatory fashion, they created a spatial overlap of racially differentiated residential and economic mobility.

While individuals benefited or suffered under this pattern, the cities they inhabited also were affected. Most of the new cities in the county had lower costs because they had newer infrastructure and populations with lower social service needs. And, as will be discussed further below, the practice of securing public services by contracting out to the county saved these new cities even more, enabling "contract cities" as a class to charge their residents much lower tax rates for comparable city services than traditionally organized cities (G. J. Miller, 1981, p. 82). Older, traditionally organized suburban cities and newer, contract cities followed increasingly divergent paths. The political and economic causes and effects of that divergence are discussed below, particularly in regard to the question of whether politics or the market was responsible. At present, it is important to note merely that suburbanization and the Lakewood Plan appeared to some contemporary observers to be a means by which the region's white middle class secured economic security and privilege relative to the rest of the county, racial minorities in particular.

The metropolitan consolidation agenda of the early 1960s was eclipsed by other theories during the 1960s and 1970s, falling out of influence in Los Angeles as well as nationally. However, many of the premises of metropolitan integration were revived in the 1990s and 2000s in social science fields referred to variously as new regionalism, regional equity, or, in the term I will use, metropolitics.[2] Scholars of metropolitics, who may identify as sociologists, economists, policy analysts, or political scientists, have renewed normative claims about metropolitan inequality, suggesting that efforts to achieve metropolitan equity represent "the new civil rights movement" (Pastor, Benner, & Matsuoka, 2008, p. 15). Metropolitics is distinguished by its attention to the relationships between metropolitan places and an effort to identify the mechanisms by which resources are distributed (or maldistributed)

---

[2]The term *metropolitics* was used in the title of Orfield's influential work on the subject, which pointedly argued that spatial inequalities were produced and protected by politics and public policy (Orfield, 1997, 2002). Regional equity and "new regionalist" scholarship is more likely to focus on regional development and interregional strategic initiatives than on intraregional competition, and thus it focuses more on simple growth as a goal rather than development and distribution (Pastor, Benner, & Matsuoka, 2008).

spatially. Where historians have been reluctant or disinclined to draw connections between metropolitan places, metropolitics scholars argue that regions are a necessary scale of analysis. Regions form relatively cohesive economic units. Though the wealthy or the educated might engage in residential migration, and employers might relocate their facilities within a region, the layered concentration of human capital and infrastructure in "sticky" nodes within regions prevents the complete functional disintegration of a region. Different people and different places in a metropolitan area thus depend upon each other. One regionalist argues "it makes no more sense to talk about suburban independence from central cities than it does to talk about the head being separate from the stomach" (Dreier, 2004, p. 75).

Metropolitics analysts do not, however, disregard differences between head and stomach. Boundaries in a metropolitan area often work at cross purposes to the functional integration of a region, dividing resources and obligations at smaller spatial scales. While demonstrating that development may improve all parts of a region, they warn that impoverishment or unmet social needs in particular places can function as a drag on the prosperity of the region as a whole. An example of such a drag might occur when inner-city school systems fail because local school taxes systematically underfund them relative to suburban schools, preventing regional businesses from accessing an adequate labor supply. Metropolitics scholars thus appeal to rich areas to participate in regional economic equity initiatives out of enlightened self-interest (Dreier, 2004; Orfield, 1997; Pastor, 2000, 2001). They also acknowledge, however, that a region's existence as an integrated whole is counterbalanced by institutional, cultural, and social factors that favor more parochial, local interests in opposition to regional ones. As this body of scholarship has matured, scholars have begun to question how the particular character of local places affects metropolitan processes. Pastor et al. (2008) have recently emphasized that strong and aggressive social movements rooted in local concerns and social identities may be necessary to create political, moral, and rhetorical support for regional initiatives for growth, sustainability, and equity because the principle of localism exerts such strong influence over political consciousness.

This occurs because suburbs have become "great sorting machines for separating Americans along the lines of class, race, ethnicity, religion, and lifestyle" (Dreier, 2004, p. 52). Those who occupy positions of privilege (both spatially and socioeconomically) in their local communities are likely to perceive regional equity as an attack on their interests. To the extent that metropolitics analysis defines problems in terms of politics and culture, rather than simply economics, it demonstrates that the crux of the metropolitan problem is not simply "fragmentation" but complex *relationships* between metropolitan places that structure, protect, and justify inequity. Municipal boundaries are key structural components of these relationships; metropolitics scholars argue that boundaries define political communities of interest and delimit the sharing of resources in ways that have a profound effect on the production of communities of opportunity.

Behavioralism and Public Choice Theory

Metropolitics is by no means the only social scientific perspective on metropolitan formation. A counterweight to metropolitics can be found in two interrelated social science theories, behavioralism and rational choice. As with the perspectives of urban and suburban history, understanding these competing views of metropolitan formation requires understanding their genesis in scholarly and disciplinary practice at specific historical moments. Both behavioralism and rational choice theory developed in the 1950s as social sciences sought to establish claims to empirical rigor and prestige in the academy. Behavioralism, as applied to political science practice, describes an empirical orientation and a core assumption of methodological individualism (a strong analytical preference for aggregating observed individual behavior). This has also been reflected in the colonization of many social science fields by the economic perspective of rational choice theory, which assumes the rational pursuit of self-interest by individual actors. In combination, these two movements have diminished regard for place, community, and collective action in social science analysis (Ethington & McDaniel, 2007, p. 130). This places them sharply at odds, for different reasons, with NSH and metropolitics.

Public Choice Theory and Public Policy

Theoretical disagreements in many social science disciplines between rational choice theory analysts and others are often entangled with larger political debates. In political science, economics, or public administration, this entanglement has been exacerbated by the fact that scholars in these disciplines are far more likely than historians to apply academic research to advocate particular public policies. The development of public choice theory, the subfield of rational choice theory applied to analysis of governmental organization, exemplifies this pattern.

Public choice theory can be traced to Tiebout's (1956) efforts to integrate public administration practices with theories of private market behavior. Like contemporaries who advocated for metropolitan consolidation, Tiebout and his followers were profoundly aware of the pressures suburbanization posed to existing forms of government and administration. However, they held different normative assumptions and viewed metropolitan fragmentation as an opportunity to address a problem that had vexed neoclassical economists. Public goods like police and fire protection, public education, or street sweeping were generally provided by local government agencies or utility companies with monopolistic licenses and were not "excludable" (a paved street could benefit many drivers and not only the ones taxed to pay for it). Furthermore, because large cities or consolidated service districts assessed taxes and administered services at broad scales, Tiebout argued that there was no reliable means of pricing by which residents could pay for services according to their own individual and rational preferences, or indicate by their purchasing behavior how much of those goods local governments should supply.

Viewed through economic rationality, the proliferation of local governments in metropolitan areas represented an opportunity to bring the practices of public administration more closely in line with the ideal of efficient allocation of resources by market dynamics. The more local governments in a region, the greater the likelihood that individuals could choose to live in a jurisdiction that offered levels of taxation and public services that met their individual tastes (V. Ostrom, Tiebout, & Warren, 1961; Tiebout, 1956). The Tiebout hypothesis inverted the normative assumptions of scholars who favored metropolitan consolidation. Whereas others had sought to create government agencies at larger scales to equalize service levels, the public choice perspective suggested that metropolitan areas should be broken up into more separate cities, and that the differences between those cities would enable individuals the greatest freedom to choose to live in areas that suited their preferences. Where proponents of consolidation were concerned about exclusion and a broad public interest, public choice advocates defined that public interest in terms of the aggregate satisfactions of individuals.

Public choice theory has a superficial congruence with historical trends. The new suburban jurisdictions created in Los Angeles County were generally internally homogeneous, but municipal boundaries demarcated cities with varied demographic profiles across jurisdictional boundaries. Because public choice scholars presumed that people with similar demographic characteristics might have similar "tastes" for services (like families with young children seeking school quality or public parks), this demographic homogeneity suggested that this sort of choice was at work. Further, the "tax revolt" that began in California in the 1960s and culminated with the 1978 passage of Proposition 13 suggested that suburban homeowners strongly preferred low taxes. However, this superficial congruence masks serious limitations of the theory with regard to the way it frames political consciousness, social agency, and the relationship of individuals and communities. The local case studies produced by suburban historians offer rich narratives that suggest that individual decisions about where to live involved complicated causes and consequences beyond the ability of public choice theory to address.

Normative and Analytical Critiques of Public Choice Theory

This theoretical and methodological conflict is an outstanding example of the need for integrative inquiry because it entails a conflict between seemingly irreconcilable analytical perspectives, each of which has some identifiable merit. Unfortunately, most criticisms of the assumptions of public choice theory have focused on its normative impact, arguing that it was merely ideological cover for public policies that promoted metropolitan stratification by income and by race. There is no doubt that many influential public choice theorists were concerned with the political impact of their research. Vincent and

Elinor Ostrom and Robert Warren tended toward economic libertarianism and hoped to steer local government administration away from metropolitan consolidation. They succeeded by articulating normative preferences for decentralization with empirical descriptions of the efficiency gains in administration that decentralization of local government and public services produced (Mitchell, 1988; V. Ostrom et al., 1961; V. Ostrom & E. Ostrom, 1971; Tiebout, 1956). The logic of public choice theory also led to an indirect normative conclusion about homogeneity within cities; moral considerations aside, social clustering of similar people would make the allocation of public goods more efficient (V. Ostrom & E. Ostrom, 1971). Although its advocates did not explicitly support overt economic or racial segregation, public choice theory did create room to consider social and geographical stratification as benign or even salutary phenomena during a period when civil rights, fair housing, and antipoverty movements were attracting strong academic support.

Other critiques have focused on the implicit definitions of city and citizen embedded in public choice theory. If the metropolitan resident was like the consumer of any other good, the role of cities accordingly contracted; rather than a polis, a city could be understood as a marketer of packages of public services at the lowest possible costs in taxes, a view that has become deeply entrenched and influential (Briffault, 1990; Peterson, 1981). Accordingly, public choice ideas have been strongly associated with a political and social order defined by the rejection of civic obligation by the privileged and political consciousness rooted in narrow self-interest (Briffault, 1990; Dreier, 2004; Frug, 1999; G. J. Miller, 1981). One overdrawn criticism has observed that if more boastful proponents are right, "public choice theory could well take credit for most of the neoconservative policies encouraged during the Reagan era" (Petracca, 1991, p. 292). As with many academic controversies, rigorous debate about the validity of public choice has been obscured by more general political antagonisms.

By focusing on the *normative* or value-based assumptions and potential political relevance of public choice, critics have left unanswered important questions of an *ontological* nature. Does the theory adequately describe human agency and the process of metropolitan formation? The public sector economist Gary Miller's critique of suburban incorporation in Los Angeles County is a prime example. Miller's research was encouraged by Elinor Ostrom and retains an economistic sense of historical change expressed in two core propositions: that the "invisible hand" of residential choice was institutionally biased in favor of the rich, and that the incorporation of new suburban cities in the 1950s and 1960s enabled the rich to suburbanize in the pursuit of low taxes (G. J. Miller, 1981, p. 134). These claims have proven influential on studies of Los Angeles, including Mike Davis's widely read *City of Quartz* (1990), a scathing indictment of the region's political economy (pp. 169–170). Although these critiques lament the equity outcomes of public choice practices, they do not question whether public choice theory fully explains residential decisions.

The normative critique of public choice resonates with normative critiques of suburbanization itself. Many scholars resist economic explanations of human behavior in general. Yet, they appear to be willing to accept that economic rationality accounts for suburbanization, possibly because this explanation supports a negative image of suburban people as selfish and suburban communities as islands of privilege. In part, this is due to unreflective acceptance of an image of suburbs as devoid of communal culture, collective politics, or of much substantive sociability at all. Although many NHS scholars, most notably Nicolaides (2006), have challenged this historiographical prejudice, historians have, until relatively recently, accepted the notion that suburban migration was motivated by the pursuit of individual advantage, the rejection of taxation and social obligation, and hostility to the prospect of having minority neighbors. New regionalists, concerned with the inequities they associate with public choice ideas, may be served by imagining that this political rationality is an inherent component of the nature of *homo economicus suburbanus,* whose destructive effects must be contained by reorganizing government.

This normative focus is unfortunate because public choice's limitations as a description of the world are many. These can be categorized in terms of the theory's conceptualization of government, its interpretation of relevant political agency, and its assumptions about power and choice in market conditions where access to resources is unequal and dependent upon past distributions. Public choice theory tends to reduce the dense and multifaceted concept of "city" to a market. It "hardly acknowledges that local governments are governments, and does not recognize the concept of local citizenship at all" (Briffault, 1990, p. 415). According to public choice, the most important citizens, and indeed the ones to whom local governments would be most at pains to cater, are the ones least attached to place and most likely to move. This is directly contradicted by historical evidence of strong communal bonds uncovered by NSH scholars. Public choice also ignores what the geographers Brenner and Theodore (2002) call the "path-dependency" of local governance. Governments make policy within procedural and structural limits imposed by the past and by the present spatial distribution of wealth and taxable property. This path-dependency also extends to local culture, communal identity, and the structural contexts of individual choices (Dreier, 2004; Frug, 1999).

Critical Legal Studies: The Power of Local Government and Boundaries

There is, however, one important strength of public choice theory that must be acknowledged: its attention to the significance of boundaries separating metropolitan jurisdictions as a foundational element of differences and inequality between them. Though the theory approaches spatiality in a reductive way, its acknowledgment of the importance of relationships between metropolitan places provides a needed counterpoint to the tendency of historical studies to view metropolitan places in isolation from each other. The institutional and distributional patterns described by metropolitics and the legal structure of local autonomy animating public choice overlap considerably with a strain of critical legal studies that evaluates the legal status of local governments.

American municipalities are a form of corporation chartered by state governments. Although business corporations enjoy a broad range of powers, courts have sharply limited the powers that cities may exercise. In legal doctrine and jurisprudence, these powers and restrictions apply equally to all localities, but legal scholarship has exposed the ways that most central cities are less empowered by law than many suburbs. Influential early scholarly treatments of the subject sought to explain the "urban crisis" of the late 20th century by reference to cities' lack of power over business, taxation, and regulation (Frug, 1980). Such analysis appeared well suited to explain the problems of large cities but not the prosperity of many suburbs, which appeared to have legal powers ideally suited to their needs.

More recent legal scholarship emphasizes two significant points. First, the majority of the places legally defined as "cities" are, according to popular and historical understandings, "suburbs." Second, the legal powers allotted to American municipalities much more neatly correspond to the governing needs, social composition, and cultural orientations of affluent suburbs. Whereas cities can be defined inclusively by the presence of diverse social, economic, and land use elements, the local empowerment of suburbs operates on an exclusionary basis. Localities may influence who or what occupies space within their boundaries by enacting exclusionary zoning, may maintain control over many locally collected tax revenues, and may prevent outside authorities from altering their boundaries (Barron, 2002).

Because local government powers are nominally equal and uniformly limited, different local governments cannot create situational responses to the path-dependent or residual effects of past decisions about land use relating to industry, housing, roads, or other infrastructure. The United States Supreme Court's 1926 decision in *Euclid v. Ambler Realty Co.* upheld the use of municipal zoning; local governments could exclude industrial development for the purpose of preserving community character. But the decision allowed local governments to act only within their own boundaries, while pressures for economic or industrial development, housing, and stratification operate historically and in the present across those boundaries. All cities had the nominal power to exclude industry, but only some cities would be able to bear the economic consequences of doing so. Accordingly, wealthy and poor people, desirable and stigmatized land uses, and valuable and burdensome properties are unevenly distributed in metropolitan areas (Barron, 2002; Briffault, 1990).

Explaining, let alone remedying, that distribution thus points to the necessity of interdisciplinary integration. Because there is no inherent legal reason for spatial inequality or uneven metropolitan development, the problem is less a matter of legal doctrine than one of the interface of law with other forces and influences. Such phenomenological overlap has prompted critical legal analysts of local government law to seek some measure of disciplinary integration in order to appreciate the way that the law is formed in a social context. That is, "political, economic, and social distinctions that divide cities from suburbs are as significant as the common legal status that unites them" (Briffault, 1990, p. 356). Because many American suburbs are strongly associated (symbolically, if not always in fact) with forms of social identity (including whiteness, middle class status, home ownership, and nuclear family structure) that are valued in the dominant culture, local government in its emergent suburban form can be understood as a means of providing protection for a privileged segment of society (Briffault, 1990, p. 392; Dreier, 2004, pp. 209–213).

Accordingly, critical legal analysts have converged on a conclusion that has been developed in other fields: The legal doctrine of "home rule" that supports narrowly local government powers relative to regional ones is, in fact, a political and rhetorical formation that Self (2003) has called "the rule of homes" (p. 8). The rule of homes is a mutually reinforcing loop. Homeowners use local government to protect their perceived interests, and, because homeowners hold both cultural and political privilege, the utility of the system to protect single-family homes validates it as just, reasonable, and democratic. Because "home rule" is not an absolute legal doctrine but a product of political and ideological considerations, its critics in legal studies advance a normative claim that local government powers can and ought to be revised. In this view, state governments would be entitled to create regional governments and redistribute power to them from municipal authorities in order to achieve ends like environmental protection or regional economic equity (Barron, 2002). In this respect, the field of critical legal studies is normatively in line with metropolitics and strongly at odds with public choice. Findings from critical legal studies are mirrored by findings from metropolitics that the region, rather than the locality, is the most appropriate scale of government authority to address important social problems that transcend local boundaries.

The Limits of Social Science Perspectives on Metropolitan Formation

The explanatory constructs of history, metropolitics, public choice, and critical legal studies can be compared in terms of their spatial framings, attention to process, and interpretation of boundaries as sociopolitical structures (see Table 3.1). This comparison is a precursor to the integrative techniques of organization and theory expansion, both of which involve systematic evaluation of the theoretical and conceptual underpinnings of scholarly arguments

(Repko, 2008, pp. 281, 289). In practice, the boundaries between these techniques are imprecise. In this context, the application of theory expansion involves extending the theoretical notions of the spatial and temporal nature of social life into the domain of multiple disciplines where it is differentially acknowledged. The technique of organization places the particular spatial framings held by different disciplines in a comparative framework that ensures that spatiality can be logically connected to each. In this chapter, the application of both techniques depends upon the relationship of secondary research findings to primary evidence.

Applying this method of organization shows that metropolitics, public choice, and critical legal studies operate on different interpretations of spatiality and historical contingency. Critical legal studies offers the closest connection to historical arguments about process and contingency, while public choice and metropolitics are weaker historical theories that are at odds with historical evidence and accounts of how metropolitan residents viewed and experienced their communities. None of these perspectives is wholly adequate. One of the premises of new regionalist analysis, for example, is that self-interested political rationality may be harnessed to produce regional integration that expands economic activity, reduces inequality, and elevates political authority to broader spatial scales because this is ultimately in the self-interest of all regional residents, even those in affluent areas who typically regard regional initiatives with suspicion.

Table 3.1   Perspectives on Scale, Boundaries, and Power

	History (urban and NSH)	Metropolitics	Public Choice	Critical Legal
Scale	Local case study	Metropolitan area	Metropolitan area	Metropolitan area
Role of boundaries	Define limits of social processes	Serve to divide and distribute resources and power	Serve to differentiate market areas where different "tastes" for services can be served	Mark the limits of local government power and social and cultural identity
Temporal process	Complex and contingent; actions at one moment affect later possibilities	Static, focus on inequality at given moments; change is viewed in terms of patterns of inequality	Places remain stable as people move among places; change viewed in terms of shifts in market behavior	Places change to the extent that their legal powers conform (or not) to local needs

This path has not been taken. Therefore, it is necessary to return to historical perspective and the idea of process in order to consider how rewards and incentives in particular spatial and temporal contexts have supported the establishment over time of home rule as a parochial form of the "rule of homes." In Tilly's (1996) terms, these contexts are essential "laboratories for the investigation of historical contingency—the way that social action in a given time and place constrains what will happen next there and in adjacent places, what will happen after that, and so on through long strings of path-dependent processes" (p. 715). The use of the plural forms of "strings" and "processes" suggests that the problem of metropolitan formation requires theoretical expansion to examine the ways that political, legal, and economic dimensions of social life, along with emotional, cultural, and symbolic attachments to places, are embedded in the metropolitan landscape.

_____ The Social Production of Metropolitan Los Angeles

The growth and development of metropolitan Los Angeles has been subjected to analysis by scholars in all of the perspectives discussed above. Urbanists in multiple disciplines who write of an "L.A. School" of urban studies contend that greater Los Angeles represents a paradigmatic metropolitan area; understanding developments there provides insight into nationally and even globally significant patterns of metropolitan development in the latter half of the 20th century (Dear, 2002; Scott & Soja, 1996; Soja, 1996). This study is less concerned with whether Los Angeles is a model site for understanding metropolitan areas than with how studies of any metropolitan area might make use of more integrated theory and methods.

In the course of searching for and evaluating secondary sources to illuminate primary source research, I found that the metropolitan political landscape that was produced through postwar suburbanization and municipal incorporation in Los Angeles County diverged in significant ways from the individualistic and economistic assumptions of public choice theorists. The landscape also confounded the spatial framings of historical studies of cities and suburbs, in which thick descriptions of local process were not systematically connected to consider relationships among metropolitan places. Finally, though the contours of equality and inequality explored by metropolitics analysts and critical legal scholars were clearly discernible, evidence from primary sources defied the expectation that past legal, social, and political patterns in the metropolitan area could be easily reformed. An integrative understanding of metropolitan formation requires leveraging insight from each of these perspectives to produce a more complete and holistic understanding of the process (Mansilla, 2005).

Leveraging the insights of history, public choice, metropolitics, and critical legal studies requires a theory capable of extending across disciplinary domains to address the spatial assumptions of each perspective. Lefebvre's

(1991) theory of the social production of space through mutually reinforcing patterns of ideas (ideologies, values, ideals), political power (over institutions and over the validation of particular ideas), and social practices supports a more integrated form of metropolitan study. In the case of Los Angeles County, residents created local government institutions that protected the socially privileged (contract cities). These institutions reflected and promoted cultural values that supported white middle-class autonomy (the discourse of "home rule"), and they ensured that the experiences of white suburbanites (enjoying good services at low tax rates) reinforced and symbolized the goodness of the system and solidified homeowners as a political constituency that effectively defended its privileges. Each of these domains (institutions, ideas, and experiences) penetrates the others.

Theory also must be connected to research methods that can provide the kinds of evidence required to evaluate theoretical predictions. The case study methods used by historians may produce the kind of detailed descriptions that connect ideas, politics, and practices, but care must be taken to avoid the spatial limits of past applications of the method. The research discussed in the remainder of this chapter applies integrative methods of theory expansion and organization to these concepts through a strategically altered form of the local case study. This method extends Massey's (1997) conceptualization of place as "social relations stretched out" to make regional, statewide, and national events and processes part of the domain of local history and emphasizes the effects that actions in one place may have on other places. Primary research sources are assessed within this expanded spatial framing to explain how housing markets, local and state politics, community, and academic knowledge contributed to a particular kind of metropolitan formation and why that formation has been resistant to change.

Theory, Practice, and Metropolitan Space: The Career of Public Choice Theory in Los Angeles County

The Lakewood Plan or contract system is an appropriate object for such an expanded case study methodology. The Lakewood Plan connected several of the multiple factors influencing suburbanization, ensured the economic viability of individual cities, organized and structured conflicts between types of cities, and became a focus of political and ideological conflict at the local, regional, and state levels. For both Lakewood and its successors, the contract services plan was indispensable for municipal incorporation. In Lakewood, the contract plan alleviated tensions regarding tax obligations between the modest-income residents of the area and the development company that had mass-produced the area's housing and streets beginning in 1950 and continued to own the most important property in the city, the shopping mall (Connor, 2008; G. J. Miller, 1981). Lakewood officials also worked aggressively with the county to promote the contract plan, inspiring the wave of new municipal incorporations in the county. Thirty-two new contract cities formed by 1970, with more than 700,000 residents (Hoch, 1981; G. J. Miller, 1981; Waite, 1957; Will, 1962).

As noted above, the Lakewood Plan not only encouraged new municipal incorporations, it allotted new cities a means for securing services at low cost that older cities in the county, which operated their own municipal service departments, did not enjoy. By 1970, all but one of the pre-Lakewood cities in the county levied a municipal property tax of more than fifty cents per $100 assessed value, while 24 of the 32 new cities charged less (G. J. Miller, 1981, p. 82). Contract services in Los Angeles County rapidly became a mechanism for distributing resources between parts of the metropolitan area. By placing the contracting system in historical perspective, research can address the evolution of the system, identify episodes of conflict and, following the demands of metropolitics, demonstrate a precise mechanism by which some metropolitan places benefited at the expense of others.

Contemporary observers may associate contracting out for public services with a competitive market of private contractors. Under the Lakewood Plan, however, the most important and expensive services (police and fire protection) could only be provided by agreements between governments, making Los Angeles County in practice the exclusive provider. Political incentives were more influential than market imperatives in the setting of rates. If the county minimized contract rates and convinced new cities to join the system, it would prevent the underutilization of equipment or personnel in its large service departments. Older cities, which had invested in their own service departments, were unlikely to dismantle them to join the contract system. So long as contract service rates remained low, few contracting cities were likely to withdraw to form their own service departments. The contract cities and the county realized a common interest, and for most of the period of this study, the county used general fund revenues (collected from taxpayers in the county at large) to subsidize contract service rates (Kirlin, 1973; Schiesl, 1982; Shoup & Rosett, 1969). As the 1960s progressed, contracting became not a neutral administrative device but a channel for the distribution of resources away from older cities and toward newer ones. This spurred rhetorical and political conflict between the two blocs of cities.

In this context of political conflict, academic ideas that could present the political consequences of the Lakewood Plan as neutral or apolitical gained great influence in state policy circles. The Task Force on Local Government Reform, convened in 1973 by Governor Ronald Reagan, embraced public choice ideas and reversed the recommendations of Governor Brown's 1961 commission (Governor's Task Force on Local Government Reform, 1973). These changes reflect obvious ideological differences between liberal Democratic and conservative Republican administrations, but they also reflect the political and symbolic values attached to and expressed by places, the political impact of the rise of suburban cities, and the shifts in politics and policy analysis that corresponded to social and political change. The 1973 report shows that public choice ideas had become the ruling ideas of the state and an institutionalized expression of the "rule of homes."

It was fitting that those metropolitan changes began locally in Lakewood. That city, often referred to as the "Levittown of the West Coast," embodied the rule of homes because its middle-income, home owning citizens viewed their local government as an essential guardian of their investments. Other area suburbs did not resemble Lakewood in every social or physical aspect. However, the expansive case study method employed here enables analysis of the way that events and ideas from outside the community influenced Lakewood and that Lakewood exerted concentrated influence on the surrounding region. Lakewood's local officials most influenced regional dynamics by their aggressive promotion of incorporation and the contract services system. In the 1961 report of the Commission on Metropolitan Area Problems, Lakewood's first mayor, Angelo Iacoboni, argued that incorporation as a contract city enabled Lakewood to achieve both local home rule and efficient provision of government services. Iacoboni's references to home rule and efficiency connected his office, his city, and his constituents to an emergent common sense about metropolitan regions.

By 1973, state politics and academic analysts had both caught up to Iacoboni's position, reflecting a changed common sense about the ideal relationship of places in a metropolitan area. The theorists on the Reagan panel included Vincent and Elinor Ostrom, Robert Bish, and Robert Warren, all of whom were affiliated with the Workshop in Political Theory and Policy Analysis at Bloomington, a hotbed of public choice theory applied in local government administration (Mitchell, 1988). The panel's report, "Public Benefits from Public Choice," praised the Lakewood Plan. The panel also formally connected the public choice principle of devolving authority to more and smaller local government to state policy (Tiebout, 1956; V. Ostrom et al., 1961).[3] The role of these scholars as both analysts and proponents of policy change underlies one of the key findings of this study: Public choice ideas were less a description of market dynamics than a structural component of those dynamics. The application of public choice ideas through the Lakewood Plan tilted the metropolitan playing field in favor of the new suburbs, expanding choice for some and constricting it for others.

Scholarly literature on the Lakewood Plan suburbs is substantial, and I have analyzed it at length elsewhere (Connor, 2008). Here, I will reference much of it in tabular form, in order to demonstrate the ways that historical spatial practice highlights particular shortcomings of the theories discussed

---

[3]I realize that the attention given to Elinor Ostrom's work on the cooperative regulation of the commons in the wake of her recent receipt of the Nobel Memorial Prize in Economic Sciences may provoke a reasonable criticism of my analysis—that public choice as a body of theory has evolved and adapted. For present purposes, I will stipulate that I am discussing the state of public choice theory in 1973 at a moment of political influence in California, and I suggest that much of Ostrom's later work reflects efforts to address the inadequacies of a strictly individual rationality and allow for the social construction of interest (E. Ostrom, 1998).

above. Though Table 3.2 makes an explicit comparison to public choice theory, it should be noted that the descriptions of historical spatial practice in Los Angeles County also work to highlight deficiencies in the spatial or theoretical framings of other disciplinary literatures.

To begin with the most fundamental departure from free market conditions, residential location in Southern California was structured by exclusionary practices and privileges that originated and operated at various scales. The single-family tract houses built in the postwar generation of suburbs were

Table 3.2 Theory and Historical Practice

	Public Choice Theory/Advocacy	**Historical Spatial Practice**
Kind of housing market	"Free," without restrictions or proximity factors related to work	Based in layered policy decisions for subsidies, exclusions, industrial locations
Variety of market	Variegated service levels and tax price points	Trend to homogenous levels of service and low taxes; bifurcation of tax levels between old and new cities
Quality of local government	Independent jurisdictions; no externalizing of costs of services	Two blocs: a metropolitan confederation of "contract cities" under the county blending local autonomy and dependence on county, and traditionally organized cities operating their own services
Regional effects	"Efficient" allocation of costs through individual locational choice; resolution of differences through exchange market serves different "tastes"	Antagonism between favored and unfavored blocs of cities; mismatch between service needs and resources; differences provoke and are decided through conflict
Valuation of outcomes	Market outcomes best possible	Political outcomes are contested, part of a social contract
View of localism	Necessary, essential characteristic of good government	Pragmatic, flexible, established over time as an effective political value
Kind of citizen	Rational, detached, mobile; established class position	Oriented toward homes as economic, cultural, social capital; homes enable multiple connections to neighbors and government
Stakes of politics	Taxes, economic rationality dominant	Multiple, experiential, possible to renegotiate social contract in response to the rationality supported by social order

heavily subsidized by federal government mortgage guarantees that privileged the white working class over workers of color, and thus underwrote the ascendancy of a broad American white middle class by enabling white skilled workers (like those drawn to Lakewood by jobs in aircraft plants and refineries in nearby Long Beach and Signal Hill) to build wealth in suburban home equity. This pattern prevailed in Southern California as it did nationally, with the locations of new suburban residences closely mirroring the locations of newly created industrial and technical jobs that supported this middle class (Hayden, 2003; Hise, 1997; Jackson, 1985; Lipsitz, 1995).

Although the 1948 U.S. Supreme Court decision in *Shelley v. Kraemer* invalidated racially restrictive covenants as a means of preserving residential segregation, new suburban developments were constructed and sold en masse, giving realtors and developers tremendous power to create and enforce white homogeneity based on the rationale that racial integration imposed a disastrous neighborhood effect on property values. Large tracts like Lakewood followed national trends in this regard (Baker, 1999; Freund, 2007). Newly formed city governments had no legal power to mandate racial segregation, but they didn't need such power because they were incorporated within a preexisting landscape of residential subdivisions that had been formed by a thoroughly racialized housing market that established racial homogeneity as a matter of common interest within the community, even though it was seldom openly acknowledged or discussed (HoSang, 2007).

The "market" of local places opened up by the Lakewood Plan also departed from the form that theory assumed and prescribed. Although suburban cities in the county had different demographic profiles and very different kinds of housing stock, different levels of amenities were largely built into these areas before local governments formed. Since FHA, VA, and other federal programs established guidelines for the size, price, and construction of houses and for the financial means of eligible buyers, many of the tracts that became Lakewood Plan suburbs were fairly homogenous, part of the San Gabriel Valley area that captured the majority of inexpensive single-family home construction in the late 1950s (Hoch, 1981, pp. 108–110). The low-tax promises of the Lakewood Plan were essential to building coalitions for incorporation that neutralized taxes as a potentially potent source of local controversy. The Lakewood plan provided a common ground between homeowners of modest means and business property owners by promising to maintain lower taxes for both groups. Thus, contracting prevented budget politics in which a powerful minority might have balanced a city budget on the backs of homeowners or home owning populists might have tried to soak the largest landowner in town (Hoch, 1981; G. J. Miller, 1981). In this sense, political considerations intruded on the market even before new cities were formed.

The levels of services new Lakewood Plan governments purchased from the county also tended toward uniformity, with 15 of the first 16 contract cities electing to buy an identical service plan that minimized costs by procuring the lowest level of services allowed by law (Kennedy, 1958). Rather than facilitating diverse choices or catering to locally specific needs, the County promoted a sharply circumscribed form of local choice in which it provided standard services for a growing metropolitan confederation of contract cities. This confederation constituted one side of a growing metropolitical division between contract cities and traditionally organized cities. This latter group included Los Angeles; relatively large satellite cities like Long Beach, Pasadena, and Santa Monica; wealthy residential enclaves; and blue-collar cities like South Gate and Compton. As much as these cities differed from each other, each one (save Los Angeles, whose role as a regional power center was challenged by the county government) had a roughly comparable counterpart among contract cities—roughly comparable except for the fact that the regional political system shunted resources from one set of cities to the other through fiscal subsidies for contract services.

Although the contracting system and the general fund subsidies that supported it reduced homeowners' tax bills in the Lakewood Plan cities, the political culture of those cities was not reducible to narrow economic rationality (Rose-Ackerman, 1983). Residential mobility was high in Southern California during this period, but a large proportion of the residents who voted to incorporate Lakewood and the officials of the new city who promoted the Lakewood plan to other areas were clearly committed to their new city (Bopf, 1965, pp. 47–52; Kennedy, 1958; Todd, 1958). Their advocacy reflected a hope that their actions were creating robust civic life along with the efficient provision of services.

The Rule of Homes: The Culture of a Public Choice Metropolis

Even before incorporation, Lakewood residents and incorporation advocates developed a coherent and enduring civic mythology organized around successive iterations of "The Lakewood Story," a narrative that emphasized participation, voluntarism, community ties, and civic commitment. One 1970s-vintage incarnation of the civic mythology was subtitled "How Neighbors and Volunteers Made a City" (City of Lakewood, n.d.). One historian has gone further, arguing that "The Lakewood Story" was more than civic propaganda; it served as a social contract that expressed the multilayered attachments and investments that residents had in their homes, their neighborhoods, and their communities as venues for raising children (Baker, 1999).

This kind of social contract reflected the power of the idea that the rule of homes was the experiential foundation of suburban political populism (Barron, 2002; Self, 2003). In Lakewood, citizen interaction with government was organized by home ownership. The material value of property and the ability of houses to connect residents to a pleasant lifestyle were the cores of a local social contract (Baker, 1999). Residents were keenly aware that although their government did not operate most of its own departments, it did retain the prerogative of local zoning and land use regulation. Those residents were vigilant monitors of local government's ability to restrict multiple-family housing, absentee-owned rental property, and the decline of housing stock.

Although these concerns were, of course, consistent with rational individualism, evidence from community surveys in the 1960s also suggests that residents understood that membership in a community of blue-collar workers defined standards for housing quality and imposed necessary limits on the building regulatory power the city should exercise. One of the most popular aspects of the city's building regulations was a tolerance for self-repair of homes. In the 1970s, the City Council overstepped these limits, passing an ordinance requiring a city inspection of all homes before a sale. This disregarded the sweat equity of residents, insulted the pride many felt in their craftsmanship, and raised fears of community collapse if local houses were suddenly made unsalable (City Planning Commission, Lakewood, California, 1969; Baker, Stover, & Waldie, 2004, p. 60).

These were not actions reasonably attributed to people looking to pull up stakes and move to secure the slightest advantage or a response to a minor crisis. Indeed, public history projects inspired by the city's 50th anniversary demonstrated the deep roots established by the city's original residents and the influence of the old settlers on the expectations passed on to new arrivals. The collected remembrances of longtime and new residents reflect many themes that were part of the city's official civic narrative of a city of homeowners, families, and local democracy. The stability of Lakewood's residential population and the civic narrative over the years indicates that civic mythology was consistent enough with residents' experiences to remain plausible and compelling as an explanation for why Lakewood was a good place to live (City of Lakewood, 2003).

This thick set of social and political relationships placed local government in the context of a "communicative rationality" in which place, community, and large-scale political forces and ideas exerted complex influence on political consciousness, and no decision could ever be perfectly individual (B. Miller, 1992, p. 27). This process was contradictory. Individual residents experienced contradictory demands posed by neighbors and by the market. Local governments encountered contradictory mandates defined by their residents and by state law and sought to set policies for taxation, services, and land use that maximized political legitimacy and cohesion. Policy debates and public discourse also followed a contradictory pattern in the way that they addressed, or more accurately failed to address, the diversity of suburban cities in the county. Although all cities in the county differed in some respects, state policy and political ideology were strongly informed by the example of Lakewood, meaning that all cities, regardless of local conditions, were affected by the policies that were developed and proven to be functional in one highly visible place.

The Image of Homes Mediates Political Contradictions

As an administrative prescription subject to political negotiation, public choice depended on its advocates' ability to focus attention on particular places as representations of the metropolitan area proponents hoped to create and their ability to argue that the system that supported the city of Lakewood was, therefore, a benefit to the metropolitan region as a whole. As the New Suburban History tells us, there was no perfectly "typical" suburb anywhere. However, Lakewood sufficed as a symbol of suburban life because it fit a nationally recognized image of communities and lifestyles defined by modest affluence, family orientation, and homogeneity without overt social strife. It had attracted regional attention as the first of the new incorporations, and the contract services plan prominently bore its name. Lakewood—an actual, observable place with many positive connotations—was thus linked to the abstract representation of a metropolitan system proposed in theory. Theories of administration and cultural understandings of the kinds of metropolitan places that public policy should nurture and protect were not neatly separable in political practice, or in historical and spatial development.

The communicative political rationality of metropolitan formation reinforced the administrative prescriptions of public choice theory because it encouraged citizen demands for low taxes, cheap public services, and single-family zoning as the most obvious steps that local governments could take to protect homes and homeowners. The rule of homes demanded that the governments of contract cities work not just locally but at the county and the state levels to defend these prerogatives. Local governments succeeded in winning reforms that protected local autonomy and could, in turn, justify those reforms as serving a metropolitan greater good. For example, state legislation established subventions from vehicle licenses and other state fees to local governments and a uniform 1% sales tax for all local jurisdictions. Under this provision, incorporated cities could keep the revenue for themselves, but taxes on sales in unincorporated areas would be controlled by the county government and could be spent anywhere. Both of these reforms proved essential to the fiscal stability of small, residence-intensive suburbs and the contract cities in particular and were strong incentives to further incorporation (Crouch, 1963, pp. 115–116; Todd, 1958). These state policies were directly informed by demands for the protection of local governmental autonomy as an opposing principle to the consolidation of authority for taxing and budgeting at broader geographical scales.

Metropolitan Political Conflicts Under Public Choice Theory

As the division between older and newer cities became more pronounced, the rates the county charged for contract services became the focus of increasingly contentious metropolitics. Predictably, Los Angeles and other traditionally organized cities challenged the legality of subsidized contract rates. This prompted the California Contract Cities Association (CCCA), formed in 1958 as the collective lobbying agent for the Lakewood Plan cities, to take a more aggressive posture. In 1973, the CCCA successfully sponsored legislation that defined the accounting formulas that county governments used to set contract rates in a way that established subsidized rates as state law. Political practice and a selective representation of space based in public choice theory converged in the legislative battle over the Gonsalves bill (named for its sponsor, an Assemblyman from the contract city of Norwalk) and subsequent legal challenges to it (Canary, 1972, p. SE1; G. J. Miller, 1981, pp. 25–26; Smith, 1975, 1973, p. SE1). The legislation harnessed public choice's call for reform of the state's relationship to local government by privileging suburban fiscal strength and increased local independence over metropolitan consolidation.

Debate on the bill raged just as Reagan's commission was reaching its prescriptive conclusions, and there is a historical convergence of the political interests reflected in the bill and in the commission's report. The new suburban contract cities were the chief beneficiaries of local autonomy. They were also strongholds of support for Reagan, making it perhaps inevitable that what was good for the Lakewood Plan suburbs in particular would be conflated with a general public good. This ideological position was not exclusive to the governor or members of the state legislature, however. Legal challenges to the legislation brought by Los Angeles and other older cities were rejected by the courts in 1976. In these challenges, judges essentially ruled that the creation of a two-tiered system of cities in the state, with one tier enjoying a privileged fiscal position, was an acceptable outcome of state politics and not a violation of equal protection guarantees (*City of Los Angeles v. City of Artesia*, 1977; "County Contract Services," 1976, p. SE3; Todd, 1976). In rejecting Los Angeles's claims, appeals court judge Harry Hupp prefaced his decision with reference to "the latest chapter in the continuing saga of that remarkable government development universally known as the 'Lakewood Plan'," suggesting that his own sympathies lay with continuing the advancement of suburban autonomy. Hupp also affirmed that the plan created "efficiencies" (in disregard of evidence that the efficiencies reflected in contract city budgets were artificially subsidized by county taxpayers at large) and expressed his contentment to allow any political dispensation by the legislature of the benefits of those efficiencies (Lane, 1976, p. SE1; Oliver, 1976, p. OC-A5).

Arguably, this was the sense in which the Reagan commission's work was most important. Though it named no particular cities in its advocacy of increased local autonomy, its references to the interests of the public, rather than to the interests of business or industry, suggests that its writers made a strategic effort to focus on the "choice" available to suburban homeowners and to leverage the populist image of Lakewood in support of that policy imperative. As much as it claimed a positive, descriptive, and analytical intent, the report was inseparable from a political context in which normative ideas about ideal forms of cities and citizenship were pervasive. In 1961, Governor Brown's metropolitan commission had associated the principles of local municipal independence in greater Los Angeles with the efforts by localities to hoard resources. Commissioners identified the City of Industry as a metropolitan place that exemplified this view. Industry was a grim concentration of factories and refineries. It had only the minimum population state law required to incorporate a city, and the purpose of its existence was to prevent other cities from taxing industrial property (Sherwood, 1961, p. 16). Industry was no more typical of the metropolitan area than was Lakewood. Like Lakewood, however, it was deployed as a symbol in debates about policies that affected the region as a whole.

By the 1970s, however, judges and legislators had learned to identify home rule with the image of Lakewood: a city of homes and homeowners. This image helped to establish the relative privilege of homeowners there as a legitimate outcome of neutral market forces, rather than the product of political conflicts. The court rulings validated a form of metropolitics in which historical layers of place-based and place-creating actions by developers, industry, and governments established a privileged class of white, middle-class, suburban homeowners who were empowered to protect that privilege through local and state government out of proportion to their numbers or economic means. This politics was premised on a set of understandings of value and investment—meant in both the financial and cultural senses of the words—in homes. Homeownership quite literally provided suburban residents with a "place" in the metropolitan region, but in multiple related senses of the word. Having a place meant occupying a dwelling, but it also meant holding a piece of property; occupying a position in a community of neighbors; having standing to speak as a citizen; and, for those holding a place in a privileged community, having one's community enjoy prestige, influence, and favorable access to metropolitan resources in relation to other places.

Conclusion

This case study reinforces and demonstrates that although particular academic disciplines may use the concepts of spatiality and place overtly, and others implicitly, traditional disciplinary approaches fail to integrate the multiple, overlapping, and occasionally conflicting elements of the essential relationship between places and social life. In the U.S. context, suburbanization and home ownership have connected individuals and families to historical changes in social class, racial differentiation, and political interest. However, historians have typically been limited by a spatial framing of social processes that seldom transcends the presumed division between urban and suburban places. Metropolitics and public choice approaches in the social sciences supply frameworks for assessing social processes that cross municipal boundaries but provide starkly different assessments of which social mechanisms—politics or the market—best account for differentiation between metropolitan places. The field of critical legal studies provides a systematic critique of municipal boundaries as political, symbolic, and economic dividers between places and people. Because research in this field focuses very diligently on the processes by which legal principles of local control have evolved in legal doctrine, critical legal studies points to the need to consider the way that policy or legal doctrines have emerged in particular historical contexts and influenced the course of events in those times.

Integrating the theoretical insights of these fields also requires expanding the characteristic methods of local history. A more spatially and analytically open case study methodology employed here addresses the qualities of individual places, but it also pays attention to the nonlocal factors, like ideology, law, and public policy, affecting metropolitan places. In addition, it pays attention to the ways in which local places are not separate but affect each other. The Lakewood Plan, for example, shaped the metropolitan area, but that influence depended on the very particular qualities of Lakewood as a symbol of the positive values of local autonomy. Public choice ideas, because they have been influential in governing as well as in scholarship, merit special scrutiny in this framework. The history of metropolitan formation in Los Angeles demonstrates the partial validity of these ideas. Under the conditions of the rule of homes, suburban residents in the Lakewood Plan cities acted in ways that were consistent with rational self-interest: advocating for low taxes, demanding better services, and seeking to exclude neighbors or land uses that threatened the value of property. Under the political and cultural conditions that have prevailed in the United States and in Los Angeles in particular, it has also been rational for relatively affluent suburban areas to reject common obligations with other metropolitan places. However, this rationality is neither an inherent part of human nature nor a complete explanation for the political and social patterns of metropolitan formation. Rather, it was formed in the context of historically produced legal, social, and political frameworks that made certain behaviors, orientations, and outlooks productive (Petracca, 1991; Zuckert, 1995). Public choice theory has, in fact, been more important as a shaper of public life than as a descriptor of it.

These frameworks of incentives and justifications are not inevitable, but they are powerful, and they have been constructed and reinforced over time through the political rationality they support. In Los Angeles County, homeowners, local and state officials, judges, realtors, bankers, and builders produced new places in the county, attached certain social privileges to favored places, and protected those privileges against claims that they were unfair or unjust. These agents worked through institutional and cultural channels at local, metropolitan, and state scales to create what was visible in hindsight: a white middle class, multiple municipal jurisdictions that could insulate portions of that class from taxation or service obligations, and perhaps most important, the sense that this division was a legitimate component of politics that reflected not exclusion or segregation but "choice."

Los Angeles County has its own particular history, making generalizations about other metropolitan areas problematic. It should, however, be possible to use a case study method involving Los Angeles to propose a methodology for evaluating the particular factors influencing metropolitan development elsewhere. Metropolitan areas nationwide exhibit comparable political division, social inequality, and privilege for affluent homeowners, regardless of the particular path of development, and researchers should devote attention to the ways that institutions, ideas, and experiences (in their particular local incarnations) have interacted to shape development. It is beyond the scope of this essay to recommend policy changes that can promote greater metropolitan equity, though metropolitics scholars offer many suggestions. Rather, by demonstrating that inequality is part of a long process of metropolitan formation with roots in many dimensions of social life, this essay suggests the limits of narrow policy solutions, which are likely to provoke intense opposition and unlikely to secure political legitimacy in the current metropolitan climate of the United States. As Gerald Frug (1999) observes, a fragmented metropolitan area is "perpetuated by the kind of person this fragmentation has nurtured" (p. 80). Reform proposals for regional equity are unlikely to succeed without substantial efforts to unravel dominant values and ideals about place and community in metropolitan America, ideals which have coalesced around the priority given to local interests and the rule of homes.

References

Baker, A. L. (1999). *The Lakewood story: Defending the recreational good life in postwar Southern California suburbia, 1950–1999* (Doctoral dissertation). University of Pennsylvania, Philadelphia.

Baker, A., Stover, M., & Waldie, D. (2004). *The Lakewood story: History, traditions, values.* Lakewood, CA: City of Lakewood.

Barron, D. J. (2002). Reclaiming home rule. *Harvard Law Review, 116,* 2257–2386.

Bigger, R. (1961). The role of California local government in metropolitan areas. In E. Engelbert (Ed.), *Metropolitan California* (pp. 83–88). Sacramento, CA: Governor's Commission on Metropolitan Area Problems.

Bigger, R., & Kitchen, J. (1952). *Metropolitan Los Angeles: A study in integration: Volume II, How the cities grew.* Los Angeles: Haynes Foundation.

Bopf, W. L. (1965). *An analysis of the Lakewood Plan's influence on the cities that incorporated in Los Angeles County since April, 1954* (Master's thesis). University of California, Los Angeles, Public Administration.

Brenner, N., & Theodore, N. (2002). Cities and the geographies of "actually existing neoliberalism." *Antipode, 34*(3), 349–379. doi:10.1111/1467-8330.00246

Briffault, R. (1990). Our localism: Part II—Localism and legal theory. *Columbia Law Review, 90*(2), 346–454. doi:10.2307/1122776

Canary, P. (1972, August 20). In wake of Reagan veto: Hopes raised on city contracts. *Los Angeles Times*, SE1.

Chauncey, G. (1994). *Gay New York: Gender, urban culture, and the makings of the gay male world, 1890–1940*. New York: Basic Books.

City of Lakewood. (n.d.). *The Lakewood story: How neighbors and volunteers made a community and a city* [Pamphlet]. Local History Collection, Angelo M. Iacoboni Library, Lakewood, CA.

City of Lakewood. (2003). *Take your place in history community essays*. Retrieved from http://www.lakewoodcity.org/about_lakewood/community/writestuff.asp

City of Los Angeles v. City of Artesia, 73 Cal. App. 3d 450 (1977).

City Planning Commission, Lakewood, California. (1969). *Community survey*. Local History Collection, Angelo M. Iacoboni Library, Lakewood, CA.

Cohen, L. (2003). *A consumer's republic: The politics of mass consumption in postwar America*. New York: Knopf.

Connor, M. A. (2008). *Creating cities and citizens: Municipal boundaries, place entrepreneurs, and the production of race in Los Angeles County, 1926–1978* (Doctoral dissertation). University of Southern California, Los Angeles.

Countryman, M. (2006). *Up south: Civil rights and black power in Philadelphia*. Philadelphia: University of Pennsylvania Press.

County contract services to cities upheld by court. (1976, April 25). *Los Angeles Times*, SE3.

Crouch, W. W. (1961). The general status of research in metropolitan affairs. In E. Engelbert (Ed.), *Metropolitan California* (pp. 33–37). Sacramento, CA: Governor's Commission on Metropolitan Area Problems.

Crouch, W. W. (1963). *Southern California metropolis: A study in development of government for a metropolitan area*. Berkeley: University of California Press.

Davis, M. (1990). *City of quartz: Excavating the future in Los Angeles*. New York: Verso.

Dear, M. J. (Ed.). (2002). *From Chicago to L.A.: Making sense of urban theory*. Thousand Oaks, CA: Sage.

Deloria, P. J. (2009). Broadway and Main: Crossroads, ghost roads, and paths to an American studies future. *American Quarterly, 61*(1), 1–25.

Dreier, P. (2004). *Place matters: Metropolitics for the twenty-first century. Studies in government and public policy* (2nd ed.). Lawrence: University Press of Kansas.

Engelbert, E. (Ed.). (1961). *Metropolitan California*. Sacramento, CA: Governor's Commission on Metropolitan Area Problems.

Ethington, P. J. (2007). Placing the past: "Groundwork" for a spatial theory of history. *Rethinking History, 11*(4), 465–493.

Ethington, P. J., Frey, W. H., & Myers, D. (2001, May 12). *The racial resegregation of Los Angeles county, 1940–2000*. Retrieved from http://www.usc.edu/schools/sppd/research/census2000/race_census/research_reports/research_reports.htm

Ethington, P. J., & McDaniel, J. A. (2007). Political places and institutional spaces: The intersection of political science and political geography. *Annual Review of Political Science, 10*, 127–142.

Fishman, R. (1987). *Bourgeois utopias: The rise and fall of suburbia*. New York: Basic Books.

Fogelson, R. M. (1993). *The fragmented metropolis: Los Angeles, 1850–1930*. Berkeley: University of California Press.

Freund, D. M. (2007). *Colored property: State policy and white racial politics in suburban America*. Chicago: University of Chicago Press.

Frug, G. E. (1980). The city as a legal concept. *Harvard Law Review*, 93(6), 1057–1154.

Frug, G. E. (1999). *City making: Building communities without building walls.* Princeton, NJ: Princeton University Press.

Gonzalez, J. B. (2009). *"A place in the sun": Mexican Americans, race, and the suburbanization of Los Angeles, 1940–1980* (Doctoral dissertation). University of Southern California, Los Angeles.

Gordon, C. (2008). *Mapping decline: St. Louis and the fate of the American city.* Philadelphia: University of Pennsylvania Press.

Governor's Task Force on Local Government Reform. (1973). *Public benefits from public choice.* Sacramento, CA: Author.

Grossman, J. R., & Katz, S. N. (2008). *The history major and undergraduate liberal education: Report of the National History Center Working Group to the Teagle Foundation.* Retrieved from http://www.teaglefoundation.org/learning/pdf/2008_nhc_whitepaper.pdf

Halberstam, J. (2009). Beyond Broadway and Main: A response to the presidential address. *American Quarterly*, 61(1), 33–38.

Harris, R., & Lewis, R. (2001). The geography of North American cities and suburbs, 1900–1950: A new synthesis. *Journal of Urban History*, 27(3), 262–292. doi:10.1177/009614420102700302

Harvey, D. (1989). *The urban experience.* Baltimore, MD: Johns Hopkins University.

Harvey, D. (1990). *The condition of postmodernity: An enquiry into the origins of cultural change.* Cambridge, MA: Blackwell.

Hayden, D. (2003). *Building suburbia: Green fields and urban growth, 1820–2000.* New York: Pantheon Books.

Hise, G. (1997). *Magnetic Los Angeles: Planning the twentieth-century metropolis.* Baltimore, MD: Johns Hopkins University Press.

Hobbs, F., & Stoops, N. (2002). *Demographic trends in the 20th century. U.S. Census Bureau, Census 2000 Special Reports.* Washington, DC: U.S. Government Printing Office.

Hoch, C. M. (1981). *City limits: Municipal boundary formation and class segregation in Los Angeles suburbs, 1940–1970* (Doctoral dissertation). University of California, Los Angeles, Urban Planning.

HoSang, D. W. (2007). *Racial propositions: "Genteel apartheid" in postwar California* (Doctoral dissertation). University of Southern California, Los Angeles, American Studies and Ethnicity.

Iacoboni, A. M. (1961). Statement. In E. Engelbert (Ed.), *Metropolitan California* (pp. 55–56). Sacramento, CA: Governor's Commission on Metropolitan Area Problems.

Jackson, K. T. (1985). *Crabgrass frontier: The suburbanization of the United States.* New York: Oxford University Press.

Keating, A. D., Moehring, E. P., & Tarr, J. A. (1985). *Infrastructure and urban growth in the nineteenth century.* Chicago: Public Works Historical Society.

Kennedy, H. (1958, April 8). *County viewpoints on metropolitan government: Is the Lakewood Plan the answer?* Fletcher Bowron Collection (Box 47). Huntington Library, San Marino, CA.

Kirlin, J. (1973). The impact of contract services arrangements on the Los Angeles Sheriff's Department and law-enforcement services in Los Angeles County. *Public Policy*, 21, 553–584.

Kruse, K. M., & Sugrue, T. J. (2006a). Introduction. In K. M. Kruse & T. J. Sugrue (Eds.), *The new suburban history* (pp. 1–10). Chicago: University of Chicago Press.

Kruse, K. M., & Sugrue, T. J. (Eds.). (2006b). *The new suburban history*. Chicago: University of Chicago Press.

Lane, L. (1976, May 2). Court decision reinforces city use of county service contracts. *Los Angeles Times*, SE1.

Lassiter, M. D. (2004). The suburban origins of "color-blind" conservatism: Middle-class consciousness in the Charlotte busing crisis. *Journal of Urban History*, *30*(4), 549–582. doi:10.1177/0096144204263812

Lassiter, M. D. (2006). *The silent majority: Suburban politics in the sunbelt south*. Princeton, NJ: Princeton University Press.

Lefebvre, H. (1991). *The production of space*. Oxford and Cambridge: Blackwell.

Lipsitz, G. (1995). The possessive investment in whiteness: Racialized social democracy and the "white" problem in American studies. *American Quarterly*, *47*(3), 19.

Malpas, J. (1998). Finding place: Spatiality, locality, and subjectivity. In A. Light & J. M. Smith (Eds.), *Philosophy and geography 3: Philosophies of place* (pp. 21–44). Lanham, MD: Rowman & Littlefield.

Mansilla, V. B. (2005). Assessing student work at disciplinary crossroads. *Change*, *37*(1), 14–21.

Massey, D. (1997). A global sense of place. In T. Barnes & D. Gregory (Eds.), *Reading human geography: The poetics and politics of inquiry* (pp. 315–323). London: Arnold.

McGirr, L. (2002). *Suburban warriors: The origins of the new American right*. Princeton, NJ: Princeton University Press.

Miller, B. (1992). Collective action and rational choice: Place, community, and the limits to individual self-interest. *Economic Geography*, 22–42.

Miller, G. J. (1981). *Cities by contract: The politics of municipal incorporation*. Cambridge, MA: MIT Press.

Mitchell, W. C. (1988). Virginia, Rochester, and Bloomington: Twenty-five years of public choice and political science. *Public Choice*, *56*(2), 101–119.

Mohl, R. A. (1998). City and region: The missing dimension in U.S. urban history. *Journal of Urban History*, *25*(1), 3–21. doi:10.1177/009614429802500101

National Center for Suburban Studies. (n.d.). *The diverse suburb: History, politics, and prospects–Hofstra University*. Retrieved January 22, 2010, from http://www.hofstra.edu/Community/culctr/culctr_events_suburb.html

Nicolaides, B. M. (2001). The quest for independence: Workers in the suburbs. In T. Sitton & W. F. Deverell (Eds.), *Metropolis in the making: Los Angeles in the 1920s* (pp. 77–95). Berkeley: University of California Press.

Nicolaides, B. M. (2002). *My blue heaven: Life and politics in the working-class suburbs of Los Angeles, 1920–1965*. Chicago: University of Chicago Press.

Nicolaides, B. M. (2006). How hell moved from the city to the suburbs: Urban scholars and changing perceptions of authentic community. In K. M. Kruse & T. J. Sugrue (Eds.), *The new suburban history* (pp. 80–98). Chicago: University of Chicago Press.

O'Connor, A. (2008). The privatized city: The Manhattan Institute, the urban crisis, and the conservative counterrevolution in New York. *Journal of Urban History*, *34*(2), 333–353. doi:10.1177/0096144207308672

Oliver, M. (1976, April 14). L. A. county wins service cost fight. *Los Angeles Times*, OC, A5.

Orfield, M. (1997). *Metropolitics: A regional agenda for community and stability*. Washington, DC: Brookings Institution Press.

Orfield, M. (2002). *American metropolitics: The new suburban reality*. Washington, DC: Brookings Institution Press.

Ostrom, E. (1998). A behavioral approach to the rational choice theory of collective action: Presidential address, American Political Science Association, 1997. *The American Political Science Review*, 92(1), 1–22.

Ostrom, V., & Ostrom, E. (1971). Public choice: A different approach to the study of public administration. *Public Administration Review*, 31(2), 203–216.

Ostrom, V., Tiebout, C. M., & Warren, R. (1961). The organization of government in metropolitan areas: A theoretical inquiry. *The American Political Science Review*, 55(4), 831–842.

Pastor, M. (2000). *Regions that work: How cities and suburbs can grow together*. Minneapolis: University of Minnesota Press.

Pastor, M. (2001). Looking for regionalism in all the wrong places: Demography, geography, and community in Los Angeles County. *Urban Affairs Review*, 36(6), 747–782. doi:10.1177/10780870122185082

Pastor, M., Benner, C., & Matsuoka, M. (2008). *This could be the start of something big: How social movements for regional equity are reshaping metropolitan America*. Ithaca, NY: Cornell University Press.

Peterson, P. E. (1981). *City limits*. Chicago: University of Chicago Press.

Petracca, M. (1991). The rational choice approach to politics: A challenge to democratic theory. *The Review of Politics*, 53(2), 289–319.

Reece, J., Rogers, C. A., Gambhir, S., & powell, j. a. (2007). *Communities of opportunity*. Columbus, OH: Kirwan Institute for the Study of Race and Ethnicity, The Ohio State University.

Repko, A. F. (2008). *Interdisciplinary research: Process and theory*. Los Angeles: Sage.

Rose-Ackerman, S. (1983). Beyond Tiebout: Modeling the political economy of local government. In G. R. Zodrow (Ed.), *Local provision of public services: The Tiebout model after twenty-five years* (pp. 55–83). New York: Academic Press.

Ryan, M. P. (1997). *Civic wars democracy and public life in the American city during the nineteenth century*. Berkeley: University of California Press.

Schiesl, M. (1982). The politics of contracting: Los Angeles County and the Lakewood Plan, 1954–1962. *Huntington Library Quarterly*, 45(3), 227–243.

Scott, A. J., & Soja, E. W. (1996). *The city: Los Angeles and urban theory at the end of the twentieth century*. Berkeley: University of California Press.

Self, R. O. (2003). *American Babylon: Race and the struggle for postwar Oakland*. Princeton, NJ: Princeton University Press.

Sherwood, F. (1961). Some major problems of metropolitan areas. In E. Engelbert (Ed.), *Metropolitan California* (pp. 15–20). Sacramento, CA: Governor's Commission on Metropolitan Area Problems.

Shoup, D. C., & Rosett, A. I. (1969). *Fiscal exploitation of central cities by overlapping governments: A case study of law enforcement finance in Los Angeles County*. Los Angeles: Institute of Government and Public Affairs, University of California.

Sides, J. (2003). *L. A. city limits: African American Los Angeles from the Great Depression to the present*. Berkeley: University of California Press.

Sides, J. (2004). Straight into Compton: American dreams, urban nightmares, and the metamorphosis of a black suburb. *American Quarterly*, 56(3), 583–605.

Sides, J. (2009). *Erotic city: Sexual revolutions and the making of modern San Francisco*. New York: Oxford University Press.

Singh, N. P. (2009). Disciplining American studies? A response to the presidential address. *American Quarterly, 61*(1), 27–32.

Smith, S. (1973, November 25). County review likely of contract system. *Los Angeles Times,* SE3.

Smith, S. (1975, April 6). Cities prove to be potent lobbyists in Sacramento. *Los Angeles Times,* SE1.

Soja, E. W. (1994). *Postmodern geographies: The reassertion of space in critical social theory.* London: Verso.

Soja, E. W. (1996). *Thirdspace: Journeys to Los Angeles and other real-and-imagined places.* Cambridge, MA: Blackwell.

Stansell, C. (1987). *City of women: Sex and class in New York, 1789–1860.* Urbana: University of Illinois Press.

Sugrue, T. J. (2008). *Sweet land of liberty: The forgotten struggle for civil rights in the north.* New York: Random House.

Tarr, J. A. (1996). *The search for the ultimate sink: Urban pollution in historical perspective.* Akron, OH: University of Akron Press.

Teaford, J. C. (1979). *City and suburb: The political fragmentation of metropolitan America, 1850–1970.* Baltimore, MD: Johns Hopkins University Press.

Teaford, J. C. (2006). *The metropolitan revolution: The rise of post-urban America.* New York: Columbia University Press.

Tiebout, C. M. (1956). A pure theory of local expenditures. *The Journal of Political Economy, 64*(5), 416–424.

Tilly, C. (1996). What good is urban history? *Journal of Urban History, 22*(6), 702–719. doi:10.1177/009614429602200603

Todd, J. (1958, March 6). *Lakewood Plan: A presentation to the Board of Directors of the Los Angeles County Division of the League of California Cities.* Retrieved from http://www.lakewoodcity.org/civica/filebank/blobdload.asp?BlobID=2538

Todd, J. (1976). *Memorandum April 13, 1976.* Local History Collection, Angelo M. Iacoboni Library, Lakewood, CA.

Waite, C. (1957). *Incorporation fever: Hysteria or salvation?* Retrieved from http://www.lakewoodcity.org/civica/filebank/blobdload.asp?BlobID=2642

Warner, S. B. (1973). *Streetcar suburbs: The process of growth in Boston, 1870–1900.* New York: Atheneum.

Wiese, A. (2004). *Places of their own: African American suburbanization in the twentieth century.* Chicago: University of Chicago Press.

Will, A. (1962, July 11). *Another look at Lakewood: Municipal services provided by contract by county to smaller units of government.* Fletcher Bowron Collection (Box 47). Huntington Library, San Marino, CA.

Wood, R. C. (1961). *1400 Governments: The political economy of the New York metropolitan region.* Cambridge, MA: Harvard University Press.

Zuckert, C. (1995). On the "rationality" of rational choice. *Political Psychology, 16*(1), 179–198.

4

Mektoub

When Art Meets History, Philosophy, and Linguistics

Mieke Bal

Introduction

The objects of study in many of the humanities are generally works of art and their historical, philosophical, and theoretical contexts. Traditionally these were works of "high art," but nowadays more widely circulating cultural objects (often referred to as "popular culture") have also come into play. This simple fact prescribes a research agenda a bit different from that in other fields. First, the artworks—literary, theatrical, cinematic, visual, musical—demand to be treated with due respect as complex artifacts that were made by people for people, in order to intervene in the cultural life of communities. Second, the examination of their cultural role also demands a critical perspective, which frequently leads to evaluative assessments. Third and most important, at a certain, more or less arbitrary, moment in history, their genre affiliations have dictated the formation of disciplines and their methods. With the advent of artifacts that can no longer be confined to categories such as "painting," "sculpture," or "film," the awareness has grown that not only now but always, many artworks fit uneasily in the disciplinary categories designed for their study (just think of opera). Finally, the fact that these objects are made by people for people gives them a historical position as well as a social function. The need to understand that position and that function is a fourth reason why research in the humanities tends to exceed the disciplinary frameworks designed to understand these objects.

In ways I hope to indicate, through their very difference from other domains of knowledge, the humanities can become a kind of model of interdisciplinarity, specifically in the way one can develop a research question outside of any a priori established discipline. At the same time, models of interdisciplinarity that work well for other domains may not be the most productive to address the specific research questions humanists develop.

In particular, both the respect due to the objects and the need to analyze critically whether and how they serve the people they address in the most adequate way are two requirements potentially in tension with each other. Tension, therefore, is indispensable and sometimes overrules the wished-for integration. Here lies, in my view, the specific contribution of the humanities to our reflection on how to do interdisciplinary research.

How to Develop a Research Question

A research question focused on "art"—a literary text or a work of visual art, the body of works by an artist, an artistic movement—must develop from the principles outlined above: respect and criticism. Furthermore, there is another reason for a somewhat peculiar "need" of humanistic research. To announce where my analysis will be going: *The artwork sets the terms of the approach best suited to understand it.* In the case at hand—my case study—I argue that the key term the work proposes is the Arabic word *mektoub.* This means both "writing" and "fate," two meanings that come together in the phrase "the handwriting on the wall." And, as I will demonstrate, this power to set the terms entails neither freedom nor a pre-established confinement; it bypasses that dichotomy. Nor is it circular, as I will work hard to argue. Just consider the following historical event out of which I developed a research question.[1]

In January, 2008, the Jeu de Paume, a prestigious Parisian museum of film and photography, inaugurated an extensive exhibition of works by the Finnish artist Eija-Liisa Ahtila. It was her first "retrospective" exhibition in France. For the occasion, a new work had been commissioned, called *Where Is Where?* In many ways—in space, length, and scale, as well as in subject matter—it is the most monumental of her works to date. On no fewer than six screens, four of which surround the viewer for most of the duration, the history of the Algerian war—France's Vietnam—is presented in a mix of documentary footage and fiction, set in both Algeria and in Finland.[2]

Described in this way, the historical event involved, but was not limited to, a specific work of art, as well as the other way around: The historical situation was framed by the artwork, yet the artwork was not limited to the historical situation. An artwork framed by a historical situation is a typical

---

[1]*Mektoub,* thus, joins my earlier analysis of a graffito, which Allen Repko has thoughtfully woven through his book on interdisciplinarity. The graffito was remarkable because it is both painting and writing, pertaining to both popular culture and "high art" (it was a fragment from a literary poem). *Mektoub,* likewise, is double-edged, as will become clear later. The graffito and the Arabic word emblematize for me what triggers interdisciplinarity.

[2]The French occupation of Algeria started in 1830. In 1954, the National Liberation Front (*Front de Libération Nationale,* or FLN) started what became an eight-year-long war of liberation. For Algeria as for France, the war has remained traumatic. See Shepard (2006) for a historical-political overview.

object for research in the humanities. As soon as we approach this work "in its event" in 2008, the humanities meet psychology and postcolonial theory. For *Where Is Where?* is based on a fragment, a "case history" of psychiatrist Franz Fanon (1968), drawn from his passionately anticolonial 1956 treatise *The Wretched of the Earth*. Ahtila's video installations, often in large formats, offer an intense experience of heterogeneity, bringing together things that are usually separated and considered incomparable and incompatible. It is no coincidence that this statement is very close to the way we think of interdisciplinarity: bringing together academic disciplines and approaches usually applied separately and frequently even considered incompatible. It also suggests that Ahtila's works exemplify the potential of art to generate social experiences that are different from the customary ones. Innovative yet also appealing to the image repertoire of her spectators, Ahtila subverts well-known images. Her works are aesthetically engaging, affectively intense, and politically complex. They are also intellectually challenging, offering food for thought, often on par with academic reflection. According to this description, the work I chose exemplifies the task of art in society and the need to understand that task and its fulfillment from an interdisciplinary perspective.

For, clearly, this ostensibly simple situation requires an interdisciplinary approach. Here are the terms the work sets for us. A Finnish artist brings her work to France; she engages with one of the most painful moments in French history. If I may highlight the terms that refer to disciplines: This work raises questions of *history* and of *politics*, triggering international cultural sensibilities. Her work is *cinematic* and *theatrical*—thus soliciting responses from two disciplines simply by its own medium. Moreover, it uses *language* in *literary* forms and raises profound *philosophical* questions. According to this brief summary, to understand, interpret, and review this work critically, one must responsibly call upon at least seven different disciplines, plus the interdisciplinary domain of cultural sensibility in international relations. Seven. Just as this interdisciplinarity is inevitable, it is equally impossible to make full use of the entire paradigms and methodological packages of these disciplines. Nor is it possible for any individual to be knowledgeable in the canonical texts whose importance these disciplines tend to take for granted. This confronts us with the primary challenge interdisciplinarity poses.

But the work poses yet another challenge. As I will explain below, the remarkable force of *Where Is Where?* and of the artist's entire body of work resides in its *integration* of aesthetic, affective, and political dimensions. Hence, not only aspects of at least seven disciplines, but also the integration of those aspects—indeed, the integrative thrust itself—requires a thought-through interdisciplinary research process. Like scientists, who often encounter complex situations that require interdisciplinary analysis, humanists also confront situations of great complexity. Frequently, even their very objects are, by definition, already complex in this sense. With the involvement of so many disciplines comes a need, for the analyst, for limitation. But these cannot be the limitations of disciplinary method, as in "normal science."[3]

I propose that in order to grasp what this difficulty entails for scholars in the humanities and what opportunities it opens up, they can follow the lead of the artworks themselves. This is quite tricky; it may become a (vicious) circle. Of course, we never approach an artwork "neutrally." But if we bracket that other circular argument—art pertains to what art history, or literary theory, says we should see in it—and instead, see it with an open eye for the different academic contexts that might help understand it, it becomes easier to see how the work addresses issues that pertain to a range of different disciplines. Such an approach is less predictable than "normal"—say, disciplinary—scholarship, which would limit the analysis, for example, to either an aesthetic or a historical approach. Yet, the proposed manner of heeding the artwork's own implications is still shareable and teachable because it requires constant feedback between the analysis the scholar is performing and the work itself.

To demonstrate both the difficulties and the potential of all this with an example, I propose to build limitation into the research question. That is, I propose an interpretation of Ahtila's *Where Is Where?* that is *partial* in both senses of the word. Partiality enables the interpretation to avoid circularity, liberating it from the confinement of the work itself. It is partial in the sense that I magnify a detail, an aspect of the work rather than the whole work, because the latter is too rich to fully account for here; hence, it is a part-interpretation. My interpretation is also partial in the sense that I have selected a single aspect that I consider of key importance without claiming it to be the most important; consequently, my reading is subjectively motivated. Both meanings of *partial* insure that the interpretation remains at some distance from the work. But the word *subjective* needs some qualification.

My interpretation may be subjective, but it is not individualistic. It is also *inter*subjective, and I use that term from philosopher of science Karl Popper (2002) on purpose, to align a whole range of uses of "inter." By intersubjectivity, Popper meant that terms and concepts, theories and interpretations would have the same meaning for all researchers. It was his alternative to objectivity, which he deemed impossible. In my interpretation of the term, it means that we can understand each other. Terms and concepts must be explicit and clear, but they need not mean the same for all. Only when this is the case is the procedure of the analysis replicable. The challenge I am facing in this article is to persuade my readers that this work requires interdisciplinary analysis, but also that it is itself a model of interdisciplinarity of a special kind—and that this starting point can be assessed intersubjectively. The artwork

---

[3]Thomas Kuhn (1962) proposed a distinction between "normal science" based on methods and axioms commonly accepted and "revolutionary science," in which those methods are no longer deemed adequate to tackle the problem under analysis. A new methodology, or "paradigm," results from such moments.

draws its audience into an integrative process; the interdisciplinary humanist makes that explicit and foregrounds connections that the artwork builds on.[4]

Rather than bundling together (elements from) disciplinary methodologies, as in multidisciplinarity, the work espouses different discourses and brings them together. But it does not so much do so in integration, at least not a neat one without leftovers (Repko, 2008; Klein, 2001). Integration, which is a key methodological element in interdisciplinary methodology, means that the contributions from different disciplines are not unconnected but are engaged with one another. This remains key to any interdisciplinary search. But connections need not be harmonious and blending. I propose to see them, where applicable, as a dialogue, an interaction. Discrepancies and even polemics are included, both in the work and in the interdisciplinary approach to it. The relationship among disciplines need not be synthetic. Nor do the participating disciplines have to be on equal footing. This is my first generalization—to be tested in the course of my analysis—concerning a specific humanities kind of interdisciplinarity. This does not mean only humanistic disciplines are involved, only that the special relationship between artwork and analysis—leading to a *respectful* and *critical* way of *opening up*—necessitates a close affiliation between artifact and researcher.[5]

One obvious feature of artworks already stipulated is that studying them is, by definition, an interdisciplinary endeavor. Artworks are made for people; their reception is the works' point. With the respect and criticism due to the work comes the obligation to both artwork and its public to account for reception, which brings in sociological and psychological issues, either implicitly or explicitly. Some artworks address this interdisciplinary nature of art in and of themselves. Ahtila's work is such a case. But even poems or paintings need to be framed as live objects circulating in culture, and they are thus equally interdisciplinary, whether or not the artist aims to foreground this. Hence, in order to do justice to the need to base not simply results but even a starting question in the public that processes the artwork, as well as to avoid circularity in another way, I have taken as my starting point some of the reactions that I overheard during the first days of Ahtila's exhibition in Paris (remember that my object is the historical event, not the artwork alone). Simply put, many people there and then expressed doubt about the appropriateness of the topic the artist had chosen for her most recent work.[6]

The interview in the exhibition catalogue suggests that Ahtila appears to take a turn toward more overtly political art in her recent work. With obvious reluctance, the artist concedes the point to some extent. I would not have

[4]I have developed an argument for intersubjectivity in my book on "traveling concepts" (Bal, 2002).

[5]This relationship does emphatically not include the artist; her or his intentions are irrelevant for the social function of the work.

[6]For examples of this point—that all artworks require interdisciplinary analysis due to the nature of art as cultural object—several analyses in my own books can be instructive (Bal, 1991, 1999).

conceded it at all if I were her—not because this recent work is not political, but because her work always has been. This is an issue of the place of this recent work in the artist's oeuvre. The first research question, then, can be framed as an inquiry into the degree to which and the way in which this artwork is, and functions as, "political" qua art. A second, related question concerns the coherence of this political aspect in the body of Ahtila's work.[7]

I consider her new work to be the provisional but entirely logical outcome of an oeuvre that, while constantly innovating and transforming itself, is impressively coherent in its search. Here I wish to submit a second generalization: This is the paradox typical of all "great art"—of art that matters. The paradox is that each new work contains, retrospectively, something that was already present in what preceded it, albeit marginal, subliminal, and hardly noticeable. This, in turn, can be seen as a model for history. The political potential is perhaps more subliminal in those earlier works, but no less powerful than in their monumental conclusion. Since *Where Is Where?* positions the Algerian War as a present issue and even as a creation of the present, nothing seems more logical than continuing that temporal reversion by beginning my account of Ahtila's work with the ending of her last video installation to date. This positioning in the present, which entails a chronological reversal, further sharpens my research question—to make sense of the historical event. This sense I am looking for has to be connected to the *political* work art can do; there lies the relevance of the bond between present and past the work posits.[8]

This strategy of limiting my analysis to a single (and here, last) image is a form of *zooming in* on the here and now. After the chronological reversal, zooming in is a second strategy of developing a research question. Consistent with this conceptual metaphor, I discuss the cinematic result of a zoom, the close-up, as a strategy to achieve the same. This use of concepts from the field of cinema studies helps to keep in sight the art aspect of this work and, with that, its medium specificity, in and through its political side. It also requires the two to be integrated. Hence, my third generalization: The research question espouses the strategy of the work under scrutiny.

The creation of history in the here and now does not let us escape into fiction. Yet, this artwork is fully fictional and full of fiction. Following another of the work's strategies, I explore the different ways of *authenticating* the created history, even within a work of fiction. The most obvious of these ways is the work's use of archival footage, but the citation of authoritative texts the

---

[7]See the interview by Doris Krystof (Ahtila, 2008). Not all the people I heard expressing doubt or rejection were French chauvinists. Some were highly sophisticated art critics. An artist's oeuvre is the common object of research in the humanities, hence the frequent output of monographs.

[8]This simple decision already entails a specific conception of history. I have written at length about this approach to history, in which the present is a starting point for a "re-visioning" of the past (Bal, 1999). Unfortunately, the limits of space for this paper do not allow me to develop this point through an analysis of Ahtila's earlier work.

work alludes to—termed *intertexts*—is important as well. Strategies such as these contribute to the build-up of a cultural network, a spider web of *responsibility* in which we are caught. This cultural network in which art and its audiences are caught together is the deep reason why artworks and literary texts cannot be confined to monodisciplinary study.[9]

This, in turn, leads to the inquiry that the title of Ahtila's work solicits, the question of *location*—geographical, social, psychic, and political. Now we realize that the title already frames all the questions that have come up so far. This is also where the criticisms of the alleged political turn of Ahtila's work must be situated. It was French history that Ahtila's work engaged, and this happened in France, backed by French funding. Moreover, the retrospective approach goes hand in hand with the retrospective engagement of the medium. I argue that it is the dissociation of image from sound that keeps medium and politics bound together. Finally, it is in the genre of tragedy— alluded to, staged, and yet held at bay in that emblematic word *mektoub*— that the unique combination of video-graphy, the writing of visions, takes place. This is where the word-concept *mektoub* will receive its meaning. To sum up, a strategy of zooming in, an issue of responsibility, and a question of location are the three key elements in this work, to which the research question must answer. Given the great number of disciplines the work engages, which I mentioned above, it is impossible to construct an approach using any single discipline.

In the practice of research, initial research questions tend to change and evolve along with the growing insights of the researcher. In the course of the preceding discussion, my research question has evolved into the following: What does the historical event—the opening of Ahtila's *Where Is Where?* in Paris in 2008—mean, how does it acquire the significance it has, and how are different disciplinary fields involved in this meaning making? In other words, if one approaches an artwork with an open mind to the cultural event it triggers, different disciplinary contributions become prominent, and a monodisciplinary analysis becomes less and less adequate. But the form of interdisciplinarity that results is neither a piecemeal borrowing from disciplines, nor a neat and equal integration without leftovers. Instead, it is a method that is fully loyal to its object, while enabling the disciplines whose subject matter the work itself invokes to formulate a critical assessment of it. These include, as I have argued, history and the medium of cinema, language and philosophy, literary history and art history. We will see that, through the source text of Fanon, psychology is also invoked. As I have mentioned above, only in terms of the medium and its deployment in this work, at least seven disciplines are involved, some from the humanities, some from other areas. But what is more, the path the work indicates leads to a kind of integration in which one discipline illuminates another, sometimes by means of a discussion.

---

[9]The word *authentication* refers to strategies—artistic and otherwise—by which a certain content is made to be believable, to be, in a sense to be specified, "true."

This is best expressed through the preposition "of," for example, a philosophy *of* cinema and, conversely, a cinema *of* philosophy.

The End: Philosophy of Cinema

Produced for the occasion of this major exhibition, *Where Is Where?* is both site-specific and time-specific, pertaining to the here and now, to Paris in 2008. The English subtitle of the final sentence is "You do what you have to do." It is uttered by a young Algerian boy who, together with another boy, has killed a friend, simply because the friend was European. This boy is a fictional character in Ahtila's story; he was a real patient in Fanon's practice. Fifty years later, the artwork attempts to make specific—logical, philosophical—sense of what Fanon could not explain otherwise than with general reference to the situation of war that induces madness. The image is an extreme close-up projected on the huge screen of the installation (see Figure 4.1). The result is as imposing as it is impressive. The image-sentence is an invitation to gauge the aesthetic politics (or the political aesthetic) in this work and, by extension, the body of work by Eija-Liisa Ahtila.[10]

Figure 4.1 The Final Line in *Where Is Where?*

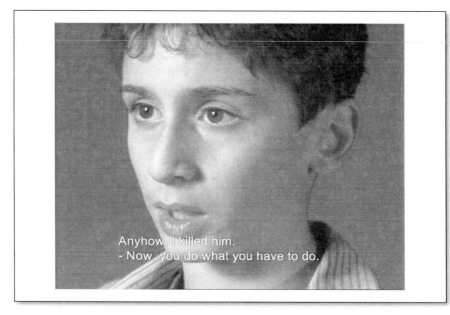

SOURCE: Eija-Liisa Ahtila. Photographed by Marja-Leena Hukkanen at Jeu de Paume, courtesy of Marian Goodman Gallery, New York and Paris. © 2008 Crystal Eye—Kristallisilmä Oy.

---

[10]"Site-specific" is a term from modern art history; "time-specific" alludes to the dogma of that discipline that requires a historical understanding of artworks.

Let me show how different disciplines come in to deal with this situation.
Cinematographically, the close-up creates what is termed an *affection-image*.
This term refers to a category of movement-images that suspend the time of
the story or diegesis. Its theory was developed by philosopher Gilles Deleuze
(1986) in an endeavor to write a "philosophy *of* cinema." Deleuze's (1986,
1989) two books on cinema demonstrate a consistent effort to integrate the
two disciplines involved. In a very useful book on Deleuze's endeavor, which
unpacks the phrase "philosophy of cinema," philosopher Paola Marrati
(2003) points at the crucial function of the affection-image—the type of
image that is closest to both the materiality of the image and to the materiality of subjectivity. She writes tersely: "Between a *perception* [emphasis added]
that is in certain ways troubling, and an *action* [emphasis added] still hesitant,
affection emerges" (p. 48). This short formulation indicates the way art can
be political.[11]

As a photograph, this image has an "Arab effect"—the boy looks Arab.
The affection-image establishes an "inter-face," both with other people, such
as viewers, and with other times. Its typical incarnation is the close-up. An
image with an "Arab effect" that is also an affection-image and simultaneously stops or slows down time: the combination alone is worth dwelling on,
as it puts us smack in the middle of the contemporary world. This artwork
drives home the point that art is not separate from the world.[12]

It is important to realize that this type of image does not mediate between
the work and the spectator, nor is it an enticement to action. These two nega-
tions are of crucial importance to understand what this work proposes,
namely, what *political* art can be and what it can do. This, then, must be my
refocused research question: How does political art work, and how can this
question at the same time illuminate this particular artwork as an aesthetic
object? What the affection-image does is provoke a confluence, even if conflicted, between subject and object, without canceling out their heterogeneity
or falling into a deceptive harmony. Affect, in this conception, is a medium,
not a message.[13]

The affective force of the image is enhanced by the acting style. Thus we
reach a domain in which theater and cinema studies cannot be distinguished,
but instead must be integrated. What we see is the young actor Allaedin
Allaedine suspending all emotion. How to interpret this acting style? In
Fanon's passionate anticolonialist text, the interview is a transcription of a
psychiatric evaluation, so that the psychiatrist implicitly interprets the lack
or suspension of emotion as a particular disturbance—what we now call

[11]The most succinct formulation of these three types of "movement-images" is in *Cinema I*
(Deleuze, 1986, pp. 66–70).

[12]Paola Marrati (2003, p. 46). On the affection-image, see also Pisters (2003, pp. 66–71). On
temporality in the movement-image, see Rodowick (1997). "Affect" is my term; Deleuze speaks
of "affection" in the same sense.

[13]For the idea that affect can function as a medium, see Hansen (2003). On affect, and
specifically the need for affect to be untied to meaning, see Ernst van Alphen (2008).

Post-Traumatic Stress Disorder (PTSD). In Ahtila's visual artwork, in contrast, it signals avoidance of the pathetic. These are two distinct ways in which emotion, or the lack of it, is *framed*. The addressee in Fanon is the psychiatrist whose questions the boy is answering. In the installation, the addressee is the spectator. Framing, here, replaces integration. The difference between framing and integration is that in framing, the difference between frames remains visible and pertinent, whereas integration would offer a synthesis that makes the different frames invisible.[14]

Cinema and theater are central, then, and so is, indirectly, psychiatry (on which more later). Then there is language. The language in which the sentence is uttered is Finnish ("Tehkää te nyt mitä tahdotte"). The sentence itself is . . . what, exactly? It could be Martiniquan (at the time, under French rule) if we go by the nationality of the quoted author, Frantz Fanon. But it is also "French," the language of the quoted text, *Les damnés de la terre*. It is Algerian, too, by virtue of its place of utterance in the diegesis. Finally, it is also American English by way of the translation, which resonates with that language's popular diffusion of ideology in political discourse, fictional cinema, and literature. Interdisciplinarity, here, touches on *interdiscursivity*.

Between the American English that resonates so strongly in "you do what you *have to* do" and the French of Fanon, "*Maintenant, faites ce que vous voulez*" (do what you *like*) a wide gap opens. The Finnish sentence follows the French. This gap alone is a testimony to the way in which the political is embedded in language as such; thus, for those who know both French and English, this subtitle would call on the discipline of sociolinguistics. The English sentence appeals to a sense of duty while the French sentence appeals to free will and individual choice. At the same time, with diction and context taken into consideration, the sentence can also express indifference, for example, when accompanied by a shrug. Tension thus emerges between the triangular elements of national interest, individualism, and indifference. The performance of the actor and the close-up of the cinematographer conspire to leave this triangulation undecidedly suspended. Let us follow the work's lead and suspend any disciplinary priorities, even the priorities of interdisciplinary integration.

It is crucial for the artwork that the three possible interpretations remain undecided. The work leaves an unresolved tension; it foregrounds it. This compels the viewer to choose, to decide, and thus to perform the integration in a specific way. The scholar, in contrast, would leave the possibilities open. Through this tension, the artwork positions itself as an intervention in the social domain, where viewers cannot simply enjoy the work as the dilemma

[14]The concept of framing is one of the concepts I have proposed in a concept-based methodology for interdisciplinary analysis (Bal, 2002). To understand the careful and subtle way in which Ahtila has reworked the text, the passage in Fanon is best taken literally, hence, in the French (2002, p. 261). Fanon does act as a psychiatrist, but his diagnosis concerns the colonial situation, not the "patient."

enforces a choice. Thus, the work proclaims the mission of art, especially contemporary art: to make viewers fully involved performers of the work.

Let me rephrase this tripartite dilemma in an attempt to reconnect what I have just separated, as a provisional interpretation of the image and its subtitle. Indifference emerges when individualism is forged between free choice and conformism—the escape from responsibility in the sense of duty. There lies the root of the indifference of the contemporary Western world. In Ahtila's work, however, the sentence simultaneously protests against this ideological triangulation by way of its overdetermination. Protest emerges from the use of grammatical tense (linguistics) and from the situation at a certain point in time (history). Linguistically, the imperative determines the mood of the sentence, and so its tense and time are inevitably the present. It speaks of the responsibility of each and everyone, here and now, whether this responsibility is inspired by a belief in duty or by free will. This is beginning to look like a philosophical or political position of the work itself. We are suddenly confronted with an ethical choice. Here lies the potential integration: Beyond different disciplines, this ethical choice makes an appeal to every viewer's agency, calls on every viewer as a social being. The choice is not made for us; in that sense, the work is about freedom. But we cannot refrain from taking a position, not even one mapped by the work. In that sense, the work says that freedom comes with responsibility, so we must exercise our social-political agency.

There is another dimension to this temporality. Posed in the present, the question of the work's title (Where is where?) makes sense. Before the act of murder the boy and his friend commit, we see a group of three interrogators in the work room of a character called the Poet. One of them says, "Every act is weak when seen from a distance. While every thought transcends the limits of time and space." There is more talk about acts and the importance of acting before the murder than after it. This suggests that there is a hypothetical continuity in the transition from thought, which transcends time and space, to action. This becomes clear in relation to what both this boy, Adel, and the Poet as the main character say in response to the question of the title. As it happens, the question concerns death: the negation of the here and now.[15]

The artist's work explicitly speaks of war, violence, and History with a capital H. It refers to a specific historical war, the Algerian war of independence, which still weighs heavily on French memory and collective consciousness. This invocation of the traumatic past—traumatic entailing the impossibility to say it—caused the upset at the exhibition in France, the historical event that is my case. As if to foreground the explicit engagement with History, the work contains documentary footage of that war, borrowed from documentaries made by French filmmaker René Vautier. Because we tend to attribute authenticity to the aesthetic of documentary footage, these

---

[15]It seems ludicrous to begin citing specific literature on death, but still, the recent book by Kaja Silverman (2009) offers brilliant and highly relevant reflections on death in contemporary art. See also Bronfen (1992).

quotations *authenticate* the relation to history. This documentary aesthetic is also the aesthetic of early cinema; consequently, the black-and-white and luminous points refer to the history of the medium.

The old films, like all war journalism, were shot under dangerous circumstances and are therefore heroic by definition. The documentary fragments include the sound of airplanes, gunshots, and executions, which adds a sonoric interdiscourse to a political and cultural déjà vu. This political and cultural déjà vu binds the work of fiction to a reality it cannot disavow.

The borrowed images also authenticate the work itself as cinematographic. The filmmaker's mastery of the medium was impressive for the period in which these shots were made. In their will to authenticity, the images, like war journalism in general, are always contemporary: Both are complicit in and testimonial of the historical violence of the colonial wars that ravaged the world in the middle of the 20th century. Philosophy of cinema, then, is not a philosophy as a master-discourse explaining cinema as a cultural field. Rather, the phrase positions cinema as philosophical; "of" is used here to mean "belonging to," "inhering in," rather than "about." This qualifies the specific form of interdisciplinarity at stake here. To "give" philosophical status to cinema is different from explaining cinema philosophically. The former is a gesture of interdisciplinary integration; the latter of multidisciplinarity.

Poetry: A Cinema of Literature

Something similar emerges in another disciplinary pairing. The relationship to history as well as the history of the medium is pursued on the textual level. As if to foreground the authenticity of the archival footage in its relation to history, *Where Is Where?* literally quotes from an interview transcribed by Fanon in its final sequence. *Where Is Where?*, with its strongly political theme, is first and foremost a poetic work. It is visually poetical, and, as if to enhance this aspect, it is also poetic as a literary work. Not coincidentally, as is the nature of literary, cinematic, and visual works, it is replete with allusions—linguistic as well as visual and diegetic—to other texts and, in this case, to masterpieces from the literary canon.[16]

First, there is the obvious allusion of the key event in the story to Albert Camus's *L'étranger* (1942), a novel in which the central event is the inexplicable and arbitrary murder of *"L'arabe"* by the protagonist, the antihero Meursault. *"C'était à cause du soleil"* (It was because of the sun), he insists. A spark of sunlight on a knife and the Arab is erased, killed without even having that label of personhood that is the proper name. In *Where Is Where?* the situation is both repeated and reversed. This time it is an Arab who kills a

---

[16]*Diegetic* means pertaining to the story. For this and other narratological terms, see Bal (2009). For a systematic conversion, or conversation, between narratology and cinema theory, see Verstraten (2009).

European. And the logic of arbitrariness is reiterated, yet brought back down to earth—and to logic. The young victim does not get a proper name either.

In another allusion, the right to the proper name is foregrounded: "My name is Ishmael" is the first sentence uttered by one of the two boys who commits the murder, to which the other boy replies, "I am Adel." For those with knowledge of literary history, the intertextual allusion to the opening sentence of Herman Melville's 1851 novel *Moby Dick*—perhaps the most frequently quoted literary sentence—would enrich their reception of *Where Is Where?* The fact that this is a novel exploring the evil of fanaticism also bears on Ahtila's work. The relationship to the intertext works for some—given the widespread fame of that sentence, for many—subconsciously or consciously. But even for those who do not recognize the sentence, the use of "call me Ishmael" in the opening sequence asserts and stages the person's right to bear a proper name that individualizes him; it confirms that he *is*. The universe of the perverted fanatic Captain Ahab in Melville's novel is invoked through archival images of a ship on sea battling with the elements. So those who have not read the novel may have seen the film and may pick up on the Melville allusion.

As an emphatically poetic work, *Where Is Where?* also frequently alludes to the highlights of Western poetry. It invokes a poem by T. S. Eliot about time, a poem in which poetry meets philosophy. The complex relationship to history warrants the enquiry into modernist time—fitting the period Ahtila's story is set in. Hence, it comes as no surprise that Eliot's poem becomes, so to speak, the theoretical starting point of the work's project to adopt the past into the present—the starting point, but not the end point.

Time present and time past

Are both perhaps present in time future.

And time future contained in time past.

If all time is eternally present

All time is irredeemable.[17]

Although it does not quote this poem literally, the Finnish work seems to belabor and critique the conceptions of time that underlie Eliot's modernism. Thus, the artwork is "doing" philosophy, blurring the boundaries between art and the study of it in the humanities in this act. I contend that art does this all the time. In the approach I am advocating here—treating art as an event—this blurring becomes visible. This is why the researcher is bound to that double commitment of respect and critique. Among the many reflections on time that *Where Is Where?* includes, the following seems to respond to the modernist poem, integrating into the philosophical discourse of the poem a subjective touch that brings in death:

---

[17]T.S. Eliot, "Burnt Norton," the first poem of *Four Quartets,* quoted in Durand (2008, p. 182).

that unexpected moment in time,

When timelessness and time meet.

A pause, a fit of absent-mindedness,

a lapse into recollection

At the same time, the reflections on time join those of William Faulkner, especially those in *Absalom, Absalom!* (1936), a novel that distances itself from Eliot's poetry as it verges toward the postmodern.

This tipping over into postmodernism is significant here because, according to the interpretation of the American literary critic Brian McHale (1987), the primary issue of modernism is epistemological doubt, while that of postmodernism is ontological doubt, a radicalization of the modernist doubt. And as it happens, Ahtila's Poet wavers between these two doubts, so that ontology (What was and what *is* the historical event of the Algerian War?) becomes epistemology again (What do we know of the past?), and vice versa. When the Poet counts backward, she appears to take up an action from Faulkner's novel.[18]

As has hopefully become clear from this discussion, this abundance of allusions to other artworks is again a way in which the work posits its need for an interdisciplinary approach. It does this through the deployment of another use of the preposition "inter" in intertextuality. Both intertextuality and interdisciplinarity are based on contact among different elements—texts or disciplines—without stipulating whether that contact leads to integration, dialogue, or (polemical) discussion. Through the deployment of the cinematic-theatrical tool of character speech, the *literary*, specifically poetic intertextual moments of the work lead to *philosophical* positions bearing on contemporary *politics*; here, we catch three disciplinary fields in the act of connecting. The work opens with the Poet's near-literal quotation of "Enfance," a prose poem by Arthur Rimbaud from his book *Illuminations*. The first words the Poet utters are the following:

In the woods there is a bird, his song stops you,

and makes you blush.

An unforeseen moment in time, one that destroys,

one with everlasting consequences.

There is a desert behind which the sun is falling

There are two churches rising, and a sea,

and thought cold as snow.

---

[18]On Faulkner's postmodern tendency in *Absalom, Absalom!*, see McHale (1987).

Even though these poetic lines appear to be innocuous, the political is already insinuated. Why else would a bird's song make one blush, if not to contrast indifference to responsibility, and why do deserts appear here, and why should thought be cold? The desert in Finland: That is only possible if the two countries, Algeria that consists for a large part of desert, and the Nordic Finland, are merged here.

With color, we reach another use of "inter": *interdiscursivity*. While intertextuality concerns relations between identifiable texts, interdiscursivity entails a relation between different discourses. Both blushing and the setting sun evoke the color red, the color against which the work's title is set, and a key color in the study of visual art. This establishes an interdiscursive relationship between poetry and visual art. Red is the predominant color in the first screen of the work, which offers a kind of prologue. The images on that first screen are animated drawings, prefiguring the main junctures of the story on the next four screens. The drawings in red prefigure the bloodshed to come. Moreover, the color red is subject to dispute between the Poet and the allegorical figure of Monsieur la Mort. When he asks the Poet for words, he adds, "Pour some red in." The Poet denies that possibility: "There is no red in this space." He replies, "That is a mistake—look outside," and the image shows a staged garden with red walls. The same red constitutes the backdrop of the final image with which I began. Finally, red is the color of the gown worn by the floating figure of the guardian angel/devil as she guides the two boys to the ranks of immigrants and to their destiny (*mektoub*) in prison. This is a surreal scene, which I will discuss further later on. The poetic lines quoted above already encompass all of these elements.[19]

In addition, the tense connections between modernist and postmodernist conceptions of time are embedded in this passage when the violent and destructive power of time is evoked. Time is thus included in the indictment by the color red. And as if to underscore the relevance of these poetic lines, a copy of Rimbaud's book is on the Poet's desk and is made visible later, right before the pages she has written come out of her printer.

The passage quoted earlier as a response to Eliot, "that unexpected moment in time, when timelessness and time meet," suggests the temporality of accidents while calling attention to the ravages wrought by a moment of inattention in the grand junctures of time. The desert landscape and the religion of the two churches, the sea and the "cold thought," all "place" that single moment that changes everything: This is poetry, also, in that every word counts for what follows. The artist has woven a dense network of things literary, with a weight that equals that of history. The underlying statement about

---

[19]Red is, of course, a historically burdened color. A particularly powerful deployment of red in the history of political cinema is Chris Marker's 1977 film, *Le fond de l'air est rouge*. See the François Maspéro edition of the script (Marker, 1978). This film blends together events of war, violence, and revolution—three connotations of the color.

merging or integrating fields is that art can express a view of the world as potent as that of the discipline of history.

This bit of poetry is not without recalling the enigmatic title of the work. As I briefly mentioned already, *Where Is Where?* poses questions that concern death: Where are you when you die? Where are you when you are dead? Adel, the boy who pronounces the (final) sentence "you do what you have to do" also utters the question of the title:

Is death always a private death?

When you die where are you?

And where is where?

The voice-off of the Poet responds, taking it upon herself to find an answer to the enigma of death:

A second's inattention,

disobedience,

a half-guessed hint.

And there are no distances,

everything is the same side of the same

and nobody knows where is where.

This is also the question the work itself raises in the very manner in which the video art is installed. To remind you, *Where Is Where?* is exhibited on six screens, and four screens surround us, lock us up for the duration of the screening. Where are we indeed? Cinema, here, rewrites poetry in ways that poetry cannot. Thus, this is a cinema of poetry, a poetics inherent in the cinematic work, analogous to Deleuze's philosophy of cinema.

Where Are We? Geography of Setting

It is important that we are inside the head of a fictional Finnish writer who is a wordsmith, a narrator, and a creator of historical images that are fictional as well. We are in Finland, too—in Europe, or a corner of Europe that used to be colonized rather than acting as home of a colonizer, but which is, nevertheless, complicit today in the postcolonial aftermath. These are only two of the many possible answers to the question of the title. Where is where in contradictory time and in contradictory space? And where is where now, in postcolonial Europe? Again, the ethical question remains unresolved, so the viewer can be a full participant in the discussion (see Figure 4.2).

Figure 4.2   The Poet

SOURCE: Eija-Liisa Ahtila. Photographed by Marja-Leena Hukkanen at Jeu de Paume, courtesy of Marian Goodman Gallery, New York and Paris. © 2008 Crystal Eye—Kristallisilmä Oy.

"Where?" is a question that, in a work of fiction consisting of visual images, deserves a literal answer about setting as geography; in other words, a geography of setting, as the bond between fiction and reality. Long sequences position us in the Finnish landscape, with its pine trees, wooden houses, and lakes. This landscape soon begins to alternate with Algerian deserts and casbahs. In the final part of the work, we are in the psychiatric hospital ward of a prison, where well-meaning doctors are put in charge of determining the meaning of responsibility and guilt, as if politics is a medical issue. Between the Finnish houses and the Algerian hospital, we also enter a church staffed by a female priest with an androgynous voice and the tone of an official. As fictional as the work is, these settings are clearly heavily real, anchored in historical reality.

Under the guidance of this figure, and thanks to a theatrical prop, we also momentarily find ourselves in an immigration office. The priest character now floats above the ground, dressed in the red of a Jan van Eyck painting, or the red of devils. The allusion to red queuing ropes also suggests museums. Curiously, immigration offices and museums share this crowd control tool to keep people at bay. We are confronted by an image: two Algerian boys are plucked from the 1950s, pushed forward by a figure who might be a guardian angel or a devil (as in the Christian religious tradition), passing along the queues of contemporary immigration offices (see Figure 4.3). "Where is where?" now becomes a question about the work's situation in space and in time, in something between literal and extended senses, and in thrust. This leads back to the

Figure 4.3   Two Algerian Boys Preceding the Priest

SOURCE: Eija-Liisa Ahtila. Photographed by Marja-Leena Hukkanen at Jeu de Paume, courtesy of Marian Goodman Gallery, New York and Paris. © 2008 Crystal Eye—Kristallisilmä Oy.

question this work posed to its visitors, which I overheard many times: Is it too political or not political enough? Now, we are just chatting as visitors to an exhibition. This ordinary social occurrence is also part of that larger interdisciplinary adventure; we cannot deny who we are in "real life."

This work may seem overly political because it is so explicitly focused on the Algerian War, suggesting that this war is still present after 50 years. It is as if the work is accusing us, the people who live in the present and who are ignorant of those past atrocities, of still bearing guilt for them. This is the first misunderstanding this work sets itself up for, in order to trouble us more effectively. Yet, at the same time, one can just as easily claim that this work is not political enough. In the wake of this chatting, ordinary discussion, we embark on that part of the mission of the humanities that aims to engage artworks *critically*. To begin with, there are long sequences set in Finland devoted to the personal problems and poetic expressions of a woman poet. From the visit of Monsieur la Mort and the conversation with the Priest, we surmise she has lost a person dear to her. Sad as this is, there is nothing particularly political about such losses. Then, the work sometimes seems to get close to a highly theatrical excess of aesthetization and fictionality. That this can immediately be reversed, however, becomes especially clear in the scene I just discussed, of the devilish Priest pushing the future assassins through the immigration queues toward their destiny.

Or is this work not political enough when the Poet sings a religious song and all four screens turn sky blue? This scene would be skirting kitsch if the military marching music to which the Poet sings did not render it so deeply disturbing. The marching music, which is literally drummed up by an onscreen drummer, is set in the same melody as an earlier whistle that could be heard when the Poet called up Satan and defied the Priest in a crucial discussion about guilt, forgiveness, and responsibility. The drumming that accompanies the singing brings in Brecht's political theater, especially his anti-war manifesto *Mutter Courage und ihre Kinder* (1939). Thus, this highly aestheticized scene refers to the history of the attempt to articulate how art, and specifically theater, can be political. This question is no longer confined to this singular artwork but concerns the mission, or work, of art in society. I contend that the emphatic aesthetic is not an escape from the political but, on the contrary, a foregrounding of it: It functions as an argument in the discussion.

Then, there is the artificial, theatrical setting of Monsieur la Mort's garden, where the Algerian dead rest peacefully and some sheep are bleating, reminding the viewer of the symbolism of the sacrificial animal that Christianity and Islam share (Figure 4.4). This religious common ground is set against the almost excessive aesthetization of the moment when a blue china vase with red flowers in it slowly falls, breaks, repairs itself, and floats back up onto the desk in a repeated and reversed take that displays cinematographic mastery, digital tricks, and the inversion of time that belongs to the philosophical

Figure 4.4   Monsieur la Mort's Garden

SOURCE: Eija-Liisa Ahtila. Photographed by Marja-Leena Hukkanen at Jeu de Paume, courtesy of Marian Goodman Gallery, New York and Paris. © 2008 Crystal Eye—Kristallisilmä Oy.

underpinning of the work; it sides with postmodernism in its polemical relationship to modernism. In other words, far from distracting from the political, beauty is used to visually enact the reversal of time, as in the Eliot-Faulkner "debate." Simultaneously, the aesthetic marks the turning point of history, suggesting that our contemporary and allegedly "postcolonial" world is moving backward to colonial violence.

The breathtakingly beautiful landscapes, the extremely precise close-ups, the brilliantly composed long shots, the slow gestures of a naked woman drying herself after a swim in the lake, and the multiple-camera *trucages* that continue a scene from one screen to the next: These scenes are all splendidly beautiful. The question is, does this beauty detract from the work's political force, or is it one of its tools? Clearly, our initial research question is being fleshed out through the confrontation between the artwork and the different disciplinary tools brought to bear on it.

Take, for example, aesthetics. In Ahtila's case, beauty does not determine the extent of the political impact any more than the evocation of a politically influential event determines, in and of itself, the political power of the artwork that seeks to stage it. Another possible answer to the question of the title is we are inside the question of political art, where no clear answer is possible as of yet, where no single discipline can be of decisive help, but the question is more urgent than ever. Fictional setting engages geography, similar to the way Deleuze's philosophy engages cinema. Perhaps we can call this "fiction of geography."

Schizophrenia: Psychiatry of Cinema

In some works, Ahtila stages a double schizophrenia such as manifests itself in psychosis. Significantly, a salient feature of this condition—the discrepancies between sound and image—is inherent in cinema, and it is these discrepancies that Ahtila frequently exaggerates to make them all the more visible. In this way, the works enact a generalized psychosis on all levels. This is not, as one may think, in order to make a theater of fantasy but, as we can hardly fail to notice from Ahtila's 2002 work *The House/Talo* on, in order to resituate the person literally beside himself or herself. Her 1993 work *Me/We, Okay, Gray* already stages an anti-individualistic politics that implicates the medium and its history. It stages the impossibility for an individual to maintain the boundaries of the self: It demonstrates how the individual necessarily bleeds over into the social domain where space and media are shared with others. The madness in this work is not the cause of that hallucinatory extension of the self but the necessary condition of such an extension.

It is in this respect that *Where Is Where?*, the newest work, retrospectively revises our understanding of earlier works such as the black-and-white triptych *Me/We, Okay, Gray*. The earlier work poses the condition of a subjectivity that endorses its schizophrenia as a means to exist in "culture," a domain where subjectivity extends its tentacles to others. This is why the subjectivity I posited at the beginning to characterize my approach is not idio-syncratic but potentially intersubjective. In a similar way, *The House/Talo* prefigures *Where Is Where?* in that it already harbors an anti-individualistic politics. As if teasing out a small element from *Me/We, Okay, Gray* and developing it, it is *The House/Talo* that gives the most incisive presentation of such politics.[20]

The psychosis of the image is produced in a decentering cinematography that is sustained by the installation setup. Such decentering is not just a cri-tique of a naturalized perception of cinema, but also, according to a com-mentary on Deleuze by Paola Marrati (2003), a fundamental characteristic of that medium: "The mobility of the camera, the variability of angles of framing always reintroduce zones that are a-centered and de-framed in rela-tion to any 'perceiving subject'" (p. 51). In the very act of centering—producing the illusion by means of the meticulous method of filming and foregrounding it through the screens—the image decenters. And this decen-tering unmoors us, too; the more so as decentering is a fundamental side effect of interdisciplinarity.

So, what do we do with psychiatry as another, quite remote discipline? Three elements characteristic of schizophrenia that are present in Ahtila's work prefigure *Where Is Where?* These elements are the inversion of the med-ical context, where mental illness becomes a model of coherence; the analogy with cinema that, in turn, contributes to the naturalization of schizophrenia; and the impeccable, inevitable, and merciless logic that advocates this natu-ralized schizophrenia as simply logical. As in *Where Is Where?*, the acting style in these earlier works is both intense and expressionless. The actors care-fully avoid hysteria or pathos, so as not to distract us from the work's conta-gious intensity. This is precisely what *affect* is: intensity without particularizing expression, so that the viewers can experience the affect on their own terms. Only then can affect be relational, the experience of art be subjective, and art still be political.

Indeed, by using the medium of affect rather than thematizing affect, Ahtila's work enters the domain of political efficacy. The moment when the alleged mental illness becomes the royal road to wisdom makes the shift between the discourse of madness and that of political agency. In such shifts, the interdiscursivity explained above becomes a source of polemical discus-sion rather than integration. Such moments raise the question about the placement of the subject. "Where is where?" is a question raised when the fragile boundaries between self and other are melting. As in earlier works, what is at stake is the transfer or—to use a term from psychoanalytic discourse—transference from individual to social psychosis.

---

[20]I use the word "presentation" to avoid the loaded one of "representation," as well as to begin insinuating what characterizes the political of this art: the sense in which presentation presupposes an involved addressee. For a more extensive analysis of *The House/Talo*, see Bal (2007).

Political art, in this sense, derives its efficacy from the act of exposing by means of affect, so that spectators are enabled to engage with and even melt into subjectivities that defy current delimitations and hierarchies. Boundaries between the "I" and the other humans, as well as between "us" and animals, and nature at large, become fluid. The meeting between art and politics facilitates an understanding of this possibility. And to understand this fully, the humanist must engage psychology, philosophy, and political science. This engaging of interdisciplinarity is not a free choice anymore; without it, the work and the historical event that framed it in 2008 make no sense. In this heterogeneous extension lies the primary political thrust of Ahtila's work.

Emphatically, to get at the political efficacy of the work, the scholar must do justice to its artistic properties. Ahtila's works tend, for example, to contain the sound of rustling leaves, the abnormally loud sound of lapping water, and the sound of a barking dog. This is an artistic achievement, a psychological statement, and an assessment of the medium. We can now conclude that Ahtila's excursus into psychiatry "treats" not the people but the medium. The relationship between the two disciplines is more complex here. The one is not simply juxtaposed against the other, but instead performs it. Through performing a psychiatric "treatment" of cinema, the artwork intimates not only that psychiatry inheres in cinema in the form of the madness that is the former's object, but also that cinema, once itself aware of this madness, can "treat" psychiatry by drawing it out into the social domain.[21]

Tragedy: Ethics of Theater

The individualism habitual in psychiatry, Ahtila seems to say, makes us blind to the madness in culture itself. And that misrecognition is the tragedy of history, which has become extreme in our time. In the context of this exploration of Ahtila's work, tragedy implies tradition, death, and theater. Of all literary genres, tragedy is the most longstanding and prestigious; it is truly traditional. The tradition of art, especially politically resonant art, is doubly emphasized in the many references to literary and cinematic masterpieces, as well as in self-reflexive references to the media of both arts. Death is present in the articulations of mourning that, in turn, resonate with other moments— visual as well as linguistic—that either resemble mourning or hint at its overcoming. This leads up to the massive presence of death in *Where Is Where?* But the work also possesses a strong, exuberant theatricality. Again, theater studies is a disciplinary field that needs to be brought in here, but neither integrated nor simply added, it remains a stubborn "discussant."

---

[21]Lyotard has advocated heterogeneity as early as 1971. For Lyotard's vision on the media, see Rodowick (2001); for his insistence on heterogeneity as a political necessity, see Readings (1991). I am currently working on the need for psychiatry to become more social in a film project with Michelle Williams Gamaker, *Mère Folle*. See www.crazymothermovie.com.

The use of light, the backdrops, and the acting style all work together to emphasize theatricality. Other elements insure that we can at no moment forget this. The backdrop at the beginning of *Where Is Where?*, for example, foregrounds its own constructedness. It consists of two churches, drawn in crayon, between which the Poet stands. The church on her left looks Christian, the one on the right has understated "oriental" features. Auditory effects also mark theatricality, for instance, when the barking of a dog performs the transition from Finland to Algeria, which is soon followed by the horn of a ship when Egypt is mentioned. Clearly, in addition to cinema and its history, theatricality is an important element of Ahtila's work, which has a suspended fiction-reality complex. Note that this complex, central to so many artifacts the humanities considers its objects, can neither be captured nor skipped by any of its disciplines. The inextricable knot of fiction-and-reality that is characteristic of the arts requires reflection on ontology that extends its relevance beyond the arts. This is resonant with the both-and thinking in interdisciplinary research, as opposed to the either-or of more limited approaches.

Theatricality is visible in the relentless passage of time, an attribute shared by theater and cinema alike. At key moments in Ahtila's work, the setting is a podium with folding chairs around it. This is a visual topos in the ending of *Where Is Where?*, when Adel's final sentence is spoken to three screens of such empty chairs. The figure of Death, in a highly theatrical costume and illuminated in such a way that we barely ever see anything more than his mouth, reminds us that theater "touches" life. And while most of the speeches directly address the spectator, the scene where Death and the Poet sit together at the breakfast table looks like an amateur theater performance in a small town venue. It is precisely because most of the speeches appear to be performances of poetry-like philosophy (or philosophical poetry) rather than drama that the prison hospital scenes, in which the boys talk to the doctors on the other screens, stand out by contrast. Thus, these moments foreground the theatricality of the four-screen disposition.

However, the notion that the disposition of *Where Is Where?* in four screens represents a theatrical setting must immediately be qualified. Because these screens are positioned in a square, traditional theater is, in fact, reversed; the work does not take place in front of us but surrounds and absorbs us. In relation to the work, we, its spectators, are on stage. This has an obvious consequence. As Raymond Bellour has pointed out in a lecture about the exhibition, *Where Is Where?* poses a great paradox. Perhaps we should call on the discipline of logic here, not to "apply" it but to confront its autonomy as abstraction. Logic is confronted with ethics: The fact that the boys are logically right does not justify their act. Or does it? Moreover, the logic is confronted with bodily experience. Although the work is based on an implacable logic, it is impossible to follow this logic "logically." This impossibility is embodied by the environment of four screens one cannot simultaneously observe. From this paradox another one emerges: Far from contradicting or mitigating it, the very theatricality of this piece, including its emphatic artificiality, *constitutes* its political force. The work is able to make History enter art, and thus end the unfortunate and damaging opposition between fiction and reality. This is one way art addresses and confronts disciplines that focus on a definition of truth as reality—called "realism."[22]

Ending that opposition, even as a nonpolarized distinction, is a condition sine qua non for political art. Not to establish a preferred presence of "reality," but to literally suspend the distinction and thus keep fiction present in a never-resolved dialectic. Suspension, or bracketing, of seemingly self-evident "truths" or "givens" is a very useful technique to get at unexpected results. Precisely on the basis of the indispensable co-presence of fiction and reality as indistinguishable categories—fiction is part of reality, and so is language—it becomes possible to approach "art" beyond the fatigue of an all-pervasive, powerless habit of critique. To make the case for the political force of Ahtila's work, we first need to resituate the political in and of art. This is a central interdisciplinary move. The political is taken out of political science and firmly put into the humanities. But, rather than being integrated, it is put there as a question. Otherwise, we cannot avoid the great aporia already put forward by Adorno (2003) in his essay "Commitment": "Art that seeks to speak of politics becomes propaganda and ceases to be art—it loses any political efficacy—but art that only wishes to be art is political in its refusal of politics" (p. 258).

Taking this aporia as a starting point, we know that neither a rhetorical nor a thematic focus will work, for both pertain to "propaganda" and not to "art." This aporia requires the interdisciplinary move of taking the political into the humanities. Resituating the political in art happens where we least expect it: in the avowed, self-conscious artifice of the theatrical. This is an uneasy, yet integrative placing of the political, which transforms both it and theatricality. This is, in my view, what *Where Is Where?* sets out to do. And it does so in a way that retrospectively illuminates the works that precede it, deploying "preposterous history" as a model for the integration of history and aesthetics. Theater, writes Maaike Bleeker (2007), "presents a *staging* of the construction that is also constitutive of the real." Theatricality is a vision machine that stages possible forms of looking around us from a culturally and historically specific consciousness, on the basis of a destabilization of the relationship between the act of looking and what is staged. It thus becomes a master discipline, transformed by and transforming the other humanistic disciplines (Bleeker, 2007).[23]

Around us, *Where Is Where?* once again takes this phrase literally, surrounding us with images that we look at with such sharp awareness that we cannot see them all. It imposes a certain physical restlessness on spectators. It forces them to turn around so that their bodies are implicated in the act of

---

[22]Raymond Bellour, gallery talk, Musée du Jeu de Paume, January 22, 2008.

[23]Bleeker discusses Barbara Freedman (1991) here.

looking. This embodied quality of the experience resonates nicely with inter-disciplinary visions in the humanities. This emphasis on the bodily nature of artistic reception can be considered a cautionary footnote to all those disci-plines, especially in the sciences, that traditionally tend to consider knowledge disembodied, "pure," and abstract. The ethical dilemma that remains after we must acknowledge the unassailable logic through which the boys explain their act is so forcefully touching that it keeps us imprisoned in that bodily restlessness.

To understand how this literal embodiment of theater works in conjunc-tion with Ahtila's other aesthetic engagements, we only need to realize what cinema and theater have in common. This is a moment of what Repko (2008) calls the creation of a common ground, as a step toward integration. As I have suggested above, this work is emphatically cinematographic, with its breath-taking beauty as well as its references to early cinema. But in its theatrical dis-position it is also emphatically opposed to the illusionism of theater and cinema that is encouraged when spectators comfortably sit in the dark, look-ing straight ahead and forgetting their bodies. To this illusionism it opposes a "critical habitat." We sit or stand there, physically unable to remain abstract and distant—whatever our critical reflections, we cannot disentangle ourselves from what we critique.[24]

Theatricality enforces on the spectator an activity already visible in the physical installation of the piece, which compels us to bend over to see the images on small, low-standing monitors. And it is also present in the implau-sible acts and acting style, which allow us to merge fiction and reality on the condition that we agree to situate ourselves in and submit ourselves to trou-bled minds and an equally troubled medium. When a woman sings a song on stage in *Where Is Where?*, the backdrops are empathically aesthetic, includ-ing even a four-screen reddening sky at sunset that could easily have come from a Hollywood props department. But the artist carefully stages not only the fiction that allows, to invoke a category from psychology, "heteropathic identification" (identification with another on his or her, not our own, terms; Silverman, 1996), but also the artifice that construes and thus destabilizes and undermines it, against the odds of illusion and transparency.

The main character, who is a poet, sets the tone of this multiple evocation of the tragedy of the transgenerational transmission of violence. At this moment, she incarnates the need for interdisciplinarity, as the emphasized words below suggest. She is a woman who seems real, but whose interlocutor is an allegori-cal figure, as in biblical and medieval *literature*. *Cinematographically*, the shadow of Ingmar Bergman is visible here. In a *theatrical* dialogue, she conducts a discussion with Monsieur la Mort, who asks her to give him words, the stuff

---

[24]Apter (2002) defines a critical habitat as "art informed by geopolitics; by an ecologically engaged conceptualism; . . . that critiques the relationship between media and environment and explores forms of global identification" (p. 22). Ahtila's work also requires reflection on installation as an art form, which cannot be addressed in the scope of this paper. On installation, see Reiss (1999).

of *poetry*. Later, words fly from a newly printed page, as an image in which *art history* would have an interest. But this interdisciplinarity is only the natural habitat of the interdiscursive issues the Poet brings up.

One wonders where the written pages go and where that where is. Boundaries between the Poet and Death, between her and the boys, the water-tight boundaries of the individual, as well as those of periods and countries, have melted. One gets the feeling that these words, which have flown away, enable a kind of shamanistic communication. Visually, they do not look like poetry at all. They are in Finnish, so non-Finnish speakers have no way of see-ing what they mean. But the graphic disposition of the words on the page looks more like a script than a poem. A script of a play, enhancing the the-atricality of the destabilization that affects even the printed word. Or is it the script of the work we are watching, in a self-reflexivity that foregrounds, by way of the Poet, the artist's endorsement of her own complicity?[25]

I believe it is both—the play that destabilizes, and the script of *Where Is Where?* that puts us in the presence of that destabilization. What is at stake in this critical reexamination of boundaries—between artistic media and between the disciplines needed to understand it—is responsibility in the pre-sent. This is both the temporality of video installation as well as the tempo-rality of the close-up, the shot that suspends linear time and positions affect instead. In an unsettling passage of philosophical discussion in which she is talking to the Priest, the Poet rejects a pardon that is too easily granted:

I don't understand how I can be forgiven

for what happens to other people?

Other people's deaths.

—If we are always forgiven,

that makes us illiterate.

The word "illiterate" is particularly striking in this context. It puts knowl-edge, the epistemology of our present responsibility, at the heart of the work. It is here, in this particular rejection, that the political is located—in a responsibility that is too easily transformed into conformism. It is in the name of the nation state that conformism develops. We saw it in the English translation of Fanon's sentence, "You do what you have to do," which in turn leads to the powerlessness and indifference of the French translation, "Faites ce que vous voulez." "Illiterate," then, is whoever refuses the chal-lenges this work poses to any attempt to confine it—in disciplines, in coun-tries, in times. Instead, it is when those boundaries are allowed to melt that the work can touch us—body and mind, in ways that only artworks, and only some of those, manage to do.

---

[25]The layout of the words on the page is undeniably according to the scriptwriting software Final Draft.

And, indeed, in the name of the misunderstandings that surround the idea of the political, the Priest insists,

Why don't you want to receive his pardon?

To this, the Poet answers with her own version of the implacable logic that dominates this piece:

What is left if everything is forgiven and will be forgiven? Then evil becomes invisible and good is just *indifference* [emphasis added] to evil.

We ourselves could continue the discussion, insisting on the unbreakable bond between art and death: Tragedy itself would become invisible and hence impossible, for it exists in order to be *seen*.

Seeing, in the context of tragedy, becomes witnessing. The empty chairs at the ending are asking for witnesses to *take place* and, to allude to our cultural holding environment, cure the stage of its indifference. This, rather than treating individuals, is psychiatry's task. Witnessing as a possibility comes up several times in this work. In the inserted archival footage, there is a proleptic image: the shot of a doll, signifier of children, lying on top of a book. The book is a signifier of the fate and the written, which I sum up below with the word *mektoub*. Whoever sees these images of violence must become a witness to that from the past, which threatens to return in the future if we do not shed our indifference.

The attack that the boys later mention as the explanation for their act—the overnight extermination of 40 inhabitants of the village of Rivet—is enacted at the home of the Poet. We see one of the victims pushing his small daughter behind him. She hides her face against the wall and survives so that she can become a witness. After the massacre, girls carry the corpses away, from screen to screen, bringing in the figure of Antigone and the dispute between the *raison d'état* and the subjective needs of life. Like many other moments, these scenes invoke tragedy with the tone of an almost solemn seriousness.[26]

After integrating, peacefully or polemically, partly or wholly, all the elements from different disciplines, discourses and media, we are left with an ethical dilemma that, perhaps, it is our fate or destiny to have to confront. This is not an ethics of theater, posing limits to the freedom of representation in the theater. Nor is it an ethical examination of tragedy's "moral lesson." Instead of such a traditional, "normal science" approach, here we see an artwork, itself a tragedy of sorts, pose an ethical aporia that suspends the

---

[26]A filming technique that depends on using several cameras from different angles is employed in moments when the action is carried over from one screen to the next. The effect is a sense of continuity within the artificially constructed four-screen space. This raises the question of the title in yet another way. On the dispute in the myth of Antigone, see Butler (2000). A more straightforward thematic analysis is offered by George Steiner in *Antigones* (1996).

possibility of judgment. The boys are right; the boys are wrong. But the suspension of judgment as a position we are compelled to step into, body and mind, does not let go of ethical deliberation in the very form the medium of installation video makes possible.

Mektoub

Tragedy, an ancient genre that has traversed the West for millennia, is updated here. The appeal to myth is now set in the present, the present of a problematic postcoloniality and of digital technology, of cynical politics of indifference and of video installation as a medium that allows no monodisciplinarity to account for it. The job of the Poet is to write—with words. Her creator, the artist, also writes, with that strange mixture of words, images, and sounds whose sense flies away that is videography. There are, in my view, two reasons why Ahtila stages the historical tragedy of the Algerian War through the creative mind of a fiction-maker. The first reason concerns theatricality—theatricality, that is, as a machine of visions that fictionality allows to develop for the benefit of the world. That is the artist's job, her destiny. The second is the suffix "graphy" of videography, which stipulates the importance of writing, in all the languages we have at our disposal, in order to articulate the stakes beyond the sole individual, or the sole group of belonging. This political conclusion implies and includes the obligation to deploy all instruments of knowing the various disciplines involved have been seen to offer.

The word-artist already pierces the boundaries of the subject and communicates beyond traditional boundaries, including those considered "natural." The Poet is the personification of an artist engaged in the practice of *abduction*—she abducts fiction to use it as weapon in and for the reality of which it is an integral part. Perhaps, following her example, instead of seeking integration we can explore abduction as a strategy for interdisciplinary research. Abduction, as in stealing live elements and holding them until they yield their contributions. Tragedy is both the genre that has endured throughout history—with its strong presence of death and destiny kept alive and, hence, changeable in words—and the genre that has politics at its very core.

The handwriting on the wall: The expression signifies both destiny and the written—destiny as that which is written. The phrase also harbors a warning; it points at the gloom of doom not far away. *Where Is Where?* does not fall back on this Western cliché. Yet, the bond between what is written and what inevitably brings us death is foregrounded in many other ways—when the Poet's sentences fly away, for instance, which undermines her power over the writing of the past. The most subtle, subliminal, and therefore most powerful of these indications I saw in a barely noticeable image.

Close to the beginning of *Where Is Where?*, when Algeria gradually penetrates Finland and its Poet's mind, we briefly get to see a beautiful image of a sign with the name of a street inscribed on it (Figure 4.5). The sign is framed by an ornate white Arabic architecture. I would like to propose this image as an emblem of my doubly partial interpretation of *Where Is Where?* The sign has Arabic letters at the bottom, and the top is formally identical to signs still in use today in Paris's 7th arrondissement. The first time I saw this double writing, it brought the double meaning of the Arabic word *mektoub* to my mind. *Mektoub* means "that which is written," including the mundane inscriptions on such signs. It also means "destiny"—the great destiny staged by tragedy.

Destiny is insinuated in this banal sign that, as much as it is a historical trace of the colonial times in which the story is set, is more importantly a forward-projecting trace—a Derridian one.[27] It is a trace of colonization, but also, today, a trace of the double culture that resulted from it. It points forward to that culture in which the Poet lives, mourns, and overcomes her mourning; it is the culture to which the Priest/Guardian/Angel/Devil in red pushes her young charges.[28]

The writing is bilingual, bi-scripted, and for Western spectators, only half-understandable. Yet, the half we do not understand belongs there; the readable French half does not. A trace, then, of a world, fictively staged in *Where*

Figure 4.5   Street Sign in Algiers

SOURCE: Source: Eija-Liisa Ahtila. Photograph courtesy of Marian Goodman Gallery, New York and Paris. © 2008 Crystal Eye—Kristallisilmä Oy.

---

[27]Derrida's first internationally influential book, *Of Grammatology* (1976), is devoted to this conception of writing as trace that points forward.

[28]The reference to this culture is meant to invoke Michael Hardt and Antonio Negri's books *Empire* (2000) and *Multitude* (2004). With all the criticism that these books have elicited, they have marked a turning point in the academic indifference to that culture.

Is Where?, in which "where?" is indeed no longer a determinate place, a protected site, or an isolated location, but rather a question mark of the future. Of course, with this intuitive sense of the importance of this particular image, I needed to find out what the Arabic script means. I did, and was stunned. The street indicated in this instance of *mektoub* is called, as if "by chance," to use that loaded phrase one more time, "Street of the Detained." Is it honoring the two boys and their logic that exposes the perversion of logic in colonialism?[29]

Mektoub: the word itself is a trace of destiny, a "graphy" as trace. As that which is (already) written, it is the trace where temporalities become complex. It is the concept—only visually presented in this modest street sign—that makes sense of such enigmatic speeches as when the Poet says, attempting to put her mourning into words, "Stretching, hanging, lacking the courage to notice time passing. Face adrift, the two sides extending across each other, held aloft upon time, will it hold?" It makes sense of that strange word "illiterate" in "If we are always forgiven, that makes us illiterate." The written, and our capacity to process it, is our responsibility for destiny, so that forgiveness becomes meaningless.

Mektoub stands in the face of death. This pondering on death, following up on Adel's wondering whether death is always a private death, is resonant with Antigone's dilemma. The Poet brings death in contact with the complex temporality of history that makes us responsible even if we are not guilty personally. Her poetry binds death to time and its nonlinearity: "How do you know this is not that unexpected moment in time when timelessness and time meet?" In connection with these deeply tragic thoughts and in its very banality, the street sign inscribes the presence of death in the everyday—of life, of cinema, or, as Elisabeth Bronfen says in the catalogue, of both life and cinema at the same time. The boundaries between those two domains have, after all, been melted as well.

Conclusion

I have not answered the question of "how to do" interdisciplinarity with a set of recommendations and prescriptions. The preposition "of," taken in its ambiguity outlined above, is enough of a guideline. My aim has been to demonstrate that the choice to espouse what an artwork requires can be a mode of being loyal to the complex and culturally important objects that constitute the object-domain of the humanities—loyal, as well, to the many important guidelines in the disciplinary divisions of the humanities, without being confined by any party thereof.

---

[29]The street is in Algiers. I thank Tarek Mehdi for this small lesson in Arabic language and culture, along with many other such small lessons he has given me over the years of our friendship.

References

Adorno, T. W. (2003). Commitment. In R. Tiedemann (Ed.) & S. W. Nicholsen (Trans.), *Can one live after Auschwitz? A philosophical reader* (pp. 240–258). Stanford, CA: Stanford University Press.

Ahtila, E. (2008). *Entretien de Doris Krystof avec Eija-Liisa Ahtila* (pp. 176–197). Paris: Hazan.

Apter, E. (2002, Winter). The aesthetics of critical habitats. *October, 99,* 21–44.

Bal, M. (1991). *Reading Rembrandt: Beyond the word-image opposition.* Cambridge: Cambridge University Press.

Bal, M. (1999). *Quoting Caravaggio: Contemporary art, preposterous history.* Chicago: University of Chicago Press.

Bal, M. (2002). *Travelling concepts in the humanities: A rough guide.* Toronto: University of Toronto Press.

Bal, M. (2007). What if? The language of affect. In G. Beer, M. Bowie, & B. Perrey (Eds.), *In(ter)discipline: New languages for criticism* (pp. 6–23). London: Modern Humanities Research Association and Maney.

Bal, M. (2009). *Narratology: Introduction to the theory of narrative* (3rd ed., rev.). Toronto: University of Toronto Press.

Bleeker, M. (2007). *Limited visibility.* Retrieved from http://home.medewerker.uva .nl/m.g.bal/bestanden/Bleeker%20paper%20Migratory%20Aesthetics%20text %20READER%20OPMAAK.pdf

Bronfen, E. (1992). *Over her dead body: Death, femininity and the aesthetic.* Manchester: Manchester University Press.

Butler, J. (2000). *Antigone's claim: Kinship between life and death.* New York: Columbia University Press.

Deleuze, G. (1986). *Cinema 1: The movement-image* (H. Tomlinson & B. Habberjam, Trans.). Minneapolis: University of Minnesota Press.

Deleuze, G. (1989). *Cinema 2: The time-image* (H. Tomlinson & R. Galeta, Trans.). Minneapolis: University of Minnesota Press.

Derrida, J. (1976). *Of grammatology* (G. C. Spivak, Trans.). Baltimore, MD: Johns Hopkins University Press.

Durand, R. (2008). Where is where? Atmospheric drama. *Eija-Liisa Ahtila* (pp. 180–184). Paris: Hazan.

Fanon, F. (1968). *The wretched of the earth* (C. Farrington, Trans.). New York: Grove Press.

Fanon, F. (2002). *Les damnés de la terre.* Paris: La découverte/Poche.

Freedman, B. (1991). *Staging the gaze: Postmodernism, psychoanalysis, and Shakespearean comedy.* Ithaca, NY: Cornell University Press.

Hansen, M. B. N. (2003). Affect as medium, or the "digital-facial-image." *Journal of Visual Culture, 2*(2), 205–228.

Hardt, M., & Negri, A. (2000). *Empire.* Cambridge, MA: Harvard University Press.

Hardt, M., & Negri, A. (2004). *Multitude: War and democracy in the age of empire.* London: Penguin.

Klein, J. T. (2001). Interdisciplinarity and the prospect of complexity: The tests of theory. *Issues in Integrative Studies, 19,* 43–57.

Kuhn, T. (1962). *The structure of scientific revolutions.* Chicago: University of Chicago Press.

Lyotard, J. (1971). *Discours, figure.* Paris: Klincksieck.

Marker, C. (1978). *La fond de l'air est rouge: Scènes de la troisième guerre mondiale*. Paris: Editions François Maspéro.

Marrati, P. (2003). *Gilles Deleuze: Cinéma et philosophie*. Paris: P.U.F.

McHale, B. (1987). *Postmodernist fiction*. London: Methuen.

Pisters, P. (2003). *The matrix of visual culture: Working with Deleuze in film theory*. Stanford, CA: Stanford University Press.

Popper, K. (2002). *The logic of scientific discovery*. New York: Routledge.

Readings, B. (1991). *Introducing Lyotard: Art and politics*. New York: Routledge.

Reiss, J. H. (1999). *From margin to center: The spaces of installation art*. Cambridge, MA: MIT Press.

Repko, A. F. (2008). *Interdisciplinary research: Process and theory*. Los Angeles and London: Sage.

Rodowick, D. N. (1997). *Gilles Deleuze's time machine*. Durham, NC: Duke University Press.

Rodowick, D. N. (2001). Presenting the figural. In D. N. Rodowick (Ed.), *Reading the figural, or, philosophy after the new media* (pp. 1–44). Durham, NC: Duke University Press.

Shepard, T. (2006). *The invention of decolonization: The Algerian War and the remaking of France*. Ithaca, NY: Cornell University Press.

Silverman, K. (1996). *The threshold of the visible world*. New York: Routledge.

Silverman, K. (2009). *Flesh of my flesh*. Stanford, CA: Stanford University Press.

Steiner, G. (1996). *Antigones: How the Antigone legend has endured in western literature, art, and thought*. New Haven, CT: Yale University Press.

Van Alphen, E. (2008, Spring/Autumn). Affective operations of art and literature. *RES: Anthropology and Aesthetics, 53/54*, 20–30.

Verstraten, P. (2009). *Film narratology* (S. van der Lecq, Trans.). Toronto: University of Toronto Press.

PART III

Approaches to Integration

Integrating Theory-Based Insights on the Causes of Suicide Terrorism

5

Allen F. Repko

_____ **Introduction**

One of the most insidious forms of terrorism is suicide terrorism. This is the "intentional killing of oneself for the purpose of killing others in the service of a political or ideological goal" (Hronick, 2006, p. 2).[1] Since the attacks on the World Trade Center on September 11, 2001, research on terrorism has increasingly focused on suicide terrorism because these attacks have increased in frequency and ferocity, with more than 180 occurring each year since 2001. From 2000 to 2004, there were 470 suicide attacks in 22 countries, killing more than 7,000 people and wounding tens of thousands, including women and children. Since 2005, suicide attacks have spread to Afghanistan, Britain, India, Pakistan, China, and Spain. More troubling still is that the great majority of these attacks are carried out by adherents of a fundamentalist arm of Islam, one of the world's four major faith traditions (Judeo-Christianity, Islam, Buddhism, and Hinduism) whose adherents are found in most countries of the world. Suicide terrorism is becoming a global phenomenon because of the geographical spread of attacks and because participants come from countries across the Middle East and Europe (Atran, 2006, p. 127). Consequently, scholars and policy makers are anxious to develop a more comprehensive understanding of this phenomenon.

---

[1] Hronick's study summarizes the proceedings of a conference held in October 2004 and hosted by the National Institute of Justice (NIJ), the research, development, and evaluation agency of the U.S. Department of Justice. Conference participants included Ariel Merari of Tel Aviv University, who advanced the definition quoted here in an attempt to distinguish suicide terrorism from high-risk terrorist missions.

To this end, some have used a multidisciplinary approach in which expert views from different disciplines are juxtaposed, but they make no attempt to integrate these conflicting insights.[2] While potentially helpful, these multidisciplinary efforts fall far short of the interdisciplinary approach that Ian Pitchford (2003) calls for:

> The key to understanding suicide terrorism is to identify a theoretical framework capable of explaining the disparate facts on which the majority of researchers are agreed and of extending our understanding by establishing links to other bodies of knowledge [i.e., the disciplines]. (p. 1)

Developing "a theoretical framework" and "establishing links" across disciplinary knowledge domains requires creating common ground and performing integration, which are distinguishing features of interdisciplinarity. Analyzing the causes of suicide terrorism, therefore, requires an interdisciplinary approach, for several reasons. First, the problem is complex, meaning that it has several components and that each component has a different disciplinary character. Second, important insights into the problem have been produced by experts from multiple disciplines: These are narrowly focused and thus often conflict. Third, no single disciplinary expert has been able to address this problem comprehensively, much less offer a holistic solution to it. Fourth, suicide terrorism is a pressing societal/public policy/foreign policy problem that urgently requires a more comprehensive understanding of its causes so that policy makers can develop effective countermeasures. Fifth, the problem falls within the research domain of several disciplines (Repko, 2008, pp. 151–155).

The purpose of this chapter is to show how the application of the interdisciplinary research process delineated in Repko (2008) can illuminate a complex problem, such as suicide terrorism, in which the expert views are typically theory based. Though most of the steps of the integrated model of research process are used, the primary focus of the chapter is on Steps 7 to 9, concerning how to perform causal integration of conflicting theoretical explanations.

Drawing on Disciplinary Insights (Steps 1 to 6)

After framing the research problem or question (Step 1) and justifying the use of an interdisciplinary approach to investigate it (Step 2), several decisions need to be made. These include deciding which disciplines are most relevant to the problem (Step 3), which disciplinary literatures to mine for insights (Step 4), how to achieve adequacy in each relevant discipline in terms of the elements (i.e., assumptions, theories, and concepts) that pertain to the problem (Step 5), and how to analyze the problem and evaluate each insight into it (Step 6).

---

[2]Examples of multidisciplinary approaches include the following: Walter Reich (1998), Wadsworth/Thomson Learning (2004), and Rex A. Hudson (1999).

Identifying the Most Relevant Disciplines (Step 3) and Conducting the Full-Scale Literature Search (Step 4)

Step 3 of the research process calls for identifying those disciplines, subdisciplines, and interdisciplines that are *potentially* relevant to the problem because it falls within their research domains. These include economics, psychology, history, sociology, communications (an applied field), international relations (a subdiscipline of political science), cultural anthropology (a subdiscipline of anthropology), religious studies, and cultural studies (an interdiscipline).[3] This list was generated using the perspectival approach (i.e., relying on each discipline's unique perspective on reality). This preliminary list was checked for completeness against a list generated from Szostak's (2004) classification approach, which links particular phenomena (including theories) to particular disciplines. Both approaches are discussed in Chapter 4 of Repko (2008).

Narrowing this list to those disciplines most relevant to the problem requires conducting a full-scale literature search (Step 4). This involves querying the major databases such as Academic Search Complete, JSTOR, and WorldCat using the keywords "terrorism" and "suicide terrorism." This search serves two critical functions. It shows that the most important insights into the problem have been produced by psychology, political science, history, and cultural anthropology, based on their theories, concepts, assumptions, and research methods. These disciplines are the *most relevant* to the problem because they "are most directly connected to the problem, have generated the most important research on it, and have advanced the most compelling theories to explain it" (Newell, 1992, p. 213). The second function of the search is to establish whether the problem is researchable in an interdisciplinary sense. It is *if* the search yields insights or expert views from two or more disciplinary perspectives (Repko, 2008, p. 350). Notably, the literature search on the problem of suicide terrorism met these criteria and revealed a substantial number of insights, many of which are theory based.

---

[3]This describes the "perspectival approach" to conducting a literature search. There is a second way to identify the most relevant disciplines using Rick Szostak's (2004) classification approach, which links most topics readily to one or more broad categories of phenomena (such as genetic predisposition and individual differences) that cut across disciplinary boundaries. Each of these categories links to a more detailed list of second-level phenomena, and each of these, in turn, links to a still more detailed list of third-level phenomena. The researcher using the classification approach should be able to identify connections to neighboring phenomena that may touch on the research question but that may have been overlooked using the perspectival approach. At minimum, this approach provides an effective way to determine whether the initial list of potentially relevant disciplines is, indeed, complete. For example, the problem of suicide terrorism definitely concerns individual differences (one of the broad categories in Szostak's first level of phenomena). But it *may* also concern the broad category of genetic predisposition that explains, among other things, motivations (including aggression and group identification) and emotions (including anger, fear, jealousy, and emotional display). If so, then the literature search (Step 4) must be broadened to include the biological sciences. In the case of suicide terrorism, the expanded literature search failed to reveal any published peer-reviewed research.

Developing Adequacy in Each Relevant Discipline (Step 5)

Once the disciplines most relevant to the problem are identified, the next task is to develop adequacy in them. "Adequacy" in an interdisciplinary context means knowing enough about the discipline to have a basic understanding of how it approaches the problem and how it illuminates and characterizes the problem (Klein, 2005, p. 68).[4] The perspectives of the most relevant disciplines on suicide terrorism are as follows:

- Psychology's overall perspective on human behavior is that it reflects the cognitive constructs that individuals develop to organize their mental activity and motivate their behavior. Applied to suicide terrorism, this perspective suggests that suicide terrorist behavior reflects inherent personality traits and/or cognitive constructs that are possibly cultivated by terrorist leadership.
- Political science tends to view the world as a political arena in which individuals and groups make decisions based on the quest for or exercise of power. Politics, at all levels and in all cultures, is typically viewed as a perpetual struggle over whose values, not just whose interests, will prevail in setting priorities and making collective choices. When applied to suicide terrorism, this perspective views suicide terrorism as motivated primarily by strategic and power/political considerations.
- Cultural anthropology views individual cultures as organic integrated wholes with their own internal logic. By "culture" is meant the sets of symbols, rituals, and beliefs by which a society gives meaning to daily life. This perspective views suicide terrorism as a complex phenomenon deeply rooted in some variants of Islamic culture.
- History tends to view events past and present as expressions of trends and developments leading up to them and as the result of both societal forces and individual decisions. Consequently, this perspective tends to view suicide terrorism as the product of events and developments that have shaped, and continue to shape, the course of Muslim civilization for more than a thousand years (Lewis, 2002, p. 1).

Developing adequacy in the most relevant disciplines may also include identifying important theories advanced by disciplinary experts to explain the phenomenon. This is especially true when working in the social sciences, which are typically theory laden. Because suicide terrorism has attracted the

---

[4]Developing adequacy involves asking questions of these disciplines, such as how much knowledge, and what kind of knowledge, is required from each discipline. Beyond knowing the cognitive map of the disciplines involved, not much specialized knowledge is required. Indeed, the problem can be adequately illuminated using a handful of introductory-level elements from each of the relevant disciplines. These include its assumption(s), theories, concepts, and research methods. See the discussion of adequacy in Repko (2008, pp. 189–194).

most scholarly interest from the social sciences, and because the most important insights are generally theory based, developing adequacy calls for identifying these theories, which are shown in Table 5.1.[5]

The interdisciplinarian must be open to the possibility that one or more of these theories may not be as important as first supposed, and/or that further searching may reveal the need to add one or more new theories to the list.

Analyzing the Problem and Evaluating Each Insight Into It (Step 6)

Closely associated with achieving adequacy in the relevant disciplines is analyzing the problem from the perspective of each relevant discipline and evaluating each important insight into it, particularly the theory that each expert advances. The evaluation focuses on each theory's explanation of the causes of suicide terrorism, its key assumption(s), and its strengths and weaknesses as an explanatory model. This work is foundational to creating common ground and to performing integration.

The Theory-Based Insights of Psychology

Psychology typically sees human behavior as reflecting the cognitive constructs individuals develop to organize their mental activity. Psychologists

Table 5.1   Important Theories on the Causes of Suicide Terrorism

Relevant Discipline and Subdiscipline	Writer	Theory
Psychology	Post	Terrorist psycho-logic
	Bandura	Self-sanction (moral disengagement)
	Merari	Martyrdom
Political Science	Crenshaw	Collective rational choice
	Rapoport	Sacred terror
	Monroe & Kreidie	Religious identity theory
Cultural Anthropology	Atran	Fictive kin
History	Lewis	Modernization

---

[5]Since 9/11, the literature on terrorism has grown exponentially, which greatly complicates the interdisciplinarian's task of identifying the most relevant insights and the most important theories.

also study inherent mental mechanisms, both genetic predispositions and individual differences. Experts typically see suicide terrorism in terms of individuals whose behavior is the product of mental constructs and cognitive restructuring. They attempt to identify the possible motivations behind a person's decision to join a terrorist group and commit acts of shocking violence. They tend to agree that there is no single terrorist mindset, a finding that greatly complicates attempts to profile terrorists groups and leaders on a more systematic and accurate basis (Hudson, 1999, p. 22). Among the several psychology-based theories that researchers have advanced to explain this phenomenon are the theories advanced by Jerrold M. Post, Albert Bandura, and Ariel Merari, which are frequently cited by other experts.

1. Post (1998) argues that suicide terrorists reason logically but employ what he calls "a special logic" or "psycho-logic." According to this theory, terrorists do not *willingly* resort to terrorism as an intentional choice. Rather, "political terrorists are driven to commit acts of violence as a consequence of psychological forces, and . . . their special psycho-logic is constructed to rationalize acts they are *psychologically compelled to commit* [emphasis added]" (p. 25). In other words, terrorists are born with certain personality traits that can predispose them to engage in terrorist acts, including suicide attacks. Post's theory challenges other research on suicide attackers, which shows that "most suicide terrorists are psychologically normal, in the sense that psychological pathology does not seem to be present and the attacks are virtually always premeditated" (Cronin, 2003, p. 6). His theory assumes that attackers are born, not made. A major weakness of Post's theory is its narrow focus on the "special logic" of individual terrorists, which does not allow room for those terrorists whose behavior may be motivated by something other than this "special logic." The implication of his theory is that suicide terrorists may themselves be "victims" because they have no control over their particular personality traits.

2. Bandura (1998) is interested in how terrorists rationalize their acts of violence. He assumes that terrorists are made, not born. According to his self-sanction theory, terrorists use four techniques to insulate themselves from the human consequences of their actions: (1) imagining themselves as the saviors of a constituency threatened by a great evil, (2) viewing themselves as functionaries who are merely following their leader's orders, (3) minimizing or ignoring the actual suffering of their victims, and (4) dehumanizing their victims (p. 161). A principal strength of his theory is that it addresses causal factors external to the individual attacker, including political factors, the influence of culture on one's sense of identity, and the influence of sacred beliefs. A major weakness of the theory is its silence concerning a person's cognitive predisposition and personality traits that may influence decision making.

3. Merari (1998) rejects the notion that suicide attackers are mentally unstable and assumes, with Bandura, that attackers are made, not born. They need, he says, a very specific mindset to carry out a suicide bombing. According to his martyrdom theory, this mindset is shaped by four factors: culture (including religion), ideas (i.e., indoctrination by terrorist organizations), politics, and the attacker's personality. He rejects the widely held view that this brand of terrorism is the exclusive domain of religious fanaticism, noting that "in most cases the perpetrators sacrificed themselves in the name of a nationalistic rather than a religious idea" (pp. 196, 204–205). He argues that personality factors, especially the psychological impact of a broken family background, seem to play a "critical role in suicidal terrorism" but attributes primary responsibility to recruiting organizations and their charismatic trainers (p. 207). As with Post's theory, this theory fails to address the causal factors of politics, culture, and religion that research outside psychology has shown to be highly influential in the development of a suicide attacker.

These psychological approaches focus on individual terrorists, their motivations and behaviors, their recruitment and induction into terrorist groups, their personalities, their religious beliefs, their family ties, and other influences that can possibly explain their actions. Conflicting assumptions underlie these theories. Post (1998) assumes that suicide terrorists are inherently predisposed to commit acts of terrorism, whereas Bandura (1998) and Merari (2007) assume that they are the product of factors external to the individual.[6] All three theories share the deeper assumption basic to psychology: that group behavior can be reduced to individuals and that understanding the behavior and motivations of individual suicide terrorists is best achieved by examining their personality traits.

The Theory-Based Insights of Political Science

Whereas psychologists are interested in the mental life of the individual terrorist, political scientists are interested in the political contexts of terrorist groups. They typically view suicide terrorism as a purposeful or rational mode of political expression and focus on the terrorists' ideological convictions and strategic and power-motivated political considerations. However, newer approaches are focusing on the role of religion in politics and religious perceptions of political reality.

---

[6]Rex A. Hudson (1999) questions the widely held Olson hypothesis, which "suggests that participants in revolutionary violence predicate their behavior on a rational cost-benefit calculus" and the theory's conclusion that prevailing social conditions explain why violence is often seen as "the best available course of action" (p. 19).

Political scientists Martha Crenshaw, David C. Rapoport,[7] and Kristen Renwick Monroe and Lina Haddad Kreidie view suicide terrorism as a form of political expression of competing values, worldviews, and interests.[8]

1. Crenshaw (1998), a pioneer of terrorist studies, concedes that psychology is, indeed, important in determining terrorist behavior, but she contends that the nonpsychological—that is, the instrumental—bases of terrorist actions must be accorded equal weight. For Crenshaw, terrorist behavior is a product of strategic choice and an expression of political strategy (p. 7). Strategic choice theory is a variation of rational choice theory that holds that people calculate the likely costs and benefits of any action before deciding what to do. All kinds of actions, even those that may appear to be irrational or nonrational, such as suicide attacks, are explained as rationally motivated and calculated. The theory assumes that the individual decision maker is "typical" or "representative" of some larger group. It also makes two other assumptions: that the terrorist is "maximizing utility" by choosing this preferred alternative, and that the presence of constraints makes the decision to use suicide attack necessary (Green, 2002, pp. 4, 7). Crenshaw's (1998) theory of collective rational strategic choice offers three advantages: (1) it permits the construction of a standard by which degrees of strategic reasoning modified by psychology and other constraints can be measured; (2) it suggests important questions about the preferences or goals of terrorist organizations; and (3) it offers a useful interpretation of reality. The resort to terrorism need not be viewed as an aberration, she says. Rather, it may be "a reasonable and calculated response to circumstances" (pp. 9–10). The main problem with her theory is its "assumption that terrorist actions and motivations are purely results of strategic choice—that it is logical thinking that is aimed at achieving rational, strategic ends" *that are essentially political.* However, the theory fails to account for the varieties of terrorist motivations, that is, "the ways in which certain belief systems, particularly ideological and religious ones, contribute to world views that make terrorism attractive to some persons" (Reich, 1998, p. 3).

2. Rapoport (1998) is a leading analyst of the relationship between terrorism and religion, particularly within Shia and Sunni Islam. His particular focus is on the revival of terrorist activities to support religious goals or

---

[7]Rapoport is a political scientist *and* a historian.

[8]Bruce Hoffman's *Inside Terrorism* (2006) is widely viewed as the seminal work for understanding the historical evolution of terrorism and the terrorist mindset. In it, he argues that terrorism in general, and suicide terrorism in particular, are ways to pursue, acquire, and use power to achieve political change (p. 2). Suicide terrorism, he says, is an "entirely rational and calculated choice, consciously embraced as a deliberate instrument of warfare" (p. 132). His use of rational choice theory to understand the causes of suicide terrorism differs from Crenshaw's (1998) use of it in this critical aspect: Hoffman's approach makes room for religious and theological justifications for using this form of terrorism. Still, there is more similarity than difference between Hoffman's approach and the approaches of Crenshaw and Rapoport to justify his inclusion.

terror justified in theological terms, a phenomenon he calls "holy" or "sacred" terror. The main difference between sacred and secular terror, he says, derives from the special justifications and precedents each uses. Whereas secular terrorists produce cultures in which participants feel free to take their lessons from anyone, sacred or religiously motivated terrorists ground their approach in events in Islam's founding period and the commentaries of religious sages. According to these sages, sacred terror is the duty of true Muslim believers and will reverse Islam's humiliation and decline (1998, pp. 98–111). Rapoport's theory of "holy" or "sacred" terror is broad enough to account for terrorist political aspirations and to explain how culture and religious values may motivate a person to become a suicide terrorist. Yet, it fails to address how a person's mind may be predisposed, susceptible to, or shaped by these complex influences and motivated to commit such a horrific act.

3. Monroe and Kreidie (1997) say that part of the scholarly failure to understand the growth of Islamic fundamentalism and to explain the phenomenon of suicide terrorism "results from a failure to recognize the importance of cognitive differences in worldviews held by fundamentalists and secularists" (p. 19). This fundamentalist worldview is completely different from rational choice decision-making models, which are Western and secular. Rather than superimpose this model on suicide terrorists, Monroe and Kreidie turn to identity theory, which is based on the psychological concept of "cognitive-perceptual framework," to explain how Islamic fundamentalists perceive reality and what motivates their behavior. The term "cognitive-perceptual framework" is a compound idea that includes the concepts of cognition and perspective. Cognition "refers to that particular part of an individual's beliefs about how the world works which is used to organize and make sense of reality." Monroe and Kreidie "assume that the development of a person's cognitive-perceptual framework is influenced by societal norms and culture." In turn, "culture helps shape the human mind and gives meaning to action" (p. 23). Perspective conveys the visual idea of locating oneself on a cognitive map, much as one locates oneself in a landscape. In a psychological sense,

> perspective contains the idea that we all have a view of the world, a view of ourselves, a view of others, and a view of ourselves in relation to others. Perspective implies that there is a particular way in which the world is seen. . . . It incorporates our worldviews and our identities. (p. 25)

Identity theory shows that the Islamic fundamentalist way of life "takes precedence over all else, even one's own children, and even their own life" (Monroe & Kreidie, 1997, p. 37). Consequently, politics, for suicide terrorists, is merely one aspect of an all-encompassing religious faith. Power is sought and exercised for the purpose of extending the reach of religion. Achieving, maintaining, and extending power is a moral (in a theological sense) imperative.[9] Therefore, it is a mistake for Western policy makers to view Islamic fundamentalists as rational actors but then dismiss them as irrational when they do not act as predicted by traditional cost/benefit models such as rational choice theory. Islamic fundamentalism, argue Monroe and Kreidie, is not simply another set of political values that can be compromised or negotiated. Nor is it a system of beliefs or ideology, such as socialism or communism, in which "traditional liberal democratic modes of political discourse and interaction are recognized." Rather, "Islamic fundamentalism taps into a quite different political consciousness, one in which religious identity sets and determines the range of options open to the fundamentalists. It extends to all areas of life and respects no separation between the private and the political" (pp. 19–20, 41). Though the theory is interdisciplinary in that it borrows concepts from psychology, it fails to probe the psychological mechanisms that enable terrorists to do what they do as deeply as some psychology theories (such as Post's) do.

Crenshaw (1998) and Rapoport (1998) view suicide terrorism primarily as a political phenomenon, whereas Monroe and Kreidie (1997) seek broader understanding and thus borrow heavily from research outside their discipline. Nevertheless, all four writers believe that the root causes of terrorism can be found in influences such as international events and national environments (home and foreign) as well as subnational causes such as the influences of local schools and foreign universities (Hudson, 1999, p. 16). These theories share two assumptions: that factors external to the terrorists explain their motivation and behavior, and that groups and organizations exercise a determinative role on the transformation of a person into a suicide terrorist.

The Theory-Based Insight of Cultural Anthropology

Cultural anthropology typically views individual cultures as organic integrated wholes with their own internal logic. A "culture" is the set of symbols, rituals, and beliefs—including religious beliefs—by which a society gives meaning to daily life. When religion is a very strong element in a society, culture may include values that are considered sacred. For cultural anthropologist Scott Atran (2008), fictive kin theory trumps almost every other explanation for suicide terrorism.[10] *Fictive kin* refers to a family-like

---

[9]One could place this in cost/benefit terms: They believe that their acts will gain them eternal life. Monroe and Kreidie (1997) show that there is a "cognitive collision between Western and fundamentalist worldviews" (p. 22).

[10]Atran has changed his mind about why people are willing to become suicide terrorists and die for a cause. He has "moved from thinking that individual cognition and personality factors, influences from broad socio-economic factors, and devotion to a religious or a political ideology were determinant, to seeing friendship and other aspects of small group dynamics trumping almost all other factors." See Atran (2003c).

group of friends—campmates, workmates, and soccer buddies—who share a cause and a devotion to each other and to their mentors. Atran finds that "support for suicide actions is triggered by moral outrage at perceived attacks against Islam and sacred values." Though millions may express this sense of outrage, only a few thousand are willing to commit violence. These few thousand arise within specific "scenes" such as neighborhoods, schools, workplaces, and common leisure activities (soccer, mosque, café, online chat rooms) and act in small groups "consisting mostly of friends, and some kin" (p. 2). Suicide bombers are not born but made, says Atran. They have been indoctrinated by groups who are able to manipulate emotions, which "creates a deep commitment equal to the one a mother feels when she sacrifices herself for her child" (2003b, p. 10). A limitation of fictive kin theory is that it fails to explain how inherent psychological constructs and external political events may frame a worldview that makes suicide terrorism attractive to some persons.

The Theory-Based Insight of History

Historians believe any historical period, including our own, cannot be adequately appreciated without understanding the trends and developments leading up to it. Historical events, including current ones, are the result of both societal forces and individual decisions. History sees a historical period, person, or event in the context of the trends and developments leading up to it and as a product of societal forces and individual decisions. Consequently, historians tend to view a phenomenon such as suicide terrorism as the product of historical developments, societal forces, ideas, and individual decisions.

Bernard Lewis (2002), one of the foremost Western authorities on Islamic history and culture, applies this perspective to the problem of suicide terrorism, seeing it deeply rooted in the history of Islam and the decline of its culture and economic and military prowess vis-à-vis the West. His approach to this problem is to place it in the broadest possible historical context. He goes all the way back to 1683 when the Ottoman Turks laid siege to Vienna, Austria but were repelled and later defeated by an alliance of European states. That defeat, says Lewis, was the turning point for Islam and the beginning of centuries of culture clashes between Christian Europe and the Islamic Middle East. Lewis explains the rise of Islamic fundamentalism in our own day and the phenomenon of suicide terrorism as a result of Islam's loss of civilizational leadership and retreat from modernity (p. 159). He uses modernization theory to explain what went wrong as Islamic countries suffered successive stages of military, political, and economic decline. In the most general terms, this cross-disciplinary theory attempts to explain the process of historical and cultural change and why some cultures "modernize" or transform themselves politically, economically, and technologically following the Western model while others do not. However, the idea that all states would become Western has been largely discredited, as Asian and other societies have developed economically without adopting a wide range of Western cultural attributes.

A Taxonomy of Theory-Based Insights

At this point in the interdisciplinary research process, the problem is how to organize effectively the rapidly accumulating data. The approach used here is to develop a taxonomy of the most relevant insights and their key elements, as shown in Table 5.2. These elements are the theory's name, the insight of

Table 5.2 Theory-Based Insights Into the Problem of Suicide Terrorism

Theory	Insight of Theory Stated in General Terms	Insight Into the Problem	Concept	Assumption
Terrorist psycho-logic	Political violence is not instrumental but an end in itself. The cause becomes the rationale for acts of terrorism the terrorist is compelled to commit (Post, 1998, p. 35).	"Individuals are drawn to the path of terrorism to commit acts of violence . . . as a consequence of psychological forces, and . . . their special psycho-logic is constructed to rationalize acts they are psychologically compelled to commit" (Post, 1998, p. 25).	Special logic (Post, 1998, p. 25)	Humans organize their mental life through psychological constructs.
Self-sanction	"Self-sanctions can be disengaged by reconstruing conduct as serving moral purposes, by obscuring personal agency in detrimental activities, by disregarding or misrepresenting the injurious consequences of one's victims, or by blaming and dehumanizing the victims" (Bandura, 1998, p. 161).	"Self-sanctions can be disengaged by cognitively restructuring the moral value of killing, so that the killing can be done free of self-censuring restraints" (Bandura, 1998, pp. 164, 171–182).	Moral cognitive restructuring (Bandura, 1998, p. 164)	

Theory	Insight of Theory Stated in General Terms	Insight Into the Problem	Concept	Assumption
Martyrdom	"Terrorist suicide is basically an individual rather than a group phenomenon; it is done by people who wish to die for personal reasons . . . Personality factors seem to play a critical role in suicidal terrorism. . . . It seems that a broken family background is an important constituent" (Merari, 1998, pp. 206–207).	"Perpetrators of suicidal attacks . . . are not the exclusive domain of religious fanaticism in general. . . . In most cases the perpetrators sacrificed themselves in the name of a nationalistic rather than a religious idea" (Merari, 1998, p. 205).	Indoctrination (Merari, 1998, p. 199)	
Collective rational strategic choice	This approach permits the construction of a standard that can measure degrees of rationality, the degree to which strategic reasoning is modified by psychology and other constraints, and explain how reality is interpreted (Crenshaw, 1998, pp. 9–10).	Terrorism can be understood as an expression of political strategy (Crenshaw, 1998, p.7).	Collective rationality (Crenshaw, 1998, pp. 8–9)	"Terrorism may follow logical processes that can be discovered and explained" (Crenshaw, 1998, p. 7).
"Sacred" terror	"Holy" or "sacred" terror is "terrorist activities to support religious purposes or terror justified in theological terms" (Rapoport, 1998, p. 103).	"Sacred" or "holy" terrorists justify the means they use on the basis of sacred writings and/or on certain theological interpretations of these writings (Rapoport, 1998, pp. 107–130).	"Holy" or "sacred" terror (Rapoport, 1998, p. 103)	
Identity	"Religious identity sets and determines the range of options open to the fundamentalist. It extends into all areas of	Religious identity (in an Islamic fundamentalist sense) redefines what is meant by		There is no separation between religion and politics.

(Continued)

| Table 5.2 | (Continued) | | | |

Theory	Insight of Theory Stated in General Terms	Insight Into the Problem	Concept	Assumption
	life and respects no separation between the private and the political" (Monroe & Kreidie, 1997, p. 41).	"politics" (Monroe & Kreidie, 1997, p. 41).		Religious identity explains "political" behavior.
Fictive kin	Loyalty to an intimate cohort of peers who are emotionally bonded to the same religious and political sentiments (Atran, 2003a, pp. 1534, 1537).	Suicide terrorists act out of a universal heartfelt human sentiment of self-sacrifice for the welfare of the group/culture (Atran, 2003b, p. 2).	"Religious communion" (Atran, 2003a, p. 1537)	Personal relationships shape people's ideas about what is good.
Modernization	Explains the process of historical and cultural change and why some cultures "modernize" or transform themselves politically, economically, and technologically following the Western model while others do not (Lewis, 2002, p. 59).	Suicide terrorism is an expression of extreme frustration caused by the humiliation that the Islamic world has experienced at the hands of the West and particularly the United States (Lewis, 2002).		

the theory stated in general terms, the theory's insight into the problem stated in the writer's own words, the key concepts that express the theory, and its core assumption(s). Experience has shown that condensing and juxtaposing this critical information aids in creating common ground and performing integration. As a rule of thumb, it is better to err on the side of including too much information than too little, for the simple reason that it is impossible to know with certainty what information will ultimately prove critical to creating common ground and performing integration.

Integrating Causal Explanations (Steps 7 to 9)

The second part of the research process, and the primary focus of this chapter, is to perform causal integration. *Causal* refers to the different theoretical explanations of the behavior of a particular phenomenon.

Integration is a cognitive process that involves making a series of decisions, each of which correspond to Steps 7 to 9 of the research process: identifying conflicts between insights and locating their sources (Step 7); creating common ground between these insights (Step 8);[11] and constructing a more comprehensive understanding of the phenomenon under study (Step 9).

Identifying Conflicts in Insights and Locating Their Sources (Step 7)

There are several possible sources of conflict that one typically encounters when working with insights from multiple disciplinary literatures. The first is that which naturally arises when viewing the problem from the distinctive perspective of each relevant discipline. Because disciplinary perspectives conflict, it is natural that expert insights written from different disciplinary perspectives also conflict (Newell, 2007, p. 256). These conflicts stand in the way of creating common ground and, thus, of achieving integration (Wolfe & Haynes, 2003, p. 153). The task of the interdisciplinarian is to identify these conflicts and locate their sources so that common ground can be created and integration can proceed. The approach taken here is to identify in serial fashion the conflicts between the theoretical explanations written from the perspective of each relevant discipline and locate the sources of these conflicts.[12]

Conflicting Disciplinary Perspectives

The first possible source of conflict in insights is at the most general level, namely, between the overall perspective of each group of experts from the same discipline. These conflicts in perspective, noted earlier in the discussion of Step 6, are summarized in Table 5.3.

Conflicting Disciplinary Assumptions

A second possible source of conflict between these insights is the assumptions that underlie each discipline. An assumption is something taken for granted, a supposition. These assumptions are accepted as the truths upon which the discipline is based. Stated another way, a discipline's defining elements—its theories, concepts, and methods—are simply the practical outworking of its assumptions. Grasping the underlying assumptions of a discipline

---

[11]Concerning Step 8, I state elsewhere, "Creating common ground is undoubtedly the most challenging aspect of interdisciplinary work because it requires original thought that draws on close analytical reasoning and creative thinking. But it is achievable if one takes a systematic approach, pays attention to the nature of the challenge, and chooses an appropriate integrative technique" (Repko, 2008, p. 271).

[12]Perspectives on each relevant discipline are drawn from the taxonomy in Chapter 3 of Repko (2008).

Table 5.3   Conflicting Disciplinary Perspectives

Discipline	Perspective
Psychology	Views terrorist behavior as reflecting the psychological constructs of individuals
Political Science	Views suicide terrorism as a political phenomenon involving groups and institutions
Cultural Anthropology	Views suicide terrorism as a cultural expression of religious sharing and empowerment
History	Views suicide terrorism as an individual and cultural response to political, military, and economic loss

as a whole provides important clues to the assumption underlying the writings of its experts on a particular problem and may prove useful in creating common ground (Repko, 2008, p. 89). Concerning the problem at hand, Post (1998), Bandura (1998), and Merari (1998) share an assumption of psychology that individual human behavior can be ascertained by examining a person's mental life. By contrast, Crenshaw (1998), Rapoport (1998), and Monroe and Kreidie (1997) share an assumption of political science that terrorism in any form follows logical processes that can be discovered and explained (Crenshaw, 1998, p. 7). These assumptions conflict with an assumption underlying cultural anthropology and the work of Atran (2003a): that people's ideas and values (and thus behaviors) are largely the product of their culture. They also conflict with an assumption underlying social history and the work of Lewis (2002): that cultural clashes involving marginalized peoples and cultures are the product of deeply rooted historical developments.

Conflicting Disciplinary Theories

A third possible source of conflict between the insights under review is the theories they advance. A theory is "a generalized scholarly explanation about some aspect of the natural or human world, how it works, and why specific facts are related that are supported by data and research" (Repko, 2008, p. 352). Theory-based insights are "insights that are informed by or advance a particular theoretical perspective" (p. 255). The sources of conflict between theory-based insights fall into two categories: those produced by the same discipline, and those produced by different disciplines.

Sources of Conflict Between Theory-Based Insights Produced by the Same Discipline. Theories produced by the same discipline are likely to have far less conflict between them because, as noted earlier, they typically share the discipline's basic assumption that personality factors and psychological constructs explain suicide terrorist motivation and behavior. However, these theories conflict over the role that religion and culture play in shaping an individual's psychology. Post (1998) and Merari (1998) tend to discount both influences, whereas Bandura (1998) argues that religion plays a significant role because it is used to "cognitively restructure the moral value of killing, so that the killing can be done free from self-censuring restraints" (p. 164).

Just because experts writing from the same disciplinary perspective share the discipline's basic assumptions does not mean that differences in their theory-based approaches will be muted. Political scientists Crenshaw (1998), Rapoport (1998), and Monroe and Kreidie (1997) view Islamic fundamentalism as a political force. However, they disagree sharply over the role played by religious belief. Crenshaw (1998) explains suicide terrorist behavior in terms of "strategic reasoning" that "is modified by psychology and other constraints" and minimizes the role of religion (pp. 9–10), whereas Rapoport (1998) and Monroe and Kreidie (1997) emphasize the strong influence of religion in this reasoning.

Religion is the central focus of Rapoport's (1998) sacred terror theory as well as Monroe and Kreidie's (1997) identity theory. "Holy" or "sacred" terror, explains Rapoport (1998), is designed to "support religious purposes or terror justified in theological terms," and "is most striking in Islam among both Shia and Sunni" (p. 103). He is careful to distinguish between sacred terrorists and secular terrorists. The former draw from events in Islam's founding period, from its sacred writings, and from the commentaries on them by religious sages, especially *The Neglected Duty*, which sees jihad as the essential means for reviving Islam. The latter feel free to draw from anyone, even from non-Islamic sources. Sacred terrorists, he says, are on a mission to purify Islam from all non-Muslim influences and are willing to kill to achieve this goal (p. 129).

Sources of conflict between the three political science theories extend beyond the role of religion, however, to include the role of perception, cognition, and intrapsychic traits. These concepts, borrowed from psychology, form the core of Monroe and Kreidie's (1997) identity theory and enable it to transcend the narrow focus on politics and power typically associated with political science work on terrorism. Indeed, the theory serves as a bridge between the insights of political science and those of psychology. Moreover, by recognizing that the self is situated in a cultural context, the theory includes the important factor of culture and the equally important factor of religion. For suicide terrorists, politics is subsumed under an all-encompassing religious faith.

Sources of Conflict Between Theory-Based Insights Produced by Different Disciplines. Once the most relevant insights from the same discipline are identified and the sources of conflict between them are located, the next task is to identify the sources of conflict between insights produced by different disciplines. It is usually *easier* to *identify* conflict between disciplines because the contrast is greater, but *harder* to *mitigate* it to create common ground (because the conflicting positions have less in common). If the insights are theory based, as they are in the case of the causes of suicide terrorism, identifying the sources of conflict involves examining each theory in terms of its explanation of the problem and ferreting out its underlying assumption(s). Having examined the important psychology and political science theories and how these conflict, it remains only to evaluate the theories advanced by Atran (cultural anthropology) and Lewis (history).

Atran (2003a) rejects the notion that suicide terrorists have an "appreciable psychopathology" as Post and other psychologists claim. It is a "fundamental attribution error," he says, for people to explain this behavior in terms of individual personality traits—that is, as not rational and not deterred by rational concepts—for two reasons. First, research shows no instances of religious or political suicide terrorism stemming from "the lone actions of cowering or unstable bombers."

> Suicide terrorists exhibit no socially dysfunctional attributes (fatherless, friendless, or jobless) or suicidal symptoms. They do not vent fear of enemies or express "hopelessness" or a sense of "nothing to lose" for lack of life alternatives that would be consistent with economic rationality. (p. 1537)

Second, explaining suicide terrorist behavior in terms of individual personality traits ignores "significant situational factors in the larger society at work" as well as the root causes of terrorists' perceptions. These factors and perceptions include "a collective sense of historical injustice, political subservience, and social humiliation . . . as well as countervailing religious hope." The idea that religion must struggle to assert its control over politics is something that is radically new to Islam. In fictive kin theory, Atran finds a more plausible explanation of the "critical factor" determining suicide terrorism behavior: "loyalty to an intimate cohort of peers, which recruiting organizations often promote through religious communion" (Atran, 2003a, p. 1537).

> Through indoctrination and training and under charismatic leaders, self-contained suicide cells canalize disparate religious and political sentiments of individuals into an emotionally bonded group of fictive kin who willfully commit to die spectacularly for one another and for what is perceived as the common good of alleviating the community's onerous political and social realities. (p. 1534)

Fictive kin theory assumes that suicide terrorism should be approached as a complex cultural phenomenon that requires understanding its historical, political, social, and religious contexts.

Lewis (2002) views the problem of suicide terrorism through the lens of modernization theory. This theory explains the rise of religious fundamentalism as "an antidote to the dislocations resulting from rapid change or modernization" and a defense against threats posed by modernization to Islam's traditional identity (Hudson, 1999, p. 42). The root of Muslim rage, says Lewis (1990),

> goes beyond hostility to specific interests or actions or policies . . . and becomes a rejection of Western civilization as such, not only what it does but what it is, and the principles and values that it practices and professes. These are indeed seen as innately evil, and those who promote or accept them as "the enemies of God." (p. 48)

The phenomenon of suicide terrorism, then, is the inevitable result of Islam's failure to embrace Western institutions and values. Modernization theory also rejects the idea of religious fundamentalism as pathology. The theory shares with rational choice theory the view that unequal socioeconomic development is the basic reason for the discontent and alienation that fundamentalists experience. Caught between an Islamic culture that provides moral values and spiritual satisfaction and a modernizing and secularizing Western culture that provides access to material improvement, many Muslims find an answer to resulting anxiety, alienation, and disorientation through an absolute dedication to an Islamic way of life (Lewis, 1990, pp. 59–60).[13] Modernization theory assumes that a combination of material improvement, technological advancement, democratization, and secularization is the key to ending the cognitive collision between Western and fundamentalist worldviews. The theory also shares the basic assumption of rational choice theory that suicide attackers generally make choices and are not impulsive or "crazy."

Summary of These Theories and How Their Assumptions Conflict

Before performing integration, it is useful to summarize the sources of conflict between the relevant theories in terms of their underlying assumptions, as shown in Table 5.4.

Juxtaposing the assumptions of each theory shows that some of these assumptions are shared by more than one theory. For example, the psychology theories of terrorist psycho-logic, self-sanction, and martyrdom share the assumption typical of psychology: understanding the behavior and motivation of suicide terrorists requires studying the mental life and psychological constructs of individual terrorists. The theories of collective rational choice,

---

[13]Just how many or what proportion has huge implications for policy. The focus of this chapter, however, is on causes.

Table 5.4	Sources of Conflict Between Relevant Theories in Terms of Their Underlying Assumptions

Theory	Assumption(s) of Theory
Terrorist psycho-logic	Understanding the behavior and motivation of suicide terrorists requires studying primarily the mental life and the psychological constructs of individual terrorists.
Self-sanction	
Martyrdom	
Collective rational strategic choice	Suicide terrorists follow logical processes that can be discovered and explained. The primary focus of research should be on terrorist groups rather than on individuals.
"Sacred" terror	
Identity	Religious identity is (at least in this instance) an effective way to explain the "political" phenomenon of suicide terrorism. Terrorist behavior is essentially rational.
Fictive kin	Suicide terrorists are largely the product of identity with and loyalty to a culturally cohesive and intimate cohort of peers that recruiting organizations often promote through religious indoctrination.
Modernization	Poverty, authoritarianism, and diminishing expectations inevitably breed alienation and violence. Suicide terrorism is the inevitable result of Islam's failure to embrace Western institutions and values.

sacred terror, and identity share the assumption that suicide terrorists follow logical processes that can be discovered and explained. These theories also assume that the primary focus of study should be the behavior of terrorist groups rather than the behavior of individual terrorists. But only sacred terror theory and identity theory assume that a terrorist's religious affiliation is an effective way to explain the "political" phenomenon of suicide terrorism. Fictive kin theory assumes that the determining factor in shaping the development of a suicide terrorist is the terrorist's loyalty to an intimate cohort of peers, all of whom share an intense devotion to religious dogma. This theory shares with identity theory the assumption that religion is an important factor in understanding the development of a suicide terrorist. Finally, modernization theory rests on the assumption that suicide terrorism is the result of Islam's failure to embrace Western institutions and values.

There are two practical benefits of focusing on assumptions in this case. The first is to identify the possible sources of conflict between the theory-based insights and to reduce the number of these conflicts to as few as possible. The second is to make it easier to create common ground by working from the "bottom up" with assumptions while working from the "top down" with theories.

Creating Common Ground (Step 8)

Having identified the most relevant theory-based insights and located the sources of conflict between them, the process of creating "common ground" (Step 8) can proceed. Interdisciplinary common ground is one or more concepts and/or assumptions by which conflicting disciplinary insights, including theoretical explanations, can be reconciled and integrated (Repko, 2008, p. 272). Paying careful attention to this step will make integration possible.[14]

A good place to begin is with assumptions. As noted earlier (and summarized in Table 5.4), the assumptions underlying the various theories conflict. For example, a key assumption of self-sanction theory is that understanding the behavior and motivation of suicide terrorists requires studying *primarily* the mental life and the psychological constructs of *individual* terrorists. By contrast, the key assumption of identity theory is that understanding the behavior and motivation of suicide terrorists requires studying their cultural as well as their religious identity, but not at the expense of taking into account personality traits (inherent and acquired). However, a deeper probing of the assumptions of both theories reveals a commonality that both share, namely, the *goals* of suicide terrorists. These are not defined in terms of self-interest, as rational choice advocates would have it, but rather as "moral imperatives" or "sacred duties." This deeper assumption is also shared by the theories of fictive kin, strategic rational choice, "sacred terror," martyrdom, terrorist psycho-logic, and modernization. The common ground assumption shared by all of the theory-based insights to varying degrees, then, is that the goals of suicide terrorists are "moral" and "sacred"—and thus, rational—as defined by Islamic fundamentalism. The more comprehensive understanding should reflect this assumption.

Constructing a More Comprehensive Understanding (Step 9)

When working with theories, there are two possible approaches. The first, and preferable, approach is to piece together the "good parts" from each of the most relevant theories to form a new comprehensive theory. This approach is appropriate when each theory is deeply rooted in the discipline from which it emerges because it prevents the problem of either/or thinking—of having to choose one theory and reject the others. The second approach (and the one used here) is to add parts from several theories to extend, and thus maximize, the explanatory power of one of the selected theories. *Extension* is an integrative technique that addresses conflict between disciplinary concepts

---

[14]Creating common ground is undoubtedly the most challenging aspect of interdisciplinary work because it requires original thought that draws on close analytical reasoning and creative thinking. But it is achievable if one takes a systematic approach, pays attention to the nature of the challenge, and chooses an appropriate integrative technique.

or assumptions by extending the meaning of an idea beyond the domain of one discipline into the domain of another discipline (Newell, 2007, pp. 258–259; Repko, 2008, p. 341). The integrative technique of extension is used when one of the theories already has parts that come from more than one discipline.[15] The best practice is to use the former approach and avoid the latter, *except when one of the theories is already interdisciplinary, though imperfectly so, as in the present case.* "Already interdisciplinary" means that parts of the theory are borrowed from other disciplines. What is missing, and what theory extension provides, are one or more additional parts—that is, causal factors—from the other relevant theories that will enable it to account for all the known factors causing the problem.

One way to proceed is to identify all the causal factors and then categorize them under the fewest possible headings. The categories include (1) *personality traits* (i.e., the cognitive constructs of individual terrorists), (2) *power seeking* (i.e., power/political aspirations), (3) *cultural identity* (i.e., the perception that the culture is under threat), and (4) *sacred values* (i.e., a belief system based on religious doctrine). It so happens that these factors correspond closely to the assumptions noted earlier. The causal factor of *personality traits* refers to cognitive constructs that may predispose a person to become a suicide terrorist as well as influences on a person's mental development. These traits include "justification" (an even stronger, more compelling moral claim that overrides one's natural repugnance to engage in suicide terrorism), and strong "emotion" (triggered by traumatic memory or regret for not exacting vengeance on an enemy; Reisberg, 2006, pp. 465–470). The causal factor of *power seeking* refers to the influence of institutions, both domestic and foreign, on individuals, on particular groups, and on society as a whole. Such influence may include the policies and activities of Western corporations, UN agencies, foreign military forces, Western support of oppressive regimes, American support of Israel, and the countervailing influence of terrorist organizations such as Al-Qaeda. Each and any of these influences may trigger or exacerbate a collective or an individual sense of political oppression and/or historical loss. The causal factor of *cultural identity* refers to having a shared sense of place and identification with a race, ethnic group, history, nation, and/or religion. Cultural identity may also include emotional bonding based on a way of life, traditions, behaviors, values, and symbols. The causal factor of *sacred values* refers to a fundamentalist faith tradition that relies on sacred

---

[15]Integrative techniques are discussed by Newell (2007) and include the following: *redefinition,* which involves modifying or redefining concepts and assumptions; *extension,* which extends the meaning of an idea beyond the domain of one discipline into the domain of another discipline; *transformation,* which uses continuous variables when concepts or assumptions are not merely different (e.g., love, fear, selfishness) but opposite (e.g., rational, irrational); and *organization,* which identifies an underlying commonality in meaning of different disciplinary concepts or assumptions and redefines them accordingly and organizes the redefined concepts or assumptions to bring out a relationship among them (pp. 258–259). Applications of each technique are found in Repko (2008, pp. 280–292).

writings and charismatic leadership to determine an individual's motivations and actions. This factor includes the idea that religion must struggle to assert (or reassert) its control over every facet of life. The perspective of history is subsumed under culture, politics, and religion.

With these key causal factors broadly stated, the next task is to examine the relevant insights and their theories to see which causal factors each includes. The result of this evaluative process is shown in Table 5.5.

Table 5.5 shows that all the theories focus on at least two of the causal factors, with the exception of sacred terror, self-sanction, and identity, which attribute the causes of suicide terrorism to three factors. Rapoport's theory of "holy" or "sacred" terror explains suicide terrorism as a political problem caused by terrorist political aspirations. Even so, it takes into account how culture and religious values may motivate a person to become a suicide terrorist. But because the theory has not borrowed from psychology, it is unable to explain how a person's mind may be predisposed, susceptible to, or shaped by these complex influences and motivated to commit such a horrific act. So rather than force the theory to explain what it was not designed to explain—namely, the shaping of a person's personality and cognitive development—it is better to consider the possibilities offered by the other two.

Bandura's (1998) self-sanction theory explains how terrorist organizations convert "socialized people" into dedicated combatants by "cognitively restructuring the moral value of killing, so that the killing can be done free

Table 5.5	Theory-Based Insights Into the Causes of Suicide Terrorism, Showing Key Causal Factors			
	Key Causal Factors			
Theory of Suicide Terrorism	**Personality Traits**	**Power Seeking**	**Cultural Identity**	**Sacred Beliefs**
Terrorist psycho-logic	Yes	No	No	No
Self-sanction	No	Yes	Yes	Yes
Martyrdom	Yes	No	No	No
Collective rational strategic choice	Yes	Yes	No	No
"Sacred" terror	No	Yes	Yes	Yes
Identity	Yes, if expanded	Yes	Yes	Yes
Fictive kin	No	No	Yes	Yes
Modernization	No	Yes	Yes	Indirectly

from self-censuring restraints" (p. 164). The process of moral cognitive restructuring involves using religion, politics, and psychology to construe suicide attacks narrowly. This involves using (a) religion to justify such acts by invoking "situational imperatives," (b) the political argument of self-defense to show how the group is "fighting ruthless oppressors" who are threatening the community's "cherished values and way of life," and (c) the psychological device of dehumanization to justify killing "the enemy" (pp. 161, 174, 180–182). Though the theory does not borrow from other disciplines, it explains how cultural and political factors are integrated into the mental process of construal and inform individual decision making. One weakness of the theory is its silence concerning individual personality factors that may influence the would-be terrorist's decision-making process. But because the theory is a psychological theory, this weakness can be overcome by borrowing from other psychology theories so that it can include the influence of personality traits and dispositions.

If it were not for identity theory, the best approach would be to piece together the good parts from each of the theories to form a new comprehensive theory. However, because identity theory is already interdisciplinary (though imperfectly so), it is appropriate to extend it by adding one or more parts from the other theories so that it is inclusive of all the key causal factors. Identity theory has two primary strengths. First, it already addresses three of the four factors—cultural identity, sacred beliefs (i.e., religion), and power seeking (i.e., politics). Identity theory includes religion by showing that the Islamic fundamentalist conception of religion is, in fact, an all-encompassing ideology that erases all lines between public and private. This theology-based ideology is based on religious writings and commentaries on these writings that are viewed by its most devoted followers as sacred, inviolable, nonnegotiable, and worth dying for. As a "sacred ideology" (Marxism never achieved this lofty status), Islamic fundamentalism redefines politics and power. As Monroe and Kreidie show, politics for Islamic fundamentalists is subsumed under an all-encompassing religious faith and is sought and exercised for the purpose of extending the faith. Achieving, maintaining, and extending power is a sacred duty that has priority over all other obligations, including family. Because the theory holds that the self is culturally situated, it is able to explain how culture influences identity formation.

Second, the theory requires the least amount of "stretching and pulling" (i.e., extending) to include the fourth key factor of personality traits. This is because identity theory, as noted earlier, is based on the psychological concepts of cognition and perspective. These concepts address personality traits in a way that is inclusive of the psychology theories already examined. Monroe and Kreidie (1997) use the concept of cognition in a developmental way, meaning that they are concerned to show how persons are influenced by factors external to themselves—namely, culture and societal norms—rather than focusing on individual cognitive abnormalities, as Post does, to argue that some persons are psychologically predisposed to commit acts of suicide terrorism. Only slight "stretching" or extending is necessary to have identity theory include personality factors intrinsic to the individual suicide terrorist. Monroe and Kreidie's application of "perspective" to explain suicide terrorist behavior is also helpful in this regard because it effectively delineates the options that terrorists perceive as being available to them (p. 26). The act of committing a suicide attack in the service of a fundamentalist conception of *jihad* "emanates primarily from the person accepting their identity which means that they have to abide by the tenets of their religion" (pp. 26, 36). By borrowing these concepts from psychology, identity theory offers an understanding of human behavior that is based on the interplay of mental constructs in tandem with the exogenous variables of politics, culture, and religion.

The process of using the common ground assumption to reconcile or integrate the various discipline-based insights is straightforward and proceeds serially, beginning with the three psychology-based theories. Terrorist psycho-logic theory attributes the cause of terrorist behavior to "their special psycho-logic" that enables them to construct rationalizations for their actions that they are "psychologically compelled to commit" (Post, 1998, p. 25). According to Post, this built-in psychological compulsion simply awaits triggering by one or more external stimuli. In the case of suicide terrorism, the external stimulus is typically Islamic fundamentalism, which provides a comprehensive and compelling perception of reality and life goals that are "moral" and "sacred." Borrowing as it does from psychology, identity theory is able to explain the interplay between these innate cognitive traits and the exogenous factors of power, culture, and religion. Consequently, both theories agree that personal rationalizations determine terrorist action. They differ, however, over the reason for these rationalizations: Terrorist psycho-logic theory attributes them to innate psychological compulsions (that are at some point triggered by one or more exogenous factors); identity theory says that they result from a deep and abiding commitment to Islamist fundamentalist religious doctrine.

Self-sanction theory explains how terrorist organizations can disengage self-sanctions by cognitively restructuring the moral value of killing. This enables the individual terrorist to act free from self-censuring restraints (Bandura, 1998, p. 164). This process involves terrorist organizations using the exogenous factors of religion, politics, and psychology to enable the recruit to (1) reconstrue suicide attacks as serving moral purposes, (2) disregard or misrepresent the injurious consequences to one's victims, or (3) blame and dehumanize the victims (p. 161). Identity theory, by borrowing from psychology, is also able to explain the role that mental accounting and emotion play in terrorist motivation. The common ground shared by both theories is acknowledging that because the goals of suicide terrorists are grounded in Islamic fundamentalism, terrorists can disengage self-sanctions because they perceive their actions as "moral" and "sacred."

Martyrdom theory attributes the cause of suicide terrorism to individuals who are willing, if not eager, to die while simultaneously committing violence against others. The theory explains that these persons "wish to die for personal reasons" based on a variety of "personality factors" and circumstances such as "broken family backgrounds" (Merari, 1998, pp. 206–207). As a product of cognitive psychology, the theory takes into account exogenous factors such as the influence of culture and the indoctrination of suicide terrorists by various political and religious organizations. The theory assumes, as noted earlier, that understanding the behavior and motivation of suicide terrorists requires studying primarily the personalities of individual terrorists. This assumption is very close to that underlying identity theory: Understanding suicide terrorism requires knowing how terrorists perceive themselves and their actions. For both theories, this understanding requires close examination of how the exogenous factor of religion, primarily Islamic fundamentalism, determines terrorist goals that they perceive as "moral" and "sacred."

The common ground assumption that reconciles identity theory with the theory-based insights of psychology can also be used to integrate the theory-based insights of political science. Crenshaw's (1998) collective rational strategic choice theory explains the cause of suicide terrorism as the product of a sophisticated political strategy *whether in pursuit of secular or religious goals*. Her theory admits that there are "important questions about the preferences of the *goals* of terrorist organizations" (p. 9; emphasis added). Though she assumes that terrorist goals are primarily secular and strategic, Crenshaw leaves the door open to the possibility that there may be "varied degrees of rationality" in some cases and that the "strategic reasoning" of terrorists may be "modified by psychological and other constraints" (p. 9). "Other constraints" could very well include religious constraints. These caveats leave room in the theory for the possibility that *some* suicide terrorists pursue goals which *they* would consider to be "moral imperatives" or "sacred duties." It bears repeating that these terms are freighted with religious meaning derived from the theology of Islamic fundamentalism. The theory of collective rational choice shares with identity theory (at least to some extent) the assumption that the goals of some suicide terrorists are those which *they* consider to be "moral imperatives" or "sacred duties" according to Islamic fundamentalism.

"Sacred" terror theory focuses on the role of mental accounting, emotion, "special justifications, and precedents" used by religiously motivated terrorists. Paramount among these "special justifications" are religion and the sacred writings of select religious scholars, which are used to dispel the doubts of recruits concerning the importance of martyrdom and jihad (Rapoport, 1998, p. 122). The theory finds common ground with identity theory at two levels. At the level of theory, both argue that religion permeates all areas of the suicide terrorist's life and respects no separation between the private and the political. At the level of assumptions, both theories assume that suicide terrorists engage in a rational process of decision making, even though it is largely determined by religious dogma and values. (Rapoport, 1998, p. 107; Monroe & Kreidie, 1997, p. 41).

The common-ground assumption that the goals of suicide terrorists are "moral" and "sacred" as defined by Islamic fundamentalism can also be the basis for reconciling identity theory with fictive kin theory. The latter holds that suicide terrorists act out of a universal heartfelt human sentiment of self-sacrifice for the welfare of the group or culture (Atran, 2003b, p. 2). The theory explains how psychological and cultural relationships, rooted in rationality, are "luring and binding thousands of ordinary people into the terrorist organization's martyr-making web" (Atran, 2003a, p. 1538). However, the theory is conflicted concerning the role that religion plays in causing suicide terrorism. On the one hand, it rejects the notion that religion "or even religious-like motivation" can *by itself* explain this phenomenon; on the other, it assigns a determining role to "culture," a term that is notoriously vague and can be defined in terms of a wide range of attitudes and behaviors, some of which can certainly be attributed to the influence of religion. Given the elasticity of the term "culture," fictive kin theory can be reconciled with identity theory on the basis of what each assumes to be the role that religion plays in causing suicide terrorism: that persons who become suicide terrorists identify with and develop a deep sense of loyalty to a culturally cohesive and intimate cohort of peers based (at least in part) on adherence to religious dogma.

It is more challenging to use the common-ground assumption (that the goals of suicide terrorists are "moral" and "sacred" as defined by Islamic fundamentalism) to reconcile identity theory with modernization theory. This theory argues that the rise of suicide terrorism stems from the failure of the peoples of the Middle East to embrace Western notions of secularism, individualism, and liberal democratic capitalism. This supposed "failure" points up the powerful and persisting influence of religious, cultural, political, and historical factors that are contributing to the clash of civilizations and that are producing the downward spiral of "hate and spite, rage and self-pity, poverty and oppression" (Lewis, 2002, p. 159). The theory focuses on how religion, culture, politics (internal and external), and history are fueling a desire for retaliation against the West and against the U.S. in particular. Of the theories examined, this one is the most difficult to reconcile with identity theory because it treats Islam and Islamic fundamentalism as just another set of political values or beliefs or ideology that is squarely at odds with secular liberal democratic modes of political discourse and interaction. Perhaps the best way to proceed is to focus on the goals that both theories assume are embraced by suicide terrorists. For modernization theory, the goals of suicide terrorism should be viewed *through the lens of Western values and interests.* This shows them to be primarily secular, material, and self-serving. For identity theory, the goals of suicide terrorists should be *viewed through their own eyes,* the eyes of their fictive kin, and the eyes of their recruiting organizations. Viewing them from the "inside out" rather than from the "outside in" shows them to be "moral" and "sacred" as defined by Islamic fundamentalism.

Clearly, using the assumption concerning the goals of suicide terrorists to reconcile or integrate the various conflicting theories and their assumptions does not erase all differences. Instead, it focuses on the fundamental commonality of almost all the theories, namely, that the goals of suicide terrorists are largely determined by Islamic fundamentalism.

A Statement of the More Comprehensive Theory Itself

Having created common ground and performed causal integration, it remains to state the comprehensive theory itself. In its original form, identity theory was already interdisciplinary because parts of it came from outside political science. The theory was broad enough to include the causal factors of culture and the influence of fictive kin. Both factors are known to shape an individual's cognitive-perceptual framework. As a theory grounded in political science, identity theory included the causal factor of politics in all of its expressions at all levels (local, national, and international) and explained how it influences individual terrorists' perceptions of themselves, their goals, and their actions. The theory also included the causal factor of religion, explaining how Islamic fundamentalism provides the foundation for daily living and shapes an individual's perspective on all basic issues. And because the theory borrowed the concepts of cognition and perception from cognitive psychology, the original conception of identity theory was able to explain how a variety of external factors influenced the development of an individual's personality over time. Chief among these factors, according to Monroe and Kreidie (1997), is Islamic fundamentalism and how it attracts individuals by providing them with a basic identity and worldview. In its original form, the theory made two assumptions: that religious identity is an effective way to explain the political phenomenon of suicide terrorism; and that terrorist behavior is essentially rational, in the sense that individuals make choices within the confines of their fundamentalist identity.

Though interdisciplinary, identity theory was *narrowly* so because it excluded the insights of Post (1998) and Lewis (2002). As noted earlier, Post's terrorist psycho-logic theory explained how some terrorists are possibly born with a predisposition to commit acts of violence, awaiting only some triggering event to cause them to commit horrific acts. Lewis's conception of modernization theory explained that suicide terrorism may well be a rational reaction against modernity (i.e., referring to Western secular culture and material dominance) and even be, in some cases, a pathological retreat from this prevailing reality. Both insights can be accommodated, however, by modifying these assumptions to include the psychological concept of "varying degrees of rationality."

The way to do this is to extend the definition of rationality so that it includes factors (such as religious belief in an afterlife) normally excluded from discussions of rationality. Instead of accepting normal either/or thinking that treats rational thought and religious belief as completely separate, the interdisciplinarian is able to engage in both/and thinking, which is a recognized feature of interdisciplinary integration. Once extended, the definition of rationality permits the inclusion of the factors that Post and Lewis examine.

The comprehensive statement of identity theory, then, may be stated as follows: Suicide terrorism is caused by a complex interaction of variables that are both endogenous and exogenous to the individual. Endogenous variables include psychological predispositions and cognitive constructs developed over time; exogenous variables include the combined influences of culture, politics, and religion, with Islamic fundamentalism providing the perceptual framework that determines an individual's identity, motivation, and behavior. Suicide terrorists manifest varying degrees of rationality in pursuing goals that they consider "moral" and "sacred" according to a theologically based cost/benefit calculus.

Lessons for Interdisciplinary Practice

The foregoing analysis has, I hope, demonstrated the utility of first establishing common ground before attempting to integrate theoretical explanations of the phenomenon. The strategy used here was to work up from assumptions (i.e., creating common ground) and down from theories (i.e., constructing the more comprehensive understanding). In the case of the causes of suicide terrorism, one of two approaches could be used: the perspectival approach that focuses primarily on integration when different disciplines provide conflicting insights, and the classification approach that uses the strategy of integrating insights along different causal links. Until someone applies the latter approach to the same problem and the same set of theory-based insights, it is impossible to determine which approach yields the better results. Meanwhile, it is hoped that the scope of understanding of this problem is extended by the approach used here.

The focus of analysis has been on certain defining elements of the most relevant disciplines, specifically theories (both disciplinary and interdisciplinary) and their assumptions. What is striking about the theoretical explanations examined here is that the writers typically fail to critically analyze competing theories and their assumptions and, consequently, other methods of approaching the problem offered by experts from other disciplines. Consequently, it falls to the interdisciplinarian to identify the strengths and weaknesses of these theoretical explanations, evaluate them, and assume the responsibility for performing integration and constructing a more comprehensive understanding. It bears emphasizing that creating common ground is a critical step in the integrative process.

The analysis has also shown that research on problems centered on human activity needs to include endogenous factors from inside the individual as well as exogenous factors from outside the individual. In the present case, linkages need to be examined between these two sets of factors (as well as linkages between clusters of external variables), and ways need to be found to measure their relative influence on terrorist activity.

The Final Step (Step 10)

Integration is often seen as the ultimate goal of the interdisciplinary enterprise, but an instrumentalist understanding of interdisciplinarity argues that the ultimate goal should be the ability to test or assess the understanding and communicate it to appropriate audiences. To be interdisciplinary, the understanding must integrate the conflicting theories and thereby produce a "cognitive advancement"—that is, an understanding that is new and more comprehensive. "More comprehensive" means that the understanding would not be possible using single disciplinary approaches. "Cognitive advancement" may include explaining the phenomenon, proposing a solution to the problem, or raising a new research question. As well, the interdisciplinary understanding is the product of, but distinct from, the various disciplinary insights into the problem (Boix-Mansilla, 2005, p. 16).

One way to test the new understanding is to use it as a benchmark against which to evaluate current policy. Though it is beyond the scope of this chapter to propose a new policy approach that draws on the full implications of the new understanding, it is appropriate to make two observations. The first concerns the reluctance of many disciplinary experts to take the reality of religion and the power of theology seriously. Of the theory-based insights examined, only Monroe and Kreidie's (1997) religious identity theory and Rapoport's (1998) sacred terror theory fully acknowledge the centrality of religion in the lives of suicide terrorists and the vast majority of the peoples of the Muslim world. This failure has contributed in no small measure to America's tragic approach to nation-building in Iraq and to the conduct of the War on Terrorism.

For this reason, Islamic fundamentalism should not be dealt with simply as another set of political values that can be compromised or negotiated, or even as a system of beliefs or ideology—such as socialism or communism—in which traditional liberal democratic modes of political discourse and interaction are recognized. Rather, the foregoing analysis suggests that the first step toward coexistence and peace with this strident branch of Islam calls for Western policy makers to develop the capacity to view the world as they see it.

Conclusion

It is useful to conclude by briefly reviewing the key theoretical arguments and benefits of using an interdisciplinary approach to the problem:

- Producing an interdisciplinary understanding of the causes of suicide terrorism is clearly not possible without the foundational work produced by experts from different disciplines. Rather than taking a reductionist approach whose purpose is to push into the background, mute, or even ignore the multifaceted and cross-disciplinary character of the problem, the interdisciplinary approach and resultant understanding accepts the fact that the problem is complex and beyond the ability of any single discipline to understand comprehensively.

- Identifying the most relevant theory-based insights and locating the sources of conflict between them (Step 7) is a defining characteristic of the interdisciplinary research process and one way that it differs from disciplinary or multidisciplinary approaches. The latter approach merely juxtaposes disciplinary insights but omits the hard work of ferreting out the sources of conflict, let alone attempting integration. It is left to the interdisciplinarian to perform this essential task. This work often reveals gaps in expert understanding as well as the extent to which certain theories (such as rational choice theory) and their assumptions color expert understanding of the problem.

- Creating common ground between conflicting theory-based insights is critical to the integrative process. Without it, producing an interdisciplinary understanding would be impossible to achieve. In the present study, the resultant common ground assumption bridged the differing explanatory theories and enabled me to produce an understanding that is more comprehensive than any single disciplinary explanation.

- The integrative process revealed that the disciplines tend to view suicide terrorism through the lens of a Western and secular conception of rationality. Western policy makers tend to dismiss suicide terrorists as irrational actors when they do not act in accordance with cost/benefit models such as rational choice theory or utility theory. However, reason-based choice theory, for example, claims that we make decisions only when we see compelling reasons for that decision. Therefore "*any reason* that influences our thinking in general (our ability to make judgments, our ability to reason) should have a direct impact on decision making" (Reisberg, 2006, p. 464). "Any reason" includes religious-based reasons and those based on deeply held sacred values. For this theory, identity theory, and sacred terror theory, the only justification for an immoral action such as suicide terrorism is an even stronger, more compelling moral claim based on religious values (p. 470).

In many instances, it is religious *experience* far more than detached appraisal that plays a pivotal role in terrorist decision making. On this basis, secular cost/benefit models are too narrow as descriptive theories of how people actually make decisions, especially the decision to become a suicide terrorist.

References

Atran, S. (2003a, March 7). Genesis of suicide terrorism. *Science, 299,* 1534–1539.

Atran, S. (2003b, July 8). *Islam and rationality.* Retrieved August 14, 2006, from http://interdisciplines.org/terrorism/papers/1/14/printable/discussions/view/782

Atran, S. (2003c, March 7). Suicide bombers made, not born: Scientist. *News in Science.* Retrieved November 20, 2008, from http://www.abc.net.au/cgibin/common/printfriendly.pl?/science/news/stories/s801530.htm

Atran, S. (2006). The moral logic and growth of suicide terrorism. *The Washington Quarterly, 29*(2), 127–147.

Atran, S. (2008). *The religious politics of fictive kinship.* Retrieved November 20, 2008, from http://edge.org/q2008/q08_9.html#atran

Bandura, A. (1998). Mechanism of moral disengagement. In W. Reich (Ed.), *Origins of terrorism: Psychologies, ideologies, theologies, states of mind* (pp. 161–191). Washington, DC: Woodrow Wilson Center Press.

Boix-Mansilla, V. (2005, January/February). Assessing student work at disciplinary crossroads. *Change, 37,* 14–21.

Crenshaw, M. (1998). The logic of terrorism: Terrorist behavior as a product of strategic choice. In W. Reich (Ed.), *Origins of terrorism: Psychologies, ideologies, theologies, states of mind* (pp. 7–24). Washington, DC: Woodrow Wilson Center Press.

Cronin, A. K. (2003). *Terrorists and suicide attacks.* Washington, DC: Library of Congress, Congressional Research Service.

Green, S. L. (2002). *Rational choice theory: An overview.* Paper prepared for the Baylor University Faculty Development Seminar on Rational Choice Theory. Retrieved January 15, 2009, from business.baylor.edu/steve_green/green1.doc

Hoffman, B. (2006). *Inside terrorism.* New York: Columbia University Press.

Hronick, M. S. (2006, July). Analyzing terror: Researchers study the perpetrators and the effects of suicide terrorism. *National Institute of Justice Journal, 254,* 1–5.

Hudson, R. A. (1999). *The sociology and psychology of terrorism: Who becomes a terrorist and why?* Washington, DC: Library of Congress.

Klein, J. T. (2005). *Humanities, culture, and interdisciplinarity: The changing American academy.* Albany: State University of New York Press.

Lewis, B. (1990, September). The roots of Muslim rage. *The Atlantic Monthly,* 47–60.

Lewis, B. (2002, January). What went wrong? *The Atlantic Monthly, 289,* 1. Retrieved July 25, 2002, from http://www.theatlantic.com/doc/200201/lewis

Merari, A. (1998). The readiness to kill and die: Suicidal terrorism in the Middle East. In W. Reich (Ed.), *Origins of terrorism: Psychologies, ideologies, theologies, states of mind* (pp. 192–210). Washington, DC: Woodrow Wilson Center Press.

Merari, A. (2007). Psychological aspects of suicide terrorism. In B. Bongar, L. M. Brown, L. E. Beutler, J. N. Breckenridge, & P. G. Zimbardo (Eds.), *Psychology of terrorism* (pp. 101–115). New York: Oxford University Press.

Monroe, K. R., & Kreidie, L. H. (1997). The perspective of Islamic fundamentalisms and the limits of rational choice theory. *Political Psychology, 18*(1), 19–43.

Newell, W. H. (1992). Academic disciplines and undergraduate interdisciplinary education: Lessons from the school of interdisciplinary studies at Miami University, Ohio. *European Journal of Education, 27*(3), 211–221.

Newell, W. H. (2007). Decision making in interdisciplinary studies. In G. Morçöl (Ed.), *Handbook of decision making* (pp. 245–264). New York: Marcel-Dekker.

Pitchford, I. (2003, July 3). *Genesis and future of suicide terrorism.* Retrieved August 14, 2006, from http://interdiciplines.org/terrorism/papers

Post, J. M. (1998). Terrorist psycho-logic: Terrorist behavior as a product of psychological forces. In W. Reich (Ed.), *Origins of terrorism: Psychologies, ideologies, theologies, states of mind* (pp. 25–40). Washington, DC: Woodrow Wilson Center Press.

Rapoport, D. C. (1998). Sacred terror: A contemporary example from Islam. In W. Reich (Ed.), *Origins of terrorism: Psychologies, ideologies, theologies, states of mind* (pp. 103–130). Washington, DC: Woodrow Wilson Center Press.

Reich, W. (1998). Introduction. In W. Reich (Ed.), *Origins of terrorism: Psychologies, ideologies, theologies, states of mind* (pp. 1–4). Washington, DC: Woodrow Wilson Center Press.

Reisberg, D. (2006). *Cognition: Exploring the science of the mind.* New York: W.W. Norton & Company.

Repko, A. F. (2008). *Interdisciplinary research: Process and theory.* Thousand Oaks, CA: Sage.

Szostak, R. (2004). *Classifying science: Phenomena, data, theory, method, practice.* Dordrecht: Springer.

Wadsworth/Thomson Learning. (Ed.). (2004). *Terrorism: An interdisciplinary perspective* (3rd ed.). Belmont, CA: Wadsworth/Thomson Learning.

Wolfe, C., & Haynes, C. (2003). Interdisciplinary writing assignment profiles. *Issues in Integrative Studies, 21,* 126–169.

6

An Interdisciplinary Analysis of the Causes of Economic Growth

Rick Szostak

Introduction

With billions of people still living in poverty in the world, there is perhaps no more important question in human science than what are the causes of economic growth. Moreover, it is a very complex question, for economic growth is influenced by interactions among a host of economic, political, social, cultural, and geographical phenomena. This chapter discusses how a process for interdisciplinary research can usefully be applied to the study of economic growth. It is thus simultaneously an exploration of how to do interdisciplinary social science and how to develop a more comprehensive understanding of economic growth. It shows how a variety of distinct research programs across all social science disciplines can be integrated to enhance our understanding of the causes of economic growth.

This chapter is organized according to the steps in the interdisciplinary process.[1] Although the chapter will review each of the various steps ideally involved in interdisciplinary analysis, the presentation focuses primarily on

---

AUTHOR'S NOTE: My chapter summarizes and comments upon my book *The Causes of Economic Growth: Interdisciplinary Perspectives* (Szostak, Rick, 2009, Berlin: Springer).

[1]This chapter draws on Szostak (2009). That book is organized according to the 12 steps identified in Szostak (2002). In this chapter, they are combined into four sets of steps. My process is broadly similar to that in Repko (2008), though I tend to stress the identification of relevant phenomena, theories, and methods more than Repko, and I also rely more than Repko on classifications of phenomena, theories, and methods in evaluating disciplinary insights. Yet these are differences in emphasis only; Repko and I concur regarding the broad outlines of the research process. In the book, I address the question of whether growth is "good." For rich countries especially, I urge the definition and measurement of growth in terms of output per hours worked (and thus growth might just mean more leisure time) and with due regard to environmental repercussions. I also stress that only some goods and services add to human well-being.

how "common ground" can be achieved among disciplinary insights that conflict, notably with respect to the role of government, the role of international trade relationships, and the process by which economic institutions are and should be developed. Lessons are drawn for each step regarding both our understanding of economic growth and how best to perform interdisciplinary research.

The question addressed in this chapter is both very complicated and very broad. Both characteristics increase the difficulty of performing any of the steps as completely as one might like (though perhaps especially the literature survey). The question is complicated because a variety of phenomena combine to influence economic growth. By asking the question at the general level rather than with respect to a particular time and place, we broaden the scope of inquiry significantly: We could forget about questions of basic property rights if we focused on only the rich world, for example. That is, the breadth of the question forces us to engage its full complexity. We thus need a broader literature survey, and we need to identify, evaluate, and integrate across a much broader set of disciplinary insights than would normally be the case. One possible exception may be the first step: It may be just as easy to frame a broad question as a narrow one. Indeed, it may be easier, for the narrow question requires detailed definition of the boundaries of the question.

Identify an Interdisciplinary Research Question _____

We have selected our question: What are the causes of economic growth? It is then necessary to ask whether this question is suitably interdisciplinary in nature. Can economic growth be understood by relying only on the insights of one discipline? Or does our understanding increase markedly if insights from many disciplines are integrated? Economic growth must, in the first instance, involve an increase in the resources devoted to production—broadly, labor, capital, and natural resources (including land itself)—and/or the productivity with which these resources are combined to produce output. These four variables—labor, capital, natural resources, and productivity—are commonly termed the *proximate* causes of growth, and economists (and economic historians, who are treated as a separate discipline here) dominate the study of the question of which of these is most important in driving particular episodes of economic growth. As we shall see, economists are far from achieving consensus on this basic question. Moreover, economists have long appreciated that this question then invites a more complicated set of questions, such as the following:

- Why is labor more skilled in some countries than in others?
- Why is there more (saving and) investment in some countries than in others?
- Why do some countries use resources more productively than do others?
- Why is productivity higher in some countries than in others?

These questions tend naturally to invite interdisciplinary speculation. How does a society's culture or social structure or politics influence its educational attainment, work effort, saving rate, or environmental policy? The study of these deeper causal influences is pursued across the human sciences (see below).

Special mention should be made here of *institutions* and *technology*. The formal rules of a society—its legal system, economic regulations, firm structure, and so on—have a profound influence on its economic performance, and yet such institutions arguably (see below) emerge from a historical process involving political, social, and cultural influences. Likewise, technological innovation is an important source of (at least modern) economic growth, and again, it seems likely that the rate of innovation in a society may well be influenced by a host of non-economic factors.

Even the statistical analyses of economists point toward interdisciplinary analysis. Political, institutional, and social variables are often found to be important in cross-country analyses of postwar growth experience (Snowdon, 2002, pp. 97–99)—and this despite the twin facts that such variables are often hard to measure and likely exert their effects over a very long time. Surveying this evidence and the widely divergent growth experiences of postwar economies more generally, Snowdon concludes:

> To understand why some countries have performed so much better than others with respect to growth it is therefore necessary to go beyond the proximate causes of growth and delve into the wider fundamental determinants. This implies that we cannot hope to find the magic bullet by economic analysis alone. (p. 100)

The observation that it is crucial to look beyond proximate causes provides an important insight regarding interdisciplinary research more generally. Economists have, until recently, been able to view the causes of economic growth as a strictly disciplinary question by looking only at the interaction of a handful of economic variables. Interdisciplinarians need to be sensitive to the precise wording of their focus question (and be prepared to revise it as they perform later steps), in order to ensure that relevant disciplines are not arbitrarily excluded from examination. Even though we are striving to explain movements in an economic variable, our question becomes interdisciplinary once we embrace a wide range of potential causes.

Identifying Relevant Phenomena, Theories, Methods, and Disciplines

The next step or steps must involve the gathering of relevant disciplinary insights. How does the researcher know where to look? There are two complementary strategies identified in Repko (2008). One is to reflect on the character of different disciplines and identify those that are likely to have something to say about the issue of concern. The second—and the one pursued in this chapter—is to ask what phenomena, theories, or methods are implicated, and then ask which disciplines study each phenomenon identified and/or apply each theory or method. This approach reduces the risk of favoring the larger and most familiar disciplines (Szostak, 2002). Szostak (2004) develops exhaustive classifications of phenomena, theory types, and methods to facilitate the latter approach: In the absence of these, it is all too easy to assume that the subset of relevant theory, method, or phenomena pursued by disciplines is somehow appropriate. Repko (2008) identifies the defining elements of disciplines in terms of these and other classifications. One challenge the interdisciplinary researcher will face is that library catalogues are organized by disciplines, and different terminology is used in different disciplines to refer to the same phenomenon, theory, or method (Szostak [2007, 2008] addresses how a classification suited to interdisciplinarity might be developed).

In the case of growth, it is embarrassingly easy to identify phenomena that, at least potentially, influence growth but lie outside the (at least until recently) narrow gaze of economists. These include cultural attitudes, political institutions, geographic constraints, and ethnic tensions, among others. It is thus straightforward to implicate (parts of) all social science disciplines as well as the humanities in this study.

As for types of theories, economists rely almost exclusively on methodological individualism: Only individuals are causal agents. Yet, surely the alternatives of relationship or group agency[2] matter for at least some of the proximate causes of growth. Historians have long since abandoned the idea of the heroic innovator working in isolation in favor of an appreciation of the networks in which innovators operate; the same logic applies to entrepreneurship and trade more generally, and surely institutional change cannot be fully appreciated without recourse to relationships and groups.

Economists also stress rational decision making. Yet, the history of institutional change suggests that rationality likely plays some role in institutional design—agents consciously design institutional improvements—but also that tradition does—agents are cautious in moving away from existing institutions. Historians of both science and technology have long appreciated that a

---

[2]These are the three possible types of "intentional agency" or "nonintentional agency" identified in Szostak (2004). They together form one of the five dimensions in the typology of theory cited in Repko (2008, pp. 198–200). Others are addressed below. Durkheim had distinguished sociology from economics and psychology by emphasis on methodological holism. "Methodological holism in sociology has been an obstacle to acceptance of the choice-theoretic approach underlying the new institutional paradigm"—it has isolated sociology from changes in other social sciences (Nee, 1998, p. 11). But while this approach has dominated, many analyses, from Tocqueville and Weber to today, have emphasized "rational action bounded by institutions" (p. 4). Rather than debate individualism versus holism, "a more constructive approach is to model the reciprocal interaction between purposive action and social structure" (p. 5). In other words, these approaches can be integrated.

mix of reason and intuition is involved: The investigator consciously gathers relevant information, but insight comes subconsciously as novel connections are drawn. Moreover, in a world awash in information, who can doubt that economic agents often follow decision-making rules ("Buy when the market is rising") rather than attempt rational calculations? Perhaps most important, both investment and innovation decisions must be made under uncertainty—people simply cannot know the likelihood of particular outcomes—and people cannot fully rely on rational decision making when faced with uncertainty (as economic theory admits), but necessarily follow hunches or decision rules or mimic others. Various sorts of nonrational decision making have long been studied outside economics, especially in sociology. Psychologists have long argued for different types of decision making; brain imaging shows that different parts of the brain are activated at different times and make decisions in different ways (Cohen, 2005).

Economists model growth solely in terms of steady-state (constant) growth rates. Yet, growth occurred in the West much more rapidly in the 19th century than ever before and more rapidly in the first postwar decades than before or since. In both the 19th and 20th centuries, one can discern multiple periods of a decade or so in length in which growth was relatively slow (by the standards of those centuries) or negative. The growth experience of other regions of the world is even more diverse. These diverse experiences suggest that theories with either cyclical or stochastic elements—allowing growth rates to both rise and fall—should be important. The fact that growth rates are, at least potentially, much higher than a mere two centuries ago (or alternatively, common prognostications that growth will soon decline) suggests that theories positing dynamic change in one direction may also have a role to play.

Various theories more commonly employed outside rather than within economics are thus important in understanding economic growth (though each of these has its own limitations). Alternative theories worth exploring include the following:

- Evolutionary theory can potentially embrace all types of agency, decision making, and time path.
- Systems theories (or structuralism/functionalism more generally) can also reflect a variety of types of agency and decision making. In practice, systems theorists have tended to emphasize system stability (equilibrium) and thus have had less to say than they might about dynamic processes of change.
- Social constructionist theories stress the importance of attitudes and beliefs. This provides a useful complement to the focus of most social science theory on actions, though social constructivists often see their theories as substitute rather than complement.
- Modernization theories in the early postwar period posited that all countries would move toward "Western" economic, political, and cultural realizations. These gave way to more pessimistic dependency and

world systems theories (inspired in part by Marxian analysis) that suggested that poor countries would remain poor. These theories can each be valued for detailing possible links among economic, political, cultural, and other phenomena without adopting their assumptions about the inevitable outcome of these systems of interaction.

- Complexity theories can generate all types of time path. They are perhaps particularly valuable in stressing stochastic outcomes. Complexity theories often emphasize system-level emergent properties at the expense of careful specification of individual causal links.
- Various theories stress how culture shapes behavior. These theories are often characterized by vague terminology and fail to appreciate how cultures evolve.
- Psychological theories support the insight that decision making is not always rational, but these theories have not often been carefully applied to economic decisions. (The emerging field of behavioral economics aspires to change this.)
- Literary theory may also be useful. In studying technological diffusion, scholars have long appreciated that people, not just blueprints, generally have to move from one locale to another. There is a range of tacit knowledge that is imperfectly captured by the most careful instructions. This observation is the same as that long made by theories of texts in general: There is always a divergence between the textual signifier and that which it is presumed to signify.

A similar analysis could be performed with respect to research method. One of the key insights of Szostak (2004) was that each method is better at investigating some theory types than others, and disciplines thus choose mutually compatible sets of theory and method (and phenomena). Various case study methods—observation, textual analysis, interviews—are better suited to the investigation of many of the theories listed above than are the statistical analyses favored by economists. Moreover, different methods shed different light on different theories: We should have the greatest confidence in a theory that is supported by different methods. When examining a complex historical process such as economic growth, which involves many causal interactions, recourse to multiple methods is particularly important.

There are four criteria for identifying a causal relationship: establishing correlation, establishing temporality (the cause should generally appear before the effect), ruling out alternative explanations of the result, and showing how the causal relationship unfolds in practice (including identifying intermediate variables; Singleton & Strait, 1999). The methods of economists excel with respect to the first two. Their lack of attention to alternative theories limits the third. With respect to the fourth, economists are often attracted to mathematical models even when the evidence for particular causal relationships is quite limited. The latest type of economic growth models—called unified growth models—attempts to model the course of economic performance over the last *millennium*. These models posit that small changes (in the first models, changes in population density, but later models treat other variables) eventually surpass some threshold where they begin to have dynamic effects on growth. But of course, one can develop mathematical models such that any cause can have any effect, if one assumes that small changes achieve big results. The creation of these models should not enhance one's confidence in such a relationship in the absence of careful case study evidence.

Disciplinary perspectives will be treated briefly here. As both Szostak (2003) and Repko (2008) have stressed, preferences with respect to theory and method and phenomena are critical components of disciplinary perspective. Ideological, ethical, and epistemological predispositions need also to be appreciated in evaluating disciplinary insights. In these latter respects, the following can be noted:

- On average, economists believe in markets more than other social scientists do. Although economic theory suggests a variety of market imperfections that may arise, the average economist may, nevertheless, tend to downplay the role of governments in the process of economic growth. In turn, other disciplines may underestimate the role of markets in fostering growth.
- Economists are generally consequentialist in ethical orientation, while other disciplines place greater emphasis on tradition, virtue, or intuition. Economists in particular tend to think that economic growth is good, while scholars in other disciplines are more likely to critique at least some elements of growth. Although questions regarding the desirability of growth can be distinguished from questions about causes, thoughts about one naturally influence thoughts about the other.
- Economists tend to be realists and assume that scholars can obtain reasonably accurate understandings of a fixed external reality. Other disciplines, especially in the humanities, cast a useful, if often exaggerated, skepticism on the possibility of human understanding. They thus encourage scholars to be more careful in both their theorizing and policy advice. In particular, these other disciplines are suspicious of broad generalizations and encourage careful context-dependent research.

The preceding analysis has illustrated the following points regarding these steps in interdisciplinary analysis:

- Interdisciplinarians should be careful of curtailing the scope of their research unwittingly by following major currents in the existing literature. In the case of economic growth, which other disciplines have rarely stressed as a topic, it is particularly likely that scholars may produce valuable insights that are relatively unheralded within their own discipline.

- Nevertheless, interdisciplinarians can usefully focus on particular disciplinary subfields. The danger of missing relevant literature will be reduced if they also reflect on what theories and methods might be relevant to the issue at hand.
- Interdisciplinarians must evaluate disciplinary insights in the context of disciplinary perspective and with attention to the (complementary) strengths and weaknesses of different theory types and methods.

Evaluating Disciplinary Insights

The interdisciplinary researcher must next evaluate the disciplinary insights generated by the relevant theories and methods. This is an exercise in critical thinking. Interdisciplinarians must know how to distinguish argument from assertion and assumption from evidence. In addition to standard strategies for the critical analysis of any text, interdisciplinary analysis suggests several important strategies for critique:

- In what ways might a particular disciplinary insight be shaped by the particular "perspective" of that discipline?
- More concretely, how might the insight be altered if the researcher(s) had examined a wider set of phenomena?
- Likewise, what are the strengths and weaknesses of the theories and methods used by the discipline, and how might the insight in question be shaped by these?
- Do the insights of one discipline point to possible weaknesses in the insights of another? Insights from outside the academy can also be quite useful here.

The analysis of the causes of economic growth provides examples of each of these evaluative strategies. As we have seen, economists are likely to stress the role of individuals and rationality and may thus overlook the actions of groups and/or various types of nonrational behavior. Economists have focused on a narrow set of economic variables while downplaying the importance of, for example, culture. Economists stress equilibrium or steady-state outcomes in their modeling exercises (in large part because this makes the math more tractable, but also because of the emphasis of economists' general equilibrium theory on system stability); in the real world, of course, growth has never been steady. Economic historians, sociologists, and political scientists often stress that different countries have differing experiences of economic growth; this provides a useful counterpoint to the economist tendency to identify central tendencies.

The interdisciplinarian can be heartened by the observation that other disciplines avoid at least some of these biases in economic analysis. Yet, the interdisciplinarian should never forget that all disciplines have limiting perspectives:

- The other social sciences have long stressed group or relationship agency (or viewed individuals as constrained to act in a certain way by culture or institutions), without detailing how these constraints emerge. In sociology, this approach has, in recent decades, been supplemented by individual-level analysis, but syntheses of these approaches are rare. The interdisciplinarian must be prepared to integrate insights that have rarely been juxtaposed in the past.

- Various sorts of nonrational behavior have been investigated in sociology and other social sciences. As in economics, particular types of decision making are often assumed rather than established empirically. The interdisciplinarian must thus be prepared to reflect on what sorts of decision making motivate people in particular situations. This task is made more difficult by the fact that these are often mixed in practice: An investor may only act if gut instinct, rational calculation, and the actions of others all point in the same direction. The analyses of many social scientists present a further challenge: They celebrate the "irrationality" of certain behaviors without carefully identifying what sort of nonrational decision making is at work.

- The social sciences (including psychology) collectively employ each of the dozen methods utilized in the scholarly enterprise. Yet, each of these is applied to only a subset of appropriate questions. The interdisciplinarian, aware of the biases of one method, may look in vain for the application of alternative methods to particular questions. For the present inquiry, this problem—of difficulty in identifying work that applies different methods to the same question—is exacerbated by the fact that scholars in other disciplines have rarely addressed economic growth itself.

- Other social sciences often assume processes involving sustained change in particular directions, just as economists assume equilibrium outcomes. The important possibility of stochastic (unpredictable) outcomes is much less commonly explored. The growth process likely entails elements of each. Investment decisions at times seem to follow herd behavior and at times seem inexplicable, and yet there is an amazing stability (lack of volatility) in average rates of return over time. As with types of decision making, the interdisciplinarian generally has recourse to few previous attempts to integrate insights reflecting these different perspectives.

- Political scientists and sociologists often assume the superiority of governments over markets. Only a minority of scholars in any discipline carefully compares the advantages of one or the other for particular types of decisions (e.g., identifying the reasons why science is publicly funded but technology is largely left to markets and the potential difficulties with each approach), and only a minority appreciates that the ideal balance likely varies across time and place.

The lesson for interdisciplinary practice here is that the evaluative step should not be conflated with the next step of finding common ground (even if, in presentational terms, it proves useful in this chapter to discuss evaluation while outlining common ground). That is, disciplinary insights should not just be critiqued when they conflict. The mere fact that different disciplines have asked different questions, and thus often not directly disagreed with each other, should not render the interdisciplinarian sanguine about these disciplinary insights. Interdisciplinarians can thus suggest useful clarifications or extensions to theories even in the absence of a direct contrast among disciplinary insights.

Creating Common Ground

The almost-final step(s) involve finding some "common ground" that integrates (elements of) various disciplinary insights. The role of creativity, intuition, and inspiration may loom large here. However, certain straightforward techniques can be applied to find common ground:

- One can first ask to what extent seeming differences in disciplinary perspective are apparent rather than real: Differences in terminology may mean that different disciplines are not actually talking about the same causal process even when they appear to be. The interdisciplinarian can often redefine concepts or extend a concept from one discipline to the subject matter of another.
- When concepts conflict, they can often be placed on a continuum: The tendency of economists to stress rationality and of sociologists to stress irrationality can be handled by evaluating the degree of rationality that individuals may display in a certain situation (Newell, 2007).
- One can then ask whether remaining differences can be overcome by small alterations in disciplinary assumptions.
- The easiest path to creating common ground involves relaxing the assumption made by each discipline that only its phenomena matter: Economists try to explain growth by focusing on a handful of economic variables, while sociologists stress matters of culture and social structure (happily, these attitudes are starting to change). In this simplest situation, the insights of different disciplines can often be added together: Innovators may respond both to the economic incentives stressed by economists and the cultural values emphasized by sociologists. Different disciplines are highlighting different aspects of the question under investigation, but they are assuming other aspects do not exist. Of course, integration is still required in order to identify how these different causes interact in different circumstances.

- When different disciplines reach different conclusions regarding the same phenomena, the problem is often one of excessive generalization, and it can thus be solved by more carefully expressing the range of applicability of the theories involved.

Examples of each technique can be readily provided. Economists use the word "investment" quite differently from business scholars, for example: To economists, it means the actual production of buildings or equipment that are then used in the production of other goods or services. Business scholars are likely to include any effort to make a profit, such as speculation in various markets, in the term investment. Economists have ignored certain things such as the influence of culture, the importance of networks, and the uneven path of technological innovation. At times, the insights of other disciplines in these areas can simply be added to the insights of economists—after each has been carefully evaluated in turn. Economists often assume that a particular institution is optimal, while sociologists and political scientists show that institutions operate in a complex web of social interactions: The different traditions can together strive to identify how well different institutions serve economic growth in different contexts.

Rather than organizing this section in terms of the type of integration pursued, it will be more useful to organize it by topic. Common ground will be found along a variety of different causal links generating economic growth. Within each topic, though, care should and will be taken to identify the integrative strategies utilized.

This approach—examining different causal links in turn (but not losing sight of emergent properties of systems)—is different enough from the standard practice in economics of formally modeling several links at a time that it deserves some comment. There are difficulties in applying the methodology of models to open systems—ones which are clearly linked causally (as the economy surely is) to phenomena outside the model. Although these problems do not destroy the model-building exercise, it is nevertheless true that such models rely on an unrealistic assumption that the relationships observed in a system can remain fixed through time. Notably, complexity theory takes a different approach, allowing different causal forces to operate along different links, and does not assume any particular organizing principle (such as equilibrium) at the outset.

It should also be noted that this emphasis on causal links is not common to all efforts to identify best-practice processes of interdisciplinary analysis. Interdisciplinarians often stress the importance of emergent properties (e.g., Bammer, 2005). It is argued here that the two approaches are complementary and thus best pursued in tandem. This strategy accords well with the general inclination toward integration by interdisciplinarians. As well, interdisciplinarians have often said vaguely that there are different "facets" to complex problems. The emphasis here on causal links provides a means of clarifying what might be meant by the vague term "facet." Since different causal links tend often to be the focus of different disciplines, the strategy of placing diverse causal links within an overarching structure can be a powerful technique for interdisciplinary analysis. The causal link approach helps us identify when different disciplines are, in fact, speaking about the same thing, and thus it sets the stage for integrating disciplinary insights link by link.[3]

The Proximate Causes Themselves

Economists have devoted an enormous amount of effort to "growth accounting" over the past decades. These empirical exercises attempt to identify the relative importance of the proximate causes of growth: How much is due to investment as opposed to innovation, for example? These exercises have been valuable: In particular, economists in the 1960s were shocked by the fact that investment in physical capital accounted for only about a third of economic growth over the previous century—and they were guided to pay more attention to education and innovation as a result. Yet, these exercises rely on a rarely voiced assumption: The effect on growth found for each proximate cause in one study should at least be a central tendency for all economies at all times. This assumption is dangerous: Easterly (2002), an applied economist, describes how the World Bank was led to a number of naïve policies over the years as a result, such as calculating the "required investment" needed for certain target rates of growth and channeling those sums into countries ill-prepared to utilize them productively.

Historians and economic historians have stressed the particularities of different cases. Economic historians have long hypothesized that different generations of industrializers faced different challenges, and thus that they necessarily developed in different ways (The classic argument was that of Gerschenkron [1962] ; see Sylla & Toniolo [1991] for an update). The same concern has been voiced, albeit using quite different theories, by dependency and world systems theorists in sociology and other social sciences. But these scholars did not (to my knowledge) directly address the assumptions of growth accounting, and thus it remains for the interdisciplinarian to make the connection.

The assumption has a corollary: The proximate causes act independently. The main reason that the World Bank strategy failed was that the return on investment in a country depends on many things: levels of education, infrastructure, technology, and so on. Complicated relationships among such supposedly independent variables are hard to capture within standard statistical procedures. That is, it is easy to estimate how investment affects growth and education affects growth, but it is harder to establish how they combine to do

---

[3]Some scholars would worry about the number of distinct causal links that would need to be investigated in any complex study. We can hardly hope, though, for a simple understanding of a complex process. Szostak (2009) shows how the causal link understandings can be organized into a coherent whole through reference to an exhaustive classification of phenomena.

so. And thus a more nuanced understanding of how proximate causes interact will depend on detailed case studies.

This adjustment in our understanding of the relationship between investment and growth is entirely in accord with the strategies for interdisciplinary analysis outlined above: Growth accounting regressions naturally omit many variables that condition this relationship; the structure of those regressions does not allow for independent variables to act in concert; the approach reflects a disciplinary tendency to identify supposedly enduring causal relationships without careful concern for the set of conditions in which these might hold; and the growth accounting analyses thus represent a widespread tendency in scholarship to assume greater generality for one's results than they deserve.

Trade and Growth

Solow (2005, p. 4) argues that there has been less modeling of growth in open economies than he would have expected 50 years ago. Growth models tend to focus entirely on the internal dynamics of the growth process. This is unfortunate. Static economic analysis suggests that free trade is good because by pursuing their comparative advantage, countries will be able to increase the value of their total output. They will export goods that they are relatively good at producing and import goods that they are relatively poor at producing. This is one of the most powerful insights in all of economics. But what if productivity (output per labor and capital input) is advancing fastest in the goods a country imports? It will still benefit by being able to import more as the international price of these goods falls, but it will not benefit as much as it would if its own economy was experiencing rapid productivity growth. And thus there is a theoretical possibility that a country may benefit in the long run by sacrificing some of the short-term gains from importing and exporting in order to encourage production of goods where productivity advance is more likely.

Empirical research by economists has often suggested that the benefits from openness to trade are much greater than static theory can explain: They thus point to dynamic benefits such as increased technology transmission or greater competitive pressures on local firms. Yet, these empirical results have been questioned even by economists, who note that they are not always obtained when different definitions of "openness" are used or different time periods investigated. Economic historians, sociologists, and political scientists have stressed that all successful developed economies have been protectionist early in their development process. They have theorized that protectionism encouraged growth (see Miller, 2008).

Most economists will not readily accept a suggestion that openness to trade is not necessarily a good thing (even this author finds it difficult). Yet, we have just seen that economists have proven willing to accept arguments that the dynamic gains swamp the static comparative advantage gains. If arguments for huge dynamic advantages are allowed, then arguments for dynamic disadvantages cannot simply be ignored. Given the limited degree of theorization of dynamic effects, heavy weight must be placed on the empirical evidence. The statistical analysis is not conclusive. The historical evidence points toward a role for protectionism. But the historical record is also full of failed efforts to protect, of governments that allowed protected industries to focus their energies on maintaining government support rather than becoming internationally competitive. Case study analysis is tricky here: It is much easier to identify the many failed infant industries—those that received protection from government but failed to grow up—than to observe industries that developed behind tariff protection *and establish that they could only have done so behind such protection.* In the second case, a counterfactual—what would have happened without protection—needs to be carefully tested.

Although both theoretical and empirical analyses are thus more muddled than we might like on the grand question of openness, some answers to narrower questions seem clearer:

- If a country protects, it must ensure that firms face clear incentives to enhance productivity.
- Countries with incompetent and/or corrupt bureaucracies should be particularly wary of managed trade.[4]
- The inflow of information about technology and institutions should be encouraged, and trade in goods is one way of doing so.
- Tariffs are not the only, and perhaps not the best, strategy for supporting industrial development.

These important insights (which emerge from integrating insights from different disciplines) can be thought of as "common ground" in the debate between advocates of openness and advocates of trade barriers. That is, although it is difficult at present to sketch a common ground on the larger question of whether free trade is good for growth, it is at least possible to identify certain circumstances under which this result is more or less likely. These results, although limited, nevertheless carry important policy implications.

---

[4]Economists, as we shall see, worry a great deal about the quality of institutions when discussing institutions in general. That is, they recognize that countries differ a great deal in how well they manage/enforce institutions that may look quite similar on paper. In the realm of trade policy, however, analysis tends to proceed with respect to a dichotomy between openness and managed trade. There is usually an implicit or explicit assumption that countries cannot manage trade very well. Kohli (2004), a political scientist, argues that the key difference in developmental prospects is between countries that can manage/enforce *any* institutions well and countries that can manage/enforce *no* economic institutions well. He argues, for example, that South Korea effectively managed several years of import substitution as well as decades of export promotion (i.e., the government was not "captured" by private industries and encouraged them to improve productivity under both regimes). On the other hand, Nigeria failed miserably with respect to both types of policies (both were perverted to reward friends of the government, and productivity advance was not encouraged; p. 376). The broader literature on "the developmental state" makes similar arguments.

Technology and Growth

As noted above, economists were surprised when early efforts at growth accounting showed that investment in physical capital could account for at most a third of the growth observed in developed countries. Economists were guided to look elsewhere and came to stress the importance of education (i.e., investment in human capital), technology, trade, and institutional changes that might enhance economic efficiency. The earliest growth models treated technological innovation as *exogenous:* something that happened outside the models. The latest generation of *endogenous* growth models try to bring technological innovation inside the models; they argue that technological innovation results from another sort of investment—in research and development—and thus can be explained in terms of economic variables. These models have been valuable in encouraging economists to devote greater attention to the causes and effects of technological innovation. Yet, the tendency to assume that the rate (and direction) of innovation can be understood entirely as a function of economic variables carries the obvious danger that other influences on innovative activity will be ignored.

Scholars of technology, whether historians of technology or scholars of science and technology studies (STS), have certainly stressed a wide range of noneconomic influences on both the rate and direction of innovation. Most obviously, historians of technology have traced how each innovation builds on preceding innovations. Opportunities for innovation at any point in time (and space) are thus conditioned by the existing body of knowledge. This insight, long appreciated in economic history, has begun to be voiced in economics itself. The literature on General Purpose Technologies stresses that occasional "big" innovations set the stage for a series of minor but cumulatively important follow-up innovations. There was thus more innovative potential in the decades after the development of internal combustion (or steam) engines than in the decades before. Not only was there scope for many small improvements to these engines, but they were applied to an increasing range of uses, from factories to cars and planes.

Economists have shown less interest so far in the variety of other causal links identified by scholars of technology.[5] It is often thought—and not without cause—that STS scholars often assume, rather than identify, cultural influences. When STS scholars claim that innovation is entirely a cultural product, unconstrained by whether it reflects how the world works (an argument more often made with respect to science than technology), skepticism is invited. This should hardly restrain other scholars from respecting more nuanced arguments, and the evidence for them, that culture interacts with

---

[5]Historians of technology give roughly equal attention to the technological, economic, political, and sociocultural influences on innovation. They increasingly pay attention to the long period of development after a breakthrough innovation. They note that as technological systems harden, they limit human choices about technological innovation (Nye, 2006).

technological potential—and a host of other psychological, political, and social influences—to determine especially the direction but also the rate of innovation.

In the case of technology, different disciplinary insights can largely be integrated by dropping the "only these things matter" assumption. Different scholars have examined different causal influences on innovation, all of which likely have a role to play. The popularity of extreme assumptions—that only economic, or cultural, or technological influences matter—serves as a warning that scholars may assume rather than establish the importance of different causal links. And thus, the interdisciplinarian attempting to evaluate the relative importance of different links will need to carefully evaluate the arguments of all scholars. And he or she will also need to be sensitive to the fact that—as with growth above—the relative importance of these links likely changes across time and space.

Meeus and Hage (2006) edit an interdisciplinary handbook on innovation precisely because they believe that management specialists, economists, sociologists, historians, political scientists, and others need to integrate their efforts. They note that political scientists tend to stress government policies, management scholars look at firm behavior, economists and sociologists emphasize industry-level analysis, and STS scholars stress scientific innovation (but that until recently, very few scholars in any discipline have looked at behavior in research laboratories); they urge a co-evolutionary perspective in which the interactions among different levels of analysis are appreciated (p. 4).

Institutions

Do the right sort of institutions encourage growth (and if so how), and which sorts of functions are most necessary for institutions to perform? Because there is abundant evidence that institutions are indeed important, the question then arises how beneficial types of institutional change can be encouraged.

How important are institutions? Although economists have, in recent years, included many institutional measures in growth regressions, it has proven difficult to establish any relationship empirically. This outcome reflects, in part, the facts that different economists emphasize different theoretical arguments and that they disagree over the precise definition of institution and which particular institutions might be most important. Measures of social capital and social structure (see below) are often deemed "institutional." These analyses emphasize political over economic institutions, yet the former, for the most part, influence economic growth only indirectly through the latter. Although there may be direct effects of political stability (e.g., on investor confidence), the primary effect of stability and especially more mundane questions of electoral practices or executive powers will be to shape the nature of economic institutions. Why not, then, stress economic institutions in growth equations (with perhaps other equations linking economic and political institutions)? A further problem is relevant here: It is all too easy for incompetent or corrupt governments to create the appearance, but not the essence, of good institutions. Just as autocrats often glory in meaningless elections, so in the economic sphere they can proclaim the protection of property while actively interfering with property rights. They might expropriate property from citizens through fake legal proceedings or simply fail to enforce private contracts. Economists thus stress the quality of institutions (but a very limited set of them). But, of course, quality is always hard to measure. Finally, the various institutional variables may interact with each other and reflect feedback effects from growth itself, but simple regressions ignore these possible effects (see Aron, 2000). Because different variables are strongly correlated, different economists identify different institutional variables as most important (Lal, 1988).

Moreover, Aron (2000, pp. 100–101) worries that statistical analyses of growth in general face serious problems of data, methodology, and identification. These are generally more severe than statistical analysis elsewhere in economics. Although some of the problems identified by Aron can be alleviated by more careful definitions and theoretical specifications, others cannot. Institutions are not particularly well-suited to statistical analysis. Institutions are inherently unique. Countries may differ along various dimensions: The courts may be fair but the police incompetent in one country, while rights may be enforced without much recourse to courts in another. Such complexities call for comparative case studies and suggest that efforts to describe a type of institution in terms of one numerical indicator are likely to be fraught with difficulty.

Economic historians have, indeed, investigated the relationship between institutions and growth using comparative case studies. They have identified certain key institutional functions: protect property, enforce contracts, facilitate financial intermediation, and so on. Even economic historians are sometimes less careful than they could be: The right to property is actually a complex of rights (to earn income from, to use, to change, to sell, to rent, etc.), and financial institutions serve several important functions. The connection between institutions and growth has been little studied in other disciplines, with the important exception of the literature on the role of government in economic development. One area in which much more research is needed across disciplines is identifying the types of institution that serve various institutional functions. Institutions differ a great deal across successful developed countries, and China has experienced rapid growth against a backdrop of very peculiar institutions. Yet, it is clear that there are limits to the range of supportive institutions.

The major insight of the literature on "the developmental state" (primarily in political science, but also sociology) can be briefly summarized: "Sterile debates about 'how much' states intervene have to be replaced with arguments about different kinds of involvement and their effects" (Evans, 1995, p. 10). That is, we must move past attempts to identify best institutions to look at how well different institutions are enforced. Scholars of the developmental state (such as the political scientist Kohli, 2004) tend to argue that effective governments are necessary for *any* growth strategy to be effective. This insight has not been ignored in economics, but in practice it is often neglected: It is generally much easier to identify whether a rule exists than whether it matters. As noted above, the literature on trade and growth in economics has largely eschewed the question of whether countries have the capability to manage whatever trade regime they pursue. And thus, the literature on the developmental state can serve as an important reminder of the importance of institutional quality.

Although the connection between institutions and growth has received limited attention in most disciplines, the course of institutional change itself has been investigated across a range of disciplines (interest in institutions was reawakened in many disciplines in the 1980s). This wide range of approaches is potentially complementary, at least once some extreme assumptions are pruned from them:

- Evolutionary theorists might posit that institutional change reflects selection over random institutional changes, while rational choice theorists and functionalists (and social utilitarianism within sociology) might assume that institutions represent the farsighted intentions of their creators. Institutions are likely not the result of either perfect foresight or no foresight at all. So, then, it is an empirical question to what extent agents know what they are doing and whether the institutions created serve the purposes intended. Some scholars within all of these traditions relax assumptions of perfect foresight or no foresight. Game theoretic analyses assume that agents feel their way toward institutional solutions that work. While this is usually done in an equilibrium framework, this element can be relaxed so that institutional change is viewed as a never-finished project.
- Whether equilibrium is assumed or not (but especially if it is not), path dependence—such that small events can have important effects on the results of evolutionary processes—becomes possible and can be used in explaining a variety of types of suboptimal outcomes of historical processes. Path-dependent processes are important not just in economic history but in historical institutionalism in political science, where interactions among a variety of institutions (including influences of political on economic institutions), and among agents of unequal power, generate path-dependent processes. The objection to path dependence comes only from rational choice scholars who assume optimal outcomes.
- Once we move away from assumptions that institutions are purposely designed to serve societal goals, scope is created for a variety of causal arguments. Most obviously, the relative power of different agents comes into play. Power is stressed in sociology and political science and by economists such as Knight or Acemoglu. And economic historians have a long tradition of appreciating the role of power (e.g., in analyses of the feudal system; Greif, 2006). Political scientists tend to tell

both good stories of purposeful pursuit of beneficial institutional change and bad stories of the exercise of power; these are likely complementary explanations rather than substitutes.

- The exercise of power is often obscured from view: Those exercising power generally wish not to encourage an angry reaction and thus pretend to have other motives. Analyses of power, then, are entirely compatible with analyses of legitimation. Both sociologists and political scientists speak of legitimation. But as game theory analysis of institutional change suggests, cultural attitudes are not easy to change purposefully. Scholars can usefully investigate, then, the degree to which processes of legitimation serve the interests of the powerful or have a momentum of their own. Social constructionism provides one useful hypothesis here: that institutions solidify over time into a form that comes to seem natural. Another sociological hypothesis is that political institutions themselves shape which other institutions are viewed as legitimate. Both could well capture important aspects of legitimation.

- Sociological treatment of "ideas" encourages a broader exploration of the influence of culture on institutions. If culture is not shaped entirely by the powerful, then cultural values may exert a range of influences on which institutions are thought to be desirable. The normative approach in political science is similar. The "ideas" approach is particularly unique in emphasizing the role that social science might play in establishing the desirability of certain institutions. The seeming reticence of other social scientists to engage this line of argument is remarkable.

- Network analysis in sociology argues that agents are constrained by their networks: Institutional change is only possible if supported actively by a sufficient network. Such an approach needs to look at the resources that different network members bring, and it is thus compatible with an emphasis on power (and culture). The business-labor analyses in political science can be seen as a particular approach to network analysis, looking at how particular coalitions, whether within or across groups, were formed and able to achieve change. Organizational institutionalism in sociology alternatively examines the different motives of agents within an organization.

- Historical institutionalism is not alone in stressing the causal links between institutions. Both structural institutionalism and social institutionalism emphasize the effects of certain sorts of institutions on others.

These theories address links to institutions from each of the major categories of phenomena identified in Szostak (2003, 2004), with the exception of the nonhuman environment and the two psychological categories. Because each of these theories tends to be pursued in one or two disciplines, interdisciplinary integration promises a more holistic outlook than any one discipline can provide. The treatment of cultural and social phenomena tends to be too broad and diffuse and needs to more carefully focus on particular cultural and social elements. Beyond this need for greater clarity, there are no obvious missing variables from the set of theories as a whole.

In terms of theory types, different theories emphasize individuals (rational choice), relationships (game theory, networks), groups (legitimation, cultural and social arguments), and nonintentional agents (historical institutionalism's emphasis on interactions among institutions). There are hopeful signs of increased flexibility within theories on this point: Although rational choice theory used to stress individuals and historical institutionalism used to stress groups, both increasingly relate the behaviors of aggregates like unions to those of members (Thelen, 1997, p. 378). Theories of institutional change naturally stress actions (more rarely passive reaction, in some evolutionary and historical approaches), but some note the intermediate role of ideas or values. Rational decision making is mentioned most explicitly, but game theory and evolutionary approaches often refer to an intuitive groping for improvement. Structural institutionalism emphasizes how decision-making processes or rules influence outcomes, but at the level of political institutions rather than individual agents. Organizational institutionalism in sociology stresses the role of routines in behavior. Legitimation approaches have a central place for virtue-based decisions. Path-dependent theories have an obvious place for traditions, though agents need not argue explicitly from tradition in order to generate path-dependent outcomes. Rational choice and game theory analyses stress equilibria (but not necessarily), but most other approaches embrace dynamic or stochastic outcomes. In terms of theory types, then, the major omission is in terms of decision making: More explicit attention to intuitive and traditional, and especially virtue- and rule-based decisions, would be useful. These types of decision making are rarely found in the disciplines that have studied economic growth the most, but they are commonly explored in anthropology and the humanities.

In establishing common ground, we would wish to know which theories or causal links are the most important—and whether the relative importance varies by time or place or type of institution. Unfortunately, the relative strengths of different theories are rarely compared in practice, for the simple reason that most researchers favor and master only one.[6] The empirical evidence collected in support of each theory is strong enough, arguably, to urge the dismissal of the extreme arguments noted above that only one

---

[6]The value of integrating these approaches has occasionally been appreciated in the literature. Thelen (1997, p. 370) suggests that rational choice theorists can appreciate historical circumstances while historical institutionalists can think more about why actors do what they do (and the importance of collective action problems); all can recognize the role of norms in supporting institutions. Thelen's main argument is that scholars cannot understand change without also understanding stability. Both the coordination emphasized by rational choice theory and the shared cultural understandings of sociological institutionalism allow us to understand continuity better than change (p. 386). Historical institutionalism, on the other hand, invokes sunk costs and vested interests, and thus is good at identifying critical junctures that send countries on different trajectories, but worse at explaining continuity.

theory is correct. Legions of political scientists and sociologists and economic historians have been fooling themselves, if assumptions of perfect foresight or functionalism are entirely correct. The debate regarding path dependence is more subtle: Although it is clear that path dependence is important over some time periods, the question of whether optimal institutions are inevitably selected in the end is hard to establish uncontrovertibly, though the diversity of economic institutions in countries of similar levels of development suggests otherwise.

Culture and Growth

It is noteworthy at the outset that the theories of institutional change referred to above almost all had some role for culture. This insight accords with casual empiricism: Laws against littering or drugs are almost impossible to enforce if many members of society view them as illegitimate. Yet, although economists admit the importance of culture in this way, they tend to stop short of explicit cultural analysis. Greif (2006, pp. 8, 19–20) provides a good example of both attitudes. He not only recognizes that we must understand why rules are enforced and obeyed, and cannot thus simply study the development of formal rules in isolation, but goes so far as to define "institution" as a complementary complex of formal rules (what we and most others would call institutions) and cultural elements.[7] Institutional change is slow and path dependent because institutions depend on "poorly understood and often unintentional processes of socialization, internalization, learning, and experimentation," including beliefs and ethical attitudes (p. 190). Yet, Greif worries that cultural elements are largely unobservable, and he despairs of cultural explanations of anything for this reason: Because ad hoc appeals to unobservable cultural elements can explain everything, they explain nothing (p. xv). He thus focuses his analysis almost entirely on the observable formal rules, assuming that when these seem to work, supporting cultural values and beliefs must be in place.

To argue that culture cannot be operationalized is to suggest that scholars of culture across a range of disciplines and interdisciplinary fields have been wasting their time. Surveys are the most common source of measures of cultural attitudes. Interviews and observation can usefully clarify whether survey questions are both understood and answered honestly. In some cases, indirect quantitative measures are possible: Trust can be defined as whether agents

---

[7]Greif (2006) notes that different disciplines define institutions differently: as rules, as norms, as functional solutions to particular problems. He urges the integration of these definitions. From our holistic perspective, this is best done not by conflating quite distinct phenomena but by capturing in different causal links both the influence of culture on institutions and the role of institutions in solving particular problems. Greif's own wish that different definitions be viewed as complements (p. 40) is best achieved in this manner. Greif's definition encourages an emphasis on culture over other causal influences on/of institutions, while inviting us to treat the culture-institutions nexus as a black box.

behave as they are expected to. There are thus a variety of ways in which cultural attitudes can be operationalized.[8]

To be sure, there are problems with the existing scholarship on culture. The term itself is perhaps the vaguest in all of human science: Thousands of different definitions exist, and individual scholars rarely bother to clarify what they mean by the term. Yet, culture can potentially be defined in terms of a host of attitudes and behaviors; moreover, the works of individual cultural scholars can generally be understood as engaging a handful of these (see Szostak, 2003). The ideological content of some versions of cultural studies raises concerns that the important causal role of culture is simply assumed—but similar concerns have been raised regarding other scholarly communities above.

The sociologist Beckert (2002) provides a compelling overview of the need for sociocultural analysis of economic decisions. Economic theory itself suggests limits to the exercise of rationality in two common circumstances. The first is when cooperation among agents is required, in which case economic calculations depend on culturally conditioned expectations regarding the behavior of others. The second is when uncertainty is present: If actors cannot rationally attach probabilities to the results that their actions might produce, they must rely on various mental rules to guide behavior. Although individuals will differ in these, there will also be cultural influences (and cooperation in the face of uncertainty would depend on similar mental rules). He urges sociologists to focus on examining the social influences on those economic decisions for which rationality is particularly problematic. This recommendation would have the effect of strengthening the value of the research in each discipline to the other. He also urges sociologists to move away from references to "irrationality" and instead identify specific strategies engaged in by actors when strictly rational calculation is not feasible. This advice is similar to the advice of Newell (2007) to find common ground between economists' emphasis on rationality and sociologists' stress on irrationality by thinking of a continuum between the two. Although Beckert (2002) does not attempt to classify these non-strictly rational[9] strategies, he makes frequent

[8]In the past decades, the availability of better data and techniques has induced some economists to study culture. One popular approach is to look at whether membership in a particular ethnic or religious group affects economic outcomes. The advantage of this approach is that such memberships are easily measured and are also largely inherited: This overcomes the possible concern that any correlation between culture and economy reflects causation in the other direction. Both internationally and within countries, ethnic and religious differences do generate different economic outcomes (though within countries, studies of immigrants suggest that these will lessen over time). Moreover, these differences are correlated with different values and beliefs (trust, social mobility, fairness, hard work, fertility, thrift) in both regressions and experiments. Yet, such studies can only be suggestive of links between these values and economic growth, and these links are hard to establish statistically (Guiso, Spienza, & Zingales, 2006).

[9]Beckert (2002), in distinguishing himself from the emphasis of other sociologists on irrationality, strives to emphasize the "rationality" of other decision-making strategies. In this chapter, these can be seen as reasoned but nonrational strategies. Note that semantic confusion between narrow and broad uses of the word "rational" contribute to misunderstanding between sociologists and economists.

reference to following routines (which not only reduces costs of calculation, but increases the predictability of the behavior of others) and following cultural guidelines—including respect for widely shared values—and less frequent mention of intuition; thus, his analysis is consistent with the elucidation of the five types of decision making above.

Economists tend to believe that there is one best value set for capitalist societies (Blim 2005, p. 307). Modernization theory in sociology had also suggested that certain values, such as attitudes toward achievement, were essential (p. 308). More recently, Fukuyama has stressed trust and Harrison has urged future orientation, work effort, frugality, education, merit, trust, honesty, justice/fairness, dispersed authority, and secularism (p. 309). Blim devotes several pages to detailing differences in institutions across modern economies and then shows that these both reflect and support value differences. Different emphases on individual versus community are reflected in lifetime employment in Japan and huge CEO salaries in the United States. Values regarding competition versus collaboration are reflected in different approaches to labor/management relations (p. 316). Again, careful specification of causal relationships, in concert with careful attendance to differences across countries, produced a more complicated but more accurate understanding.

In sum, the analysis of economists suggests that cultural values may be very important causes of economic growth. Research in other disciplines has rarely addressed growth directly and has too often been characterized by vague terminology and lack of careful empirical analysis. These problems can each be overcome. At present, though, the interdisciplinarian can most usefully provide advice to disciplinarians as to how insights here can best be developed and/or clarified.

Networks

Networks of individuals serve a variety of social, political, and economic purposes. Networks are a third way of organizing economic activity—along with the markets and organizational hierarchies that economists have stressed until recently—and sociologists have shown that networks are critical in such important economic activities as finding a job or locating a business contact. Moreover, network analysis focuses on relationship agency, whereas economic analysis stresses individual agency. Network analysis is thus potentially a valuable addition to the study of economic growth. Economists have rarely used network analysis and tend, when they do, to stress a static analysis of how networks work, rather than looking at how networks evolve. Network analysis has occasionally been applied to economic interactions but not directly to the study of growth. As with culture, then, interdisciplinarians can provide advice on promising research strategies and potential pitfalls. Scholars wishing to examine the relationship between networks and growth could benefit from the following observations:

- Social capital is another vague term. There are three types of definition. The worst invites tautology (and ignores the reality of bad outcomes being possible) by defining social capital solely in terms of results. The second stresses cultural values such as trust. The third emphasizes networks and perhaps organizations. The last two can be combined: Networks generate generally beneficial outcomes by encouraging trust. This chapter will thus not address social capital, but rather address culture and networks separately.

- As with culture, useful classifications of different types of network are needed. Sociologists stress the importance of weak and/or cross-group links: Networks serve a critical role in transmitting information, and the most important links may be the less obvious and less strong links between individuals with access to quite different types of information.

- Then scholars must identify the links between different types of network and different economic activities: investment most obviously, but also innovation (which scholars of both science and technology increasingly appreciate occurs within networks) and institutional change (which is also only possible if resources are mobilized through networks). It should not be forgotten in these explorations that networks can serve to divert resources from growth; links between groups may be particularly important in generating positive outcomes.

- In particular, network analysis may provide a means (though certainly not the only means) to get a handle on the slippery concept of entrepreneurship (another topic treated more often outside economics than within). Entrepreneurs can only be successful within networks, and thus both the supply of entrepreneurs and their effectiveness will be influenced by the availability of networks that provide access to diverse sources of information and resources. Ironically, Swedberg & Granovetter (2001, pp. 12–13) observe that entrepreneurs often only succeed after migrating away from expectations within networks of family and friends (e.g., expectations that they will employ family members).

- The reasons for differences in networks across countries can be explored in a comparative fashion. Granovetter (2001) has argued that there are limits to the ability of an agent to forge links instrumentally for gain. Instead, information often flows as a side-effect of relationships pursued for social reasons. It has been hypothesized that networks are especially weak when social divisions are sharp, poverty exists without a safety net, rule of law is weak, politics is not free and without real choices, different groups do not see shared goals, war or famine undermine sense of stability, and minorities are discriminated against.

- The question of whether networks (or markets) are a substitute or complement for institutions deserves further attention: It is probably true that institutions can substitute for deficient networks in some cases but not others. This question has important policy implications for countries with limited "social capital."

Social Structure

There is a general appreciation across all disciplines that social divisions—primarily ethnic and class differences, but also gender and family divisions—can have negative economic and political effects. Writers in each discipline show how, in at least some instances, these negative effects are of enormous importance. Despite the general (and unusual) consensus on this point, there are still opportunities for one discipline to learn from another. Economists tend to downplay issues of class or inequality, while other disciplines may exaggerate these issues.

Economists rarely look at the sources of social division, and may thus too readily assume that they are intractable. Geddes (2002) warns us not to take ethnic divisions as given, for individuals have choices about how to identify themselves. People also decide whether to feel mistreated or threatened by other groups and how to respond. She argues that this focus on malleability characterizes modern political science research (p. 361).

Community Development

Among disadvantaged groups, both in poor countries and rich countries, economic growth may depend on "community development": Members of the community need to come together in order to identify strategies that enhance economic growth prospects directly or indirectly (by improving education, health, legal, or a host of other institutions and policies). Local communities often provide critical infrastructure, such as irrigation. The World Bank increasingly makes unrestricted loans to local communities (Stiglitz, 2006, pp. 51–53). Community development involves strengthening civil society (by strengthening links within the community and its interaction with sources of academic and professional advice), in order to prioritize the actions and perspectives of these communities in addressing the development of social/economic/environmental policies. It thus involves empowerment: strengthening the capacity of both individuals and community-level institutions. Community development, like the economic growth it may encourage, is best pursued in an interdisciplinary manner. This is, in part, because community development usually involves complex challenges, and thus it requires input from a variety of academic disciplines and professions. As well, the diversity of insights gives communities a freedom of choice (in how they integrate them) that they lack if presented with only one discipline-grounded policy option. Moreover, there is a synergy between cross-disciplinary integration and the integration of community insights with academic/professional insights: Both types of integration depend on respect, forging a common vocabulary, and seeking a whole that is greater than its parts. Community activists often need to oppose entrenched interests, just as interdisciplinarians must at times confront the entrenched authority of disciplines (see Butterfield & Korazim-Körösy, 2007).

Emergent Properties

We must be careful that the study of individual causal links does not divert our attention from emergent properties that might be apparent only at the level of broader systems of links. Two types of emergent properties deserve particular attention.

First, growth itself can be considered to be an emergent property of a host of independent actions, mostly undertaken without having the encouragement of growth as an objective. There is indeed a long tradition in many fields of arguing that economic growth occurs only when many causal forces are combined. "Big push" theories in economic development in the 1960s, Walt Rostow's "stages of growth" theory with its long list of necessary conditions for a "takeoff into economic growth," dependency and world systems theory (which postulate a variety of ways in which poor countries might be kept poor by their interactions with rich countries) in sociology and political science, among other approaches, have made this sort of argument.

Are the optimistic or pessimistic versions of these approaches more plausible? In terms of the three strategies for dealing with differences in interdisciplinary insights (above), it is clear that this difference is not merely semantic: Pessimists and optimists are talking about the same thing and reaching different conclusions. Do these hypotheses have different ranges of applicability? It must seem that many of the world's poor countries have achieved impressive rates of economic growth in recent decades and thus better fit the optimistic outlook. Most of sub-Saharan Africa might better fit the pessimist scenario, though again, it must be recalled that some of these countries grew rapidly in the 1960s. There might be some mechanism that ensures that at least some poor countries remain poor. This leads to the third question: Could one achieve common ground by changing some assumptions in one or the other perspective? Indeed one could. If one strips away the determination to identify without doubt the future course of history, each perspective supports and depends upon a set of causal arguments. It is entirely possible that all of these have some empirical merit, and thus whether a country grows or not depends on which causal forces are operating most strongly at certain times. And such a common ground can indeed be seen in the writings of both camps: Optimists often talk about overcoming what they see as surmountable barriers (such as the absence of property rights or decent infrastructure) to economic growth, while pessimists generally suggest that growth will only occur if dramatic changes are made (say, in trade or foreign investment policies at the global level) to the way the world operates.

Although both optimists and pessimists appeal to issues of complexity, they have not, in general, emphasized emergent properties but rather a set of mutually reinforcing causal links. This need not mean that emergent properties are unimportant: Scholars across disciplines may be biased toward making narrow causal arguments rather than appealing to emergent properties.

A second venue for emergent properties is economic fluctuations. Economic actors do not set out to generate business cycles (indeed, this result is even less intended than economic growth), but cycles emerge from the interactions among actors. Economists have struggled for decades to explain cycles precisely because it is hard to move from an understanding of how individuals behave to an appreciation of how cycles are generated. For present purposes, a few brief points can be made about fluctuations:

- In a world without growth and the structural change that accompanies it, economic cycles would be mild or nonexistent. Cycles should thus be treated as largely an emergent property of the economic growth process.
- In addition to the business cycles of a year or two in duration that economists have focused most attention on, there are longer periods—of a decade or more—characterized by significant differences in growth rates: The 1950s and 1960s saw more rapid growth in most developed countries than did the 1930s or 1970s. Notably, these periods of rapid growth tend also to be characterized by less severe cyclical behavior—perhaps because workers losing their jobs could quickly find others.
- However, economic models of growth predict a steady state outcome of some constant rate of growth. It was noticed above that other disciplines are more likely than economics to stress differences in growth experience across time and place. Interdisciplinarians should thus seek a common ground that reflects the observed reality of alternating periods of fast and slow growth. (Our appreciation above that technological innovation occurs unevenly through time might form an important component of this common ground.)

Lessons for Interdisciplinary Practice

The foregoing analysis has, I hope, provided evidence of the advantages of a strategy of integrating insights along different causal links (without neglecting the interactions among them) and also seeking emergent properties of the system as a whole. The literature on interdisciplinarity often refers somewhat vaguely to different "facets" of an issue. The stress here on causal links clarifies the focus of analysis and points again to the advantages of an exhaustive table of the key phenomena studied by scholars across all disciplines: This provides a "map" of the links addressed while also mitigating against ignoring links just because all disciplines have ignored them (or the literature survey failed to find works that did).

Interdisciplinarians have understandably focused the most on integration when different disciplines provide conflicting insights. Yet, the analysis above suggests that integrative strategies are also useful when gaps exist between disciplines. In such cases, interdisciplinarians can usefully suggest avenues for research that would bridge these gaps. The symbiotic relationship between disciplines and interdisciplinarity may then be easier to display to disciplinarians: Interdisciplinarians can point to valuable extensions to disciplinary analysis without having first to outline the deficiencies of previous research.

Reflection and Communication

Establishing common ground is the most important single step in the integrative process. Yet, the interdisciplinarian cannot simply stop at this point. As is true in specialized research, the act of insight should be followed by careful attempts to evaluate and clarify the integrative insights obtained.

Interdisciplinarians are not free of bias themselves, though they will generally be more aware of the existence of scholarly biases than specialized researchers. Interdisciplinarians as a whole may be biased toward seeing good (or not) in all approaches, and they must thus be careful to scrutinize each insight they take from any discipline. Individual interdisciplinarians may be characterized by a host of ideological, ethical, epistemological, theoretical, methodological, and other biases. They may like some disciplines more than others. All these possibilities should be reflected upon to see whether the integrative results obtained reflect such biases.[10]

The interdisciplinarian should then ask whether there are ways in which his or her integrative understanding might be tested. It may well be that a complex integrative understanding such as that sketched above cannot be tested in its entirety (though it is useful to ask whether the set of insights as a whole is useful to the policy maker). Rather, different tests may be required for different causal links. The interdisciplinarian will wish to use multiple methods to test insights. If different methods suggest different conclusions, it is necessary to revisit the strategies outlined above of interrogating assumptions and revisiting the strengths and weaknesses of different theories and methods.

---

[10]I am an economist, but one who has written methodological critiques of my discipline and my field of economic history (Szostak, 1999, 2006). I have thus had the pleasure of being critiqued by non-economists for being too much of an economist and by economists for being not quite enough of one. The reader can best judge which—likely both—is the case here. I lack practitioner-level expertise in some of the disciplines covered here, but I have considerable familiarity with most of the theory types and methods addressed. I am a self-conscious interdisciplinarian and thus likely biased toward stressing the advantages of interdisciplinary analysis. As should be clear by now, I believe in theoretical and methodological flexibility. I may thus be biased toward seeing some good in all approaches. Indeed, I do suspect that any idea pursued at length by some academic community must have some kernel of truth in it. But this need not prevent skepticism: One can appreciate that those who thought the world was flat for millennia were misguided, while appreciating the value of the ways they amassed evidence in support of their hypothesis. Still, I can imagine that disciplinarians reading this chapter will readily imagine that I have been too harsh with respect to them and not harsh enough in my treatment of others. And surely some of them will be right (but hopefully not to a considerable degree), though I know not which.

The final task involves communicating results in a format that is accessible to multiple audiences. This involves appreciating both the knowledge bases of different audiences and their interests: The results should be connected to issues that different audiences (especially disciplines) already care about.

Conclusion

In the end, did we end up with a chaos of conflicting arguments extending in too many directions? Or were we able to put enough order into our reflections to make the effort worthwhile? Hardcore disciplinarians will respond negatively: They can instill greater order by simply ignoring theories and methods other than their own. But the interdisciplinarian strives toward an order that does not arbitrarily limit insight. The cause of economic growth—and the billions of people who desperately need to experience more of this—is best served by privileging integrated insight over narrower criteria.

It is useful to close by briefly reviewing the benefits to our understanding of growth of the various steps in the interdisciplinary research process:

- The scope for interdisciplinary analysis expands markedly when we move beyond studying the proximate causes of growth to ask why some countries innovate or trade or invest more than others. Economists—and far from all of these—have only recently extended their gaze beyond the proximate causes, and they are held back by the difficulty of applying their usual theories and methods to non-economic phenomena such as culture. The importance of not arbitrarily constraining a guiding question along disciplinary lines could hardly be better illustrated.
- The second step(s) reviewed a wide range of theories and methods and established that each had strengths for the study of growth that could compensate for weaknesses in others. The appreciation of these strengths and weaknesses was invaluable when disciplinary insights were evaluated later. The analysis also served usefully to justify in advance wide-ranging theoretical and methodological explorations. For mainstream economists, the key message was that rational choice theorizing and statistical analysis need to be supplemented with other—for the most part *complementary*—theories and methods. Yet, the same message was communicated to all other disciplines.
- The identification of gaps in scholarly understanding is always a critical step in interdisciplinary analysis. It has been particularly important in the case of economic growth, for scholars of networks or culture or business cycles have only rarely addressed questions of economic growth (and vice versa), and even much of the literature on technology and institutions is oriented toward quite different questions. One of the main purposes of this research project has been to identify areas where future research is needed and how this might be pursued.

- Asking about the possibility of emergent properties led us to two important areas of investigation: poverty traps and the connection between growth and cycles.
- More generally, we were able to create a common ground across a range of causal links that is superior to the insights of any one discipline. We will not reprise those analyses here, in part not to detract attention from the other steps in the research process.
- Though we did not have space to describe the final steps in detail, our understanding of growth will be greatly enhanced if we interrogate possible biases in our analysis, test our insights empirically, and communicate them clearly to diverse audiences.

References

Aron, J. (2000). Growth and institutions: A review of the evidence. *World Bank Research Observer, 15*(1), 99–135.

Bammer, G. (2005). Integration and implementation sciences: Building a new specialization. *Ecology and Society, 10*(2), 6. Retrieved from http://www.ecology andsociety.org/vol10/iss2/art6/

Beckert, J. (2002). *Beyond the market: The social foundations of economic efficiency.* Princeton: Princeton University Press.

Blim, M. (2005). Culture and economy. In J. G. Carrier (Ed.), *A handbook of economic anthropology* (pp. 306–322). Cheltenham: Edward Elgar.

Butterfield, A. K. J., & Korazim-Körösy, Y. (2007). *Interdisciplinary community development: International perspectives.* New York: Haworth Press.

Cohen, J. D. (2005). The vulcanization of the human brain: A neural perspective on interactions between cognition and emotion. *Journal of Economic Perspectives, 19*(4), 3–24.

Easterly, W. (2002). *The elusive quest for growth: Economist's adventures and misadventures in the tropics.* Cambridge: MIT Press.

Evans, P. (1995). *Embedded autonomy: States and industrial transformation.* Princeton: Princeton University Press.

Geddes, B. (2002). The great transformation in the study of politics in developing countries. In I. Katznelson & H. V. Miller (Eds.), *Political science: State of the discipline* (pp. 342–370). New York: Norton.

Gerschenkron, A. (1962). *Economic backwardness in historical perspective.* Cambridge: Harvard University Press.

Granovetter, M. (2001). Economic action and social structure: The problem of embeddedness. In M. Granovetter & R. Swedberg (Eds.), *The sociology of economic life* (pp. 51–76). Boulder CO: Westview Press.

Greif, A. (2006). *Institutions and the path to the modern economy: Lessons from medieval trade.* New York: Cambridge University Press.

Guiso, L., Spienza, P., & Zingales, L. (2006). Does culture affect economic outcomes? *Journal of Economic Perspectives, 20*(2), 23–48.

Kohli, A. (2004). *State directed development: Political power and industrialization in the global periphery.* New York: Cambridge University Press.

Lal, D. (1988). *Unintended consequences: The impact of factor endowments, culture, and politics on long-run economic performance.* Cambridge: MIT Press.

Meeus, M. T. H., & Hage, J. (2006). Product and process innovation, scientific research, knowledge dynamics, and institutional change: An introduction. In J. Hage & M. T. H. Meeus (Eds.), *Innovation, science, and institutional change: A research handbook* (pp. 1–19). Oxford: Oxford University Press.

Miller, R. (2008). *International political economy*. London: Routledge.

Nee, V. (1998). Sources of the new institutionalism. In M. C. Brinton & V. Nee (Eds.), *The new institutionalism in sociology* (pp. 1–16). New York: Russell Sage Foundation.

Newell, W. H. (2007). Decision making in interdisciplinary studies. In G. Morcol (Ed.), *Handbook of decision making* (pp. 245–264). New York: Marcel Dekker.

Nye, D. E. (2006). *Technology matters: Questions to live with*. Cambridge: MIT Press.

Repko, A. (2008). *Interdisciplinary research: Process and theory*. Thousand Oaks, CA: Sage.

Singleton, R. A., Jr., & Strait, B. C. (1999). *Approaches to social research* (3rd. ed.). New York: Oxford University Press.

Snowdon, B. (2002). *Conversations on growth, stability, and trade: A historical perspective*. Cheltenham: Edward Elgar.

Solow, R. (2005). Reflections on growth theory. In P. Aghion & S. N. Durlauf (Eds.), *Handbook of economic growth* (pp. 1–10). Amsterdam: Elsevier North-Holland.

Stiglitz, J. (2006). *Making globalization work*. New York: Norton.

Swedberg, R., & Granovetter, M. (2001). Introduction to the second edition. In M. Granovetter & R. Swedberg (Eds.), *The sociology of economic life* (pp. 1–28). Boulder CO: Westview Press.

Sylla, R., & Toniolo, G. (Eds.). (1991). *Patterns of European industrialization: The nineteenth century*. London: Routledge.

Szostak, R. (1999). *Econ-art: Divorcing art from science in modern economics*. London: Pluto Press.

Szostak, R. (2002). How to do interdisciplinarity: Integrating the debate. *Issues in Integrative Studies, 20,* 103–122.

Szostak, R. (2003). *A schema for unifying human science: Interdisciplinary perspectives on culture*. Selinsgrove PA: Susquehanna University Press.

Szostak, R. (2004). *Classifying science: Phenomena, data, theory, method, practice*. Dordrecht: Springer.

Szostak, R. (2006). Economic history as it is and should be: Toward an open, honest, methodologically flexible, theoretically diverse, interdisciplinary exploration of the causes and consequences of economic growth. *Journal of Socio-Economics, 35*(4), 727–750.

Szostak, R. (2007). Interdisciplinarity and the classification of scholarly documents by phenomena, theories, and methods. In B. Rodriguez Bravo & L. Alvite Diez (Eds.), *Interdisciplinarity and transdisciplinarity in the organization of scientific knowledge: Actas del VIII Congreso ISKO-Espana* (pp. 469–477). Leon: University of Leon.

Szostak, R. (2008). Classification, interdisciplinarity, and the study of science. *Journal of Documentation, 64*(3), 319–332.

Szostak, R. (2009). *The causes of economic growth: Interdisciplinary perspectives*. Berlin: Springer.

Thelen, K. (1997). Historical institutionalism in comparative politics. *Annual Review of Political Science, 2,* 369–404.

7

Why We Talk

An Interdisciplinary Approach to the Evolutionary Origin of Language

Ria van der Lecq

Introduction

Questions about the purpose of language arise quite naturally. Although the advantages of having language are obvious, we may still wonder why language is such a complex ability. And if language is so useful, why have only humans acquired it? Of course, other animals have communication systems to inform each other about food or danger, but only humans can communicate about anything, whether it is present, absent, or even fictional. Then there are questions about the *origins* of human communication. Did we acquire our language capacity in one single step without intermediate forms, or did language evolve gradually through a sequence of stages?

Beginning the Research Process (Steps 1 to 4)

The first section of this essay describes the results of the first four steps of the interdisciplinary process presented in Repko (2008): (1) define the problem or state the focus question, (2) justify using an interdisciplinary approach, (3) identify relevant disciplines, and (4) conduct a literature search. It goes without saying that a preliminary literature search is necessary in order to state the focus question.

Framing the Research Question (Step 1)

Debates about the nature, origin, and development of language have engaged philosophers and scientists throughout history. Until the end of the 1980s, lack of empirical data made it difficult to draw scientific conclusions, especially about the *origin* of language. Scientists did not consider this problem a valid field of research (Aitchison, 1996). Since then, however, research in evolutionary biology, evolutionary psychology, evolutionary anthropology, and neuroscience have given the field a new impetus by providing empirical data. Even so, definitive answers are elusive, controversies are numerous, and it is difficult to detect common conclusions despite the great amount of evidence.

Even a superficial literature search makes clear that it is impossible to analyze and integrate all the insights on the origin and development of language in one book chapter, even if we were to confine ourselves to the scholarly literature of the past decade. For the task to be manageable, a focus on one aspect of this problem is therefore necessary. This study will focus on the question *What was the primary function for which language emerged?* Obviously, communication is an important function of language. But if it is its *primary* function, why do we humans need such a complex system as language to communicate, whereas other animals can survive without it? Thus, our focus question contains three subquestions: Why did language evolve? Why only with humans? Why (and how) did language evolve into such a complex system? The goal of this study is to construct a theory of the primary function of language that is more comprehensive than other available theories.

Justifying an Interdisciplinary Approach (Step 2)

Repko (2008) identifies several criteria by which to justify using an interdisciplinary approach. The problem of the primary function of language fulfils four of these criteria:

- The problem or question is complex.
- Important insights into the problem are offered by more than one discipline.
- No single discipline has been able to address the problem comprehensively.
- The focus question is at the interfaces of disciplines, in this case biology and anthropology. (p. 151ff)

These four criteria seem to be interrelated, to a certain extent. Because the problem is complex (first criterion), no single discipline has been able to address it comprehensively (third criterion), and questions that are at the interfaces of disciplines (fourth criterion) are likely to elicit insights from more than one discipline (second criterion).

Identifying Relevant Disciplines (Step 3) and Conducting an In-Depth Literature Search (Step 4)

The third step in the interdisciplinary research process is to identify *potentially* relevant disciplines; the in-depth literature search (Step 4) that follows leads to the identification of the *most relevant* disciplines. The term *discipline* is used as a shorthand descriptor that includes traditional disciplines, subdisciplines, and interdisciplines. To identify potentially relevant disciplines, students may use the tables in Repko (2008), especially those in Chapter 3 that list the overall perspectives of many disciplines. They may also use taxonomies of disciplines found on the Internet.[1] The literature search often leads to a revision of Step 1 when a research question appears to be too broad or too narrow. It may also reveal additional relevant disciplines. Repko (2008, p. 142) considers Step 4 to be a fluid process within the overall research process, especially in its early phases.

Potentially relevant disciplines are linguistics, biology (with its subdisciplines evolutionary biology, primatology, ethology, and anatomy), psychology, cognitive science, philosophy, anthropology, and archeology. They were identified before the full-scale literature search was conducted. An analysis of them shows that disciplinary boundary crossing occurs in various ways. Psycholinguistics and biolinguistics, for example, are subdisciplines of linguistics. Psycholinguistics links psychology and linguistics when it studies language and the mind. Biolinguistics links biology and linguistics in the study of the biological foundations of language. Evolutionary biology is a special branch of biology that tries to explain psychological traits such as language as evolved adaptations. Other potentially relevant subdisciplines of biology are ethology (the study of animal behavior) and primatology (the study of primates), but anthropologists also study animal communications. Neuroscience is sometimes referred to as neurobiology, but it also has a subfield called cognitive neuroscience. Cognitive science, in its turn, is an interdisciplinary field embracing philosophy, psychology, artificial intelligence, neuroscience, linguistics, and anthropology.

In many cases, it is difficult to judge which discipline a particular study "belongs" to because most researchers have multidisciplinary backgrounds. They appear to have discovered that a monodisciplinary approach to language will not yield satisfying results. Linguists were the first to realize that they needed other perspectives, especially from biology and psychology, to attain a more comprehensive understanding of the phenomenon of language.

The focus on the *primary function* of language eliminates several subdisciplines. Linguistics, for example, assumes that we need language primarily as a vehicle for transmitting complex representations (Bickerton, 1990). Obviously, this is an important function of language today, but whether it was its original primary function is another question. *Theoretical* linguists often claim to be describing language *knowledge*, rather than language *usage*; they are interested in the nature of language and in the question of whether language competence is an innate capacity or not, but the origin and development

---

[1]An interesting and useful tool is the interactive Mind Map of Academic Disciplines (http://www.gogeometry.com/mindmap/academic_disciplines.html).

of this capacity is not their primary concern. This makes *pure* linguistics less relevant for the present study.

The *most relevant* disciplines are those that have generated direct insights on the question of the primary (original) function of language and its sub-questions mentioned above. The in-depth literature search reveals that biology (including the study of primates), anthropology, and cognitive science have generated such insights. The last 40 years of research on monkeys and apes has taught us that humans are, in many respects, not unique. Primates are just as social as we are, and we can learn a lot about our own past from the study of their behavior, especially their ways of communicating. The developments in evolutionary biology have had far-reaching implications for our understanding of human (linguistic) behavior. These developments put an end to the claim of social scientists that language, being an aspect of human behavior, is a social phenomenon that lies beyond the pale of biological explanations (Dunbar, 1996). Evolutionary biologists make use of anthropological and archeological evidence to support their claims. Cultural anthropologists study language in its cultural context, and some of them appear to be interested in the origin of communication in social networks. Cognitive science studies language in relation to knowledge, which leads to distinct insights regarding the original function of language. The insights of cognitive scientists are especially helpful when it comes to addressing the problem of language complexity.

Drawing on Disciplinary Insights on the Primary Function of Language (Steps 5 to 6)

In the second section of this study, Step 5 (Developing adequacy in each relevant discipline) and Step 6 (Evaluating disciplinary insights) of the interdisciplinary research process will be performed. Interdisciplinary researchers have to develop adequacy in each relevant discipline to be able to detect salient differences in perspective. While conducting the in-depth literature search, the interdisciplinarian should be mindful of concepts, assumptions, epistemologies, research methods, and theories, as these are the elements that may be the source of the conflicts between disciplinary insights that have to be identified in Step 7 and mitigated in Step 8.

Developing Adequacy in Each Relevant Discipline (Step 5)

The literature search shows that biology, anthropology, and cognitive science are the most relevant disciplines for our study because they offer insights directly pertaining to the focus question. The overall perspectives of these disciplines are stated below:

- Biology studies the behavior (including linguistic behavior) of the living physical world. Biologists look for physical, causal explanations of behavior (such as genes and evolution) that are subject to laws of nature. Evolution is one of the cornerstones of modern biology. Evolutionary biology is a subfield of biology that also includes scientists from a wide range of disciplines. Other relevant subfields of biology are primatology (the study of primates) and ethology (the study of animal behavior). Animal studies can help us understand the computational capacities underlying language, along with the neural and genetic basis of these abilities (Tecumseh Fitch, 2007).
- Anthropology (literally "the study of human beings") has four major subdivisions that have developed as almost separate disciplines. *Physical anthropology* focuses on the evolution of humans in prehistory through the study of artifacts. Another subdivision is *archaeology*, the study of human prehistory and history. *Cultural anthropology*, the comparative study of living human groups, uses linguistic data to study the development of human cultures. *Anthropological linguistics* investigates the relationship between language and culture. Anthropologists do not deny that language is a biological capacity, but they stress the importance of cultural factors for its origin and development. The signature research method of cultural and linguistic anthropologists is participant observation, a method of collecting data by observing what people do (Selby & Garretson, 1981).
- Cognitive science is the scientific study of mental phenomena. It is an interdisciplinary field embracing psychology, philosophy, artificial intelligence, linguistics, robotics, and neuroscience. When cognitive scientists study the mind from a theoretical perspective, they view the mind as an information processor. Linguistic information is "input" into our minds from what we hear (or see). It is stored in our memories and processed in the form of thought. Our thoughts then serve as the basis of "output" in the form of speech (Friedenberg & Silverman, 2006). Cognitive science can establish a cognitive model of language behavior. With the model, it becomes possible to track backward from the structure to the biological function, which in turn enables us to define the particular conditions that made the biological function advantageous for the people who possessed it (Dessalles, 2007).

Evaluating Disciplinary Insights (Step 6)

The next paragraphs identify and evaluate the insights of the leading experts concerning the primary/original function of language (Step 6). However, because all these experts have the theory of evolution as their common background, it may be useful to start by reviewing the main points of this theory, especially since it is often misunderstood.

The Theory of Evolution

The use of the term *evolution* dates back to the ancient Greeks. In its broadest sense, the term refers to change or growth that occurs in a particular order.[2] Theories of evolution seek to explain why natural species and also cultural phenomena are the way they are. They also try to explain diversity within species and the possession by species of characteristic adaptations.[3] Modern theories of evolution insist on the significance of natural and/or cultural inheritance.

Evolution is not the same as natural selection. The theory of evolution says that species change over time because of "descent with modification." What Darwin discovered was a particular *cause* of evolution, natural selection:

> Any variation, however slight and from whatever cause proceeding, if it be in any degree profitable to an individual of any species . . . will tend to the preservation of that individual, and will generally be inherited by its offspring. The offspring also will have a better chance of surviving. . . . I have called this principle, by which each slight variation, if useful, is preserved, by the term Natural Selection. (Darwin, 1859, quoted in Pinker, 1994)

Natural selection is the process whereby any traits that make survival and reproduction of its owner more likely will tend to spread through the population over many generations. Those traits occur as a result of natural genetic variation and are supposed to be produced by a copying error in the multiplication process. Key concepts in natural selection theory are *adaptation* and *environment*. An adaptation is a replication-enhancing trait. It enhances the probability of reproduction of an organism in a particular environment. An adaptation makes a population better suited to its habitat. Each intermediate stage of the development of the trait must have a reproductive advantage for its possessor, otherwise it would not survive.

Darwin saw the history of life as a great tree with many branches. We humans belong to the branch (order) of primates. The order of primates has three branches (families): gorillas, chimpanzees, and hominids (human-like creatures). Our most ancient fossilized ancestor in the family of hominids is "Lucy." She is 4 million years old and lived in Africa. Unlike the apes, she walked on two feet. Our own genus *Homo* (man/woman) is a subdivision of the hominid family. One of our ancestors in this line is *Homo habilis* (handy man), who appeared around 2 million years ago, followed by *Homo erectus* (upright man), who lived 1.5 million years ago.

---

[2]For the history of the term *evolution,* see *The Internet Encyclopedia of Philosophy* (http://www.iep.utm.edu/evolutio/#H6).

[3]See the entry "Cultural Evolution" in *The Stanford Encyclopedia of Philosophy* (http://plato.stanford.edu/entries/evolution-cultural).

Broca's area of *Homo habilis*'s brain was already larger, but we do not know whether he used it for language as we do. About 300,000 years ago, *Homo sapiens* (wise man) arrived on the scene, followed by *Homo sapiens sapiens* (very wise man; that's us!) around 200,000–150,000 years B.P. (Before Present). It is hard to believe that *Homo sapiens* lacked language because biologically they were modern humans, and all modern humans have language (Aitchison, 1996; Pinker, 1994).

In Darwin's view, language is "an instinctive tendency to speak . . . slowly and unconsciously developed by many steps" (Wilson, 2006, p. 809).[4] Articulate language is peculiar to man, but "it is not the mere power of articulation that distinguishes man from other animals . . . it is his large power of connecting definite sounds with definite ideas; and this obviously depends on the development of the mental faculties" (p. 809). As to the origin of language, Darwin suggests that the first step in formation of a language was that "some unusually wise ape-like animal should have thought of imitating the growl of a beast or prey, so as to indicate to his fellow monkeys the nature of the expected danger" (p. 810).

Darwin saw an important relation between the development of the brain and the continued use of language: "The continued use and advancement of this power [of speech] would have reacted on the mind by enabling and encouraging it to carry on long trains of thought" (Wilson, 2006, p. 810). He thought the reason other animals do not use their vocal organs for speech "no doubt depends on their intelligence not having been sufficiently advanced" (p. 811). In Darwin's view, the expression of complex thoughts was an important function of speech, but humans did not "invent" language for this purpose. Articulate language has been "slowly and unconsciously developed by many steps" (p. 809). The development of language was closely connected with music: "The habit of uttering musical sounds was first developed, as a means of courtship, in the early progenitors of man, and thus became associated with the strongest emotions of which they were capable—namely ardent love, rivalry and triumph" (p. 1309). Darwin contended that the vocal and other sound-producing organs were first developed for sexual purposes, but once acquired, these organs could be voluntarily and consciously employed as means of communication.

For those interested in the origins of language, evolutionary issues are essential (Hauser, 1996). Language is a complex feature (Pinker & Bloom, 1990), and evolution of complex features does not occur unless it is driven by some evolutionary advantage for those who possess the feature. The principal explanation for the evolution of language must, therefore, be the same as for any complex organ: Darwin's theory of natural selection (MacNeilage, 2008; Pinker, 1994; Pinker & Bloom, 1990). As we shall see below, Darwin's ideas resonate in the theories of various contemporary scholars.

---

[4] I thank Herman Hendriks for his help in finding the relevant passages in Darwin's works.

Contemporary Theories

Because most, if not all, insights regarding this problem are based on multidisciplinary or interdisciplinary research, this study takes hypotheses and theories, not disciplines, as the starting point for the evaluation of insights.

There are many plausible hypotheses concerning the driving forces behind language evolution, but general plausibility is not sufficient. A serious theory of language evolution must also account for the absence of language in other hominids and for its evolution into a complex ability. Thus, an instrumentalist hypothesis that hunting- or gathering-related communication was the driving force behind language evolution can be eliminated because hunting and gathering are common practices among some other hominids. Another hypothesis is that language was necessary for tool use and tool making, but, although humans took tool making to a whole new level, the making of tools appears not to be limited to humans.[5] Therefore, tool making was not the *primary* cause of language development. Darwin's idea that the fitness of language is based on sexual selection is plausible but not sufficient either, unless our sex life is much more complex than the mating systems of other apes.

Hypotheses that do account for language as a unique and complex ability for humans are presented and evaluated below. They assume that humans are social animals, as are most other primates, but that we differ from the other apes in that human social groups are much larger and more complex, with correspondingly heavier demands on our ability to handle social relationships. This has implications for our cognitive makeup. Hypotheses that generate insights directly pertaining to the question of the original function of language are (1) the social brain hypothesis (e.g., the grooming and gossip theory by Robin Dunbar), (2) the political hypothesis (e.g., the linguistic relevance theory by Jean-Louis Dessalles) and (3) niche construction theory by John Odling-Smee, Kevin Laland, and Marc Feldman. In addition to these theories regarding the function of language, (4) complexity theory explains why language is so much more complex and powerful than one can account for in terms of selective fitness. In the following paragraphs, these four theories are presented and evaluated.

The Social Brain Hypothesis (Biology, Anthropology). A widely supported answer to our focus question (What was the primary function of human language?) comes from the English evolutionary anthropologist Robin Dunbar. Dunbar (1996, 1998, 2008) argues that the primary function of language is social rather than instrumental. Instrumentalist theories assume that language evolved for exchange of technical information, such as explaining how to make tools or coordinating hunts. Obviously, transmission of information is important and language is good at it, but this fact does not specify what kinds of information are involved (Dunbar, 2008, p. 13).

---

[5]See Johansson (2005) for evidence.

In the instrumentalist's view, the social use of language is just a byproduct of the instrumental use. But knowledge about the social world we live in is just as complex as instrumental knowledge about the physical world. So, if language is about exchange of information, it is just as likely to have evolved for social reasons. According to Dunbar (1998), "the need to hold large highly structured groups together has been more important than the need to solve ecological problems" (p. 94). This has led to the so-called social brain hypothesis: the claim that the primate brain is primarily a social, rather than an ecological, tool.

The social brain hypothesis is based on research among primates. Primates bond their social groups by intensive use of social grooming. Dunbar discovered that there is a linear relationship between group size and the amount of time devoted to grooming, and social groups that spend less time on social grooming than predicted by this relationship are unstable. Thus, when the groups become too large, there is not enough time for social grooming to keep the group stable. Now, in primates there appears to be a close relation between social group size and the size of the neocortex, so there is a cognitive limit to the size of social groups that primates can bond by grooming (Dunbar, 1998, 2008). The average social network size in a wide range of contemporary and historical human societies is a group of 150 (Dunbar, 1998). Primates in a group this size would have to spend almost 40% of their time on grooming, which is more than twice the average time spent grooming for any primate species. Thus, further increases in group size would be severely limited if social bonding depended on grooming alone. Therefore, Dunbar argues, a more efficient mechanism was required, and language met this requirement very nicely because language enables us to reach several individuals at the same time. Dunbar's (1996) conclusion is that human language may have evolved to replace social grooming. Instrumental use may have emerged as a property once social language was in place: "Once you can talk about something, you can talk about anything" (Dunbar, 2008, p. 20).

Language was an effective solution for several reasons. Language enables the direct exchange of information over a long distance, without physical contact. Moreover, it can be used for advertising oneself and for acquiring information about prospective partners when they are not physically present. According to Dunbar (1998), the latter seems to be especially advantageous because, unlike other species, humans can gather information about the reliability of an ally via third parties (p. 96).

Dunbar (2008) refers to recent studies on animal communication that have corroborated his conclusion that language evolved to replace social grooming. They have shown that, in primates, vocal repertoire size correlates with social group size and with time spent on grooming. Thus, as social group size has increased, there seems to have been selection pressure to increase the role of vocal exchanges as a means of supplementing grooming. Dunbar (1996) suggests that vocal grooming began around 2 million years ago with the appearance of *Homo erectus*, when group sizes began to drift upward beyond the numbers for which physical grooming works well. Eventually, even vocal grooming would have exhausted its capacity to bond groups, and a more efficient mechanism was needed. Vocalizations began to acquire meaning, but the content must have been largely social: gossip had arrived (p. 115). Thus, language evolved to allow us to gossip.

Dunbar's (1998) opinion is that not only did language evolve to exchange social information in order to facilitate bonding in larger groups, but this still *is* its primary function. In modern societies, language is also used to control social cheats and to spread malicious propaganda ("Machiavellian behavior"), but according to Dunbar, these are *consequences* of large social groups:

> It is more parsimonious to argue that language must have evolved as a bonding device first, and then later have acquired its more exploitative properties once the opportunities for exploitation became apparent, than to argue that the Machiavellian properties were the driving force. (p. 98)

Dunbar (2008) has compared his theory, which is known as the *grooming and gossip* hypothesis (or *gossip theory*), with other social hypotheses and the classical instrumental hypothesis (p. 21). As mentioned above, the instrumental hypothesis holds that language evolved for the exchange of information about the male activities of hunting and tool making. The other two social hypotheses are the *Scheherazade hypothesis* and the *social contract hypothesis*. The Scheherazade hypothesis (Miller, 1999, cited in Dunbar, 2008) says that the selective advantage that drove language evolution may have been that the better speakers were preferred as mates and thus had more offspring. The social contract hypothesis (Deacon, 1997, cited in Dunbar, 2008) considers the fact that we, unlike other apes, have a more-or-less monogamous mating system, of prime importance for the origin of language. This way of living in pairs in larger social groups, connected with paternal provisioning and male cooperative hunting, would explain the necessity of an efficient social communication system to prevent cheating. Dunbar compared the predictions of all four hypotheses with the evidence regarding some individual traits that are supposed to be characteristic of language use. The gossip hypothesis was the only hypothesis whose predictions were confirmed on all tests. Moreover, it is the only hypothesis that predicts the observed findings in a wide range of contemporary societies (1) that women spend more time talking than men, (2) that the context specificity in conversations is low[6] and (3) that the main topics in conversations are social issues. Dunbar concludes that the gossip hypothesis not only resolves the bonding problem, but also includes the other two social hypotheses and the instrumental hypothesis as emergent properties.

---

[6]The Scheherazade hypothesis and the social contract hypothesis would predict that in contemporary societies, mating and/or tool making, or their modern equivalents (sex and education?), would be the main topics of conversation, which is not the case, according to Dunbar's observed findings.

If it is true, as Dunbar (2008) argues, that language appears late (i.e., with anatomically modern humans), there is a bonding gap between what can be done with grooming and the point at which language is a serious substitute. Dunbar suggests that language may have evolved via an intermediate musical phase. This cannot be confirmed by anatomical evidence, but research on music as a communicative medium has shown that across different cultures, music performs the function of management of social relationships. Particularly in situations of social uncertainty such as grooming, music has the capacity to produce endorphins that seem to create the sense of bonding (p. 29).

The strength of the gossip theory is that it makes comprehensive sense of a number of otherwise unrelated facts: brain size, group size, grooming patterns in primates, how we use language, what we talk about, and conversation group sizes. The critical test analysis of hypotheses for language evolution shows that the theory has a high predictive value. It explains why language emerged and why only with humans (our first two subquestions). An important assumption of this theory is that there is a close relationship between social intelligence and speech (the so-called *sociality assumption*). Research in neurology corroborates this assumption by showing that there is an overlap in the brain between the language centers and the location of social intelligence (Worden, 1998). A weakness of the gossip theory, which it has in common with other social theories, is that we cannot really be certain whether what is true for us—that we mainly talk about social issues—was also true for our ancestors. Also, it doesn't explain why language is much more complex nowadays than is necessary for social bonding. Another alleged weakness (see below) is that the theory is too general, in the sense that it does not specify what humans are talking about while bonding.

The Political Hypothesis (Cognitive Science, Biology). Cognitive scientist Jean-Louis Dessalles (2007) uses another approach that draws on the insights of various disciplines. While attempting to address the question "What biological necessity is there for language?" Dessalles intends to show "how fruitful the coming together of evolutionary biology and the cognitive sciences may be" (p. x). As a cognitive scientist, he sees language as an open combinatorial system made up of arbitrary symbols; that is, we combine sounds to make words, which we combine again to make sentences using symbols that bear no similarity to the things they refer to. Although we use a small number of sounds, the combinatorial possibilities are virtually endless. Moreover, language enables us to share with others references that are remote in both space and time. Unlike some biologists,[7] Dessalles does not see language as qualitatively comparable with similar behavior among primates. On the contrary, it is a specific aptitude, not the application of a

---

[7]See, for instance, Savage-Rumbaugh, Shanker, & Taylor (1998).

general form of intelligence. According to Dessalles, our ancestors had the same linguistic abilities as we do (p. 76).

Drawing on biological insights, Dessalles (2007) makes the case that language is a biological trait and that it cannot have been a *mere* product of culture. He rejects Dunbar's social bonding theory because it does not explain why, biologically, we have the mode of communication that we have. Essentially, Dessalles argues, human beings use language for the exchange of relevant messages. A relevant message is a message that is able to produce knowledge in the minds of the hearers (p. 278). But that leads to the next question: When is a message considered relevant?

A message is relevant if speakers manage to convey to the audience that what they are saying is of interest; the message must contain a "salient" feature. Very small children start to point at salient things to draw their mother's attention to them. Among other primates, this attention-sharing behavior is unknown (Carpenter, Nagell, & Tomasello, 1998, cited in Dessalles, 2007, p. 290). Even if their attention is drawn to salient events, they never attempt to share that attention with any of their fellows. Among humans, informative conversation is universal and spontaneous. This brings Dessalles to the conclusion that it fulfills an important biological function.

Relevance implies a constraint on the behavior of the participants in a conversation: To be relevant, a speaker has to explain a certain salient fact. Speakers who fail to do so run the risk of being irrelevant. It is important to notice that Dessalles (2007) refuses to explain conversational conflicts in social terms. When people disagree about an issue, it is a *cognitive* conflict, not between individuals but between mental representations (p. 299). In this view, the social function of language is only a consequence of its primary cognitive function: communication of salient features.

What is the biological benefit speakers derive from language interaction? Obviously, to receive information about important facts benefits the listener, but what is the benefit for the speaker? Dessalles (2007) rules out the possibility that speakers are motivated by altruism when they offer useful information because altruism, he argues, would contradict Darwinian evolution. Thus, he believes he needs to find another justification. Dessalles' answer amounts to the following: *Being relevant benefits speakers because it grants them status.* The basis of this insight is a biological theory developed by Amotz Zahavi and Avishag Zahavi (1997): *prestige theory.* According to this theory, altruistic behavior of some animals is motivated by the fact that it affords them prestige among their fellows. Prestige pays off in increased chances of reproduction. Dessalles extends this theory by suggesting that the system of status granting is advantageous not only to those who benefit from it, but also for the individuals who grant the status. The biological motivation for granting status is what Dessalles calls "the coalition game," in which the prize is to become a valued member of a network.

It is not unusual for animals that live in sufficiently large social groups to form coalitions. Coalitions are essential to the survival of a large group's members. When coalitions compete with each other, political behavior becomes important. According to Dessalles (2007), politics is a basic behavioral component of our species arising from confrontations between coalitions (p. 347). The basis for forming coalitions is status. It is Dessalles' view that members of coalitions choose and grant status to each other according to their ability to speak relevantly. Performance in conversation demonstrates the ability of a speaker to get biologically relevant information from the environment. By showing their conversational qualities in an election campaign, the speakers can show that they are the best candidates to lead the coalition. On a smaller scale, "we all participate in a perpetual election campaign, the point of which is to elect our friends, our social contacts, and the people whose advice, orders, or suggestions we are going to heed" (p. 358). In this elective process, highly developed mental capacities and linguistic faculties are selection pressures.

That humans are highly political creatures was noted earlier by Aristotle, according to whom man is by nature a political animal. Aristotle thought that our capacity to speak made civic societies possible, but according to Dessalles (2007), it is just the reverse: The social organization of our species, structured through political competition among coalitions, led to the emergence of language (p. 359). Dessalles thinks that our ways of understanding and reasoning are a fortuitous product of evolution.

The relevance-for-status theory can be seen as a variation on Miller's Scheherazade theory (see above). Both theories share the political hypothesis that verbal skills can be translated into political power, which in turn enhances reproductive success (Pinker & Bloom, 1990). The strength of this hypothesis is that it explains much of what we observe, especially in scientific and political communication. In these contexts, speaking well is certainly status granting.

If the power of language is a biological rather than a cultural phenomenon, as Dessalles (2007) seems to hold, it is probable that our human ancestors used it for the same reason as we do. His assumption, however, that altruistic behavior contradicts Darwinian evolution may be doubted. As primatologist Frans de Waal (2005) has shown, altruistic behavior is natural among primates and perfectly compatible with Darwinian evolution. Another weakness is the theory's lack of explanatory power. If Dunbar is right in saying that humans spend up to 20% of their waking hours engaged in social interactions, it is hard to believe that we are motivated by gaining status all the time. In a typical conversation, speakers are often neither interested in transmitting information nor in showcasing their fitness for leadership. A last point of critique may be that Dessalles' strong emphasis on the contrast between biology and culture appears somewhat outdated, as the next theory to be evaluated shows.

Niche Construction (Biological Anthropology, Evolutionary Biology). A recent and very promising approach is the theory of cultural niche construction developed by biological anthropologist John Odling-Smee and evolutionary biologists Kevin Laland and Marc Feldman (2003). A *niche* is an appropriate combination of conditions for a species to flourish. *Niche construction* is "the process whereby organisms, through their activities and choices, modify their own and each other's niches" (Niche Construction, n.d.). According to the authors, standard evolutionary theory "has inadvertently erected conceptual barriers that make it difficult to integrate evolutionary biology with several neighboring disciplines, including . . . the human sciences" (Odling-Smee & Laland, 2008). Combined with established evolutionary processes, the process of niche construction improves understanding of human evolution. Odling-Smee et al. (2003) present the theory of cultural niche construction as an *extended evolutionary theory*. This example of theory extension is especially interesting for interdisciplinarians. Therefore, it is worthwhile to see how theory extension works in this case, before applying this theory to the evolution of language.

In standard evolutionary theory, summarized in Figure 7.1, adaptations of organisms are assumed to be consequences of natural selection in a certain environment (E). Populations of organisms transmit genes from one generation to the next, under the direction of natural selection. Processes that operate

Figure 7.1   Standard Evolutionary Theory

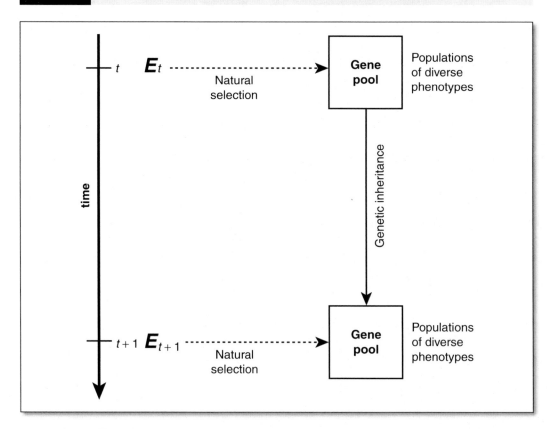

SOURCE: Niche Construction (n.d.).

independently of organisms, such as climate change, frequently change the worlds in which they adapt.

The fact that organisms can and do alter their environments is well known among biologists and ecologists, but the conventional way of thinking about niche construction is that it is a product of natural selection. However, Odling-Smee et al. (2003) argue that niche construction is best regarded not as an evolutionary product but as a co-evolutionary process in its own right. Organisms frequently create and destroy their environments by their behavior and choices. Through niche construction, organisms shape the nature of their world and, in part, determine the selection pressures to which they and their descendants are exposed. Niche construction theory takes into account that living organisms are active as well as reactive. It sees natural selection and niche construction as reciprocal causal processes in evolution involving two major inheritance systems, genetic and ecological inheritance (Odling-Smee & Laland, 2008; Odling-Smee, Laland, & Feldman, 2003). Figure 7.2 summarizes this view.

Figure 7.2   Niche Construction Theory

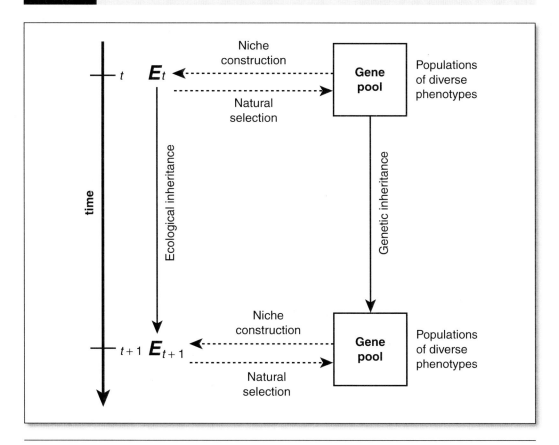

SOURCE: Niche Construction (n.d.).

Social niche construction can be fruitfully understood as a special kind of evolutionary niche construction. The social niche is

> the subset of natural selection pressures in an evolutionary niche that stems from interactions with other organisms in their social groups. It constitutes the resources (e.g., food), services (e.g., grooming), and other outputs (e.g., threats) provided by organisms for each other. It also includes all the ways in which individual organisms can actively defend themselves, compete with, form alliances with, cooperate, exploit, or manipulate other organisms, and by doing so modify some of the natural selection pressures they encounter in their niche. (Odling-Smee & Laland, 2008, pp. 106–107)

Social niche construction is relevant for the present study because it could have played a major role in the evolution of societies and the evolution of language. Living in social groups is advantageous for some species—it protects its members against predators and makes foraging more efficient—but it is only possible if the members of the group are able to communicate with each other.

Odling-Smee and Laland (2008) conclude that group living depends on two kinds of niche construction. One concerns the construction of social niches that modify conventional sources of natural selection, as described above. The other kind is *communicative niche construction,* which depends on the ability of living organisms "to convey meaningful information to and from each other through their bodies, products, or activities" (p. 108). In primates and other large-brained organisms, communication typically consists of sending and receiving meaningful messages that involve learning and cognition (p. 108).

Odling-Smee and Laland (2008) suggest that organisms can modify one or more of the natural selection pressures in their common environments by communicating. However, this does not happen overnight. For communicative niche construction to have evolutionary consequences (with some impact on human genetics), the social groups and their communication networks have to last longer than one generation. The organization of social groups over generations should correlate with a "transgenerational capacity" for communicative niche construction. Natural selection will probably favor individuals who know how to communicate effectively at low costs and with high benefits (p. 112). Obviously, language, once learned and used well, is a "cheap" way to gain high social benefits. However, this insight does not yet answer the question of why humans apparently need language to communicate, whereas other animals seem to survive very well without it.

Human language differs in two important respects from other animals' communication systems: Human language is learned and it changes rapidly, whereas communication among other animals is unlearned and it does not change very much over time. Which kind of selection pressure could have favored the shift from unlearned to learned vocalization? In answering this question, Odling-Smee and Laland (2008) argue that the context for language evolution has to be culturally constructed. They propose that there is an interaction between culture and genes, when cultural changes modify natural selection pressures. This idea of gene-culture co-evolution is visualized in Figure 7.3.

In Figure 7.3, Route 1 applies when a culturally induced change leads to an effective cultural response, with no impact on human genetics. An example may be our response to the challenge of acid rain. Human behavior probably caused acid rain, but it also was responsible for the solution to this problem. Route 2 applies when we fail to provide an effective response to a culturally induced environmental change, with changing gene frequencies as a consequence.

According to niche construction theory, the source of selection for language is not some external changing environment but a feature of the self-constructed environment. It hypothesizes that "our ancestors constructed the environmental conditions that favored hominid reliance on culture, building niches in which it paid them to transmit more information to their offspring" (Odling-Smee & Laland, 2008, p. 119). Cultural practices change rapidly. Moreover, cultural change is evidently cumulative and cultures grow more complex and diverse over time. With the generation of more cultural variants, better ways of communicating were selected for. Thus, "human language may have co-evolved with human cultural niche construction as a means of

Figure 7.3   Cultural Niche Construction

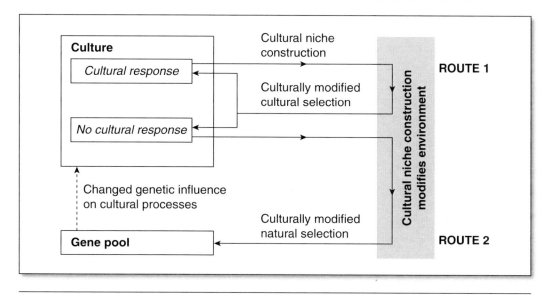

SOURCE: Niche Construction (n.d.).

facilitating and enhancing socially transmitted life-skill acquisition in young hominids, particularly in our own species" (p. 120). According to niche construction theorists, the emergence of our natural predisposition to speech is the result of gene-culture interaction that shaped our genomic architecture.

The strength of niche construction theory (i.e., extended evolutionary theory) is that it addresses the importance of human behavior and cultural processes in human evolution. It is also an interdisciplinary approach that crosses the boundaries between natural (physical) and cultural explanations of the evolution of language. A weakness of the application to language evolution may be that it is difficult to test. Odling-Smee and Laland (2008) are aware of this concern and propose some criteria for determining the validity of competing theories (p. 116), but more research has to be done.[8] The theory is based on the assumptions that language is a cultural phenomenon and that it emerged gradually.

Complexity Theory (Cognitive Science, Artificial Intelligence, Linguistics). Our third subquestion—Why (and how) did language evolve into such a complex system?—regards the development of language once it was invented. The discussion of the evolution of language takes place in the context of the famous "language-instinct" debate. This, largely theoretical, linguistic debate has its origins in the 1960s when Noam Chomsky advanced the so-called *innateness hypothesis,* holding that language is a genetically programmed system, a sort of biologically inherited coding system for our biologically inherited knowledge base, and that all languages share the same fundamental "universal grammar." Chomsky's so-called "nativist" theories had great impact, but in the 1980s his star waned. Since the 1990s, however, linguistic nativism has been back on stage again. This revival of nativism came together with a growing interest in Darwinian biological evolution. Chomsky argued that human language could not have evolved through natural selection, but he suggested that it might have emerged as an evolutionary saltation—a sudden discontinuous leap rather than a gradual development from simpler precursors (Sampson, 2005). Most other linguists, though, contend that natural selection is the only mechanism that can account for both the structure and function of human language (Hurford, Studdert-Kennedy, & Knight, 1998; Pinker, 1994; Pinker & Bloom, 1990). However, if we assume that language evolved as a substitute for grooming or for the exchange of information about hunting and tool making, language is "an embarrassment for evolutionary theory" because it is more complex, and "vastly more powerful, than one can account for in terms of selective fitness" (Premack, 1986, cited in Hurford et al., 1998, p. 3). The aim of *complexity theory* is to solve exactly this problem.

---

[8]Emphasizing their ignorance of the human language literature, Odling-Smee and Laland encourage language scholars to use niche construction theory and come up with some testable predictions.

Complexity theory says that "complex entities produced by any process of unplanned evolution, such as the Darwinian process of biological evolution, will have tree structuring as a matter of statistical necessity" (Sampson, 2005, p. 143). According to this theory, organisms that contain hierarchical ("tree") structuring have a greater chance to survive.[9] Applying this theory to the development of language, Geoffrey Sampson (an expert in natural language computing) hypothesizes that our ancestors would have begun by speaking in one-word sentences. Then, after a period when sequences of one-word sentences had quite often proved useful when uttered in succession, grammatical structure might have gradually emerged. This process leads to the hierarchical structure (tree structure) of language, with rules or grammar that modify elements of a sentence. Sampson agrees with Chomsky and other nativists that tree structure in grammar is a universal feature, but, unlike Chomsky, he sees tree structuring as the hallmark of *gradual* evolution: Hierarchical structures are created by the repeated splitting and differentiation of what begins as a single unit. The growth of a fetus after conception is the most obvious example of this repeated splitting and differentiation, but it also holds for the growth of knowledge, and even social institutions show a strong tendency to become hierarchical in this way.

Sampson (2005) holds that languages are wholly cultural constructs. As an empiricist, he insists that most concepts are developed separately by separate cultures. In his view, there is no specialized "innate" linguistic faculty or brain component specific to language; first-language learning depends on *general* human intelligence and capabilities, not on some *specialized* biological structure dedicated to language. Sampson assumes that "children learn their first language by a process of trial and error hypothesis formation based on their experience with language data made available in the linguistic community into which they are born combined with the skills provided by general human abilities" (p. 145). This assumption is relevant because, in Sampson's view, in this respect "ontogeny recapitulates phylogeny," which is the usual way to express the idea that the development of the individual mirrors the evolution of its species, not necessarily in exact detail but in broad outline. When we invented language, the preexisting vocalizing and hearing capabilities just happened to come in handy.

If Sampson is right, the development of language into a complex system can be considered as a process of unplanned *cultural* evolution. Languages, like other examples of human culture, are the result of individuals trying to master their environment. Their complexity varies over individuals' lifespan, between individuals, between cultures, and in history, as Sampson and Gil (2009) show. Like other cultural institutions (including human societies and social institutions), languages evolve in complexity over time, often becoming more complex, sometimes being simplified. The complexity of language is not

---

[9]The link between hierarchical structure (tree structuring) and evolutionary development was first made by the founder of Artificial Intelligence and Nobel Prize winner Herbert Simon (*The Architecture of Complexity*, 1962).

the result of natural selection, but there are plenty of "evolutionary" processes in the world other than Darwinian biological evolution.

The strength of this theory is that it offers a solution to the problem stated above, that language is so much more complex and powerful than one can account for in terms of selective fitness. A weakness is that it seems to rest on the assumption that languages are *wholly* cultural constructs, which seems to be an overstatement and difficult to reconcile with the alleged universality of tree structures in grammar. Furthermore, Sampson's (2005) assumption that "in this respect, as in many others" (p. 145), ontogeny recapitulates phylogeny is now discredited among biologists. Aitchison (1996) summarizes the scholarly opinion when she says that "ontogeny sometimes recapitulates phylogeny, but it does not necessarily do so" (p. 93).

The insights of the four theories, as well as their assumptions and concepts, are shown in Table 7.1. The use of data management tables is very helpful during the literature search, as were the cards and card trays in the pre-computer era. In the beginning, it is better to have too much information than too little, but revision is always necessary in a later stage of the research process. Thus, Table 7.1 contains only those insights, concepts, and assumptions that will be used later in the process.

So far, we have analyzed and evaluated theory-based insights on the problem of the primary and original function of language from four competing perspectives. We have taken theories, not disciplines, as our point of departure because the relevant theories are interdisciplinary or draw on various disciplinary insights. We have learned that grooming and gossip theory and niche construction theory see the evolutionary function of language as primarily social, whereas the political hypothesis, exemplified in the relevance for status theory, states that language is primarily a cognitive entity that developed as a means for informative communication. These three perspectives answer our first two subquestions, why did language evolve and why only with humans, in different ways. The fourth theory, complexity theory, provides an answer to our third subquestion: Why did language evolve into such a complex system? What remains to be done is to integrate these insights and produce a more comprehensive understanding. This will be done in four steps, the last four steps of the interdisciplinary research process.

Integrating Insights and Producing an Interdisciplinary Understanding (Steps 7 to 10)

The goal of this study is to construct a theory of the primary function of language that integrates the four theories discussed in the previous paragraph. In order to achieve this goal, it is important not to jump to the conclusion—that is, the more comprehensive understanding—without taking the intermediate steps of the research process. The insights analyzed above are

Table 7.1	Theory-Based Insights Into the Primary Function of Linguistic Communication

Theory	Insights	Assumption(s)	Concepts
Grooming and gossip theory (Social brain hypothesis)	• Language evolved primarily to serve social bonds by providing a substitute for social grooming. Language evolved to enable us to gossip. • The evolutionary function of language was the cooperative sharing of "displaced" (not currently perceptible) information, particularly social information. • Perceptual processing skills are all byproducts of the fact that the (primate) brain evolved to handle day-to-day social problems. • Why only humans? No other species evolved group sizes large enough to require more than grooming for social bonding. • Human social relations have a complex structure.	• Sociality assumption: man is a social animal • Development of language is a slow and gradual process (continuity hypothesis).	• Evolution • Communication • Social bonding
• Relevance for status theory (Political hypothesis) • Prestige theory (extended)	• Primary function of language: communication of salient features. • Language is closely associated with the granting of status. Language is a way of "showing off." • Biological function of language: the coalition game. • The social function of language is only a consequence of its primary function: communication of salient features.	• Language is a cognitive entity, an open combinatorial system, a digital code made of discrete and arbitrary symbols. • A relevant message produces (useful) knowledge in the minds of hearers (cognitive approach). • Speech is a component of our biological nature. • Man is a political animal. • Language is a local adaptation, not the result of a gradual process and not an outcome of intelligence.	• Evolution • Communication • Relevance • Status

(Continued)

Table 7.1   (Continued)

Theory	Insights	Assumption(s)	Concepts
• Niche construction • Extended evolutionary theory	• Language evolved as a means of facilitating and advancing the social transmission of life skills to young hominids, particularly in our own species. • The emergence of our natural predisposition to speech can be seen as the result of gene-culture interaction that shaped our genomic architecture.	• Human language is a component of human culture, socially learned and rapidly changing. • Development of language is a slow and gradual process (continuity hypothesis).	• Evolution • Communication • Cultural niche • Gene-culture interaction
Complexity theory	• Like other cultural institutions (including human societies and social institutions), languages evolve in complexity over time, often becoming more complex, sometimes being simplified. • Tree structuring is the hallmark of gradual evolution.	• Languages are wholly cultural constructs. • Popperian view of human nature, which sees the individual as making original though fallible conjectures and testing them against objective reality. • Ontogeny recapitulates phylogeny.	• Evolution • Complexity

the building blocks of our new theory. But building a theory is like building a house: It begins with creating a solid foundation. Unless this foundation (common ground) is created, integration cannot proceed. Now, "common ground is created not by modifying insights directly, but by modifying the theories, concepts, or assumptions from which the conflicting insights were produced" (Repko, 2008, p. 279). Therefore, we first have to identify the conflicts between the theory-based insights and locate their sources (Step 7), then create common ground between them (Step 8), integrate them (Step 9), and produce a more comprehensive understanding of the problem (Step 10).

Identifying Conflicts Between Insights and Their Sources (Step 7)

Conflicts typically occur between insights in a discipline and between disciplines, but also between insights resulting from interdisciplinary theories, especially in the study of language where so many disciplines are involved. It is only natural that insights resulting from different disciplinary perspectives conflict because disciplines focus on different aspects of a problem. Interdisciplinary theories, as they appear in this study, may already have solved some of the conflicts between disciplinary insights, but even then each theory represents a different view of the problem, so that new conflicts arise between the insights based on those theories. It is necessary, therefore, to identify the conflicts between the theory-based insights because they stand in the way of achieving integration.

A Taxonomy of Conflicting Insights

The theories produce different insights regarding the primary function of language that are summarized in Table 7.2.

The insights of grooming and gossip theory (GGt) and niche construction theory (NCt) are different more than opposed. NCt may be seen as *subsuming* GGt, since NCt includes grooming in the definition of "social niche." NCt is more comprehensive in that it discusses the origin of language in the broader context of cultural niche construction. A difference is that GGt was originally designed to account for the evolutionary origin of language, whereas NCt is a theory that aims to bring culture under the umbrella of standard evolutionary theory by extending this theory. GGt and NCt (implicitly) share the assumption that human language is socially learned and that it

Table 7.2   Conflicting Insights

Theory	Disciplines Involved	Primary Function of Language?	Why Only Humans?	Why Complex?
Grooming and gossip (social brain hypothesis)	• Anthropology • Biology	To serve social bonds by providing a substitute for social grooming	No other species evolved group sizes large enough to require more than grooming for social bonding.	Complexity of language is a function of complexity of social problems.
Relevance for status (political hypothesis)	• Cognitive science • Biology	Communication of salient features, the coalition game	Politics ("the coalition game") is a basic behavioral component of our species, arising from the confrontations of coalitions.	Complexity of language is a function of complexity of messages (argumentation).

(Continued)

Table 7.2	(Continued)			
Theory	**Disciplines Involved**	**Primary Function of Language?**	**Why Only Humans?**	**Why Complex?**
Niche construction	• Anthropology • Biology	To facilitate and advance the social transmission of life skills to young hominids, particularly in our own species	Human language is socially learned and rapidly changing.	Complexity of language is a function of complexity of culture.
Complexity theory	• Natural language computing • Theoretical linguistics • Cognitive science		Languages are wholly cultural constructs.	Like other cultural institutions (including human societies and social institutions), languages evolve in complexity over time, often becoming more complex, sometimes being

developed gradually from other forms of animal communication (the continuity hypothesis). Both theories leave the problem of the adaptive significance of complexity in language implicit or open.

Jean Dessalles' relevance for status theory (RSt) seems, in some respects, to be diametrically opposed to GGt and NCt because RSt states that the social function of language is only a byproduct of its primary function: communication of salient features. RSt does not see communication of relevant information as a kind of social behavior, but rather as a cognitive act: A relevant message produces (useful) knowledge in the minds of hearers. Against the continuity hypothesis, RSt stresses the uniqueness of language. It sees language as a local adaptation, not as the result of a slow and gradual process and not as an outcome of intelligence. RSt assumes that man is a political animal, whereas GGt and NCt, like Darwin, see man as a social being.

Geoffrey Sampson's complexity theory (Ct) differs from the other three with respect to its explanatory aim and power. Ct is meant to explain not why we talk but how languages evolve in complexity over time, often becoming more complex, sometimes becoming less so. In that respect, Ct can be seen as complementary to GGt and/or NCt or as an alternative for RSt where this last theory is too context specific. Unlike GGt, NCt, and RSt, which see language as part of our biological nature, Ct sees languages as wholly cultural constructs. Ct joins RSt in its cognitive approach to language.

These conflicts have their source in the overall perspective of the disciplines involved as well as in each insight's concepts and assumptions.

Conflicting Concepts

One of the most important sources of conflict is the concepts used by the various writers. In this study, it is of utmost importance to see whether the concepts *evolution* and *communication* have the same meaning in all relevant theories.

Evolution, as noted earlier, is not the same as natural selection. Evolution can have many causes and natural selection is one of those causes. Our focus question asks for an account of the adaptive significance of language, that is, an explanation in terms of natural selection. GGt and RSt use the term *evolution* in this sense: with modification by natural selection. NCt does the same, but extends the theory of evolution by natural selection in order to explain the interaction between natural and cultural events. Ct compares the evolution of linguistic complexity with the evolution of societies and cultural institutions. This kind of evolution is not likely to be the result of natural selection because selection occurs culturally rather than genetically. Thus, we have to conclude that Ct uses the concept of evolution in a broader sense than the other three theories.

Communication is also a central concept in this discussion. The theories under review see language as a form of communication, but GGt and NCt consider communication to be a social activity (the cooperative sharing of information), whereas for RSt and Ct (both rooted in cognitive science), communication is primarily a cognitive activity (producing knowledge in the minds of hearers). For GGt, perceptual processing (i.e., cognitive) skills are byproducts of the fact that the (primate) brain evolved to handle day-to-day social problems.

Conflicting Assumptions

Because the most important insights in this study are interdisciplinary, it is not necessary to identify disciplinary assumptions. Identifying the assumptions that are made within a theory, however, is particularly important.[10] Table 7.1 shows that the assumptions in this debate are several and conflicting. Dunbar (GGt) and Odling-Smee and Laland (NCt) share the sociality

---

[10]Szostak (personal communication, January, 2010) distinguishes two kinds of assumptions: theoretical assumptions, which are the precise assumptions made within a theory, and philosophical assumptions, which are the epistemological, ethical, religious, and ideological views that may inform theory construction.

assumption ("man is a *social* animal"). This may not surprise us because they all have some affiliation with anthropology, a social science. Dessalles (RSt) sees man as a *political* animal. At first sight, this is just another way of saying the same thing. After all, most people see politics as a social activity. But for Dessalles, politics is a consequence of the biological function of language: the coalition game. The social function of language is, for him, only a consequence of its primary function: communication of salient features. As a cognitive scientist, he sees communication as a cognitive activity (i.e., producing knowledge in the minds of hearers). Although Dessalles and Sampson share an affiliation with cognitive science, they could not differ more in their assumptions: For Sampson, languages are wholly cultural constructs with no biological origins whatsoever. He would, presumably, share the assumption of NCt that human language is socially learned and rapidly changing (and growing more complex).

Creating Common Ground (Step 8)

When conflicts have been identified,[11] the next step is to create common ground to overcome these conflicts. Theories on the origins of language are traditionally divided between theories that emphasize genetic evolution and theories that emphasize cultural evolution (Steels, 2008). RSt seems to belong to the first category and Ct certainly belongs to the second. GGt and NCt adopt an intermediate position, arguing that culturally evolved systems could have induced genetic modifications. Even if all these theories are coherent (i.e., internally consistent), they cannot be valid at the same time in the same respect if the conflicting elements remain unresolved. Step 8, creating common ground, is meant to resolve the conflicts as much as possible.

Creating Common Ground Using Concepts

The insights into the problem of the primary function of language have one thing in common: They take the Darwinian theory of evolution as their point of departure. Although some of the details may be open to interpretation, the outlines of this theory are common knowledge and function as a point of common ground for all four theories. Although GGt and RSt have different assumptions regarding the question *how* language developed (continuous versus discontinuous), they use the term *evolution* in its biological sense and agree that natural selection is its cause. NCt extends the Darwinian theory of

---

[11]In the second edition of his book *Interdisciplinary Research* (in preparation), Repko addresses the question Is creating common ground even necessary? The point of this would be that students need only to find common ground between theorists who are disagreeing about the same thing, not when they are talking about two different things. If theorists have at least one variable in common, then the interdisciplinarian needs to create common ground for that variable (personal communication, March, 2010).

evolution to include cultural developments insofar as they induce changes in the environment over generations. Ct appears to compare the evolution of languages with the evolution of other cultural constructs: Their evolution is not the result of natural selection but of a "natural" tendency to evolve toward more complexity. Medieval philosophers used to solve this kind of terminological problem, which they often encountered when they had to reconcile philosophical insights with religious truths, by making a distinction between a strict (or literal) sense and a broad sense of a term. In our case, we could solve the conflict by making a distinction between a strict sense of the term "evolution," meaning evolution-with-modification-by-natural-selection, and a broad sense for the evolution of knowledge, cultures, societies, and institutions. The evolution of language toward more complexity would be an example of evolution in the broad sense. This technique of "distinguishing," as it was called in the Middle Ages, is probably best described as a combination of the common ground techniques of redefinition and extension (Repko, 2008, pp. 281–283).

With the concept of *communication* we may proceed in a similar way, but in the opposite direction. Using the technique of redefinition (Repko, 2008, p. 283), we could redefine *communication* in a way that covers both its social and its cognitive function. After all, it is hard to imagine that the exchange of social information succeeds if the partners in the conversation do not understand each other's messages. This leads us to the common ground definition of communication as the cooperative sharing of information by producing knowledge in the minds of hearers.

Creating Common Ground Using Assumptions

In our study, the relation between sociality and linguistic communication appears to be a source of conflict. Is sociality a prerequisite for communication (GGt and NCt) or is it just a byproduct of communication (RSt)? Is man a social (GGt and NCt) or a political (RSt) animal? To answer these questions, we need the help of one other perspective: computer science. Based on the evidence of language game experiments with robots, Steels (2008) argues that one of the factors that make communication successful is a strong social engagement ("joint attention") of speaker and hearer. Another aspect of sociality is the ability to adopt the perspective of the other. Without this power of perspective reversal, no communication system is possible, according to Steels. Thus, if we adopt Steels' conclusions, sociality is a necessary condition for the emergence of language.

Now, what does this mean for our effort to create common ground? Is there a way to reconcile the assumption "man is a social animal" with the assumption that "man is a political animal?" Again, we may find some inspiration in medieval philosophy, this time in the work of Thomas Aquinas (1225–1274). Entrusted with the task of reconciling Aristotle's political philosophy with Christian values, he silently extended Aristotle's claim that "man is a *political* animal"[12] to "man is a *political and social* animal." Aquinas's motive must have been that for him, man is not only a citizen with civic duties, but also an individual with Christian duties. Applying this technique to our case, we could argue that humans use linguistic communication in the context of their family and friends mainly for social reasons, but on the level of the larger community, they need language to make coalitions. Thus, the common ground assumption is that man is a social *and* political animal.

Thus, the result of Step 8 is that we have created two common ground concepts and one common ground assumption. The common ground concept of *evolution* is a complex concept because it encompasses "Darwinian" as well as "natural" evolution. In our new theory, we have to distinguish between the two aspects when necessary. The common ground concept of *communication* refers to the cooperative sharing of information by producing knowledge in the minds of hearers. The common ground assumption is that man is a social *and* political animal.

Integrating Disciplinary Insights (Step 9)

Having created common ground among the relevant insights—actually, three "layers" of common ground—we can begin the process of integrating insights. Our aim is to formulate a coherent and testable theory that gives an answer to the question *What was the primary function for which language emerged?* The focus is on the original function of linguistic communication from an evolutionary perspective, but the theory will have to answer two other questions as well: Why do only humans have language, and how can language complexity be explained?

Integrating the conflicting theories involves using the technique of theory extension. We could take the useful elements of each theory in order to form a new comprehensive theory, or we could expand one of the theories by adding one or more elements of the other theories. Since we already have one extended theory (niche construction theory), the second route seems to be the most promising. The step-by-step integration runs as follows:

Niche construction theory enables us to see linguistic communication as one of the activities that may modify more conventional sources of natural selection. Group living, the theory says, depends on social and communicative niche construction. A *social* niche is a subset of natural selection pressures in an evolutionary niche that are induced by interactions with other organisms in the group (e.g., grooming). The construction of a *communicative* niche depends on the ability of living organisms to exchange meaningful information. Communication with evolutionary consequences typically involves learning and cognition. The fact that only humans use speech to communicate is explained by assuming that human language is a component

---

[12]Notice that for Aristotle, this was not an assumption but a conclusion based on two premises: (1) man is by nature a rational animal, and (2) nature does nothing in vain.

of human culture. Cultural practices change rapidly, and with the generation of more cultural variants, better ways of communicating were selected for.

Using Dunbar's grooming and gossip theory, we may add that better ways of communicating were also necessary for humans to communicate in larger groups with complex networks. This theory says that language evolved to replace social grooming when group sizes increased. Accepting the idea that grooming contributes to the construction of a social niche makes it possible to include grooming and gossip theory in niche construction theory. From grooming and gossip theory we also take the social brain hypothesis and the continuity hypothesis. Together these hypotheses propose that language (both learning and performance) evolved gradually out of primate social intelligence. Research in neurology corroborates this idea by showing that there is an overlap in the brain between the language centers and the location of social intelligence (Worden, 1998).

Accepting the common ground assumption that man is a social *and* political animal and using the common ground concept of communication as a social *and* cognitive activity, it is possible to partially integrate Dessalles' relevance for status theory. This theory sees language (performance) as a way of "showing off," its primary function being communication of salient features. Integration of this theory is possible if we accept the idea that the (primary) function of language may have been (and still is) different for different individuals.

Niche construction theory suggests that growth in cultural complexity made better ways of communicating necessary. In addition, complexity theory explains *how* languages evolve in complexity over time, often becoming more complex, sometimes being simplified. We must consider the possibility that in the beginning there was no selection pressure for complexity, but that once language existed, it quite "naturally" evolved in complexity like other cultural institutions, and then more complex language abilities were selected for. This idea is compatible with niche construction theory, when we assume that complex languages make communication about complex environmental problems and the solution to these problems possible. Language can induce changes in the environment to which organisms will adapt.

Thus, based on the common ground concepts of evolution and communication and the common ground assumption that man is a social and political animal, it is possible to extend niche construction theory in such a way that it includes Dunbar's grooming and gossip theory and the political hypothesis exemplified by Dessalles' relevance for status theory. Complexity theory can be seen as complementary to the extended niche construction theory.

An Interdisciplinary Understanding of the Primary Function of Language (Step 10)

The last step of the interdisciplinary process in this study is the formulation of the new comprehensive theory of the primary function for which language emerged. The new theory is the result of the extension of niche construction theory, which in its turn is an extension of conventional evolutionary theory. Three questions need to be answered: Why did language emerge? Why only with humans? Why (and how) did language evolve into such a complex system? From the foregoing analysis, it is possible to formulate the new comprehensive theory this way:

The emergence of our natural predisposition to speech can be seen as the result of gene-culture interaction. Humans belong to the family of primates. For primates, living in social groups is advantageous because it increases the fitness of individual members of the group. In other words, groups construct a necessary social context (social niche) for existence. The formation and maintenance of a social group depends on communication. Our ancestors were able to handle social problems by grooming, but when group sizes increased and social relations became more complex, grooming became time consuming. Moreover, it was advantageous to be able to share "displaced" information. This explains the emergence of language because with language, more individuals can be reached with less effort. Moreover, human group sizes and the complexity of human networks require more than grooming for social bonding. Social bonding is the most likely *original* function of language.

Once the possibility of linguistic communication had emerged, it may have served multiple purposes for different individuals, including mating, child-care, tool making, and hunting. For language to have an evolutionary impact in the Darwinian sense, a certain amount of learning and cognition must have been involved. So, most probably, it evolved as a means of advancing the social and cognitive transmission of life skills to young hominids. But for some (male?) individuals, it may also have played a role in the "coalition game." As we know from election campaigns, language can be used as a way of showing our talent for leadership, and strong leaders benefit all the members of the group. Thus, the primary function of language may differ for individuals in different situations and is not necessarily the same as the original function for which language emerged, social bonding.

Like other cultural constructs and knowledge, languages have a "natural" tendency to evolve in complexity over time. Language complexity does not seem to be advantageous in itself, but when environmental problems become more complex, we need complex linguistic skills (scientific reasoning) to solve them. But when we use language for "social grooming," one or two simple words may be enough.

The final question we have to answer is, How can we test this comprehensive theory?

It is impossible to test our theory in the context of this study, but we can give an indication of its strengths and weaknesses. Because the basis of our theory is niche construction theory expanded with grooming and gossip theory, the strengths of these theories also hold for our new, more comprehensive theory as long as they are compatible. The strength of the grooming and gossip theory is that it makes comprehensive sense of a number of otherwise unrelated facts: brain size, group size, grooming patterns in primates, how we use language, what we talk about, and conversation group sizes. It shows why language emerged and why it is unique for humans. It passed a critical test analysis of four competing theories (Dunbar, 2008). Regarding niche construction theory, we said that it reflects the importance of human behavior and cultural processes in human evolution. It gives language (knowledge and performance) a powerful role in the creation of communicative and cultural niches, but Odling-Smee and Laland (2008) admit that some predictions are needed to test their hypothesis for the development of language. The strength of the complexity part of our theory depends on the validity of complexity theory in general and its application to the evolution of language. If Sampson (2005) is right in arguing that tree structuring is the hallmark of gradual evolution (in the "natural" sense), this is a strong case in favor of language complexity as an evolving capability.

Lessons for Interdisciplinary Practice

In this interdisciplinary study, we have developed a comprehensive theory explaining the primary function of language in an evolutionary framework. The original aim of this project was to integrate insights on the origin and development of language, but a preliminary literature search revealed that this would be overly ambitious. Many scientists have studied language for many years, with the result that the literature is enormous. The focus on the question *why* we talk made the task manageable.

A major challenge of this project was the fact that many of the most important insights are already interdisciplinary. That made identifying disciplinary assumptions difficult and maybe even unnecessary. It appeared to be more fruitful to focus on theories, not on disciplines, and to identify the assumptions of the theories involved. The availability of a strong interdisciplinary framework, niche construction theory, made it relatively easy to construct a new theory by adding relevant factors from other theories to the theory of niche construction. With the emergence of more interdisciplinary fields, Steps 3 and 5 of the interdisciplinary research process will probably become more challenging.

Finally, it would be a good idea to pay tribute to our medieval ancestors by adopting the technique of "distinguishing" as a way of creating common ground. This technique is especially useful when different theorists use the same concept with a different meaning. Creating common ground, in this case, involves analyzing the concept to bring out the underlying non-commonality in meaning, in order to prevent confusion and achieve transparency. Discovering uncommon ground can be a route to creating common ground when the non-commonality explains why insights seem to conflict.

Conclusion

Returning to the initial issue of the primary function for which language emerged, we may conclude that the answers to this question can be divided in two groups corresponding to two hypotheses: the social brain hypothesis and the political hypothesis. The social brain hypothesis argues that language is a component of human culture, socially learned and rapidly changing, its primary function being the sharing of social information. The political hypothesis emphasizes the cognitive function of language; it sees the social function as only a consequence of its primary function: the production of relevant information in the minds of hearers. In this view, language is a component of our biological nature. An analysis of available theories revealed that it was possible to integrate the conflicting insights by extending one of these theories, niche construction theory, in such a way that it reconciles the social brain hypothesis and the political hypothesis. According to our new theory, the most likely function for which language emerged is social bonding, but, once the possibility of linguistic communication had emerged, its primary function may have differed for different individuals, as it does today. Language is used for the exchange of very complicated thoughts, but it also serves as a "bonding" instrument in various contexts, social as well as political. Further study might fruitfully examine the role of reciprocal altruism in the emergence of speech.

The focus of this study was on one aspect of the origin of language, the question of *why* we talk. There is, however, a rich diversity of perspectives regarding all aspects of language, its nature, its origin (how and when), and its development. Interdisciplinarians interested in language can use their integrative skills to create more comprehensive understandings on all these aspects.

References

Aitchison, J. (1996). *The seeds of speech: Language origin and evolution.* Cambridge: Cambridge University Press.

Bickerton, D. (1990). *Language & species.* Chicago: University of Chicago Press.

Dessalles, J. (2007). *Why we talk: The evolutionary origins of language* (J. Grieve, Trans.). Oxford: Oxford University Press.

de Waal, F. B. M. (2005). *Our inner ape: A leading primatologist explains why we are who we are.* New York: Riverhead Books.

Dunbar, R. (1996). *Grooming, gossip and the evolution of language.* Cambridge, MA: Harvard University Press.

Dunbar, R. (1998). Theory of mind and the evolution of language. In J. R. Hurford, M. Studdert-Kennedy, & C. Knight (Eds.), *Approaches to the evolution of language* (pp. 92–110). Cambridge, UK: Cambridge University Press.

Dunbar, R. (2008). Why only humans have language. In R. Botha & C. Knight (Eds.), *The prehistory of language* (pp. 12–35). Oxford: Oxford University Press.

Friedenberg, J., & Silverman, G. (2006). *Cognitive science: An introduction to the study of mind.* Thousand Oaks, CA: Sage.

Hauser, M. D. (1996). *The evolution of communication.* Cambridge, MA: MIT Press.

Hurford, J. R., Studdert-Kennedy, M., & Knight, C. (1998). *Approaches to the evolution of language: Social and cognitive bases.* Cambridge, UK: Cambridge University Press.

Johansson, S. (2005). *Origins of language: Constraints on hypotheses.* Amsterdam: John Benjamins B.V.

MacNeilage, P. F. (2008). *The origin of speech.* Oxford: Oxford University Press.

Niche construction: The neglected process in evolution. (n.d.). Retrieved from http://lalandlab.st-andrews.ac.uk/niche/index.html

Odling-Smee, J., & Laland, K. M. (2008). Cultural niche construction: Evolution's cradle of language. In R. Botha & C. Knight (Eds.), *The prehistory of language* (pp. 99–121). Oxford: Oxford University Press.

Odling-Smee, F. J., Laland, K. N., & Feldman, M. W. (2003). *Niche construction: The neglected process in evolution.* Princeton, NJ: Princeton University Press.

Pinker, S. (1994). *The language instinct: The new science of language and mind.* London: Penguin Books.

Pinker, S., & Bloom, P. (1990). Natural language and natural selection. *Behavioral and Brain Sciences, 13*(4), 707–784.

Repko, A. F. (2008). *Interdisciplinary research: Process and theory.* Thousand Oaks, CA: Sage.

Sampson, G. (2005). *The "language instinct" debate* (Rev ed.). London, New York: Continuum.

Sampson, G., & Gil, D. (2009). *Language complexity as an evolving variable.* Oxford: Oxford University Press.

Savage-Rumbaugh, E. S., Shanker, S. G., & Taylor, T. J. (1998). *Apes, language, and the human mind.* Oxford: Oxford University Press.

Selby, H., & Garretson, L. (1981). *Cultural anthropology.* Dubuque, IA: Wm. C. Brown.

Steels, L. (2008). Is sociality a prerequisite for the emergence of language? In R. Botha & C. Knight (Eds.), *The prehistory of language* (pp. 36–57). Oxford: Oxford University Press.

Tecumseh Fitch, W. (2007). The evolution of language: A comparative perspective. In M. Gareth Gaskell (Ed.), *The Oxford handbook of psycholinguistics* (pp. 787–804). Oxford: Oxford University Press.

Wilson, E. O. (Ed.). (2006). *From so simple a beginning: The four great books of Charles Darwin.* London: W.W. Norton.

Worden, R. (1998). The evolution of language from social intelligence. In J. R. Hurford, M. Studdert-Kennedy, & C. Knight (Eds.), *Approaches to the evolution of language: Social and cognitive bases* (pp. 148–168). Cambridge, UK: Cambridge University Press.

Zahavi, A., & Zahavi, A. (1997). *The handicap principle: A missing piece of Darwin's puzzle.* New York: Oxford University Press.

Understanding Human Action

8

Integrating Meanings, Mechanisms, Causes, and Contexts

Machiel Keestra

Introduction

Humans are capable of understanding an incredible variety of actions performed by other humans. Even though these range from primary biological actions, like eating and fleeing, to acts in parliament or in poetry, humans generally can make sense of each other's actions. Understanding other people's actions is called *action understanding,* and it can transcend differences in race, gender, culture, age, and social and historical circumstances. Action understanding is the cognitive ability to make sense of another person's action by integrating perceptual information about the behavior with knowledge about the immediate and sociocultural contexts of the action and with one's own experience.

Because it is necessary to integrate multiple sources of information, it is not surprising that failures to understand a person's behavior are also common. Well known is the case of the autistic professor who compares herself to an "anthropologist from Mars." Incapable of spontaneously understanding why someone cries, she has learned rules that help her to infer that people who rub their eyes while tears are running down their cheeks are weeping and probably feel unhappy (Sacks, 1995). By contrast, normal individuals automatically allow stereotypes, prejudices, self-interests, and the like to influence their understanding of a person's behavior (Bargh & Chartrand, 1999). More generally still, humans can easily misunderstand unfamiliar symbolic actions or rituals if they rely too much on their own sociocultural expertise (Gadamer, 2004). Given the importance of action understanding in every domain of human life and society, and in light of the complexities that surround it, a comprehensive scientific understanding of this capacity is needed. Apart from

5

satisfying intellectual curiosity, such insight would serve to improve our action understanding and mitigate several forms of misunderstanding. Indeed, in studying action understanding, "we as scientists are engaged in the very process that is central to our concerns" (Gergen & Semin, 1990, p. 1).

Scholars are increasingly dissatisfied with monodisciplinary approaches to understanding human action. Such one-sidedness can rest upon various motives. For example, "hermeneutic interpretations" of action understanding tend to emphasize historical and cultural influences while overlooking that ultimately such influences depend upon individual cognitive processes.[1] This has provoked criticism of the corresponding assumption that humans are born as a "blank slate" and that culture is solely responsible for all cognitive contents. However, such critique in turn easily slides into an overemphasis on the biology of human nature and a denial of sociocultural influences on cognition (Pinker, 2003).

Fortunately, recent interdisciplinary endeavors have shown that an interdisciplinary approach is preferable when investigating complex functions like action understanding. Such research often involves developing a new "interdiscipline," such as cultural psychology (Bruner, 1990), or combining insights from the social sciences and psychology (Shore, 1996; Sperber, 1996). Evidence shows that throughout human evolution there have been mutual influences between biological and cognitive processes that shape human capacities and the sociocultural influences on those processes (Bogdan, 2003; Donald, 1991; Tomasello, 1999). In addition to these interdisciplinary investigations, computational sciences and artificial intelligence research are developing computer models of human understanding that enable new types of experiments and simulations (Churchland, 1995). Such insights underscore the necessity and fruitfulness of disciplinary boundary crossing and require that various disciplinary methods, concepts, and theories be combined in innovative ways.

At present, there is a need for a theoretical framework that is capable of explaining a phenomenon as complex as human action. Such a framework requires integrating insights from multiple disciplines. The purpose of this chapter is to propose a "mechanism-based explanation"[2] of action understanding that will provide a theoretical framework for integrating various and often conflicting disciplinary insights. Proposing an integrative theoretical frame is a common practice in the sciences. Such a frame enables scientists to

---

[1]There is little room for evidence from the natural and social sciences in the hermeneutics as proposed by the influential Gadamer (2004). A theory of interpretation that gives scientific explanation a role in interpretation is proposed in Ricoeur (2008). In the social sciences, an influential approach considers human functions as stemming from actor-network interactions, without specific interest in biological and psychological conditions (Bourdieu, 1990).

[2]Such an explanation is also called "mechanistic" in the philosophy of science literature (Machamer, Darden, & Craver, 2000). It is important to realize that in an explanatory context, a mechanism is an epistemic device and plays a role in the organization of knowledge. If our knowledge of a phenomenon changes, the mechanism needs adjustments accordingly.

explain many facts that have been observed while predicting others. In the life and cognitive sciences, a specific integrative device that is often applied is this *mechanism-based explanation.*[3] As used here, *mechanism* means "an organized system of component parts and component operations. The mechanism's components and their organization produce its behavior, thereby instantiating a phenomenon" (Bechtel, 2005, p. 314).

In explaining action understanding, scientists assume that there is a complex cognitive mechanism that is responsible for this phenomenon. Such a cognitive mechanism can "produce" action understanding as it processes multiple sources of external information. Moreover, external influences can modulate or affect the mechanism itself, as is the case with sociocultural information. For instance, neuroimaging experiments in which Western and Chinese students were asked to think about themselves and then think about their mothers showed that differences in family relations are correlated with differences between the neural processes. In Western students, self-related thought activated different processes than mother-related thought, while in Chinese students the two processes were rather similar (Han & Northoff, 2008). Because action understanding involves many more different sources of information, a mechanism-based explanatory approach should be prepared to integrate insights such as these, stemming from various disciplines.

Mechanism-Based Explanation in Brief

A simple and familiar example of a mechanism is a clock with components like gears and shafts and operations like turning and oscillating. If made properly and provided with external inputs such as energy and correct initial settings, the clock will establish time accurately. However, we cannot identify the mechanism that makes the clock work just by observing its external pattern of behavior. To do that requires going *inside* the clock and investigating its various components and operations. Complex mechanisms may be analyzed at various levels. The human body, for example, is a far more complex mechanism than a clock and must be analyzed at various levels—anatomical, physiological, or biochemical—to be fully understood. Each of these levels refers to the hierarchy of the body's organization, not to the physical size of the parts that exist at each level. Given the many and often nonlinear interactions between, for example, chemical substances, organ functions, and sociocultural meanings that together can produce specific hallucinations, biological phenomena are very complex. Compared to

---

[3]Because it proved to be extremely rare to demonstrate analogues of Newton's mechanical laws for biological or cognitive systems, an alternative scientific device is considered more apt for these fields (Bechtel & Richardson, 1993; Machamer et al., 2000). Meanwhile, social scientists are discussing the fruitfulness of a mechanism-based approach as well—see Hedstrom and Swedberg (1996), for example.

the human body, a mechanical clock is not complex: Underneath the observable level of shafts and gears is the unobservable level of molecules. Note that molecular differences between clocks made from steel or from silver do not affect the way they establish time, whereas changing molecules in blood will affect human bodily functions. Biological and cognitive mechanisms are also far more complex than engineered mechanisms because of the nonlinearity of many intrinsic activities and their responsiveness to environmental factors, including the meanings of sociocultural settings and symbols.

Two strategies are used to develop a mechanism-based explanation of a phenomenon: decomposition and localization (Bechtel & Richardson, 1993). *Decomposition* means that we first analyze a given phenomenon—whether establishing time or action understanding—into components or smaller tasks that in concert are responsible for it. *Localization* means that we then try to locate these components of the phenomenon somewhere in the object or organism that displays the phenomenon. In easy cases, such as the clock, we can localize the components of our phenomenon (e.g., pointing the hours or the minutes) in separate component parts and activities of the clock. However, these parts and activities are not completely separable because they rely on the same energy source and initial settings and share many other parts and activities. Typically, therefore, our research leads to increasing specification and revision of the decomposition and localization of the phenomenon with which we started. For readers who may be unfamiliar with this approach, some clarifications are in order.

The first is that a mechanism-based explanation is *not* a complete description of a clock, an animal, or a brain. Rather, it is an explanation of a specific phenomenon, event, or behavior that is produced by the organized interaction of components and operations. A mechanism-based explanation of action understanding as performed by the brain will, therefore, contribute only in a limited sense to explanations of other functions of the brain. Because a mechanism-based explanation could be given for each function and for its components, a complete description would consist of an unmanageable multitude of mechanisms, many of which would overlap and modulate each other. Fortunately, explaining a specific phenomenon does not require this.

The second clarification is that a phenomenon may appear singular and opaque, but if we are to give a (mechanism-based) explanation of it, we must establish that it is produced by different components and operations. Cognitive operations are often called *computations*. These can be very simple, like addition, or more complex, like face recognition. Figure 8.1 shows a schema of a phenomenon, the activity of SΨ-ing.[4] It also shows components X 1–4 that, by interacting in response to an external input, produce the phenomenon. The arrows indicate the interactions that connect the components, consisting mostly of simple activation or inhibition signals. These interactions

---

[4]If the phenomenon is complex, it is useful to decompose it into in subtasks, as we will do with action understanding (see Figure 8.2 at the end of the chapter).

Figure 8.1   A Phenomenon and Its Mechanism

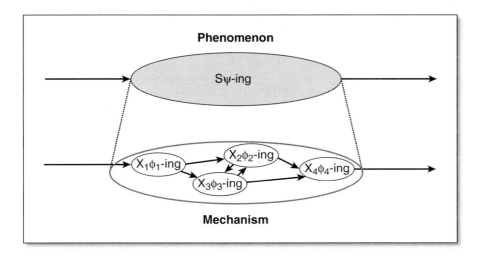

SOURCE: Craver (2007, p. 7).

often include feedback and feedforward interactions between the components and their operations. However, note that merely observing the phenomenon (from the top down) does not reveal the complex mechanism and its operation that produce the phenomenon. What appears on the surface to be a single phenomenon is, in fact, a "distributed network" of smaller actions. Note also that the phenomenon receives input (left-side arrow) and produces output, as do the components and operations at a lower level. Explaining action understanding means that we examine the cognitive processes that the human brain performs at various levels and that together form the person's capacity to understand the action or behavior of another person.

The third clarification is that such a mechanism usually is a multilevel system and can accordingly be examined at different levels. Obviously, we can study action understanding while remaining at the personal level, where we observe which types of action a person can and cannot understand, and examine the conditions that influence his action understanding. Going into the brain to a first subpersonal level, we can investigate which neural networks must cooperate to perform this function appropriately. Going down to a second level, we can investigate isolated components and activities in a particular neural area: its neurons, their interactions, and their connections to neurons in other locations. If we need to be even more specific about these neuronal activities, we can focus at a third level and describe the neurochemical activities by which neurons pass on information to each other. Going in the other direction, we can also climb one level upward and consider the person as a component; that is, consider him or her as a member of various social groups. At that supra-personal level, we are interested in the interactions between individuals and how they influence each other's action understanding, for example. For reasons discussed later, we don't need always to descend or ascend many levels when we explain a phenomenon like action understanding. The study of neurochemical interactions at the third level may still be relevant, but it is implausible that going as deep as the quantum mechanic level of the human brain yields useful insights into action understanding.

The fourth clarification, and one that is particularly relevant to all cognitive processes, is that mechanisms do not operate in complete isolation but are responsive to various factors, including contextual factors. Organisms are open to external information via their senses, but not always equally so because their motivation state, attention, and other internal processes influence this openness. Thus, the mechanism governing action understanding will be influenced by a host of contextual variables.

The fifth is that organismic mechanisms are much more flexible systems than other mechanisms. In organisms, we may observe that over time and due to learning or development or to injuries, mechanisms responsible for a particular behavior have changed or have been adapted—something a clock cannot do. Strikingly, an organism may even develop different ways to produce the same behavior or phenomenon. Automatization of a skill leads, for instance, to diminished involvement of conscious control of movements, making it possible to perform other cognitive tasks simultaneously. This can be made visible with the help of brain imaging techniques, which reveal that experts and novices in a particular skill display strikingly different brain activation patterns when performing similar tasks (Poldrack et al., 2005).

A mechanism-based explanatory approach, then, is particularly useful to interdisciplinarians because it allows them to achieve a more comprehensive understanding of phenomena such as action understanding. In applying this approach, interdisciplinarians can connect the monodisciplinary insights in specific components and operations at multiple levels and their intricate interactions that contribute to human action understanding. How this works is the subject of the next section.

Drawing on Disciplinary Insights (Steps 1 to 6)

Generally speaking, scientific efforts enable us to represent reality and intervene in it (Hacking, 1983). Scientists represent reality by using mathematical formulas, graphs, charts, mechanism-based and verbal explanations, and the like. Scientists intervene to test the adequacy of their representation or the predictions they derive from it. Depending on the discipline and the representations, such interventions range from digging for fossils in geological strata, sending particles through a cyclotron, subjecting people to experimental conditions, to adjusting variables in computational programs used for simulations of phenomena. Choosing an adequate type of representation of our insight into a phenomenon is an important matter, as is the choice of an appropriate intervention to test it.

Engaging in interdisciplinary research is an even more demanding process. A mechanism-based explanation allows us to assign disciplinary insights more or less to particular levels: Neuroscientists will focus on the neuronal and neural level, psychologists at the higher level of action understanding and its components, while sociologists will focus on the interactions between individual persons that influence the properties of this understanding. The challenge for interdisciplinary integration is to demonstrate how the components and activities that occur at different levels interact with those at other levels. However, first we must decide which disciplines are relevant for explaining action understanding. *Relevance* is thus a key term for this first part of the interdisciplinary process, if only to keep it manageable.

Defining the Problem: Decomposition of Action Understanding

Action understanding is the subject of many disciplines. This is partly the result of it being such a general and wide-ranging phenomenon with many different properties. While acknowledging its variability, it is useful to formulate a general definition. In what follows, we will consider action understanding as the result of cognitive processes that an individual—partly unconsciously—performs when making sense of another person's actions. In doing so, one person has not only to recognize the other person is acting, but also to include various sources of information to interpret that action. As a result, the action can be understood and perhaps responded to appropriately.

By putting cognitive processes at the heart of the definition, we will focus on the cognitive information processing that goes on in the brain, for which we will establish a mechanism-based explanation. This decision is in line with recent developments in both the cognitive and social sciences. Indeed, we may even speak of a "cognitive turn" in many disciplines. For instance, anthropologist Bradd Shore (1996) argues for a "cognitive view of culture" (p. 39), concurring with his fellow social scientist Sperber (1996), who argues for combining psychology with the study of culture because of our "psychological *susceptibility to* culture" (p. 57). In accordance with that susceptibility, Reyna (2002) analyzes the human mind as a "neurohermeneutic system," for which "'interpretation' is the operation of neurons to represent, and act upon, reality" (p. 112). Finally, and more extreme, is the argument that even "philosophical theories are largely the product of the hidden hand of the cognitive unconscious" (Lakoff & Johnson, 1999, p. 14). Note that putting cognition at the heart of these approaches does not imply that there is no room left for external and sociocultural influences on action understanding. Nor does it imply that the culture-specific meaning of words and symbols doesn't matter. It does, and the study of cultural determination of meaning is highly relevant. However, for such sociocultural aspects to have an influence on action understanding, they must exert this influence by affecting cognitive processes that go on in the brains of individual persons.

Having defined action understanding and put cognition at its center, we now have to take an important step. I mentioned in the previous section that we must apply two heuristics, decomposition and localization. Ergo, we should first try to decompose action understanding into smaller (sub)phenomena that can be studied more or less separately and subsequently integrate the results. Associated with that decomposition is our localization effort that involves finding responsible cognitive or brain processes that do the work. In fact, we have already localized action understanding very broadly in the individual's cognitive processes.

Having defined action understanding as a cognitive process, we can now decompose it further by classifying it according to its contents.[5] We can follow the lead of hermeneutic philosopher Paul Ricoeur, who has devoted much of his work to the theory and method of interpretation of human narrative and human action. Ricoeur (1992) pointed out that we can approach action with a set of interrelated questions focusing on, respectively, who, what, why, how, where, and when.[6] His analysis prioritizes three of those questions, which offer three different perspectives on action: *What* is the action, *why* is the action being done, and *who* is the agent? Because "Who is the agent?" refers to the agent's identity, social roles, continuous maturation, and the like, this information will generally not be captured by the other perspectives. For that reason, Ricoeur deplores that "the use of 'why?' in the explanation of action . . . became the arbiter of the description of what counts as action" (p. 61). It will become clear that to identify the relevant contexts, we need to know more about the agent "who" performed the action. Ricoeur's emphasis upon the "who" of action does not imply that contexts do not matter, but it is a consequence of the fact that contexts have to make themselves felt via an individual's cognitive processing.

So, following the lead offered by a hermeneutic analysis of understanding actions, we can decompose action understanding into three different, but probably interrelated, component tasks: understanding what an action is, understanding why an action has been performed, and a more thoroughgoing understanding of the "who" behind it. Evidence does indeed confirm the possibility of disentangling these three components of action understanding that have to do with, respectively, action recognition, intention understanding, and narrative understanding.

---

[5]Even though it is very well known that classifications and taxonomies often need corrections, revisions, or additions, they are extremely helpful in delineating otherwise overwhelming domains (Dupre, 2001). In the case of human capacities like action understanding, our preliminary classification inevitably starts from the use of our common vocabulary. This does not imply that such words that we commonly apply hold up to scientific scrutiny. Indeed, although we may expect that concepts in the domain of human experience are more robust than concepts like "ether" or "vital force," we may need to revise the former, too (Keestra & Cowley, 2009).

[6]This set of questions has also been proposed in the context of the classification of scientific theories (Szostak, 2004).

Justify Using an Interdisciplinary Approach: Action Understanding as a Multilevel Phenomenon

Because our mechanism-based explanation focuses on cognitive processes, we must first appreciate that cognitive sciences are themselves plural and that the field is interdisciplinary. This has been the case from the start, as one of its pioneers recalls: "I argued that at least six disciplines were involved: psychology, linguistics, neuroscience, computer science, anthropology and philosophy. I saw psychology, linguistics and computer science as central, the other three as peripheral" (Miller, 2003, p. 143). Note that interdisciplinary endeavors may range from a mere borrowing of concepts or tools to the establishment of a new interdiscipline with its own discipline-like contents, structures, and conventions (Klein, 1990). In our current research, different types of interdisciplinarity will be involved simultaneously.

Somewhat simplifying, I mentioned earlier that there is a link between the contribution of different disciplines and the different levels of a mechanism. This is easier to see in nonorganismic mechanisms, as they are not so complex nor flexible in their organization. From cosmology via molecular physics to quantum physics, we can distinguish different disciplines focusing on particular levels of mechanism. They use their own tools and methods and formulate different theories and hypotheses. Even though the differences between, for example, quantum mechanics, relativity theory, and classical mechanics are considerable, I believe that in the cognitive sciences, the characteristics of the different levels and the associated differences are wider ranging. To connect sociological and psychological observations, brain images, neurochemical interactions, and genetic factors, we need a wide variety of conceptual and methodological tools, whereas in the physical sciences, gaps between levels are largely bridged with mathematics.

Given this complexity and the interdisciplinary nature of our investigations, decomposing action understanding into action recognition, intention understanding, and narrative understanding will make our task more manageable. Our next step is to localize these task components somewhere "in" the individual, or rather in that person's cognitive apparatus—foremost the brain. The interaction between cognitive processes and their contexts may involve social scientific and humanistic investigations. Applying our mechanism-based explanatory perspective to the decomposed task of action understanding, we will once more approach it as a multilevel phenomenon. Of course, we already did that when decomposing the task into three components, but now we are heading for the brain and neural tissue. Indeed, we must try to assign the components and operations of our phenomenon to concrete, localizable, bodily or neural areas and activities. Generally, if we start from a particular level, we can look both upward and downward. Looking downward "involves describing lower-level mechanisms for a higher-level phenomenon" where these mechanisms are responsible for subtasks of the task or phenomenon (Craver, 2007, p. 257). Conversely, if we look upward, we may be able

to see our mechanism interacting with other mechanisms that together realize a new phenomenon at this higher level. For instance, action understanding will, in interaction with perception, motivation, and motor action,
contribute to the agent's response to another person's behavior. At that level,
it can be considered a component alongside several other components and
operations. So, in looking downward, we can treat action understanding as
an independent variable and detect changes in the associated mechanisms.
Or, conversely, we can investigate the changes in action understanding due to
influences at a higher level. Figure 8.2 at the end of this chapter may illustrate
these investigative approaches to the mechanism that we are discovering in
association with action understanding.

Interdisciplinary collaborations are involved in the investigations of such
a mechanism, bringing different intervention and observation techniques
with them. Researchers can experimentally intervene in the components or
operations at a particular level and try to detect the consequences at
another level—upward or downward. In the cognitive sciences—including
neuroscience—such interventions can be distinguished generally as interference, stimulation, or activation experiments (Craver, 2007). Stimulation
involves, for example, presenting a stimulus to a subject and then detecting
correlated activation at lower levels, down to single neurons. Interference
implies disturbing the normal mechanism, for instance by electrostimula-
tion of neurons, with subsequent detection of behavioral differences at a
higher level. Apart from such "vertically" directed interventions,
researchers can try to influence the mechanism "horizontally." By varying
the stimuli, researchers can observe at various levels whether different
mechanisms are activated, which subsequently are observable through specific properties of cognitive processing. Activation experiments can also be
combined with brain imaging techniques, which allow researchers to
observe the associated lower-level activities of the posited mechanism, its
components, and its operations. The colorful images of brain activation
patterns published in great numbers are the results of such activation experiments. Furthermore, there is also the valuable assistance of comparative
work performed by ethologists, developmental psychologists, computer
simulation scientists, philosophers, and, again, social scientists and humanists. The latter disciplines can help to investigate, for instance, whether
action understanding relies on different mechanisms in subjects from col-
lectivist versus individualist societies, or whether religious and nonreligious
subjects display a difference in focus while processing perceptual information. Clearly, limiting the number of disciplines to those that are most relevant to the problem at hand is crucial to make the interdisciplinary research
process manageable—even though empirical evidence can lead to the need
to include an originally excluded discipline.[7]

---

[7]For example, climate change models have only recently included ocean dynamics, after
marine scientists proved that it is involved in climate change.

Identify Disciplines Most Relevant to the Mechanism-Based Approach

In general, deciding which disciplines are most relevant for any given research project can be guided by three questions: Does the discipline have a well-defined *perspective* on the problem? Has the discipline produced a *body of research* (i.e., insights) on the problem of such significance that its published insights and supporting evidence cannot be ignored? Has the discipline generated *one or more theories* to explain the problem (Repko, 2008, pp. 169–170)? Although action understanding is instantiated by a multilevel mechanism, it is not surprising to find that disciplines that focus on very low levels—like quantum mechanics—have not delivered useful insights to it. Fortunately, not all events at such low levels make themselves felt at much higher levels in a relevant way. Quantum phenomena do occur in every atom of the brain, but if they affect cognition or behavior, they can do so only by influencing the functioning of specific neural areas. A cosmological phenomenon like sunspots may impact on human cognition only when it influences earthly temperatures, which have an impact on environmental conditions of humans, which finally can affect human cognitive processes. However, it is rarely the case that a single neuron seriously influences a cognitive process that involves many more neurons, or that human cognition is directly and irrevocably influenced by environmental temperature. Therefore, and in accordance with the observation that everywhere in the universe we find "local maxima of regularity and predictability" (Wimsatt, 2007, p. 209), we can restrict our multilevel system investigations to the nearest levels of our phenomenon.[8] Even though interdisciplinarians must be critical of the traditional division of labor among disciplines and keep an open eye to contributions from unexpected disciplines, the fact that we can conceive of connections between extremely divergent disciplines is never reason enough to deny differences in relevance and specificity.

Meanwhile, a first estimation of relevant disciplines for our research of action understanding can be made. Although our initial topic of action understanding implies inclusion of the full range of the cognitive sciences, the social sciences, and the humanities to account for all varieties of action understanding, our first delineation and decomposition of it has made the research more manageable. Instead of one broad phenomenon, we are now able to focus on three distinct components (action recognition, intention understanding, and

---

[8]It is also related to the intriguing phenomenon of *emergent properties:* properties that occur at a particular level and cannot be explained purely on the basis of our knowledge of lower-level components and operations. We can now say that such emergent properties are likely to depend partly on the systemic interactions between components and operations at the particular level itself, and even that higher-level ("top-down") contributions will often be involved, leaving little room for strictly reductionist explanations of higher-level properties (Bechtel & Richardson, 1993).

narrative understanding), which will lead to different questions, research methods and results, and theories.

Most straightforward is, arguably, the investigation of the first component, action recognition, which is the capability of "parsing" or sequencing continuous bodily behavior or movements into distinct actions. It is plausible both from a developmental and an evolutionary perspective that this parsing capacity is present in newborns and animals. Consequently, we may at first exclude the humanities and even social sciences from investigations of this component of action understanding. Again, it may turn out that later cognitive or speech developments affect the mechanism that carries out action parsing, but our preliminary hypothesis is that without these developments, action parsing is still being performed. With the exclusion of those sciences, there are still enough candidates for inclusion, such as neurophysiology, developmental psychology, biology, and information science.

For the second component of action understanding, intention understanding, we may need to include social sciences and humanities in our investigations. Note that we cannot straightaway exclude those sciences that assist to explain action parsing. Parsing remains generally a precondition for understanding intention, and it appears in some cases to contribute significantly to understanding the specific intentions of actions, as well. For frequently repeated actions, it has been argued that primates derive the intentional structure of complex actions purely on statistical processing (Byrne, 1999). However, it is implausible that such processing should suffice for all instances of intention understanding. How about discovering the intentions of newly observed actions, or of irregular and complex actions involving tools?

There is much evidence of humans taking a so-called "intentional stance," assigning to the observed agent the possession of mental states such as beliefs, desires, and reasons. This stance is extremely useful for predicting future behavior of relatively autonomous agents (Dennett, 1989). Experimental observations show that even young infants expect that agents are aiming rationally at a particular goal and show surprise if their behavior contradicts this expectation (Gergely, Nádasdy, Csibra, & Bíró, 1995). To explain these mental states, we need to draw in more scientific disciplines because these states involve other types of social information, often mediated by language, symbols, and so on. Social sciences and humanities can systematically investigate the interactions between such influences and action understanding.

These influences are even transmitted at lower levels of the mechanism and are correlated with the patterns of activity of so-called mirror neurons, which have turned out to play an important role in this domain. These mirror neurons were discovered some 20 years ago and have surprising properties because they respond both to perception and to observation or imagination of actions. It is interesting that their activation depends partly on prior experiences of the observers, even with socioculturally specific information. Understanding and imitating an action that is within their "vocabulary" or actions is consequently easier than if they observe it for the first time (Rizzolatti & Sinigaglia, 2008). For this component, we can draw on philosophical analysis of intentional action, on behavioral biology and psychology, on the cognitive sciences, and perhaps on social scientific research that focuses on sociocultural specific means and goals of action.

In some instances of human action, goals, objects, and instruments are perceptually visible, facilitating intention understanding. However, often the action is not or is incompletely visible, or the action is ambivalent or is temporally extended, or the perceptually available information is sparse. Not surprising, therefore, our third component of action understanding, narrative understanding, relies much more on higher cognitive processes and the use of narrative structures. We employ language, concepts, abstraction, temporal and causal relations, and the like when developing narrative structures. These are generally of an abstract nature and cannot be perceived through the senses. With the help of such structures, "we comprehend other people's minds by creating a coherent narrative or story of their actions, organized around their goals," including the conditions, the agent's plans, and possible outcomes (Read & Miller, 2005, p. 125). These coherent narratives are naturally based, in part, upon the observable properties of agents and their actions, but they also depend upon previous expertise and knowledge of the observer, including relevant sociocultural information. While making use of the insights pertaining to intention understanding, for this component we need also insights from the humanities and the social sciences about the construction and use of narratives and theories of meaning in speech and behavior. Moreover, we may want to check for cognitive scientific explanations of these phenomena as well, in order to explain why schizophrenics have difficulties delivering coherent narratives, for instance.

In sum, simple explanations of action understanding are not to be expected. Even with appropriate neural and cognitive functions, humans will face limitations in their ability to understand each other because of the variability—due to sociocultural influences—on individuals' cognitive processes. Indeed, social cognitive scientists or cognitive anthropologists argue that sociocultural-specific differences in action understanding have "two distinct moments of birth, one public and conventional and the other a subjective appropriation and integration of a conventional form by a particular person. The links between public models and personal knowledge are contingent relations" (Shore, 1996, p. 371). Such contingency applies less strongly to action recognition, as such statistical and perceptual processes will be more generally present in individuals from different cultures—even though for some sociocultural actions we may need specific expertise, such as for parsing complex ritual actions. Given the number of disciplines listed above, interdisciplinary research can benefit from prudently leaving out a discipline if it is not relevant to the specific component or operation in which we are interested.

Conduct an In-Depth Literature Search

Having exposed the scope and complexity of action understanding, it is apt to conclude that it is not a research topic but rather a comprehensive field of interdisciplinary research. However, with the help of the mechanism-based explanatory approach, we are able to narrow the scope of our research adequately. First, by decomposing the phenomenon, we have helpfully delineated three component tasks: action recognition, intention understanding, and narrative understanding. Now, we can try to limit ourselves to one of the three component tasks when we engage in behavioral, ethological, developmental psychological, or other studies at the phenomenon level. We can investigate the conditions and results of handling the task and subsequently explain what, in fact, the apparent task consists of. We can also observe whether adults, infants, and animals are doing comparably well and whether their results are correlated with their language capabilities. A more advanced subject would be the relations between the component tasks. For instance, recognition of an action is sometimes facilitated by understanding its intention. Such relations therefore complicate the mechanism.

Second, after observing the phenomenon "horizontally," we may then look at it as a multilevel mechanism and view it "vertically." Earlier I noted that we do not need to go very high or low in the investigations of associated levels. So no quantum mechanics or cosmology, but neurology, perhaps neurophysiology, and cognitive psychology should be our prime domains for the literature search.

Third, science in general and mechanism-based explanation in particular is especially interested in behavior, changes, and modifications. If nothing ever happens to a phenomenon, it is difficult to give a representation of its relevant mechanism. When investigating such a mechanism, researchers can induce changes by using the interlevel experiments that make use of the interference, stimulation, and activation techniques referenced earlier. Such experiments are relevant to our research. Literature that refers to exceptional cases or pathologies should be included with caution because the flexibility of the brain hinders generalization from such cases to normal cognitive processes. For instance, even with dysfunctional mirror neuron systems, autistic patients may be able to reach some intention understanding.

Fourth, parallel to these studies and drawing heavily upon them, in the cognitive sciences and elsewhere researchers increasingly use computational simulations of a phenomenon. When focusing on a specific component or operation, comparison with results from such simulations may be informative. For instance, when a specific mechanism is simulated in a neural network program, it can also be used for virtual—or in vitro—interference, stimulation, and activation experiments comparable to those carried out on living subjects. More extravagant still, when building and testing humanoid robots, roboticists use the insights of action understanding research. Such research may provide us with information regarding which cues facilitate humans to understand robot actions. For instance, a form of eye contact and gaze following by a humanoid robot seems to be a prerequisite for effective interaction by humans with them.[9]

Fifth, the social sciences and humanities contribute foremost to the "horizontal" investigation of action understanding itself. For instance, cross-cultural research could deliver insights into differences in action understanding properties. It is implausible that sociocultural differences have a large impact on the cognitive mechanism itself, even though there is evidence of the coevolution of language and cognition (Donald, 1991). It is plausible, nonetheless, that a singular complex and dynamic organ like the brain can develop highly divergent forms of processing corresponding to the expertise that it gathers under specific sociocultural conditions. Anyone who has observed chess masters, musicians, or hierogram readers perform their exquisite skills may doubt whether they have the same brain and use the same cognitive processes as we all do—but, yes, largely they do. Even if these distinct capabilities are only the consequence of modulations of the mechanism by such individual and external influences, the results are relevant enough to our inquiry.

Sixth, sometimes researchers have established a specific topic that appears to be representative of the phenomenon under scrutiny. In the case of action understanding, the study of imitation has turned out to be exemplary. Studying imitation, we gain insights in "two relationships that are central to understanding minds in general and human minds in particular: the relationship between perception and action and the relationship between self and other" (Hurley & Chater, 2005, p. 48). Meanwhile, imitation has been studied in various animals, infants, adults, and computer simulations. Such an example facilitates interdisciplinary research and translation efforts enormously.

As it is only after a first acquaintance with the literature that you may be able to decide about these matters, interdisciplinary research truly is "a decision-making process that is heuristic, iterative, and reflexive" (Repko, 2008, p. 137).

Develop Adequacy Concerning the Relevant Components, Operations, and Interactions of the Mechanism

After identifying the relevant disciplines, we must develop adequacy in them. Then we should be able to decide their specific relevance, what kind of knowledge we need, and how much knowledge we need from each (Repko, 2008, pp. 189–190). In the case of the component tasks of action understanding, the range of disciplines that are involved differ, leading to narrow or wider—in the case of narrative understanding—interdisciplinarity.

---

[9]See Breazeal (2004) for more on this.

This distinction reflects the methodological and conceptual distance between the disciplines (Newell, 1998). Achieving adequacy in research that involves wider interdisciplinarity and that leads to an integration of insights is obviously more difficult.

Fortunately, it is possible to reach adequacy in the case of investigations of a multilevel mechanism and its components and operations. This is due to the aforementioned fact that in such a mechanism, there are "local maxima of regularity and predictability" (Wimsatt, 2007, p. 209) even though these maxima may themselves be produced by complex mechanisms. The regular and predictable properties of atoms, for instance, hide various underlying probabilistic quantum mechanisms. Or, referring to Figure 8.2 at the end of this chapter, investigations may focus on the local maxima that are represented by particular components or operations that are included in that Figure without having to cover all the rest. As a consequence, there are many theories that describe and explain quite specific properties of the system, perhaps under specific conditions. Such "theoretical pluralism" is common in the life and cognitive sciences, granting each theory only a relative significance for its domain regarding the comprehensive or overarching problem (Beatty, 1997). Because we are interested in a particular phenomenon, action understanding or one of its three component tasks, we are permitted or even obliged to select those insights that contribute significantly to our understanding of that phenomenon: its occurrence, the components and operations that instantiate it, the conditions under which it occurs, modulating influences from other processes, and so on. Clearly, these insights will be different in kind. Some will be based upon observations of action understanding in humans, animals, or even computer simulations; others will refer to brain imaging results that suggest correlations between specific components and operations involved in relevant cognitive processes, for example.

Adequacy, in our case, must not imply presenting a complete mechanism-based explanation that comprehensively predicts and explains action understanding under all possible circumstances, as this would be extremely difficult. Instead, we have already described how we can limit our research project to just a component or an operation that contributes to it. Having done so, we can subsequently aim first to develop a mechanism sketch that explains how the phenomenon might be constituted. Such a sketch leaves room for other sketches that offer different possible mechanisms for the same phenomenon (Machamer, Darden, & Craver, 2000). Once we provide a sketch—or several sketches—starting from our preliminary definition, decomposition, and localization of action understanding, our investigations should enable us to gradually fill in the details of our mechanism-based explanation. Adequacy, then, means that we have included those insights that contribute specifically to the instantiation of our research phenomenon, while leaving out others. Given the complexity and flexibility of cognitive systems and the phenomena they produce, it is likely that future scientific developments will have an impact on what insights need to be included. I will illustrate these remarks pertaining to adequacy with an example of such a delineated phenomenon.

We observed in the previous section that distinguishing "what" an action is in some cases delivers information on "why" it is performed as well. This suggests that adequacy with respect to action recognition would also satisfy requirements for adequate knowledge of disciplinary insights for intention understanding. Because it turned out that animals and human adults and infants recognize the beginning and end of an action by noting that body movements differ unexpectedly, changing in tempo and direction (Baldwin, Baird, Saylor, & Clark, 2001), it seemed that adequacy would be relatively easy to reach. After all, in this context, achieving adequacy implies gaining insight into a relatively simple perceptual mechanism that performs statistical processing. Moreover, the visual stimuli that appear to require processing are only those that are associated with changes of tempo and direction. Consequently, the number of components and operations that are involved in these cognitive processes is limited. Thus, the number of disciplines involved is limited, and we are able to specify the insights that we need from them.

However, action recognition and intention understanding turned out not to be two completely overlapping processes in many cases. Indeed, action recognition is not always dependent upon perceptual processes alone: It is often modulated or assisted by other cognitive components. For example, conceptual knowledge of actions and specific task requirements, like the command to focus attention on specific aspects of a movie, enables subjects to recognize more reliably and faster the precise moments an action begins and ends (Baldwin et al., 2001; Hard, Lozano, & Tversky, 2006; Zacks, Kumar, Abrams, & Mehta, 2009). Apparently, the action recognition mechanism can be modulated by components and operations that subserve other cognitive processes. Consequently, adequacy here requires additional knowledge of the mutual constraints between the originally simple mechanism and the properties of such modulating influences of other cognitive processes.

This insight into the greater complexity of the action recognition mechanism forces us to reconsider our striving for adequacy. At least, it implies that we need to refine or further specify the adequacy requirements with respect to disciplinary insights. For instance, if we aim to keep the explanatory mechanism simple, we probably need to refine more narrowly those action types that can be recognized solely on the basis of this perceptual process of action recognition. Secondary to that, we must investigate whether it is plausible that this process can function in isolation at all. This seems to be the case in primate understanding and imitation of actions, where researchers believe that supplementary understanding of the aims, goals, and intentions of the agent is generally not involved (Byrne & Russon, 1998). In humans, isolating action recognition does not appear to be a plausible way to proceed because action recognition and intention understanding are different, yet more tightly connected, phenomena. Indeed, the former is generally subserving the latter:

Such initial, "bottom-up" parsing would provide appropriate units on which to base the additional processing needed to achieve ultimate understanding of the intentions at play. This type of low-level mechanism thus seems likely to be a crucial prerequisite to infants' developing understanding of the intentions motivating others' actions. (Baldwin et al., 2001, p. 715)

In the case of human action recognition, *adequacy* means the investigation of whether observers often rely upon previous sociocultural knowledge or other cognitive processes to recognize the borders of an action or between actions. If that is the case, the explanatory mechanism for action recognition must be expanded, and our adequacy requirements will be more comprehensive, too.

Sometimes, an empirical finding suggests that adequacy is within reach. For instance, the discovery of mirror neurons in the Macaque monkey motor system was not just exciting; it appeared also to bring some relief to researchers of action recognition and intention understanding. The peculiar activation of these neurons both during action perception and during action performance suggested to many researchers that action recognition and intention understanding could be adequately explained at once by referring to these neurons. Even though these mirror neuron systems are already more complex than the earlier proposed, and purely perceptual, action parsing mechanism, they did appear at first to operate in isolation from higher cognitive processes that involve speech. Indeed, they are still held to enable "that modality of understanding which, prior to any form of conceptual and linguistic mediation, gives substance to our experience of others" (Rizzolatti & Sinigaglia, 2008, p. 192). Still, the question remains: Was the promise fulfilled that adequacy with respect to action recognition and intention understanding implied having insights into the action parsing mechanism and mirror neuron systems only?

Unfortunately not, as it turned out that in human intention understanding, still more is needed. Due to the complexity of our actions, humans cannot always recognize action borders even with the additional help of these mirror neuron systems, let alone understand the intentions of complex actions. Especially, intention understanding seems to often rely on a "mentalizing" approach, which is the—silent and unconscious—application of a "folk psychology" or "theory theory" that people use to explain or understand "why" someone acts as he does. Such reasoning includes the use of implicit psychological theories about (human) actions, goals, reasons, desires, and the like (Stich & Nichols, 1993). Even though this process does not yet involve explicit and conscious verbalization, such an explanation of intention understanding does involve many more cognitive processes than those performed by the action parsing mechanism or the mirror neuron systems alone.

Not surprisingly, as soon as we include higher cognitive processes that involve language or reasoning in the explanatory mechanism, adequacy will be increasingly difficult to achieve. For instance, the "theory theory" account of intention understanding has rival theories. One of these is a "simulation" theory that suggests that subjects implicitly project themselves into the place of the agent when observing an action. The simulation theory claims to be supported by mirror neuron research because these neurons allegedly enable such silent and immediate simulation (Gallese & Goldman, 1998). The narrative approach proposes yet another and different take on action recognition and intention understanding in humans. It refers to the fact that in most cases, we ask agents themselves "why" they did "what" they did. It is then "these second-person deliveries—the narratives narrated—that do the heavy lifting in enabling us to understand and make sense of others with confidence" (Hutto, 2007, p. 21). Ricoeur (1992)—who taught us the distinction between the "what," "why," and "who" of action—explains that a narrative in fact establishes a sort of "plot" around an action, which includes the character of the agent, the events experienced, and those acted on. Together, these allow us to establish the identity of agents and their actions alike, even if such a narrative will never be complete or definitive. Such contributions of our narrative capacity to our capacity of action understanding—and of acting itself—has only quite recently gained the interest of philosophers and scientists (cf. Bayne & Pacherie, 2007; Gallagher & Hutto, 2008; Hutto, 2007; Ricoeur, 1984; Zwaan, Taylor, & de Boer, 2010). Consequently, it has not yet found definitive inclusion in the explanations of action understanding.

Developing adequacy can thus take us in different directions. It can imply revisiting the observations of the phenomenon itself, in order to find out whether we can isolate a specific class of actions that can be recognized by a simple perceptual mechanism alone. Or, adequacy may require us to expand this mechanism with the mirror neuron systems, still fencing out those cognitive processes that include speech. Unfortunately, in humans this may still not yield adequacy because our narrative and intention understanding depend mostly upon modulating factors that lie outside the scope of these perceptual and mirror neuron systems. With respect to the disciplines involved, adequacy requirements are enlarged because additional components and operations need attention. On top of that, new disciplines—such as the social sciences—need to be involved in order to reach adequacy. It is to be expected that in our next step(s) we will feel the impact of this.

Analyze the Phenomenon and Evaluate Each Insight Into It

Because research is never simply the accumulation of factual knowledge, we now need to analyze the problem from the perspective of each relevant discipline and evaluate each insight into it (Repko, 2008, p. 217). A mechanism-based explanation allows us to respect the differences between disciplinary perspectives even though we will assign disciplinary insights into a phenomenon with only a limited role in the comprehensive explanation. Disciplinary theories, methodologies, and assumptions may hold for the investigation of a specific component or operation of the phenomenon but may have only limited relevance for the overall phenomenon.

Thinking of a phenomenon as the result of the interaction of a multilevel organization of components and operations has the advantage that those components and operations may be investigated separately. Of course, it is tempting to disciplinary specialists to isolate their domain and to maintain that their domain of study and the insights it delivers are sufficient to explain the phenomenon, leaving the rest aside as irrelevant. In such a case, the assumption is that the phenomenon can be explained with reference to a specific "module" that is relatively isolated and independently responsible for all properties of the phenomenon.[10] Even though I argued earlier that there is relative autonomy of levels in a phenomenon, in organisms there are many feedback and feedforward interactions at a particular level, as well as top-down and bottom-up interactions between levels, that can influence such a "module." We must remain on the alert for this possibility, indeed.

Analyzing and evaluating the disciplinary perspectives on the phenomenon of action understanding within the mechanism-based explanatory approach is a straightforward task. Starting from a mechanism sketch, mentioned in the previous section, researchers will complete and describe the components, their operations, and indeed the interactions within the mechanism in ever more detail. This process consists partly of deciding the relevance of the contribution of different components and operations and the further arrangement of them. In our case, analysis of action understanding was already part of Step 1, where we defined and decomposed it into the three component tasks. Clearly, achieving adequacy and this task of analyzing, evaluating, and arranging insights are intimately related research tasks that need to be carried out repeatedly during the interdisciplinary research process.

The interrelated research tasks of analysis and evaluation as applied to the present case of mirror neuron research can demonstrate that the tight connection between the definition, decomposition, and localization of a phenomenon; the experimental set-up used in investigating it; and the subsequent results require much care. An inadequate definition will hamper research as much as a bad experiment. Take, for instance, the following conclusion drawn on the basis of a mirror neuron activation experiment: "To ascribe an

---

[10]A famous example of such an assumption pertains to language, which has been claimed to rest in a specific mental organ, separate from the other mental organs, and therefore also localizable in specific parts of the brain. These claims are highly implausible, if we take our earlier analysis of mechanism-based explanations for functions in complex and dynamic biological systems into account. And indeed, former language modularity proponent Chomsky wrote in an influential review in 2002, "A neuroscientist might ask: What components of the human nervous system are recruited in the use of language in its broadest sense? Because any aspect of cognition appears to be, at least in principle, accessible to language, the broadest answer to this question is, probably, most of it." (Hauser, Chomsky, & Fitch, 2002, p. 1570). In that review, the authors engage in a more modest approach, similar to the one I present here for action understanding.

intention is to infer a forthcoming new goal, and this is an operation that the motor system does automatically" (Iacoboni, Molnar-Szakacs, Gallese, Buccino, & Mazziotta, 2005, p. 533). This sweeping conclusion was drawn on the basis of an experiment in which humans were looking at images of a hand taking a cup for drinking or for cleaning and images of a breakfast table. Sure enough, the results suggested that our brain automatically includes context information in its prediction of the likeliness of the subsequent action with the cup. Nevertheless, the authors overstate the relevance of their results by defining intention extremely narrowly, while applying a very broad interpretation of the operation of the mirror neurons in this highly suggestive and restrictive task. This exaggeration is partly due to the lack of a comprehensive, interdisciplinary analysis of the phenomenon of intention understanding and consequently the lack of a rigorous evaluation of the results. As a result, the researchers suggest that these mirror neurons function as a module that, in isolation, fulfills the difficult task of intention understanding. Indeed, one of these investigators still maintains that these mirror neurons "embody the deepest way in which we stand in relation to each other and understand each other" (Iacoboni, 2008). However, in human relations we often experience our mutual deep involvement and attachment through verbal meanings, which will not always activate mirror neuron systems. Such meanings may heighten our sensitivity to some actions over others. In sum, although we know that the evidence is convincing enough to include mirror neurons in the action understanding mechanism, we still need other components to account for intention understanding.

Such overstated claims are more common than one would expect. Most research into human social action, for example, subscribes to one of two opposed theoretical positions: either "Plastic Man" or "Autonomous Man": "Whereas Plastic Man, being formed by adaptive response to the interplay of nature and nurture, is only spuriously individual, his rival is to be self-caused. . . . Where Plastic Man has his causes, Autonomous Man has his reasons" (Hollis, 1977, p. 12). Such extreme positions are often due to overestimation of disciplinary strengths and underestimation of disciplinary limitations with respect to a complex and dynamic, multilevel system. Fortunately, interdisciplinary exchanges may force researchers to integrate their insights in a much more complex, but at the same time more comprehensive, explanation.

Integrating Insights (Steps 7 to 10)

According to the model of the interdisciplinary research process that Repko (2008) presents, we would only now enter the second phase of the research process where the integration of insights takes place. Until now, the focus was accordingly on "drawing on disciplinary insights." Even though I have already looked ahead at the integration of these insights, I will follow the proposed research process and discuss the model's next steps with respect to the mechanism-based explanatory approach on offer here. Therefore, we need to identify conflicts between insights and locate their sources (Step 7) and then create common ground between these insights (i.e., discover one or more latent commonalities between them; Step 8). Using this common ground, we should be able to integrate as many of the insights as possible (Step 9). Eventually, this should bring us to a more comprehensive understanding of human action (Step 10). The mechanism-based explanation will prove a very useful instrument in these steps.

Identify Conflicts Between Insights and Locate Their Sources

Even though it is often the case that "the possible sources of conflict between insights are concepts, assumptions, and theories" (Repko, 2008, p. 250), not all forms of interdisciplinary integration are dependent upon resolving the conflicts stemming from these building blocks of disciplinary perspectives on the phenomenon. In the mechanism-based explanatory approach, conflicts of different types can occur. One source of conflict stems from the initial phase of defining and decomposing our phenomenon. In the previous section, we came across researchers who overstated their conclusion based upon an oversimplified definition of intention ascription.

A second source of conflict related to such definition and decomposition mistakes is assuming that the underlying mechanisms for different component tasks are completely separate. For instance, even though we distinguished the three component tasks—action recognition, understanding of intention, and narrative understanding—we noted that it is likely that these components are intimately related, both functionally and in their neural implementation.

Different from such conceptual conflicts are those that arise from misunderstandings of the internal arrangement of components and operations of the mechanism. For instance, interactions between components or interactions have been neglected or overlooked—as is the case when the component task of action recognition would be forgotten as a prerequisite for intention understanding.

A fourth source of conflict is the underestimation of the role of specific context features on the way an action is being cognitively processed. For instance, under favorable conditions—without time pressure, for instance—and with adequate preparation, people are able to suppress or, rather, overrule the power of stereotypical modes of understanding other people because in such cases other mechanisms are kicking in (Kruglanski & Orehek, 2007).

Fifth, conflicts can arise from the failure to acknowledge and evaluate correctly the alternative processing trajectories that may prevail in specific groups or individuals when engaging in action understanding. For instance, it is still debated whether or not autistic subjects, who have difficulties in spontaneous human action understanding and often use specifically trained theories about human behavior, suffer from disturbances in their mirror neuron systems, forcing them to rely on other trajectories (Blakemore, Winston, & Frith, 2004).

A sixth source is a combination of the latter two sources of conflicts: External, sociocultural information may have become entrenched in the explanatory mechanism and cause observable and regular differences in action understanding processing, as is the case with modulation of mirror neuron activity due to individual experience with sociocultural information (Keestra, 2008). In general, for explanations of the variability of sociocultural influences on individuals' cognitive processes, we need to draw on both cognitive and social scientific insights (Shore, 1996).

This is not an exhaustive list of the possible sources and locations of conflicts in mechanism-based explanations, but they are the most prominent. The list also demonstrates that considering a phenomenon from a mechanism-based approach is useful as a heuristic when reflecting on potential conceptual and theoretical failures and conflicts. In our domain of action understanding, such conflicts have arisen predominantly with respect to the component of intention understanding.

In particular, there has been a fierce rivalry between an explanation that is based upon tacit folk psychological theorizing by the individual and an explanation that refers to the silent simulation of the observed actor. Conflicts pertained to the definition and decomposition of intention understanding, explanations of its components' tasks, the underlying mechanisms, and their neural implementations in the brain.

The opposition between these theorizing and simulation accounts was modified somewhat as soon as tacit theorizing was no longer necessarily associated with propositions, rules, psychological causal laws, and the like because only then were animals and infants equally able to understand intentions. So when connectionist models were developed and computer tested with some success, theorizing accounts seemed to gain the upper hand in the conflict (Stich & Nichols, 1993). The balance shifted dramatically again the moment the surprising evidence of mirror neurons appeared. Simulation theorists immediately appreciated it as support for their position and took it as evidence for a neural basis for their idea that we employ similar structures to both actively engage in action and passively understand that action. This was clearly stated in a seminal article co-authored by a neuroscientist and a simulation theorist: "Thus [mirror neuron] activity seems to be nature's way of getting the observer into the same 'mental shoes' as the target—exactly what the conjectured simulation heuristic aims to do" (Gallese & Goldman, 1998, pp. 497–498).

Extensive analysis of the history of this conflict between theorizing and simulation accounts of intention understanding would show that the conflict alternately received energy from theoretical arguments, from neuroscientific evidence, from behavioral observations, and so on. As I note in the following discussion, we can meanwhile observe that the two formerly opposing positions are being successfully integrated into an overarching explanatory mechanism.

The mechanism-based approach allows us to analyze such a conflict and the different sources from which it arises. Similarly, it can function as a heuristic device that enables us to handle the conflict by employing its apparatus of phenomenon analysis, components and operations, levels, and interactions of sorts. Most important for interdisciplinary research is, of course, how the mechanism-based explanation can be adapted in such a way that it can integrate those insights or properties that appeared to be in conflict with each other, while both sides can present some evidence in support. For that, we need to take the next step, in which we are asked to create or discover common ground.

Create or Discover Common Ground via a Mechanism

Interdisciplinary investigations of human action understanding aim at the integration of insights into that phenomenon. For such integration to succeed, it is crucial to build upon a common ground that allows the integration of heterogeneous materials. In our case, this common ground should have the form of an explanatory mechanism. Language processing is unlikely to provide such a ground, for instance, as it cannot play a central role in explanations of action understanding in animals and young infants. Nonetheless, given the strong interaction between components of any comprehensive explanatory mechanism of action understanding, the explanatory mechanism that we choose as common ground will be affected by the components and operations that we will add to it. As noted above, language affects many other components of the explanatory mechanism, including action recognition.

In fact, for most interdisciplinarians who use a mechanism-based approach, finding common ground for our interdisciplinary understanding involves the identification of the most promising mechanism-based explanation among those that have already been proposed in the literature. *It is this mechanism-based explanation as a whole that furnishes common ground.* Note that this implies that generally such common ground is already "composed of *knowledge that is distributed among or is common to disciplines*" (Repko, 2008, p. 273).

After having identified a plausible explanatory mechanism as common ground, interdisciplinarians need to demonstrate how other relevant components and operations are related to it. What is implied in this endeavor is the rejection of claims that a specific explanatory mechanism independently produces the phenomenon. Embracing a mechanism as common ground can mean that it loses the exclusive explanatory force it previously had. We have observed that mirror neuron systems were believed to be the prime candidate for a mechanism-based explanation of action understanding and imitation alike. Thanks to their functional properties, these mirror neuron systems have been held responsible for enabling relationships between oneself and another and between action and perception (Hurley & Chater, 2005). Even though this makes these mirror neuron systems workable as common ground, the associated mechanisms have meanwhile been embedded in a more comprehensive mechanism, limiting their role accordingly. It is worth quoting a recent meta-analysis that argues why still other systems or submechanisms must be added to a mechanism-based explanation of intention understanding, with a central role for mirror neurons:

> First, an inconsistent or anomalous movement might be outside the perceiver's repertoire of familiar movements, so the mirror system cannot be of help. To resolve this, inferences of higher-level goals (e.g., "why did the actress fall?") or other attributes (e.g., "was she depressed?") seem to be needed, which are outside the scope of the mirror system. Second, when the perceiver reflects on a high-level intention of an action, this might necessarily engage the mentalizing system. It is possible that the mirror system is recruited for automatic lower-level goal interpretation . . . and the mentalizing system for reflection on the higher-level goals (from task goals to more general intentions). (Van Overwalle & Baetens, 2009, p. 580)

Nonetheless, various mechanism-based explanations of action understanding have been presented in which mirror neuron systems function as common ground. These systems offer, then, a common ground to different mechanism sketches or models. Authors are sometimes even updating their own earlier model, such as by

> introducing a new model of action recognition learning by macaque mirror neurons which addresses data on auditory input, a model for opportunistic planning of sequential behavior, and studies of how to embed a macaque-like mirror system in a larger ape-like or human-like circuit to support "simple imitation" and then "complex imitation." (Arbib & Bonaiuto, 2008, p. 45)

In this case, the previous model for imitation and understanding, with mirror neuron systems as common ground, was expanded with components and operations that process speech and symbol use. With that expansion, the authors are able to explain the differences between human and monkey capabilities while leaving the mechanism-based explanation of several commonalities largely intact.

What can be derived from this example is that, if possible, newly discovered insights should be integrated into an existing explanatory mechanism. Obviously, proposing a completely new mechanism is a much more demanding task. The various adjustments of an existing explanatory mechanism in order to integrate insights into a mechanism-based explanation are the subject of our next section.

Integrate Insights Into a Mechanism-Based Explanation

This chapter's argument for a central role for mechanism-based explanation is in accordance with the general observation that "at the heart of any interdisciplinary integration lies an integrative device—for example, a metaphor, complex explanation, or bridging concept—that brings together disciplinary insights" (Boix-Mansilla, Duraisingh, Wolfe, & Haynes, 2009, p. 344). I hope to have convincingly shown that a mechanism-based explanation is a useful device for achieving interdisciplinary integration. After having identified an appropriate explanatory mechanism as the common ground for explaining our phenomenon, the remaining task is to build on this when seeking integration of additional insights.

Disciplinary insights are, in that case, included as explanations of components and operations of the mechanism, or as explanations of the interactions that take place within the mechanism or between the mechanism and external factors. Given the explanatory mechanism that we have identified as common ground, integrating further insights will lead to refining or expanding it. Refining implies that we can specify the mechanism of a subcomponent or suboperation or interaction of the overarching explanatory mechanism. For instance, the action-perception interactions that mirror neurons facilitate are affected both by action-specific experiences of the subject and the task one is performing (Rizzolatti & Sinigaglia, 2008). Expanding the mechanism involves an extension with a component, operation, or interaction that has turned out to influence the mechanism in a relevant way. For instance, investigations of sociocultural influences on the cognitive processes that underlie action understanding are relatively new and may lead to unexpected extensions: Some processes turn out not to be sensitive to these influences; others are strongly affected by them (Han & Northoff, 2008).

Refining or expanding the explanatory mechanism with an additional disciplinary insight requires a careful consideration of the place within the mechanism where the addition could be located. This is especially difficult in the case of a complex and dynamic multilevel mechanism: An addition is likely to have a widespread impact on many components and operations. Figure 8.2, at the end of the chapter, demonstrates the many choices available for assigning a location to the additional insight. For instance, should we consider a sociocultural influence like religious belief as a "sociocultural model" that functions as a specific "computation" for narrative understanding, having only via that route a modulatory influence on the perceptual mechanisms that produce action recognition? Alternatively, we could investigate whether it is the imitation of religious practices, implying mirror neuron system activations, that modulate perceptual processes. So knowing that religion influences action understanding still leaves undecided where and how this influence should be integrated into the overarching explanatory mechanism. Similarly, we already mentioned that the action understanding deficits in autistic patients may or may not be wide-ranging consequences of their disturbed mirror neuron systems (Blakemore et al., 2004).

Integrating an additional insight by way of a refinement or expansion of the explanatory mechanism that we chose as common ground, therefore, requires us to specify one or more relations between previously unrelated components or processes. The results of mirror neuron research have, indeed, forced researchers to reconsider explanatory mechanisms for imitation, for action understanding, for empathy, for language processing, and for action learning—to mention the most prominent (Rizzolatti & Sinigaglia, 2008). Obviously, refining or expanding the mechanism-based explanations of mirror neuron system activities will, in that case, require a variety of techniques, depending on the specific interactions that the additional component is involved in.

In this context, it may be useful to realize that Repko (2008) mentions several integrative techniques that are commonly used for establishing common ground: (1) *redefinition* of concepts or assumptions to include or exclude phenomena; (2) *extension* of concepts and assumptions or *expansion* of a theory to cover previously uncovered phenomena, perhaps even beyond their original disciplinary domain; (3) *organization* of previously unrelated concepts or assumptions into a relationship; and (4) the *transformation* of opposing concepts or assumptions into variables of an uncovered factor (cf. Repko, 2008, pp. 282–291). Obviously, common ground depends on establishing a relationship between previously unintegrated theories. According to the present approach, it is advisable to identify a given explanatory mechanism as common ground and subsequently to refine or expand this. It is interesting that the four techniques can, in modified form, also be applied to these refinements or expansions, as discussed below.

For instance, the integrative techniques of redefinition and organization are fairly common practice in the life sciences. They are often applied in combination, as can be learnt again from mirror neuron research. Among the many consequences of the discovery of mirror neurons was the following insight:

> That rigid divide between perceptive, motor, and cognitive processes is to a great extent artificial; not only does perception appear to be embedded in the dynamics of action, becoming much more composite than used to be thought in the past, but the acting brain is also and above all a brain that understands. (Rizzolatti & Sinigaglia, 2008, p. xi)

Such rigid divides are also at stake when the integration of speech requires various refinements and expansions of the mechanism-based explanation of mirror neuron properties, which was proposed as common ground. These refinements and expansions involve a reorganization of components and operations, comparable to the third integrative technique of organization of previously unrelated concepts or assumptions into a relationship. Traditionally, language and action have been treated as separate phenomena. Now that researchers realize that mirror neurons contribute to both these cognitive processes, they are better able to explain the subtle and sometimes disturbing interactions of language and action. This requires, however, a redefinition (Technique 1) of some basic assumptions concerning the "modular" processes that were taken to underlie language and action.

Obviously, even when common ground has been established, further integration of insights into the preferred mechanism-based explanation demands careful application of various integrative techniques. Also, prudence and modesty are needed with respect to the scope of the theories or explanations that require integration. Researchers must realize that it is most unlikely that it is possible to localize cognitive functions in particular neurons or specific neuronal activities. Talk of neurons that "see" or "feel" or "infer" should, therefore, be taken to mean that these components or operations play a specific and decisive role in the comprehensive mechanism that accounts for that function—no more, and no less (Keestra & Cowley, 2009).

To conclude, a general consequence of the integration of insights should be acknowledged. Even if the focus is not on the assumptions or concepts of the associated theories, integration will have an impact on the scope of these theories. Integration of two theories has the consequence that their scope will become expanded or contracted: expanded when integration demonstrates that a mechanism has also an impact on an additional component or operation; contracted when the converse is true and, for instance, a mechanism turns out to depend on another mechanism for its operation. When the integrated theory has wide-ranging impact on the complex explanatory mechanism, both theory expansion and contraction will obtain, though with respect to different components, operations or interactions and the theories pertaining to these.

Produce a Mechanism-Based Explanation of Human Action Understanding and Test It

Often, interdisciplinary understanding of a problem will be obtained at the final stage of the research process. In a mechanism-based approach to explanation, this is somewhat different. As many—if not most—phenomena in the natural, life, and cognitive sciences do not appear contingently but reflect the behavior of a complex mechanism, there are often already interdisciplinary mechanism-based explanations available of components or operations of the eventual, overarching explanatory mechanism. Remember

the definition of a mechanism mentioned earlier: "[A] mechanism is an organized system of component parts and component operations. The mechanism's components and their organization produce its behavior, thereby
instantiating a phenomenon" (Bechtel, 2005, p. 314). When employing the
mechanism-based approach, researchers are aware of the fact that their specific research of a phenomenon should allow integration of their results into
the mechanism in the form of a further specification of a component or operation or one of its interactions.

How we represent the explanatory mechanism is dependent upon its
aim. Complex and dynamic mechanisms, with their reciprocal constraints
of components and operations and their feedback and feedforward streams
are difficult to represent as a picture. Developing a computer program that
includes such components and operations is a more feasible method.
However, if our interest is in the neural areas that are involved in the mechanism, we may settle for a neuroanatomical map with designated cortical
areas and some broad processing streams. Or, we may focus on a finer
grain of single neurons, like mirror neurons, and present the fine distribution of those in a particular area and their connections. Often, researchers
present their findings in a relatively abstract "boxology" in which boxes
and arrows refer to components and operations. In that case, we can add
labels to these that refer broadly to their neural implementations in specific
cortical areas. In Figure 8.2 below, I have presented most of the relevant
information on action understanding contained in this chapter in the mixed
form of a boxology and the diagram found in Figure 8.1. Clearly, it is far
from complete, and much more information could be added to it or integrated with it. Specification of the components and operations would
require additional layers and theoretical descriptions, but they are beyond
the scope of this chapter.

Finally, it is easy to see that a visual representation of the mechanism can
assist further research in many ways, perhaps better than a verbally for-
mulated theory would do. Let me stress that as an integrative device,
mechanism-based explanation does not exclude formulation of verbal and
mathematical theories. Such theories often focus on specific components or
operations as we find them in the mechanism. As I noted above, cognitive
scientific experiments involve the activation, interference, or stimulation of
components or operations. The consequences of those can subsequently be
detected as changes in components or operations at other levels, or indeed in
the behavior of the subject. With the help of a mechanism sketch such as
Figure 8.2, we can more specifically engage in the formulation of hypotheses or in thinking of potential interventions in it with experiments or other
treatments. We can consider horizontal interactions and their potential
effects, or we can reflect on interlevel investigations, using the interference
and stimulation techniques mentioned earlier. Such tests should lead to
refinements, adjustments, or perhaps even the rejection of the proposed
mechanism sketch.

Figure 8.2   Highly Simplified and Incomplete Mechanism Sketch of Human Action Understanding

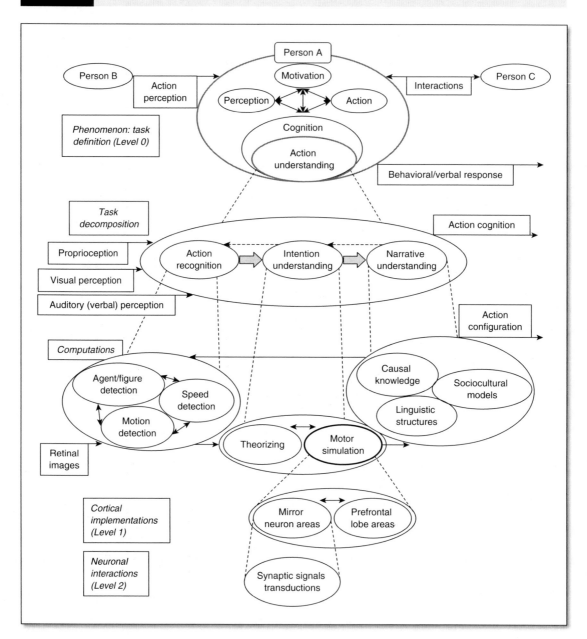

NOTE: Many dynamic (feedforward and feedback, top-down and bottom-up) interactions are left out. Further components and operations, like attention, memory, and awareness, could be added to the sketch as they modulate action understanding. Note that each component and interaction could, in turn, be investigated as a complex phenomenon on its own, requiring a mechanism-based explanation. Note, as well, that components may play a role in other mechanisms and contribute to various phenomena simultaneously. This is the case with mirror neurons, for example. Vertical dotted lines = constitutive relations.

_____ **Conclusion**

Action understanding is a complex cognitive capability performed by a complex cognitive mechanism. As we learned above, that mechanism comprises various components and operations that are themselves open to mechanism-based explanations. In developing a mechanism-based explanation of action understanding, we need, therefore, to integrate insights from various disciplines by attributing them to components or operations to be found in the mechanism or to specific interactions in which the mechanism participates. Strikingly, although there are many nonlinear processes involved, and notwithstanding the complexity of the overarching mechanism, the phenomenon of action understanding displays relatively stable properties under specific conditions.

The method proposed in this chapter requires application of the heuristics of definition, decomposition, and localization. However, not all phenomena lend themselves to this explanatory approach. If a phenomenon does not appear to behave in an orderly fashion at all, or if it turns out to be impossible—even preliminarily—to localize and identify components or operations, then we may have to look for another approach. Fortunately for us, human action understanding is a phenomenon suitable for this approach. By learning more about the complex and dynamic mechanism that underlies action understanding, we can appreciate even more this crucial capability and cope with its constraints and limitations. Indeed, rather than being satisfied with explanations of its successes, it may be even more important in our global society to acknowledge the fragility of our ability to understand each other's actions.

_____ **References**

Arbib, M., & Bonaiuto, J. (2008). From grasping to complex imitation: Mirror systems on the path to language. *Mind & Society, 7*(1), 43–64.

Baldwin, D. A., Baird, J. A., Saylor, M. M., & Clark, M. A. (2001). Infants parse dynamic action. *Child Development, 72*(3), 708–717.

Bargh, J. A., & Chartrand, T. L. (1999). The unbearable automaticity of being. *American Psychologist, 54*(7), 462–479.

Bayne, T., & Pacherie, E. (2007). Narrators and comparators: The architecture of agentive self-awareness. *Synthese, 159*(3), 475–491.

Beatty, J. (1997). Why do biologists argue like they do? *Philosophy of Science, 64*, S432–S443.

Bechtel, W. (2005). The challenge of characterizing operations in the mechanisms underlying behavior. *Journal of the Experimental Analysis of Behavior, 84*(3), 313–325.

Bechtel, W., & Richardson, R. C. (1993). *Discovering complexity: Decomposition and localization as strategies in scientific research*. Princeton, NJ: Princeton University Press.

Blakemore, S. J., Winston, J., & Frith, U. (2004). Social cognitive neuroscience: Where are we heading? *Trends in Cognitive Sciences, 8*(5), 216.

Boix-Mansilla, V., Duraisingh, E. D., Wolfe, C. R., & Haynes, C. (2009). Targeted assessment rubric: An empirically grounded rubric for interdisciplinary writing. *The Journal of Higher Education, 80*(3), 334–353.

Bogdan, R. J. (2003). *Interpreting minds: The evolution of a practice.* Cambridge, MA: MIT Press.

Bourdieu, P. (1990). *The logic of practice* (R. Nice, Trans.). Stanford, CA: Stanford University Press.

Breazeal, C. L. (2004). *Designing sociable robots.* Cambridge, MA: The MIT Press.

Bruner, J. S. (1990). *Acts of meaning.* Boston: Harvard University Press.

Byrne, R. W. (1999). Imitation without intentionality. Using string parsing to copy the organization of behaviour. *Animal Cognition, 2*(2), 63–72.

Byrne, R. W., & Russon, A. E. (1998). Learning by imitation: A hierarchical approach. *Behavioral and Brain Sciences, 21*(05), 667–684.

Churchland, P. (1995). *The engine of reason, the seat of the soul: A philosophical journey into the brain.* Cambridge: MIT Press.

Craver, C. F. (2007). *Explaining the brain. Mechanisms and the mosaic unity of neuroscience.* New York: Oxford University Press.

Dennett, D. C. (1989). *The intentional stance.* Cambridge, MA: MIT Press.

Donald, M. (1991). *Origins of the modern mind. Three stages in the evolution of culture and cognition.* Cambridge, MA: Harvard University Press.

Dupre, J. (2001). In defence of classification. *Studies in History and Philosophy of Science Part C: Studies in History and Philosophy of Biological and Biomedical Sciences, 32*(2), 203–219.

Gadamer, H. G. (2004). *Truth and method* (J. Weinsheimer & D. G. Marshall, Trans.). London: Continuum.

Gallagher, S., & Hutto, D. (2008). Understanding others through primary interaction and narrative practice. In J. Zlatev, T. Racine, C. Sinha, & E. Itkonen (Eds.), *The shared mind: Perspectives on intersubjectivity* (pp. 17–38). Amsterdam: John Benjamins.

Gallese, V., & Goldman, A. (1998). Mirror neurons and the simulation theory of mind-reading. *Trends in Cognitive Sciences, 2*(12), 493–501.

Gergely, G., Nádasdy, Z., Csibra, G., & Bíró, S. (1995). Taking the intentional stance at 12 months of age. *Cognition, 56*(2), 165–193.

Gergen, K. J., & Semin, G. R. (1990). Everyday understanding in science and daily life. In K. J. Gergen & G. R. Semin (Eds.), *Everyday understanding: Social and scientific implications* (pp. 1–18). London: Sage.

Hacking, I. (1983). *Representing and intervening.* Cambridge: Cambridge University Press.

Han, S. H., & Northoff, G. (2008). Culture-sensitive neural substrates of human cognition: A transcultural neuroimaging approach. *Nature Reviews Neuroscience, 9*(8), 646–654.

Hard, B. M., Lozano, S. C., & Tversky, B. (2006). Hierarchical encoding of behavior: Translating perception into action. *Journal of Experimental Psychology: General, 135*(4), 588–608.

Hauser, M. D., Chomsky, N., & Fitch, W. T. (2002). The faculty of language: What is it, who has it, and how did it evolve? *Science, 298*, 1569–1579.

Hedstrom, P., & Swedberg, R. (1996). Social mechanisms. *Acta Sociologica, 39*(3), 281–308.

Hollis, M. (1977). *Models of man: Philosophical thoughts on social action.* Cambridge: Cambridge University Press.

Hurley, S., & Chater, N. (2005). Introduction: The importance of imitation. In S. Hurley & N. Chater (Eds.), *Perspectives on imitation: From neuroscience to social science* (Vol. I & II; pp. 1–52). Cambridge, MA: MIT Press.

Hutto, D. D. (2007). *Folk psychological narratives: The sociocultural basis of understanding reasons.* Cambridge, MA: The MIT Press.

Iacoboni, M. (2008). *Mirroring people: The new science of how we connect with others.* New York: Farrar Straus & Giroux.

Iacoboni, M., Molnar-Szakacs, I., Gallese, V., Buccino, G., & Mazziotta, J. C. (2005). Grasping the intentions of others with one's own mirror neuron system. *Public Library of Science Biology, 3*(3), 0529–0535.

Keestra, M. (2008). The diverging force of imitation: Integrating cognitive science and hermeneutics. *Review of General Psychology, 12*(2), 127–136.

Keestra, M., & Cowley, S. J. (2009). Foundationalism and neuroscience: Silence and language. *Language Sciences, 31*(4), 531–552.

Klein, J. T. (1990). *Interdisciplinarity history, theory, and practice.* Detroit, MI: Wayne State University Press.

Kruglanski, A. W., & Orehek, E. (2007). Partitioning the domain of social inference: Dual mode and systems models and their alternatives. *Annual Review of Psychology, 58*(1), 291–316.

Lakoff, G., & Johnson, M. (1999). *Philosophy in the flesh: The embodied mind and its challenge to western thought.* New York: Basic Books.

Machamer, P., Darden, L., & Craver, C.-F. (2000). Thinking about mechanisms. *Philosophy of Science, 67*(1), 1–25.

Miller, G. A. (2003). The cognitive revolution: A historical perspective. *Trends in Cognitive Sciences, 7*(3), 141–144.

Newell, W. H. (1998). Professionalizing interdisciplinarity. Literature review and research agenda. In W. H. Newell (Ed.), *Interdisciplinarity: Essays from the literature* (pp. 529–563). New York: College Entrance Examination Board.

Pinker, S. (2003). *The blank slate: The modern denial of human nature.* London: Penguin Books.

Poldrack, R. A., Sabb, F. W., Foerde, K., Tom, S. M., Asarnow, R. F., Bookheimer, S. Y., & Knowlton, B. J. (2005). The neural correlates of motor skill automaticity. *Journal of Neuroscience, 25*(22), 5356–5364.

Read, S. J., & Miller, L. C. (2005). Explanatory coherence and goal-based knowledge structures in making dispositional inferences. In B. F. Malle & S. D. Hodges (Eds.), *Other minds: How humans bridge the divide between self and others* (pp. 124–139). New York: Guilford Press.

Repko, A. F. (2008). *Interdisciplinary research: Process and theory.* Thousand Oaks, CA: Sage.

Reyna, S. P. (2002). *Connections: Brain, mind, and culture in a social anthropology.* London: Routledge.

Ricoeur, P. (1984). *Time and narrative, Vol. 1* (K. McLaughlin & D. Pellauer, Trans.). Chicago: University of Chicago Press.

Ricoeur, P. (1992). *Oneself as another* (K. Blamey, Trans.). Chicago: University of Chicago Press.

Ricoeur, P. (2008). *From text to action: Essays in hermeneutics, II* (K. Blamey & J. B. Thompson, Trans.). London: Continuum Press.

Rizzolatti, G., & Sinigaglia, C. (2008). *Mirrors in the brain: How our minds share actions and emotions.* New York: Oxford University Press.

Sacks, O. (1995). *An anthropologist on Mars: Seven paradoxical tales.* New York: Alfred A. Knopf.

Shore, B. (1996). *Culture in mind. Cognition, culture, and the problem of meaning.* Oxford: Oxford University Press.

Sperber, D. (1996). *Explaining culture: A naturalistic approach.* Oxford: Blackwell.

Stich, S., & Nichols, S. (1993). Folk psychology: Simulation or tacit theory? *Philosophical Issues, 3,* 225–270.

Szostak, R. (2004). *Classifying science: Phenomena, data, theory, method, practice.* Dordrecht: Springer.

Tomasello, M. (1999). *The cultural origins of human cognition.* Cambridge, MA: Harvard University Press.

Van Overwalle, F., & Baetens, K. (2009). Understanding others' actions and goals by mirror and mentalizing systems: A meta-analysis. *NeuroImage, 48*(3), 564–584.

Wimsatt, W. C. (2007). *Re-engineering philosophy for limited beings. Piecewise approximations to reality.* Cambridge, MA: Harvard University Press.

Zacks, J. M., Kumar, S., Abrams, R. A., & Mehta, R. (2009). Using movement and intentions to understand human activity. *Cognition, 112*(2), 201–216.

Zwaan, R. A., Taylor, L. J., & de Boer, M. (2010). Motor resonance as a function of narrative time: Further tests of the linguistic focus hypothesis. *Brain and Language, 112*(3), 143–149.

Integrative Theory in Criminology Applied to the Complex Social Problem of School Violence

Stuart Henry and Nicole L. Bracy

Introduction

Interdisciplinarians have been very clear that they are interested in addressing problems, questions, or topics that are "too broad or complex to be dealt with adequately by a single discipline" (Klein & Newell, 1997, p. 393) and "whose solutions are beyond the scope of a single discipline" (Boix-Mansilla, 2005, p. 16; National Academies, 2005, p. 39). Single disciplinary approaches "fail to provide the truly comprehensive perspective on the problem that policymakers and the public really need. On too many issues of public importance, the disciplines tend to talk past each other" (Repko, 2008, p. 31). The charge of "disciplinary inadequacy" (p. 39) in dealing with complex social problems has been applied to crime by integrative criminologists who, like interdisciplinarians, are also concerned about the myopic analysis offered by traditional disciplines (Barak, 1998a, 1998b, 2009; Messner, Krohn, & Liska, 1989; Robinson, 2004; Robinson & Beaver, 2009); each discipline captures a narrow dimension of the crime problem but misses, or dismisses, the contributions of the rest. As a result, public policies to deal with crime, which themselves derive from disciplinary analyses or from media-driven fear (Muschert & Peguero, 2010), are also likely to be partial and fail to comprehend the complexity of the problem.

Multidisciplinary approaches that acknowledge a range of disciplinary perspectives through a process of "cognitive decentering" (Hursh, Haas, & Moore, 1998; Repko, 2008) are an advance over disciplinary approaches. Cognitive decentering "is the intellectual capacity to move beyond a single

259

center or focus (especially the innate tendencies towards egocentrism and ethnocentrism) and consider a variety of other perspectives in a coordinated way to perceive reality more accurately, process information more systematically, and solve problems more effectively" (Hursh et al., 1998, p. 37). However multidisciplinarity rarely looks at the dynamic, interactive, and cumulative effects of the complex problem over time; rather, it fragments the complexity and fails to comprehend its emergent holistic characteristics. In contrast, integrative interdisciplinary approaches to addressing complex social problems explicitly engage in "integration, synthesis, or amalgamation that attempt to produce a 'comprehensive' explanation" (Einstadter & Henry, 2006, p. 310) and move us toward holistic policies to address them.

In this chapter, we explore the last steps of Repko's (2008) research process: how to integrate insights to produce interdisciplinary understanding. We do so by examining the insights of those criminological theorists who have been attempting to develop integrative theory for the past 30 years. In the first section of the chapter, we critically review the issues that have arisen in criminological theory around what should be integrated from the disciplines beyond simply "insights." And in the second section, we show how criminologists striving for an integrated theory have applied this to explain the crime of violence. In the third section, we sketch out what an interdisciplinary understanding of school violence might look like and indicate its policy implications.

Creating Common Ground(s) and a Comprehensive Understanding in Criminology _____

For readers not familiar with the history of theory development in criminology, it is important to know that criminology has, from the outset, been profoundly influenced by the theories of other disciplines to explain why people commit crime, violate laws, or deviate from norms. In this sense, criminology is an applied science/social science. Theoretical explanations of crime causation range from the theological and demonological to economic, biological, psychological, sociological, and political; more recently, they also include a variety of feminist, postmodernist, and social constructionist theories (see Einstadter & Henry, 2006; Lanier & Henry, 2010). At different times some criminological theories have been more prominent than others, but rarely are any theoretical explanations completely expunged, with the result that criminology fits Ritzer's (1975) category of being a "multiparadigmatic" science.

However, since 1979 a subset of criminological theorists has attempted to harness the explanatory and predictive power of existing theories of crime causation by integrating the concepts and propositions present in the diverse range of disciplinary-based theories (see especially Akers, 1994; Barak, 1998a, 1998b, 2009; Bernard, 2001; Colvin, 2000; Colvin & Pauly, 1983;

Elliott, Agerton, & Canter, 1979; Fishbein, 1998; Hagan, 1989; Hawkins & Weis, 1985; Jeffrey, 1990; Johnson, 1979; Messner et al., 1989; Muftić, 2009; Pearson & Weiner, 1985; Robinson, 2004; Robinson & Beaver, 2009; Shoemaker, 1996; Tittle, 1995; Vila, 1994). This has been attempted in a variety of ways, which leads to an instructive set of issues and challenges for interdisciplinary integrative theory. The three dominant positions are advocates, critics, and moderates. Advocates see distinct advantages in integrating existing discipline-based theories. Barak (1998b) summarizes these advantages, arguing that criminologists engaging in integration do so (1) because of a desire to develop central concepts that are common to several theories; (2) to provide coherence to a bewildering array of fragmented theories, and thereby reduce their number; (3) to achieve comprehensiveness and completeness, and thereby enhance their explanatory power; (4) to advance scientific progress and theory development; and (5) to synthesize ideas about crime causation and social control policy.

In contrast, critics ask whether it is better to have a set of competing theoretical explanations, each of which responds to a different, but overlapping, set of questions, or whether it is better to combine elements of several theoretical perspectives into one integrative theory. For example, some critics have argued that criminological theories should remain "separate and unequal" and that "theory competition" and "competitive isolation" are preferable to theoretical integration (Akers, 1994, p. 195; Gibbons, 1994; Hirschi, 1979, 1989). They claim the idea that integration appears to create a more powerful or more comprehensive explanation is an illusion often resulting in theoretical confusion (Thornberry, 1989, p. 54).

We argue that these opposing positions need not be mutually exclusive; criminological theories can remain separate because the separate disciplines illuminate different aspects of the issue, problem, or question, but there are also potential benefits to be gained from integration (Newell, 2001). Our more moderate position is that we should not integrate unless there is a measurable benefit from doing so. We maintain that if integration produces a more comprehensive understanding that is not presently provided by disciplinary approaches alone, then it is a valuable process. For example, a comprehensive approach to complex social problems, such as crime, benefits from both disciplinary-based theories competing for the best explanations and integrative approaches that go beyond the single theoretical approach.

Another contentious issue is whether integration can achieve comprehensive understanding or whether, because of the increasing number of interdisciplinary combinations, it simply produces a plurality of comprehensive understandings or competing meta-theories (Einstadter & Henry, 2006; Fuchsman, 2009):

When the conditions for interdisciplinarity exist, there are then a variety of results possible from efforts to forge a synthesis. There can be full integration, no integration, partial integration, or multiple integrations. The contending discourses, synthesis, ideological disputes, plural epistemologies, and fragmentations that occur within disciplines and their subfields also make their appearance within interdisciplinarity. (Fuchsman, 2009, p. 79)

Under these circumstances, we might argue that the concept of integration as a single coherent entity may not always be possible; when there are multiple bases for integration (e.g., assumptions, concepts, or theories), partial integration may be the best that one can achieve, although full integration remains the ideal. Indeed, one recent review of integrated theories in criminology found that different integrative theories each draw on 2 to 10 of the 14 different discipline-based theories available, and their various combinations have produced 16 different integrative theories (Lanier & Henry, 2010). These come with a variety of indicative names, such as "integrated social theory," "integrated structural Marxist theory," "conceptual integration theory," "integrative systems theory," and "holistic theory." Moreover, not all discipline-based theories that constitute these new integrative theories are drawn on equally. The range of inclusions varies from 2, in the case of feminist criminological theory, to 11 or more in the case of social learning theory and social control theory (Lanier & Henry, 2010, pp. 382–391). This raises the question of whether theoretical integration should be striving for comprehensiveness or multiple more-comprehensive understandings and, in criminology, whether the new set of competing integrative theories provides theoretical clarity or "integrational chaos" (Einstadter & Henry, 2006, pp. 319–320).

Interdisciplinarians, however, might argue that the charge of integrational chaos presumes that there is no way to adjudicate between competing integrative theories. Newell's (2001) theory of interdisciplinary studies and Repko's (2008) version of the steps in the interdisciplinary research process both include a final step of testing/applying the more comprehensive theory (Boix-Mansilla, 2005). As is the case in classic theory building, the fit with empirical evidence determines which competing integrative theory is preferable or at least has more practical value (Bernard, 2001). If multiple integrated theories of crime causation exist, whether these have been arrived at by partial integration or by the integration of elements from different combinations of root disciplines, the key issue is which stands up to the evidence. As a further test, we might ask which of the different "comprehensive policies" produced by each of these different integrative theories lowers the incidence of a particular crime. In short, which comprehensive policy works best when it is implemented?

Another approach to the issue of creating more comprehensive theory comes from addressing what, precisely, is being integrated. In the criminological literature, there are four different ways that integration in criminological theory has occurred: (1) conceptual integration; (2) propositional integration; (3) causal integration; and (4) cross-level integration (Einstadter & Henry, 2006; Hirschi, 1979; Liska, Krohn, & Messner, 1989). When considering the meaning of these various integrations, it is important to be clear that social science theorists (like their natural science counterparts) typically see theories as assertions about relationships among variables. Different theories may have some variables in common, but they can be distinguished by the differences in the variables they interconnect and by the assumptions about causal relationships between the variables. There is no reason an integrative theory cannot include a wider array of variables and provide a somewhat different explanation (from those contained in any of the theories from which it derives its variables) for why those variables are included and how they are interconnected. Here, a variable is a measurable way of operationalizing an abstract or general concept; a variable is either in an equation or it isn't. For example, we might want to look at the range of variables derived from different theories that have been empirically demonstrated to correlate with the propensity of juveniles to join gangs. We might include neighborhood housing density, age, criminality of parent or siblings, degree of neighborhood disorganization, and neighborhood transience rates. These variables may be interconnected in different ways. Theories that claim community shapes the opportunities available for adolescents to make delinquent decisions present a different set of interconnections than those that claim that only juveniles who are predisposed to sensation-seeking behavior due to biological or psychological developmental processes will act on environmental opportunities. In this individual-level predisposition case, we might be including variables such as adolescent brain development, domestic abuse, traumatic brain syndrome, high sugar consumption, addictive personality, and so on. Clearly, therefore, a different comprehensive understanding would emerge, based on an integration of variables located at the micro-level of analysis (i.e., at the level of the individual), than if we integrated elements of theory based at the macro-level of analysis (i.e., at the level of the community and society) because the latter would embody the former and arguably shape its internal relations/dynamics. So the decision about the nature of the interconnections between variables affects which concepts are integrated from the different discipline-based theories.

Conceptual Integration

In order to achieve conceptual integration toward a more comprehensive understanding, concepts from different disciplines first need to be reconciled through redefinition, extension, organization, or transformation. This conceptual reconciliation is a step prior to the integration process (Step 8, creating common ground, rather than Step 9, integrating insights into a more comprehensive understanding, in Repko's [2008] schema). As we have previously argued, "integrating concepts involves finding those that have similar meanings in different theories and merging them into a common language" (Einstadter & Henry, 2006, p. 316). This technique of redefinition in interdisciplinary studies, referred to as "textual integration" (Brown, 1989), is one of the foundations for creating common ground. Abstractly, theories are generally built up from concepts, or kernels of ideas, that theorists then link together into explanations for events or phenomena. For example, high levels of immigration into cities combined with profit-seeking landlords leads to poor quality, low rent, multifamily inner-city housing with high resident turnover; the resultant neighborhood instability fragments communities, resulting in a breakdown of informal networks of social control. Fearful of being victimized, youth band together for self-protection, forming subcultures that can become territorial gangs that protect their members by instilling fear in nongang or other gang members. They maintain autonomy by engaging in a variety of delinquency, such as vandalism and drug dealing (i.e., the social disorganization theory of gang formation).

In practice, many theories start with others' explanations that they modify by creating concepts to fit, or by borrowing concepts from other theories. For example, the concept of social learning added to the theory of social disorganization extends its explanatory power. It explains intergenerational gangs by showing that gang members develop powerful rationalizations to justify their existence; define crime and violence as necessary for survival; and pass the knowledge, skills, and markets on to new gang members. Once a gang is formed in a neighborhood, youth can be socialized into the gang's subculture.

In creating common ground, then, the separate disciplinary "languages" (really, definitions of terms) reflect the differences as well as the similarities in meanings of related concepts. Those differences, in turn, reflect what distinguishes one discipline from another: most generally, its perspective or worldview. Merging concepts is not the simple task of focusing on similarities and ignoring differences. Rather, it entails figuring out how to utilize those similarities in a way that retains the integrity of the original concept.

The aim of interdisciplinary integration when creating common ground (Step 8) is to be identifiably responsive to each disciplinary perspective on which one draws, but to be dominated by none of them. Although this test for interdisciplinarians normally refers to constructing a more comprehensive understanding, it also applies to creating common ground (i.e., a concept should be redefined such that it is responsive to the perspective of the discipline into the domain of which the concept is entering). For example, Akers's (1994) "conceptual absorption" approach takes concepts from social learning and social control theory (among others) and merges them. The control theory concept of "belief," which refers to a person's moral conviction for or against delinquency, is equated to learning theory's "definitions favorable or unfavorable to crime" (differential association). It is interesting that there are parallels here to the theory of human cognitive practice known as "conceptual blending," in which humans subconsciously integrate elements and relations from diverse situations to create new concepts, a process seen by some as being at the heart of the creative process (Fauconnier & Turner, 2002; Turner & Fauconnier, 1995).

Although ultimately conceptual integration may distort, even transform, a disciplinary concept in creating a new or blended concept (Lanier & Henry, 2004, p. 342), that need not be a disadvantage so long as it does not engage in a reductionist practice, that is, to lose the integrity of the original idea through oversimplification (during Step 9 of creating a more comprehensive understanding). The appropriate test is not to remain true to disciplinary intent, but to faithfully capture the meaning of the aspect of the concept that will be utilized—its kernel of truth or essential idea. A disciplinarian should be able to look at a redefined or extended concept, for example, and agree that the part of the concept of interest to the interdisciplinarian has been accurately and adequately captured.

Propositional Integration

Having created the common ground through conceptual integration, we can now move to Step 9, creating a comprehensive understanding. If we take theoretical propositions to refer to the interconnections or relationship between two or more variables, or among a specific (and usually small) set of variables, then at least some theoretical propositions must be integrated in order to construct an integrated theory. If one of those variables is also included in the causal explanations of another discipline, propositional integration could involve the addition of another equation to a system of simultaneous equations or another independent variable to a single equation. Propositional integration "refers to combining propositions from theories or placing them in some causal order or sequence" (Lanier & Henry, 2004, p. 343) or what might simply be called organizing them logically.

> Propositional integration is a more formal effort because it entails linking the propositions and not just the concepts of two or more theories into a combined theory. . . . Rather than simply usurpation, a propositionally integrated theory must actually meaningfully connect or relate the propositions of different theories into the new theory. (Paternoster & Bachman, 2001, p. 307)

Shoemaker (1996, p. 254) has observed that propositional integration can quickly result in an exponential increase in the number of variables, making the testing of integrative theory impractical because of the sample size necessary. However, this may be appropriate—the causal factors interacting to produce crime may indeed be numerous—but it is not inevitable: Interdisciplinarians may come to realize that some variables from one discipline are being used without much success to explain an aspect of crime that is much better explained by another discipline. Those variables would then be supplanted in the more comprehensive theory by variables from the other discipline or disciplines. Along this line of thinking, Robinson (2004, pp. x–xi) advocates building integrative theory by examining the tested contribution to our understanding of crime made by "risk factors" derived from each discipline, "illustrating how risk factors at different levels of analysis from different academic disciplines interact to increase the probability that a person will commit anti-social behavior" (Robinson, 2004, p. 271). It is important to note that Robinson is disaggregating these "risk factors" from their discipline-based theories and applying the test of whether they contribute to the new integrated theory based on their empirical veracity, then combining them into a new integrative explanation for why people engage in crime, or why they engage in a particular kind of crime.

Here, we are considering what is the most appropriate mechanism or method of integrating selected theories to produce a more comprehensive understanding (Step 9). For example, is integration to take the form of one grand theory? Does integration assume a sequential, "end-to-end" process, in which various theories kick in at different stages? Does the mechanism of integration seek to provide a transcendent approach, leaving the individual theories to deal with specifics? Does the mechanism used for integration discuss the interrelationship between the component theories, showing how each of the dimensions relates, or do the integrated propositions vary depending on which crime/offender/situation is being analyzed?

Liska et al. (1989, pp. 5–15), drawing on Hirschi (1979), suggest that a key issue in generating a comprehensive understanding through integrating theory is to consider how theoretical propositions are logically related. They describe three types of relationships, though others could also be envisioned: (1) end-to-end or sequential integration, which implies a sequential causal order; (2) side-by-side or horizontal integration, which implies overlapping influences; or (3) up-and-down or vertical integration, which "refers to identifying a level of abstraction or generality that encompasses much of the conceptualization of the constituent theories" (Bernard & Snipes, 1996; Messner et al., 1989, p. 5). The danger of up-and-down propositional integration, in which one theory is subsumed by another that is claimed to be more general in its explanatory power while incorporating the explanatory power of its constituent theories, is that it can rapidly become an example of reductionism. However, in its less-often used synthetic form, it holds significant promise, which is discussed below.

First, end-to-end or sequential integration links the immediate cause of crime to a more distant cause of crime and then links that to an even more distant cause. For example, an arrest for gang violence might be the outcome of the following process of sequential causes over time: Biological deficits at birth may lead to low IQ, which leads to learning disabilities in early childhood, which may lead to an inability to follow social norms, which may lead to group and institutional exclusion, which produces reduced self-esteem and alienation, which generates anger and hostility that results in affiliations with similarly alienated peers, which leads to delinquent peer or gang formation, which leads to law violation, which is reacted to by authorities, producing criminal justice intervention and stigmatization, which results in an arrest for gang violence. In this illustration, an arrest for gang violence is explained by a series of theoretical propositions drawn from labeling theory, subcultural theory, learning theory, cognitive theory, and biological or genetic theory. No one theoretical explanation explains the whole sequence, but linked end-to-end they may do so.

Second, in side-by-side or horizontal integration, each of the theories integrated explains a different aspect of the phenomenon, in this case different kinds of crime or different types of criminal. So, one theory may explain one type of crime, such as organizational (white-collar) crime, while another will explain violent crime such as robbery, and yet another theory will explain workplace crime, and so on (Gibbons & Farr, 2001; Moffitt, 1993). Added together, the collection of theories explains a variety of crimes, and it is also possible that two or more theories may explain the same type of crime. For example, some acts of sexual assault may be explained by self-control theory, which argues that such crimes are the result of a predisposition to sensation seeking and the desire for immediate gratification, but sexual assault may also be explained by social learning theory and low self-esteem as a result of the offender being a victim of childhood sexual abuse. Of course, the question this raises is whether two acts defined by law as the same crime are actually the same or different behaviors. If different, then each theory would be explaining a different act, even though the law classifies them as the same with regard to the harm and consequences for the victim.

In side-by-side integration, "the integrated typological theory is simply all the separate explanations of crime combined" (Paternoster & Bachman, 2001, p. 308). Alternatively, one theory may explain one type of offender. A good illustration of this is provided by Terri Moffitt's (1993, 2003) theory of two types of offender: adolescent-limited offenders have a pattern of extreme antisocial behavior during adolescence, which they mature out of by early adulthood. In contrast, life-course-persistent offenders exhibit criminal activity across their life course. She argues that a different causal explanation is needed to explain the two types of offender.

> [Side-by-side integration addresses the] scope of theoretical explana-
> tion and whether the integration is intended to explain crime in general
> or a specific type of crime, or whether it is intended to explain a spe-
> cific kind of motivation across a range of different crimes. Is it intended
> to apply to the population in general or only certain sectors of it (e.g.,
> young, old, men, women, African American, Hispanic)? Is it intended
> to apply in all situations or is it situationally specific? (Einstadter &
> Henry, 2006, p. 318)

Finally, up-and-down or deductive integration attempts to explain crime by generalizing from a range of constitutive theoretical explanations. The synthetic form of up-and-down integration is consistent with the aim of developing an integrative comprehensive understanding. It involves creating a theory of sufficient generality that incorporates multiple propositions from constitutive theories, each of which explains a part of the process that is the crime. The difference between this and the other forms of propositional integration is that each of the explanations plays a part in explaining the whole crime event, but none alone explains the whole event. Consider again the example of delinquency. Several different theories offer explanations for why adolescents engage in delinquent acts. Control theory, for example, has a key concept of parental attachment, which is inversely related to delinquency (assuming parents are themselves moral and law abiding). When lack of parental attachment is combined with other elements, such as low commitment to convention and lack of involvement in conventional activities, an adolescent may do poorly in school. Conflict theory, as well as developmental theory, argues that family conflict can arise from a variety of internal family dynamics or external societal pressures and can produce alienation of the adolescent from his or her family. Low commitment to convention can also lead to underachieving in school, which in turn can exacerbate conflict and alienation in the family. Social disorganization also contributes to the alienation of some adolescents from their parents, due to a lack of identification, and social learning theory shows how alienated and underachieving students can identify more directly with underachieving peers, which in turn can create more alienation and further underachievement, as well as lead to deviant and law-breaking activity. A synthetic version of up-and-down integrated theory would argue that none of these theoretical propositions alone explains delinquency, but taken together they show how delinquency can be the codetermined outcome from the different propositions acting in the same direction. This is not because one factor causes the other, but rather because relations in the family are part of the relations in the school, and relations between peers are part of the relations of school and family. One does not cause the other to change, but when one changes, the qualities of the other are changed simultaneously. This leads us to the notion that when we are talking about integration, different causal relations are implied in each of these models of integration, which suggests that before integrating, the interdisciplinarian must think hard about how causal factors are related.

Causal Integration

Another key issue affecting the nature of theoretical integration is causality. When developing a theory of common ground (Step 8) toward a more comprehensive understanding of complex phenomena (Step 9), we need to recognize that there are different kinds of causal models that describe the relationships between variables. We can identify a minimum of four kinds of causality: (1) linear causality, which takes the form of a sequential chain of events; (2) multiple causality, which sees the phenomenon as the outcome of several different independent causes or a combination of interdependent causes (but see 4 below); (3) interactive causality, in which the effects of one event influence its cause(s), which then influences the event; and (4) dialectical or reciprocal causality, in which causes and events are not discrete entities but are overlapping, interrelated, and codetermining (Barak, 1998a; Einstadter & Henry, 2006; Henry & Milovanovic, 1996). The difference between interactive causality and reciprocal causality has to do with the way the causes and events are conceived. In interactive causality, one cause produces an effect, which subsequently acts on the original cause and affects it in an interactive cycle. In dialectical/reciprocal causality, causes and events are intertwined such that each is a part of the other. A clear example is the relationship between law and society. Law is not separate from society or from the social forms, such as family or government, to which it is related: "Law is integrally constituted in relation to a plurality of social forms" (Fitzpatrick, 1984, p. 115) and "elements of law are elements of the other social forms, and vice versa" (p. 122). The effect is not independent but instantaneous because a change in one is simultaneously a change in the other (imagine a Venn diagram). This presents a challenge to theorists attempting to examine individual causal links in turn. The interactive and dialectical/reciprocal models of causality suggest a dynamic, rather than static, form of integration, one that will be of particular interest to interdisciplinarians examining complex phenomena.

This typology leads to a series of questions:

> Should different causalities be integrated such that some are dynamic and some static? . . . Is the weight given to theories emphasizing a fixed or changing picture of social life? Do most of the theories combined assume a static or dynamic state? (Einstadter & Henry, 2006, pp. 318–319)

If we were to integrate these models of causality, some (such as those found in the more linear and static theories) might explain some stages of a phenomenon while others (that are nonlinear and dynamic) might explain the relationship between stages or how a process evolves over time and across space.

Cross-Level Integration

Finally, we need to consider the level of integration, meaning whether an integrated theory should address a micro-, meso-, or macro-level of integration, or integrate across all levels, which is called "cross-level integration" (Liska et al. 1989; Muftić, 2009). Intuitively, it seems that if comprehensiveness is the goal, then all three levels (and even a fourth global level) need to be addressed simultaneously in what has been called "multilevel" integration (Paternoster & Bachman, 2001, p. 305). The integrational levels to be considered include "(1) kinds of people, their human agency, and their interactive social processes (micro); (2) kinds of organization, their collective agency, and their organizational processes (meso); and (3) kinds of culture, structure, and context (macro)" (Einstadter & Henry, 2006, p. 319). An example of cross-level (macro-micro) integration in criminology is Colvin and Pauly's (1983) attempt to combine Marxist, conflict, and strain (macro-level) with subculture, social learning, and social control (micro-level) theories. It could be argued that considering the levels of integration takes us back to Step 1 in the interdisciplinary process, namely, the identification of the kind of complex problem to be studied, and the distinction between broad and narrow interdisciplinarity. The question about the appropriate breadth of study perhaps can only appropriately be answered for a particular instance (of crime, in this case). Still, interdisciplinarians need to be aware of these questions as they decide on the scope of the particular complex problem they want to study. This is an important consideration because without an explicit awareness that macro-micro level interactions occur, it might be seductive to believe that an integration of a range of theories is adequate, without realizing that macro-level theories have been omitted. For example, the 16 different integrated theories identified by Lanier and Henry (2010, pp. 385–389) draw on micro-level theories in greater numbers (66%) than they draw on macro-level theories (33%). Put simply, integration of discipline-based theories in criminology has typically been biased toward same-level rather than cross-level analyses.

Toward an Integrated Analysis of Violence and School Violence

In this section, we first establish that violence/school violence is a complex problem. Second, we examine the integrated causal analysis of violence/school violence, arguing that this is best explained using interactive/reciprocal causal explanations rather than single or multiple independent causality. Third, we argue that a comprehensive understanding of the phenomenon requires that we examine causation across multiple levels, and we explain how these levels are interactive and interrelated. Finally, we suggest the kind of policy that such an integrated reciprocal, multi-level causal analysis would imply.

Violence as a Complex Problem

Leaving aside for the moment the problematic status of "problems," "problem solving," and "problem solvers" (see McCormack, 2009), we need first to decide what makes a problem complex and, indeed, what are the criteria of complexity. This issue has been addressed in the interdisciplinary studies literature (Meek, 2001; Meek & Newell, 2005; Newell, 2001, 2003), has been incorporated into Step 2 of Repko's (2008) schema, and has also been explored by scholars seeking to understand the nature of complex problem solving. For example, according to Funke (1991), building on the work of Dietrich Dörner, a complex problem is defined by the following five characteristics: (1) multiple variables and decisions (complexity), that (2) interact and interrelate in nonlinear, even chaotic and dynamic ways (connectivity), that (3) achieve multiple goals or outcome states (polytely), that (4) lack clarity of content and meaning (opacity), and that (5) change over time (variable temporal dynamics), being unpredictable (temporal sensitivity) and yet occurring in waves (patterned clusters of events). Detombe (1994, 2003) says that complex social problems involve multiple people and organizations, are characterized by a lack of knowledge and data, and produce uncertain and often undesired outcomes. She says, "knowledge about the issues involved in the problem normally belongs to more than one discipline" and "belongs to the subject of study of different domains within one discipline [inter-domain problems]" (Detombe, 2003). The complexity of the issue reflects the multiple levels of phenomena that are involved, which can be "viewed from the micro-, meso- or macro-aggregation" levels and includes "persons, groups, societies, organizations, buildings, education, ministries" (Detombe, 2003). These entities are interrelated in uncertain dynamic ways, changing over time, with uncertain start and end points, and often with unexpected or unique outcomes. Definitions of the problem are lacking or conflicting, and the problem has so far defied a comprehensive understanding, which challenges any simple analysis.

Complex societal interdisciplinary problems are often embedded in a dynamic context (continuously changing environment), as a result of which the problems change continually. This, combined with the unpredictability of the effects of interventions, makes it difficult to handle the problem (Detombe, 2003).

To what extent does violence/school violence qualify as a complex social problem, according to these criteria? Clearly, from the perspective of producing unwanted outcomes, the harms of violence/school violence affect not only the victims but also the perpetrators, their families, and, in the case of school violence, the school as an institution, the learning environment, the community, and the wider society. Violence/school violence, therefore, qualifies as a social problem with multiple and variable negative outcomes. In the case of school violence, these outcomes are relatively unpredictable, both in their timing and their impact, which is especially true for the extreme forms, such as rampage shootings (Newman, Fox, Harding, Mehta, & Roth, 2004), although the outcomes may be less random and more predictable for the continual occurrence of subforms of violence that permeate urban schools. Indeed, the question of unpredictability is difficult to answer in general because, although the outcomes of complex systems are not strictly predictable, they are often quasi-predictable. And they usually produce identifiable patterns of behavior, as can be seen in the research on patterns of school violence; although those patterns do evolve over time, they don't evolve quickly or capriciously. The least predictable aspects of complex systems are the bifurcation points at which one pattern suddenly transforms into another, but those are quite infrequent. A good example here would be when a school system, such as Columbine, embodies a pattern of repeated bullying over many years, which transforms into a dramatic rampage shooting as the victims of bullying seek to destroy the school and those in it. Therefore, we argue that complex systems are relatively unpredictable if we approach them without a comprehensive understanding of their complexity, which, of course, is the point of an integrative analysis.

It is certainly the case that acts of violence/school violence are often depicted as meaningless random acts of aggression rather than acts targeted at particular persons or groups. Also, the definition of violence/school violence is contested. Some restrict it to any form of physical violence and bullying; others include psychological and emotional harm through intimidation; and still others include institutional and symbolic forms of violence as expressions of power and control by teachers, administrators, and politicians (for a review of these different definitional positions, see Henry, 2000, 2009). Finally, as we reiterate in the next section, violence/school violence is constituted through multiple causal relationships, operative on micro-, meso-, or macro-levels of society, from individual through interactive group level, institutional and community levels, to societal, cultural, and even global levels (Benbenishty & Astor, 2005; Henry, 2009; Muschert, 2007; Muschert & Peguero, 2010). In short, violence/school violence satisfies the five conditions of complexity, connectivity, polytely, opacity, and temporality to qualify as a complex interdisciplinary social problem. In the next section, we argue that violence/school violence has multiple constitutive causal variables that interact in nonlinear, chaotic, and dynamic ways to produce multiple uncertain but harmful outcomes or events, themselves subject to change in relation to the changing environments, including being transformed and accumulating over time.

Integrative Theory in Criminology as an Explanation of Violence/School Violence

Violence is defined by law as a serious crime:

> (a) an offense that has as an element the use, attempted use, or threatened use of physical force against the person or property of another, or (b) any other offense that is a felony and that, by its nature, involves a substantial risk that physical force against the person or property of another may be used in the course of committing the offense. (18 U.S.C. 16)

School violence, because of the age of the victims, is seen as a particularly heinous form of crime and has a broader definition that includes a wide range of disruptive activities seen as harmful to victims besides physical and/emotional violence, though its definition is contested (Henry, 2000).

There are approximately 12 different theoretical explanations for crime causation in the criminological literature, each tied to the following academic disciplines, fields, or schools of thought: economics, biology, psychology, geography, sociology, social constructionism, political science, philosophy, feminism, and postmodernism (see Einstadter & Henry, 2006; Lanier & Henry, 2010). However, as we have argued, several criminologists have recognized the value of taking an integrative approach that incorporates various different combinations of these causal explanations. Thus, instead of seeing crime through a single disciplinary framework, or even through multiple paradigms, integrative criminological theorists take an interdisciplinary approach defined as "the combination of two or more pre-existing theories, selected on the basis of their perceived commonalities, into a single reformulated theoretical model with greater comprehensiveness and explanatory value than any one of its component theories" (Farnworth, 1989, p. 95). Hunter and Dantzker (2002, p. 150), for example, describe "holistic" explanations of crime, which "combine multifactor perspectives" allowing "criminologists to see the entire panorama" rather than a one-dimensional picture. Robinson (2004, 2006; Robinson & Beaver, 2009) has refined the micro-, meso-, and macro-levels of crime causation while still retaining an overall holistic approach as an "integrated systems perspective." This theory "asserts that various criminogenic factors interact among all levels of analysis—cell, organ, organism, group, community/organization, and society—to produce antisocial and criminal behavior" (Robinson, 2006, p. 322).

Gregg Barak, the author of a foundational book on integrative theory in criminology (1998b), also wrote *Violence and Nonviolence: Pathways to Understanding* (2003). Here, Barak points out that in spite of clear evidence that the causes of violence are cumulatively interrelated across a range of societal levels, most analyses of violence are "un-reflexive," about the relationship between causes, or about whether forms of violence can themselves become causes of violence. This is partly because analysts tend to "focus on one particular form of violence, without much, if any, reflection on the other forms." He further argues that "these fragmented and isolated analyses seek to explain the workings of a given form of violence without trying to understand the common threads or roots that may link various forms of violence together" (p. 39; see also Barak, 2006). Critical to our purpose in this chapter is the nature of the links to which he alludes. In one sense, Barak could be talking about side-to-side linkages of the kind discussed earlier, but he is actually talking much more about both reciprocal causality and cross-level causality. Indeed, he argues that causes of violence (and nonviolence) ranging "across the spheres of interpersonal, institutional, and structural relations as well as across the domains of family, subculture, and culture *are cumulative, mutually reinforcing, and inversely related* [emphasis added]" (p. 169), but that "most explanations of the etiology of violence and nonviolence . . . emphasize the interpersonal spheres to the virtual exclusion of the institutional and structural spheres" (p. 155). He argues that we need to take account of the dynamic interrelations of these different levels in order to understand the pathways to violence (p. 170). Important to his argument is that occurrences of violence at these different levels can themselves be implicated in the causes of subsequent acts of violence as the process of violence unfolds over time. Barak (2006) observes that we need to consider the full range of behavioral motivations and sociocultural constraints that intersect with the spheres of interpersonal, institutional, and structural communication. This same multi-level, interactive, and reciprocal analysis of culminating factors can be applied to school violence, and a few scholars have attempted this approach.

Integrative Analysis of School Violence as a Cumulative Reciprocal Causal Process

Several researchers studying school violence have noted that a complex set of influences on, or multiple causes of, school violence operate at the individual, community, and national levels (Centers for Disease Control and Prevention [CDC], 2008; Garbarino, 1999; Henry, 2000, 2009; Newman et al., 2004). Muschert (2007), for example, states, "School shooting incidents need to be understood as resulting from a constellation of contributing causes, none of which is sufficient in itself to explain a shooting" (p. 68). He identifies 13 categories of "causes" of school shootings, arguing that "causes may emerge from a variety of levels, ranging from the individual causes, community contexts, and social/cultural contexts in which the events occur." These include (1) "individual" causes such as mental illness, access to guns, peer relationships, family neglect, or abuse; (2) "community" context such as youth and peer dynamics; (3) "institutional" contexts such as school-based interaction that encompasses poor student/faculty relationships, ineffective school administration, inability of communities to respond to delinquency or excessively oppressive community responses to delinquency, and intolerant community climate; and (4) the "social and cultural" level, such as the crisis in public school education, gender role violence, conservative religious political climate, gun culture, and media violence (p. 69).

Some school violence researchers have envisioned these levels not only as interacting but as incorporated, one in the other, such that the individual is incorporated into the group, which is incorporated into the society, from micro- to macro-structural levels (Benbenishty & Astor, 2005; Muschert, 2007; Henry, 2000; Welsh, Greene, & Jenkins, 1999). As Benbenishty and Astor (2005) state, school violence "is the product of many factors that are associated with multiple levels organized hierarchically (nested like a matryoshka doll): individual students within classes, classes within schools, schools within neighborhoods, and neighborhoods within societies and cultures" (p. 113). The problem with this nested analysis is that the metaphor begs the key question of the nature and strengths of the inter-level linkages.

Henry (2009), applying Barak's (2003) reciprocal cumulative analysis (itself influenced by the work of Moffitt, 2001; Sampson & Laub, 2001; and

Colvin, 2000), argued that in order to examine complex social problems such as school violence, or subsets of it such as rampage school shootings,

> we need to take a wide-angle interdisciplinary lens to the nature of what constitutes violence in schools and retain the connection between school violence and violence at various levels within the institution of the school and the wider society. We need to consider the range of different disciplinarily-based explanations in order to assess what each brings to a comprehensive analysis of school violence. (p. 1248)

He agrees that school violence is a broad phenomenon with multiple manifest forms that together constitute a continuum of violence. However, he also argues that what is critical is the ways that these causes come together over time through a culmination process that can produce a dramatic outcome of mass violence or remain as less violent forms. For example, school shooter Kip Kinkel's repeated victimization by school bullies escalated into an explosion of violence and rage when the "killer at Thurston High" shot his parents and then his fellow students. Other students may be subjected to similar repeated abuse that remains internalized as harm but does not escalate to the crescendo reached in the more extreme cases. Conventional analyses of school violence explain each subtype of school violence, without recognizing the cumulative interrelations and interaction between them. Research, however, suggests that violence is a more reciprocal process embedded in a set of mutually reinforcing ongoing causal chains that lead to episodes of violence on the pathway to more serious violence (Athens, 1992; Colvin, 2000; Hotaling, Straus, & Lincoln, 1989, as cited by Loeber & Stouthamer-Loeber, 1998, p. 112; Straus, 1994; Strassberg, Dodge, Pettit, & Bates, 1994).

> A growing body of research indicates that victims of violence are more likely than their peers to also be perpetrators of violence, and that individuals most likely to be victims of personal crime are those who report the greatest involvement in delinquent activities. (Siegfried, Ko, & Kelley, 2004)

Similarly, research on school violence shows that violent social interaction between student offenders and victims can turn some victims into offenders seeking to exact reparation or "level the score" (Furlong, Sharma, & Rhee, 2000, p. 83; Lockwood, 1997). Evidence also supports the claim that forms of violent victimization such as bullying and exclusion can eventually produce an inner sense of hopelessness and vulnerability that can lead to rampage shooting (Newman et al., 2004). However, not all rampage shooters were bullied; some may have suffered psychological trauma, and others have been influenced by witnessing violent trauma to their friends and in their neighborhoods. Henry (2009) urges,

> Consider the range of physical, psychological, and symbolic violence as cumulatively reciprocal *contributing causal elements* that can build over time to produce instances of extreme violence. From this perspective, rampage school violence is not a different crime but an extreme level of the culmination of its constitutive forms of subviolence. (p. 1252)

Henry (2000, 2009) further argues that incidents of violence in school are not only cumulative between victim and offender, but operate across multiple levels. As such, micro-level interpersonal violence can combine with symbolic images of media violence and with institutional acts of coercive power and government acts of force and violence. The expression of force through agencies of the state, whether the military or the justice system, legitimates the use of violence to deal with problems and cannot be left out of any equation seeking a comprehensive explanation for specific acts of violence, however remote may seem the direct interrelationships between these different levels. The challenge is to develop ways to assess the nature and strengths of these interrelationships over time.

Finally, using a more expansive definition of school violence, including institutional and mass mediated forms of symbolic violence, Henry (2009) identifies and locates these examples of school violence at different levels and represents them in a typological matrix, showing that instances of school violence at one level can themselves serve as causes of school violence at another level. Moreover, the effects of one form of school violence operative at one level can be both the outcome of a subset of causative processes and a contributing cause to subsequent violent outcomes, in an ongoing chain of violence. He concludes:

> It is not enough to limit the analysis of school violence to incidents of particular types of student violence. Rather, it is important to identify a range of levels of violence within the school and a wide range of violence at different levels of society that impact the school, to identify and to see how these are each reciprocally interrelated in the school setting as a cumulative process over time. In this way, we will be able to comprehend how violent acts, including extreme expressions such as rampage school shootings, are outcomes of multiple subviolent, violent, and symbolically violent processes. . . . Any adequate analysis of school violence, therefore, has to locate the micro-interactive, institutional practices and sociocultural productions in the wider political economy of the society in which these occur. Ignoring the structural inequalities of power in the wider system reduces the cause of school violence to local and situational inequalities of power, suggesting that policies can be addressed to intervene locally, such as at the level of peer subculture or school organization. While these levels of intervention are important, they alone are insufficient. (Henry, 2009, p. 1262)

Thus, in order to develop adequate policies concerning school violence, we need to identify the multiple causes of school violence, noting that some of the causes are, indeed, themselves forms of violence. We also need to locate these causes at their level of operation in a nested hierarchy of cumulative interaction, examine the linkages between the different levels of cause (micro, meso, macro), and determine the strengths of these inter-level linkages. Indeed, although the CDC (2008) sees school violence as facilitated by different level strategies, for example, individual level, relationship level, community level, and societal level strategies, it fails to recognize that systemic, inter-level linkages exist between levels that require strategies that address these linkages. Thus, the CDC argues that at the community level, in addition to local and school-based strategies that involve class management and curriculum techniques and practices, changes to "the social environment of the school . . . can reduce crime and fear" (p. 4). Further, "Schools are embedded within a larger community environment by which they are influenced. As a result, broader efforts to change the physical and social environments of communities can also benefit schools" (p. 4). Unfortunately, this policy analysis implies dealing with each level separately, which ignores the interrelationships between the levels that is fundamental to the Barak (2003) and Henry (2009) analysis discussed earlier. Although it may seem that policies that deal with each level separately would negate the need for considering the interrelationships between levels, this presumes that we can know what the relevant levels are without an analysis of these interrelationships. So part of the reason for examining this interrelationship across levels is to establish which causal factors at which levels are in need of policy intervention.

Conclusion

Our purpose in this chapter was not to arrive at a comprehensive policy for school violence, but to demonstrate the advantages of approaching a complex social problem with the tools of the integrative research process. We examined how the complex problem of violence/school violence would be analyzed from such a perspective rather than from the conventional disciplinary or multidisciplinary perspectives. We explored how integrative criminologists have struggled with the issues of which elements of the variety of disciplinary theories to include in their analysis, how they integrate concepts through redefinition, the different ways they integrate disciplinary-based theoretical propositions, and their incorporation of different kinds of causality. We also demonstrated the importance not only of recognizing different levels of analysis but of developing a holistic understanding of the strengths of interaction between these different levels as they vary over time. We determined that the most promising explanation of violence/school violence is the cumulative reciprocal theory that sees causes of violent events at different levels and also sees these very events as contributing causes of subsequent violent acts. Finally, we argued that the most promising policies for combating school violence are those that incorporate an appreciation of multiple causality operative at different levels and identify the strengths or nature of the interrelationships of the processes operative at the different levels.

Any policy based on an integrative theory must address this challenge if we are to transcend our current state of knowledge and develop the ability to address such complex social problems. One promising way forward is *The Columbine Effect* (Muschert & Peguero, 2010; Muschert, Henry, Bracy, & Peguero, in press), which examines school antiviolence policy in the context of the totality of the complexity of the problem, seeking to relate specific policies to different levels and dimensions of the problem. Rather than taking policies in isolation or as alternatives, the authors argue that effective prevention policy requires the multiple, cumulative causes of school violence to be simultaneously addressed through a comprehensive web of policies.

References

Akers, R. (1994). *Criminological theories: Introduction, evaluation and application.* Los Angeles: Roxbury.

Athens, L. H. (1992). *The creation of dangerous violent criminals.* Champaign: University of Illinois Press.

Barak, G. (Ed.). (1998a). *Integrated criminology.* Aldershot, UK: Ashgate.

Barak, G. (1998b). *Integrating criminologies.* Boston: Allyn & Bacon.

Barak, G. (2003). *Violence and nonviolence: Pathways to understanding.* Thousand Oaks, CA: Sage.

Barak, G. (2006). Applying integrative theory: A reciprocal theory of violence and non-violence. In S. Henry & M. M. Lanier (Eds.), *The essential criminology reader* (pp. 336–346). Boulder, CO: Westview Press.

Barak, G. (2009). *Criminology: An integrated approach.* New York: Rowman and Littlefield.

Benbenishty, R., & Astor, R. A. (2005). *School violence in context: Culture, neighborhood, family, school and gender.* New York: Oxford University Press.

Bernard, T. J. (2001). Integrating theories in criminology. In R. Paternoster & R. Bachman (Eds.), *Explaining criminals and crime* (pp. 335–346). Los Angeles: Roxbury Press.

Bernard, T. J., & Snipes, J. B. (1996). Theoretical integration in criminology. In M. Tonry (Ed.), *Crime and justice: A review of research* (Vol. 20, pp. 301–348). Chicago: University of Chicago Press.

Boix-Mansilla, V. (2005, January/February). Assessing student work at disciplinary crossroads. *Change, 37*(1), 14–21.

Brown, R. H. (1989). Textuality, social science, and society. *Issues in Integrative Studies, 7*, 1–19.

Centers for Disease Control and Prevention. (2008). *Understanding school violence: Fact sheet.* Retrieved January 3, 2009, from http://www.cdc.gov/violence prevention/pdf/SchoolViolence_FactSheet-a.pdf

Colvin, M. (2000). *Crime and coercion: An integrative theory of chronic criminality.* New York: Palgrave Press.

Colvin, M., & Pauly, J. (1983). A critique of criminology: Toward an integrated structural-Marxist theory of delinquency production. *American Journal of Sociology, 89,* 513–551.

Detombe, D. J. (1994). *Defining complex interdisciplinary societal problems: A theoretical study for constructing a co-operative problem analyzing method: The method COMPRAM.* Amsterdam, NL: Thesis.

Detombe, D. J. (2003). *Defining complex interdisciplinary societal problems.* Retrieved from http://www.complexitycourse.org/detombecompramh1thesis.html

Einstadter, W. J., & Henry, S. (2006). *Criminological theory: An analysis of its underlying assumptions.* Boulder, CO: Rowman and Littlefield.

Elliott, D., Agerton, S., & Canter, R. (1979). An integrated theoretical perspective on delinquent behavior. *Journal of Research on Crime and Delinquency, 16,* 3–27.

Farnworth, M. (1989). Theory integration versus model building. In S. F. Messner, M. D. Krohn, & A. Liska (Eds.), *Theoretical integration in the study of deviance and crime: Problems and prospects* (pp. 93–100). Albany: State University of New York.

Fauconnier, G., & Turner, M. (2002). *The way we think: Conceptual blending and the mind's hidden complexities.* New York: Basic Books.

Fishbein, D. (1998). Biological perspectives in criminology. In S. Henry & W. J. Einstadter (Eds.), *The criminology theory reader* (pp. 92–109). New York: New York University Press.

Fitzpatrick, P. (1984). Law and societies. *Osgoode Hall Law Journal, 22,* 115–138.

Fuchsman, K. (2009). Rethinking integration in interdisciplinary studies. *Issues in Integrative Studies, 27,* 70–85.

Funke, J. (1991). Solving complex problems: Human identification and control of complex systems. In R. J. Sternberg & P. A. Frensch (Eds.), *Complex problem solving: Principles and mechanisms* (pp. 185–222). Hillsdale, NJ: Lawrence Erlbaum Associates.

Furlong, M. J., Sharma, B., & Rhee, S. S. (2000). Defining school violence victim subtypes: A step toward adapting prevention and intervention programs to match student needs. In D. S. Sandhu & C. B. Aspey (Eds.), *Violence in American schools* (pp. 69–85). Alexandria, VA: American Counseling Association.

Garbarino, J. (1999). *Lost boys: Why our sons turn violent and how we can save them.* New York: Free Press.

Gibbons. D. C. (1994). *Talking about crime and criminals: Problems and issues in theory development in criminology.* Englewood Cliffs, NJ: Prentice Hall.

Gibbons, D. C., & Farr, K. A. (2001). Defining patterns of crime and types of offenders. In S. Henry & M. M. Lanier (Eds.), *What is crime? Controversies over the nature of crime and what to do about it* (pp. 37–64). Boulder, CO: Rowman & Littlefield.

Hagan, J. (1989). *Structural criminology.* New Brunswick, NJ: Rutgers University Press.

Hawkins, J. D., & Weis, J. G. (1985). The social development model: An integrated approach to delinquency prevention. *Journal of Primary Prevention, 6*(2), 73–97.

Henry, S. (2000). What is school violence: An integrated definition. *ANNALS of the American Academy of Political and Social Science, 567,* 16–29.

Henry, S. (2009). School violence beyond Columbine: A complex problem in need of an interdisciplinary analysis. *American Behavioral Scientist, 52*(9), 1246-1265.

Henry, S., & Milovanovic, D. (1996). *Constitutive criminology: Beyond postmodernism.* London: Sage.

Hirschi, T. (1979). Separate and equal is better. *Journal of Research in Crime and Delinquency, 16,* 34–38.

Hirschi, T. (1989). Exploring alternatives to integrated theory. In S. F. Messner, M. D. Krohn, & A. E. Liska (Eds.), *Theoretical integration in the study of deviance and crime* (pp. 37–49). Albany: State University of New York Press.

Hotaling, G. T., Straus, M. A., & Lincoln, A. J. (1989). Intrafamily violence and crime and violence outside the family. In L. Ohlin & M. Tonry (Eds.), *Family violence* (pp. 315–375). Chicago: University of Chicago Press.

Hunter, R. D., & Dantzker, M. L. (2002). *Crime and criminality: Causes and consequences.* Upper Saddle River, NJ: Prentice Hall.

Hursh, B., Haas P., & Moore, M. (1998). An interdisciplinary model to implement general education. In W. H. Newell (Ed.), *Interdisciplinarity: Essays from the literature* (pp. 35–49). New York: College Board.

Jeffrey, C. R. (1990). *Criminology: An interdisciplinary approach.* Englewood Cliffs, NJ: Prentice-Hall.

Johnson, R. E. (1979). *Juvenile delinquency and its origins.* Cambridge, UK: Cambridge University Press.

Klein, J. T., & Newell, W. H. (1997). Advancing interdisciplinary studies. In J. G. Gaff, J. L. Ratcliff, et al. (Eds.), *Handbook of the undergraduate curriculum* (pp. 393–415). San Francisco: Jossey-Bass.

Lanier, M. M., & Henry, S. (2004). *Essential criminology* (2nd ed.). Boulder, CO: Westview.

Lanier, M. M., & Henry, S. (2010). *Essential criminology* (3rd ed.). Boulder, CO: Westview.

Liska, A. E., Krohn, M. D., & Messner, S. F. (1989). Strategies and requisites for theoretical integration in the study of deviance and crime. In S. F. Messner, M. D. Krohn, & A. E. Liska (Eds.), *Theoretical integration in the study of deviance and crime* (pp. 1–19). Albany: State University of New York Press.

Lockwood, D. (1997). *Violence among middle school and high school students: Analysis and implications for prevention.* Washington, DC: National Institute of Justice.

Loeber, R., & Stouthamer-Loeber, M. (1998). Juvenile aggression at home and school. In D. S Elliott, B. A. Hamburg, & K. R. Williams (Eds.), *Violence in American schools* (pp. 94–126). New York: Cambridge University Press.

McCormack, B. (2009). The problem with problem solving. *Issues in Integrative Studies, 27,* 17–34.

Meek, J. (2001). The practice of interdisciplinarity: Complex conditions and the potential of interdisciplinary theory. *Issues in Integrative Studies, 19,* 123–136.

Meek, J., & Newell, W. T. (2005). Complexity, interdisciplinarity and public administration: Implications for integrating communities. *Public Administration Quarterly, 29*(3), 321–349.

Messner, S. F., Krohn, M. D., & Liska, A. E. (Eds.). (1989). *Theoretical integration in the study of deviance and crime.* Albany: State University of New York Press.

Moffitt, T. E. (1993). Adolescent-limited and life-course-persistent antisocial behavior: A developmental taxonomy. *Psychological Review, 100,* 674–701.

Moffitt, T. (2001). Adolescence-limited and life-course-persistent antisocial behavior: A developmental taxonomy. In A. Piquero & P. Mazerolle (Eds.), *Lifecourse criminology: Contemporary and classic readings* (pp. 91–145). Belmont, CA: Wadsworth.

Moffitt, T. E. (2003). Life-course-persistent and adolescence-limited antisocial behaviour: A 10-year research review and a research agenda. In B. Lahey, T. Moffitt, & A. Caspi (Eds.), *Causes of conduct disorder and juvenile delinquency* (pp. 49–75). New York: Guilford Press.

Muftić, L. R. (2009). Macro-micro theoretical integration: An unexplored theoretical frontier. *Journal of Theoretical and Philosophical Criminology, 1*(2), 33–71.

Muschert, G. W. (2007). Research in school shootings. *Sociology Compass, 1*(1), 60–80.

Muschert, G. W., Henry, S., Bracy, N., & Peguero, A. A. (Eds.). (in press). *The Columbine effect: Fear and the expansion of school antiviolence policy.* Boulder, CO: Lynne Rienner.

Muschert, G. W., & Peguero, A. A. (2010). The Columbine effect and school antiviolence policy. *Research in Social Problems and Public Policy, 17,* 117–148.

National Academies of Sciences, National Academy of Engineering & Institute of Medicine. (2005). *Facilitating interdisciplinary research.* Washington, DC: National Academies.

Newell, W. G. (2001). A theory of interdisciplinary studies. *Issues in Integrative Studies, 19,* 1–25.

Newell, W. T. (2003). Complexity and interdisciplinarity. In L. D. Kiel (Ed.), *Knowledge management, organizational intelligence, and learning and complexity: Encyclopedia of life support systems* (pp. 849–874). Oxford: EOLSS.

Newman, K., Fox, S. C., Harding, D. J., Mehta, J., & Roth, W. (2004). *Rampage: The social roots of school shootings.* New York: Basic Books.

Paternoster, R., & Bachman, R. (Eds.). (2001). *Explaining criminals and crime.* Los Angeles: Roxbury.

Pearson, F. S., & Weiner, N. A. (1985). Toward an integration of criminological theories. *Journal of Criminal Law and Criminology, 76*(1), 116–150.

Repko, A. F. (2008). *Interdisciplinary research: Process and theory.* Thousand Oaks, CA: Sage.

Ritzer, G. (1975, August). Sociology: A multi-paradigm science. *American Sociologist,* 15–17.

Robinson, M. B. (2004). *Why crime? An integrated systems theory of antisocial behavior.* Upper Saddle River, NJ: Pearson/Prentice Hall.

Robinson, M. B. (2006). The integrative systems theory of anti-social behavior. In S. Henry & M. M. Lanier (Eds.), *The essential criminology reader* (pp. 319–335). Boulder, CO: Westview Press.

Robinson, M. B., & Beaver, K. (2009). *Why crime? An interdisciplinary approach to explaining criminal behavior.* Durham, NC: Carolina Academic Press.

Sampson, R., & Laub, J. (2001). A lifecourse theory of cumulative disadvantage and the stability of delinquency. In A. Piquero & P. Mazerolle (Eds.), *Lifecourse criminology: Contemporary and classic readings* (pp. 146–170). Belmont, CA: Wadsworth.

Shoemaker, D. J. (1996). *Theories of delinquency: An examination of explanations of delinquent behavior* (3rd ed.). New York: Oxford University Press.

Siegfried, C. B., Ko, S. J., & Kelley, A. (2004). *Victimization and juvenile offending.* Los Angeles: National Child Traumatic Stress Network, Juvenile Justice Working Group.

Strassberg, Z., Dodge, K. A., Pettit, G. S., & Bates, J. E. (1994). Spanking in the home and children's subsequent aggression toward kindergarten peers. *Development and Psychopathology, 6,* 445–461.

Straus, M. A. (with D. Donnely). (1994). *Beating the devil out of them: Corporal punishment in American families.* San Francisco: Lexington Books/Jossey-Bass.

Thornberry, T. P. (1989). Reflections on the advantages and disadvantages of theoretical elaboration. In S. F. Messner, M. D. Krohn, & A. E. Liska (Eds.), *Theoretical integration in the study of deviance and crime* (pp. 51–60). Albany: State University of New York Press.

Tittle, C. R. (1995). *Control balance: Toward a general theory of deviance.* Boulder, CO: Westview.

Turner, M., & Fauconnier, G. (1995). Conceptual integration and formal expression. *Metaphor & Symbolic Activity, 10*(3), 183–204.

Vila, B. (1994). A general paradigm for understanding criminal behavior: Extending evolutionary ecological theory. *Criminology, 32,* 311–359.

Welsh, W. N., Greene, J. R., & Jenkins, P. H. (1999). School disorder: The influence of individual, institutional and community factors. *Criminology, 37,* 73–115.

10 Research Integration

A Comparative Knowledge Base

Julie Thompson Klein

Integration is widely regarded as the primary methodology of interdisciplinarity. In the chapter on interdisciplinary studies (IDS) in the *Handbook of Undergraduate Curriculum*, Klein and Newell (1997) called integration the "acid test" of IDS (p. 404). In his textbook *Interdisciplinary Research: Process and Theory*, Allen Repko (2008) called it the distinguishing feature of IDS. And, in the defining chapter on integration in the *Handbook of Transdisciplinary Research*, Pohl, van Kerkhoff, Hirsch Hadorn, and Bammer (2008) called it "the core methodology underpinning the transdisciplinary research process" (p. 421). Three organizations have also made integration a cornerstone of their work. The Association for Integrative Studies promotes integration as the primary methodology of interdisciplinary studies. The Swiss Academies of Arts and Sciences Transdisciplinarity Research network (td-net; see http://www.transdisciplinarity.ch) devoted a recent international conference to the topic, and the Australian-based Integration and Implementation Sciences network (http://www.anu.edu.au/iisn) provides an academic base for synthesizing pertinent knowledge, concepts, and methods in order to address complex problems (Bammer, 2005).

This chapter provides a comparative overview of approaches to integration in interdisciplinary and transdisciplinary research (IDR and TDR). It presents a historical context for the idea of integration, compares major

AUTHOR'S NOTE: I thank the following for permission to adapt parts of previous material: Matthias Bergmann and Engelbert Schramm, for J. T. Klein (2008). Integration in der inter- und transdisziplinären Forschung. In M. Bergmann & E. Schramm (Eds.), *Transdisziplinäre forschung: Integrative forschungsprozesse verstehen und bewerten*, (pp. 93–116). Frankfurt, New York: Campus Verlag; and *td-net for transdisciplinary research*, for J. T. Klein's keynote address, "Taking Stock of Integration at the Century Mark," at the *td-net* international conference "Integration in Inter- and Transdisciplinary Research," Berne, Switzerland, November 19, 2009.

approaches, and defines four principles that emerge from the overview. In the course of discussion, the chapter also situates Repko's (2008) model of IDR process for student research within the wider literature on integration. Awareness of the variety of approaches will help students in three ways. First, during and after working with Repko's guide to interdisciplinary research process, they can draw on complementary concepts, methods, tools, and models. Second, they can think more systematically about similarities and differences in forms of interdisciplinarity, including the current heightened importance of transdisciplinarity. Third, in their future careers and community lives, they can apply insights from the literature on collaborative IDR and TDR to working with others on problems of professional practice and societal needs. Integrative capacity and the ability to work in teams are coupled increasingly across all sectors of our lives, making comparative understanding of best practices all the more crucial.

Historical Beginnings

The etymology of a word is always a good place to start for definition. The *Oxford English Dictionary* (1971) traces the English word *integration* back to the Latin word *integrare,* meaning "to make whole." Over the centuries, the idea of integration has been associated with holism, unity, and synthesis. The foundation, though, differed over time. For the ancient Greeks, philosophy was the seat of a broad synoptic view of knowledge based on the study of forms and their relationships. In the medieval era, the Christian *summa* was the source of synthesis. Leaders of the Enlightenment movement in the 18th century placed their faith in the concept of universal reason. For members of the famed Vienna Circle in the 1930s, logical positivism was the foundation for the unity of science. In 20th-century physics, the search for grand unifying laws guided the search for scientific synthesis. E. O. Wilson's (1999) theory of "consilience" also stirred new hope for uniting separate ideas and methods, although Wilson favored biological reductionism as the primary ground for synthesis. Today, the ancient quest for a simple unity grounded in one theory or method has largely been given up, though the online journal *Integral Review* provides a forum for transdisciplinary and transcultural models and metatheory (http://integral-review.org/index.asp).

The earliest notable uses of the term *integration* in the modern era appeared in the late 19th century, in Alexis Bertrand's theory of integrated instruction and in books on principles of psychology by Herbert Spencer and William James. The idea of integration was also linked with the role that schools play in promoting social unity and the Herbartian movement's *doctrine of correlation*, which supplemented the *doctrine of concentration* by recognizing "natural relations" among subjects (Ciccorico, 1970, p. 60). Over the course of the 20th century, the meaning of the term expanded. At the postsecondary level, integrating disciplines and developing the "whole" person were core values in the general education movement, although proponents differed on whether the whole was located in the content of texts within a prescribed curriculum or in a process of knowing and understanding contemporary problems. At the primary and secondary levels, during the 1920s integration was associated in the U.S.A. with the Progressivists' social democratic vision of education centered on students' personal and social concerns, and the term *integrated curriculum* was also linked with the project approach. During the 1930s, it appeared in conjunction with the core curriculum movement. In the 1940s and 1950s, it was aligned with problem-centered cores as well as a broad-fields approach; skills across subjects; and child-centered, activity-based, and experience-based curricula (Beane, 1997, pp. 2–3, 28–29; Ciccorico, 1970, p. 62; Klein, 2002, pp. 5–6).

Even with differences in individual approaches, a major shift in meaning occurred during the 1930s and 1940s that lies at the heart of Repko's (2008) emphasis on integration as a *process*. Integration, Repko explains, does not derive from a predetermined pattern. It is something we must create. It also, he cautions, does not supply a universal template that is necessarily applicable beyond the specific problem, issue, or question being addressed in a particular course. The shift in meaning emphasized process over content and preexisting formulas for integration. At a 1935 meeting sponsored by the National Education Association, and in the 1937 book *Integration: Its Meaning and Application*, participants in both forums concluded that complete unity is impossible. They proposed thinking in terms of *unifying*, not *unified*, approaches. At a 1948 workshop sponsored by the Foundation for Integrative Education, participants further distinguished *content integration*, in bridging physical sciences with arts and letters, from *process integration*, in the interplay of an individual and an environment. They also distinguished *integration* as synthesizing accepted postulates from *integrative* building of new conceptual modes capable of producing a holistic experience (Ciccorico, 1970, pp. 60–61; Taylor, 1969, p. 130).

In the latter half of the 20th century, two other notable developments occurred that reinforced the new emphasis on process and expanded the contexts for integrative thinking. In the first development, writers on social science research and higher education contrasted *interdisciplinary* generalizing and connecting of current knowledge formations with constructing new *integrative* concepts that raise new intellectual questions. In some cases, such as the concepts of "area" and "gender," they have even led to the formation of new interdisciplinary fields beyond the disciplines (Beane, 1997, pp. 15–18; Klein, 1990, pp. 24–25). In the second development, the Association of American Colleges and Universities (http://www.aacu.org) and the Carnegie Foundation for the Advancement of Learning also joined forces in promoting a new Integrative Learning movement that aims to bridge multiple divides, including high school and college, general education and the major, introductory and advanced levels, theory and practice, disciplines and fields, and academic and other forms of knowledge. "Interdisciplinary studies" is a subset of integrative learning that fosters connections among disciplines and interdisciplinary fields. Yet, it also intersects with and sometimes directly complements other integrative approaches to education, such as collaborative learning, feminist pedagogy, learning communities, multicultural pedagogy, team teaching, theme- and problem-based curricula, inquiry- and discovery-based teaching, and performance-based teaching (Huber & Hutchings, 2004; Klein, 2005a).

Transdisciplinarity and the Shift to Complexity and Problem Solving

Interdisciplinarity is defined conventionally as a synthesis of ideas, data and information, methods, tools, concepts, and/or theories from two or more disciplines aimed at answering a complex question, solving a complex problem, or producing new knowledge or a product. In contrast, the term *transdisciplinarity* is often associated with the idea of unified knowledge. The term is traced conventionally to the first international conference on interdisciplinary teaching and research, cosponsored in 1970 by the Organization of Economic Cooperation and Development (OECD). It denotes a common system of axioms that transcends the narrow scope of disciplinary worldviews through an overarching synthesis, such as anthropology conceived as a comprehensive science of humans and their accomplishments (OECD, 1972, p. 26). Over time, a variety of overarching frameworks became linked with the idea of transdisciplinarity, notable among them general systems theory, structuralism, Marxism, feminist theory, phenomenology, policy sciences, and sociobiology. Holistic in intent, these initiatives aimed to reorganize the structure of knowledge, although they differed in the role accorded to disciplines (Miller, 1982, p. 21). Other metatheoretical approaches also emerged, including a model informed by the new worldview of complexity in science developed by the Centre International de Recherches et Études Transdisciplinaires (http://perso.club-internet.fr/nicol/ciret).

In recent decades, a new connotation has emerged that aligns both inter- and transdisciplinarity more strongly with problem solving and complexity. This development was anticipated in 1982, when the OECD announced that the weight had shifted from *endogenous university interdisciplinarity* to *interdisciplinarity exogenous to the university*. *Endogenous interdisciplinarity* is based on production of new knowledge with the aim of achieving the unity of science. In contrast, *exogenous interdisciplinarity* originates in real problems of the community, supplementing and enriching the *endogenous* form while calling into question its limits (OECD, 1982, p. 130). The core premise of this shift within the new connotation of transdisciplinarity is that complex problems in the *Lebenswelt*—the "life-world" in German and the "real world" in English—need to frame research questions and practices, rather than disciplines. The participation of stakeholders in other sectors of society is also assumed, requiring cooperation and integration beyond academic boundaries. This development was apparent in Europe in the late 1980s and early 1990s in Swiss and German contexts of environmental research, and by the turn of the century, case studies were reported in all fields of human interaction with natural systems and technical innovations in Europe and in partnerships for development with countries in the southern hemisphere (Klein, Grossenbacher-Mansuy, Scholz, & Welti, 2001).

Not all problems are the same. One strand of problem solving in TDR centers on collaborations between academic researchers and industrial/private sectors for the purpose of product and technology development. A different type arises when academic experts and social actors with local knowledge and contextual interests cooperate to achieve democratic solutions to complex problems, such as sustainability and risks deriving from technological modernization such as nuclear power plants. Together, though, the cumulative literature on TDR provides a rich knowledge base for integration aimed at improving problem solving and decision making. It is anchored in guidelines and case studies illustrating the roles of concepts and abstract ideas; quantitative and qualitative models; methods and tools; organizing frameworks; and products such as a technical device, database, regulation, exhibition, medical treatment, or a plan for sustainable development. The 2007 book *Principles for Designing Transdisciplinary Research* presents a synthesis of principles, concepts, and methods (Pohl & Hirsch Hadorn, 2007). The 2008 *Handbook of Transdisciplinary Research* provides a state-of-the-art overview of theory and practices, with a closing chapter on the topic of integration (Hirsch Hadorn et al., 2008). And the 2009 book *Research Integration Using Dialogue Methods* is a "methodological toolkit" of 14 dialogue methods that is useful for both IDR and TDR collaborative process (McDonald, Bammer, & Deane, 2009).

In the United States, a separate but parallel initiative arose in the late 1990s. In programs of the National Cancer Institute, TDR was defined as a collaborative form of "transcendent interdisciplinary research" that is generating new methodological and theoretical frameworks for defining and analyzing social, economic, political, environmental, and institutional factors in health and well-being (Rosenfield, 1992; Stokols, Hall, Taylor, & Moser, 2008). The areas of concern include cancer, heart disease, obesity, violence, and the environment. The emphasis is on scientific discoveries, educational outcomes, and translation of scientific findings into new clinical practices and public policies. Multiple stakeholder groups are targeted, including scientists and trainees, funding organizations, policy makers, and partners in clinical settings and community organizations. Direct participation of stakeholders is not prominent, as it is in the European formulation of TDR. Yet this initiative has enriched the knowledge base for integration. Results of and reflections on a groundbreaking 2006 conference, "The Science of Team Science," appear in a special issue of the *American Journal of Preventive Medicine* devoted to theory and practice, definitions, social and cognitive dynamics of collaboration, assessment and evaluation, leadership, training, and case studies in health sciences (Stokols et al., 2008). An April, 2010 conference explored next steps in TDR team science (http://cancercontrol.cancer.gov/brp/scienceteam/index.html; http://cancercontrol.cancer.gov/BRP/scienceteam/ajpm.html; http://scienceofteamscience.northwestern.edu/agenda).

The primary focus on integration in the U.S.-based initiative has been the personal, social, and institutional dynamics of collaboration. Collaboration readiness and antecedent conditions are crucial. The more contextual factors and institutional supports in place at the outset, the greater the prospects for achieving integration and collaboration. Key factors include leadership skills and styles of research administrators, shared office and laboratory space, electronic connectivity, and team members' experiences working together on previous projects. Key factors in the quality and scope of IDR and TDR integration in both collaboration readiness and antecedent conditions include development of integrative conceptualizations, methodological approaches, commitment to team research, mutual learning, negotiation of shared meaning, resolution of conflicts, and interactions in collaborative activities such as attending meetings with co-investigators and trainees to share and integrate ideas, as well as developing partnerships with community organizations (Stokols et al., 2008).

Means of Integration

In describing the process of integration for student research, Repko (2008) highlighted three sources of conflicts among disciplines: assumptions, concepts, and theories. The key integrative activities in his model are comparing and contrasting disciplinary insights, creating common ground, and creating a new and more comprehensive understanding of a problem. The key integrative techniques are redefinition, extension, organization, and transformation. Two or more of the four may also be combined. Others have identified similar and additional means of achieving integration. In their chapter on integration, Pohl et al. (2008) highlighted four primary means that foster integration: mutual understanding in collaboration, theoretical concepts, models, and products. Along with Pohl and Hirsch Hadorn (2007), they also call attention to the importance of language and add the role of frameworks.

Language is central to integration in both IDR and TDR. The same terms may be used in different ways, underscoring the importance of focusing on conflict in Repko's (2008) model. By not dealing with conflicts, students run the risk of privileging some definitions over others or using an ambiguous mix of meanings. Bilingualism is a popular metaphor of interdisciplinary work. However, mastery of two complete languages rarely occurs. New and redeployed terminology form the basis of a working interlanguage or metalanguage likened to two concepts from linguistics. A "pidgin" is an interim tongue, providing a trade language between groups with different languages. A "creole" is a new first language among members of a new social and cognitive community (Klein, 1996, p. 220). When research problems and questions fall within the scope of interdisciplinary fields, students have an additional obligation to learn the creoles of those fields, such as feminist theory, general systems, sustainability, and cultural analysis. In collaborative work, negotiation of common meanings is also crucial. Everyday language has a role to play. "Interdisciplinary discussions," Gerhard Frey (1973) found, typically occur at a level similar to popular scientific presentations. They become more precise as individuals acquire knowledge of other disciplines, combining everyday and specialist language. Everyday language is especially important for integrating nonacademic stakeholders into the research process.

Concepts play prominent roles in integration for both individuals and groups. Repko (2008) cited differing meanings of the concept of "efficiency" for economists, biologists, and political scientists. Comparably, Miller (1982) cites the concept of "role." It is widely used in social sciences but alternatively framed in the market model as the role of the consumer, in sociology's structural-functional model as the individual's role playing in social structure, in history as a person's role, and in one conceptual model in sociology as a role model (pp. 17–18). Both individuals and groups need to uncover different meanings in order to work toward common ground. These and other *bridging concepts* play a productive role in this process, transferring notions between fields and fostering adaptations in new contexts. In a TDR project, for instance, the bridge concept of the syndrome approach classified global change problems on the basis of indicators (symptoms) that were analogous to disease patterns (syndromes). The bridge helped to generate solutions for problems such as overcultivation of marginal land (Sahel syndrome) and uncontrolled urban growth (favela syndrome; Pohl & Hirsch Hadorn, 2007, p. 29).

Models vary along a spectrum, spanning quantitative and qualitative as well as ideal and field-based approaches. They also have different intellectual foundations. Some are based in operational theory and others in studies of human behavior; sociocultural and sociotechnical theories of group interaction; communication theory; decision theory; and hybrid psychologies of social, cognitive, educational, organizational, and industrial concerns. Repko's (2008) stage model prescribes steps in a process, though he acknowledges that individuals might begin at different points and compress steps, depending on the immediate task. Newell (2007), Sjolander (1985), and Szostak (2002) have also designated steps in a sequence. Maurice DeWachter's (1982) model of an interdisciplinary approach to bioethics bridges the gap between ideal models and the realities of practice. The ideal model assumes that individuals will suspend their disciplinary/professional worldviews from the beginning, in favor of a global question grounded in the problem to be solved. Realistically, though, they are usually unwilling to abstain from approaching a topic in terms of their worldviews. The best chance of succeeding lies in starting by translating a global question into the specific language of each participating discipline, then working back and forth in iterative fashion, constantly checking the relevance of each answer to the bioethical problem at hand. That way, no single answer is privileged. Likewise, Klein's (2005b) generic model of an interdisciplinary approach to problem solving replaces linear sequence with iterative movement back and forth across types of knowledge, approaches, and stages. All of these approaches, it should be added, share a belief in best practices and iteration.

Methods (and techniques) of integration vary as well. Some are well-known, including systems theory and modeling, integrated environmental assessment and risk management, Delphi and scenario building, simulation, concept mapping, and computer synthesis of data and information flow. Other proven methods facilitate communication and common understanding, including mental mapping of stakeholder views, consensus conferences, collaborative learning, and collaborative workspaces. New methods also emerge in the process of performing IDR and TDR. The Natural and Social Science Interface of the Swiss Federal Institute of Technology in Zurich developed the TIPS approach in a case study and teaching project on sustainable regional development. Standing for Transdisciplinary Integrated Planning and Synthesis, TIPS embeds formal, scientific, integrated planning in a real-world setting, facilitating mutual learning among scientists and stakeholders through interactions. It also utilizes other successful methods such as systems analysis and scenario constructions (Walter, Wiek, & Scholz, 2008, p. 174; Pohl & Hirsch Hadorn, 2007, p. 56).

Frameworks are overriding "idea tanks" that help to integrate different disciplinary perspectives and organizing clusters of insights while structuring the core issue of a project or program in a systematic process (Ulli-Beer, Kaufmann-Hayoz, & Schwaninger, 2008, p. 170). In describing the field of policy analysis, Joel L. Fleishman (1991) illustrated the integrative character of frameworks. Policy analysis incorporates only a fraction of the contents of participating disciplines. Policy analysts construct an integrative lens and analytic framework that fit around a particular problem, choosing portions of disciplines that appear relevant to solving it and adding useful elements from statistics, operations research, history, and ethics. The process starts where economics and political science leave off, building on disciplinary descriptions and inferences to formulate alternative solutions and project likely consequences (pp. 235–238).

Lessons From TDR Integration

Although Repko (2008) focuses on the solo researcher, parallel insights appear in the literature on IDR and TDR collaboration, while extending awareness of how social and cognitive integration are interwoven (O'Donnell & Derry, 2005, p. 60). Joint definition of a project is required, along with the core research problem, questions, research objects, and goals. Role clarification and negotiation help members assess what they need and expect from each other. Ongoing communication and interaction foster mutual learning and a sense of "teamness" and interdependence. The organizational framework should also provide for coordination of subprojects and the main project with correlated inputs, progressive sharing, and inter-active cross-testing of empirical and theoretical work. If individuals hold back during the early phase, the prospect of arriving at a shared or interfac-ing cognitive framework is jeopardized from the beginning. Teams must also grapple with differences in the status hierarchy of their members. A presti-gious person or discipline may dominate, inhibiting others from speaking, impeding role negotiation, delaying communal work, and creating social and cognitive dependence.

In defining principles for TDR collaboration, Pohl and Hirsch Hadorn (2007) adopted Rossini and Porter's (1979) scheme from the IDR literature. The four major forms of collaboration are common group learning, negotia-tion among experts, integration by a leader, and modeling. Common group learning is a cooperative process among all participants: Subquestions are dis-tributed to the most appropriate members of a larger group and then dis-cussed by everyone and related to an overall question. The process repeats in recursive fashion, with progressive mutual learning and gradual shifting of individual responsibility for subanswers to the group as a whole. Negotiation among experts begins the same way but allots responsibility for subproblems to experts followed by a bilateral exchange, mutual adaptation of answers and subquestions, then a final stage of negotiation that leads to synthesis. Integration by a leader places responsibility with a designated individual or subgroup in charge of mediating exchange and integrating subresults at the end. Modeling is situated on a continuum between quantitative and qualita-tive frameworks or schema (Pohl & Hirsch Hadorn, 2007, pp. 52–54; Rossini & Porter, 1979, p. 74). The following two case studies provide com-plementary insights for students who are now doing IDR individually but will find themselves in the future involved in collaborative learning environments, workplace projects, and community forums where the lessons of IDR and collaborative TDR can be combined.

Baccini and Oswald (2008) illustrated the role of bridging concepts and models in a TDR project involving a scientist and an architect with a com-mon interest in sustainable urban development. Two tasks were crucial: learning each other's language and understanding differing perceptions of the same words, such as "landscape," "urban," and even "project" and "process." Focusing on an area in the Swiss lowlands, they took field trips that con-tributed to mutual learning. The process repeated when the project expanded to include others. One group (morphologists) was rooted in the culture of architecture and urban planning. The other group (physiologists) was com-posed of natural scientists, engineers, and an economist. Architects consid-ered themselves urban planners and designers able to lead the project because of their competence as generalists. They viewed engineers, economists, and natural scientists as suppliers of facts, figures, models, and tools to support architectural blueprints. Natural scientists were also considered more inter-ested in theories of cognition than a concrete project, and their methods were considered inadequate for dealing with complex urban phenomena and creative synthesis. Two years of mutual learning resulted in a shared definition of "urbanity" in mixed groups of morphologists and physiologists. The bridging concept of Netzstadt ("net city") provided a common way of perceiving the agglomeration of lowlands as a network with connected knots or nodes, rather than a center. A new identity and shared convictions also emerged. In a second phase, new teams elaborated the Netzstadt model and methods along with the Synoikos method of generating cooperative majorities in participative processes.

Bergmann and Jahn's (2008) case study of an urban mobility planning project offers an extended illustration of the importance of tending to integration throughout all phases of a program's life cycle. Nearly 20 participants from various disciplines and city and transportation planners from two model cities participated in the CITY: *Mobil* project. The focus was a rising volume of motorized traffic that was generating ecological and economic problems. The challenge of *integration* was complex, spanning planning and technical aspects as well as economic, ecologic, and social goals. Cooperation was further complicated by the dispersed location of research institutes in Germany and Austria. Key integrative activities in the three-phase project are italicized in the following paragraph.

Phase A dealt with construction and description of the project and the team, *constitution of a common research object*, and analysis of the problem dimensions to be treated. Objects of TDR, Bergmann and Jahn (2008) emphasize, are not automatically specified. Constituting them at the beginning of the research process establishes an underlying "fundament" for *integration*. A detailed structuring plan also called for *close cooperation* between all subprojects and the main project with *correlated inputs*. A *coordinator was responsible for leading integration*. Contradicting disciplinary, scientific, and political claims had to be recognized and integrated into a research objective accepted as the *shared focus* for all participants, using a theoretically and methodologically *guided process of translating all single aspects* of the societal problem. The common focus was determined by *mutual agreement* on problem descriptions, resulting analytical questions, and definitions of related notions and concepts. The bridging concept of the term *mobility* functioned as a boundary object and overarching integrative term encompassing spatial mobility, socio-spatial mobility, and social mobility.

During Phase B, the emphasis was on subprojects and knowledge building, *mutual learning and linking between disciplines*, and *coordination* of researchers and project parts. A *common analytical question* had to be answered by all subprojects: "How can the strong coupling between mobility and 'auto-mobility' be decoupled?" The *interaction structure* enriched interaction and mutual learning while bringing integration down to the level of every subproject and thereby preventing a large conflict at the end of the project. Partnerships between researchers from different disciplines also facilitate *mutual control of the developing comprehensibility and integration potential* of results, publications, common systems or categories, and assessment criteria. Cognitive integration was facilitated by common foci in the main project.

The overall pathway in the main project encompassed an inventory of the transportation system and its ecological impacts, options and restrictions to mobility behavior as well as transportation infrastructure and city development, mappings of scenarios, an integrated impact assessment of strategies, an intensive phase of TD *integration*, and finally publication of a guide for communities and book of findings for the scientific community.

In Phase C, the focus was transdisciplinary integration, product/publication design, and transformation/innovation/implementation impulses. The final integration task was to integrate corresponding and differing findings from all project parts to form relevant conclusions for different target groups, the scientific community, and the urban communities. *Multiple instruments and measures* were used. Researchers in the planning perspective developed a computer learning model of the cities (MOBI*DYN*) combining three modules: transportation networks, allocation of people in different housing areas and work places, and mobility behaviour. Critical analysis of research questions and methods in traditional research on transportation planning led to development of a new approach to the ecology of transportation and analysis of traffic genesis. These approaches were investigated in four subprojects supported by a system of *coproduction, interfacing workshops, and exchange of findings with cooperation among members of several institutes and disciplines*. An empirical market research and marketing instrument targeted several groups with different mobility behaviors and attitudes; it aimed to shift them from the car to other mobility modes using a new focus and method called *mobility-style research* that supplies information to transportation planners and companies. A newly developed information system called Least-Cost Transportation Planning (LCTP) provided planners and politicians with comprehensive information about all expenses for the transport sector and its sources. A new integrated method of Action Impact Assessment facilitated ex-ante evaluation of transportation projects and their ecological, economical, and social impacts and the problems to be faced when putting them into public use.

Conclusion

Four principles of integration emerge from the comparative overview of IDR and TDR.

1. The Principle of Variance

No Universal Formula for Integration

There is no universal formula for integration because the contexts of IDR and TDR differ. The focus varies, from theoretical frameworks for integrating knowledge to specific themes, questions, and problems. Integration is also influenced by the goals of a particular program, the participants who are involved, their disciplinary and professional backgrounds, and institutional settings. Scope and complexity vary as well, ranging from "narrow-gauged," "middle-range," and "horizontal" interactions among disciplines with compatible methods, paradigms, and epistemologies to "broad-gauged," "vertical," and "grand"-scale forms involving disciplines with divergent approaches (Kelly, 1996; van Dusseldorp & Wigboldus, 1994, p. 96). The type of inter- or transdisciplinarity being practiced is a further source of variance. Method- and theory-based forms also differ in the purpose and means of integration.

2. The Principle of Platforming

Interaction Structure, Integration Potential, Fundament

Platforming is a set of actions aimed at building a foundation for integration. In collaborative work, it also entails putting into place the antecedent conditions and contextual factors crucial for both cognitive and social integration (Stokols et al., 2008). One of the most important lessons to emerge from the earlier Bergmann and Jahn (2008) case study of an urban mobility planning project was the need to tend to integration throughout the life cycle of a project or program. The *interaction structure* brought *integration* down to the level of every subproject, to prevent a large conflict at the end of the entire project. Partnerships also facilitated mutual control of the evolving comprehensibility of the task. The *integration potential* of emerging results, publications, systems, categories, and assessment criteria was made visible as well.

Although the organizational management of the project was more challenging than most student projects, students trained in using Repko's (2008) model can appreciate several crucial points of similarity. They, too, must constitute a *common research object* and a *common analytical question,* to analyze the problem dimensions that will be treated within the scope of their individual studies. Bridge concepts and common foci serve as a *fundament* for integration, and the *integration potential* of each element needs to be assessed. Students also need to address conflict in contradicting claims and sources, *translating all single aspects* of the problem or question at hand.

3. The Principle of Iteration

Moving Back and Forth, Bootstrapping, Triangulation, Reflective Balance, and Weaving

Repko's (2008) step-by-step model unfolds in a linear sequence of explanation. Integration does not appear formally until the 9th of 10 steps. Yet, he argues, the process can begin at any point, may compress some steps depending on the task at hand, and may move back and forth between disciplinary part and complex whole as tentative syntheses are reformed. Others have depicted comparable movement in the process.

- Steve Fuller (1993) argues that the interdisciplinary process requires moving from lower-level translation of disciplinary perspectives by bootstrapping up to higher levels of conceptual synthesis (p. 42).
- J. T. Klein (1990) contends that the process requires achieving balance through ongoing triangulation of *breadth* of expert materials and approaches; *depth* in pertinent disciplinary, professional, and interdisciplinary fields; and *synthesis* of common ground elements tested throughout the process (p. 52; Klein, 1996, pp. 212, 214, 222–223).
- Veronica Boix-Mansilla (2006) emphasizes reflective balance and weaving together perspectives into a coherent whole. Options must be weighed in a "balancing act" that maintains generative tensions and reaches compromises in selecting and combining disciplinary insights and standards.

Together, these movements emphasize the importance of patterning and testing throughout the research process, modifying objectives and goals as new insights are generated.

4. The Principle of Communicative Rationality

Shared Language Culture, Social Learning, Translation-Negotiation-Mediation, Intersubjectivity

The quality of outcomes, Wilhelm Vosskamp (1994) suggested, cannot be separated from development and richness of a shared language culture. Moreover, Vosskamp exhorted, the agreement/disagreement structure necessary for all communication shapes the possibility of interdisciplinary dialogue. Consent/dissent (*Alteritaet*) requires accepting the unforeseeable and productive role of misunderstanding from the outset. A final case study provides a powerful reinforcement of the importance of language and conflict in integration in both IDR and TDR, in an urban planning project to retrofit residential neighborhoods built between 1950 and 1975 on the outskirts of Québec City, Canada.

In the case study, Després, Fortin, Joerin, Vachon, and Gatti (2008) demonstrate that scientific and academic knowledge alone cannot deal adequately with the complexity of subjects and problem domains such as revitalizing neighborhoods. Following Jurgen Habermas's *Theory of Communicative Action* (1987), instrumental, ethical, and aesthetic forms of knowledge are also needed. Rational knowledge comes out of not only "what we know" but "how we communicate" it, generating a form of "communicative rationality." Stakeholders enter into a process of negotiation, confronting the four kinds of knowledge in a series of encounters that allow representatives of each type to express their views and proposals. In the process, a fifth type of knowledge progressively emerges. It is a hybrid product, the result of "making sense together." Fostering "intersubjectivity," the fifth type of knowledge requires an ongoing effort to achieve mutual understanding. Simply bringing people together and coordinating conversations is not enough. Mediation is required to define collectively what could and should be done. Each stakeholder expresses individual interests or views that are discussed and criticized by others. The role of the mediator is to extract this knowledge. As progressively shared meanings, diagnoses, and objectives emerge, individual interests and views are seen in different perspectives. Even individual students conducting solo research projects will need to be alert to the importance of communicating their results to different target audiences, requiring some awareness of their worldviews.

In closing, a set of core capacities emerges from the comparative overview of approaches to integration in IDR and TDR. Students, professionals, and citizens alike need to create an integrative framework and a more holistic understanding by comparing and contrasting multiple resources, discovering patterns, and making connections. The process is not algorithmic. It is heuristic and constructivist at heart. It also, Repko (2008) reminds us, requires analytical reasoning and creative thinking. Moreover, it requires reflexivity on the limits of the wholes they create. The emergence of a literature and networks focused in significant part on integration is an important historical development in both IDR and TDR. Skills of research integration, McDonald et al. (2009) assert, have become as essential as disciplinary skills, making competence and training in integration methods as crucial today as new digital literacies. This need is all the more important when disciplines are also undergoing tremendous change characterized by pluralistic practices, boundary crossing, openness to interdisciplinary developments, and the force of complexity and problem solving. We need integration experts as much as we need disciplinary, professional, and interdisciplinary expertise.

References

Baccini, P., & Oswald, F. (2008). Designing the urban: A transdisciplinary approach. In G. Hirsch Hadorn, et al. (Eds.), *Handbook of transdisciplinary research* (pp. 48–56). Berlin: Springer Verlag.

Bammer, G. (2005). Integration and implementation sciences, building a new specialization. *Ecology and Society, 10*, 2, 6. Retrieved from http://www.ecology andsociety.org/vol10/iss2/art6//

Beane, J. (1997). *Curriculum integration: Designing the core of democratic education.* New York: Teachers College Press.

Bergmann, M., & Jahn, T. (2008). Transdisciplinary integration in sustainability research: The case of CITY: mobil. In G. Hirsch Hadorn, et al. (Eds.), *Handbook of Transdisciplinary Research* (pp. 57–68). Berlin: Springer Verlag.

Boix-Mansilla, V. (2006). Assessing expert interdisciplinary work at the frontier: An empirical exploration. *Research Evaluation, 15*(1), 17–29.

Ciccorico, E. W. (1970). "Integration" in the curriculum. *Main Currents in Modern Thought, 27*, 60–62.

Després, C., Fortin, A., Joerin, F., Vachon, G., & Gatti, E. (2008). Retrofitting post-war suburbs: A transdisciplinary research and planning process. In G. Hirsch Hadorn et al. (Eds.), *Handbook of transdisciplinary research* (pp. 251–259). Berlin: Springer Verlag.

DeWachter, M. (1982). Interdisciplinary bioethics: But where do we start? A reflection on epochè as method. *Journal of Medicine and Philosophy, 7*(3), 275–287.

Fleishman, J. L. (1991). A new framework for integration: Policy analysis and public management. In D. Easton & C. Schelling (Eds.), *Divided knowledge: Across disciplines, across cultures* (pp. 219–243). Newbury Park, CA: Sage.

Frey, G. (1973). Methodological problems of interdisciplinary discussions. *RATIO, 15*(2), 161–182.

Fuller, S. (1993). *Philosophy, rhetoric, and the end of knowledge.* Madison: University of Wisconsin Press.

Habermas, J. (1987). The theory of communicative action Vol. 2: Lifeworld and system: The critique of functionalist reason (T. McCarthy, Trans.). Boston: Beacon Press.

Hirsch Hadorn, G., Hoffmann-Riem, H., Biber-Klemm, S., Grossenbacher-Mansuy, W., Joye, D., Pohl, C. . . . Zemp, E. (Eds.). (2008). *Handbook of transdisciplinary research.* Berlin: Springer Verlag.

Huber, M. T., & Hutchings, P. (2004). *Integrative learning.* Washington, DC: AACU.

Kelly, J. (1996). Wide and narrow interdisciplinarity. *Journal of General Education, 45*(2), 95–113.

Klein, J. T. (1990). *Interdisciplinarity: History, theory, and practice.* Detroit, MI: Wayne State University Press.

Klein, J. T. (1996). *Crossing boundaries: Knowledge, disciplinarities, and interdisciplinarities.* Charlottesville: University Press of Virginia.

Klein, J. T. (2002). Introduction: Interdisciplinarity today: Why? What? and How? In J. T. Klein (Ed.), *Interdisciplinary education in K-12 and college: A foundation for K-16 dialogue* (pp. 1–17). New York: The College Board.

Klein, J. T. (2005a). Integrative learning and interdisciplinary studies. *Peer Review, 7*(4), 8–10.

Klein, J. T. (2005b). Interdisciplinary teamwork: The dynamics of collaboration and integration. In S. J. Derry, C. D. Schunn, & M. A. Gernsbacher (Eds.), *Interdisciplinary collaboration: An emerging cognitive science* (pp. 23–50). Mahwah, NJ: Erlbaum.

Klein, J. T., Grossenbacher-Mansuy, W., Scholz, R. W., & Welti, M. (Eds.). (2001). *Transdisciplinarity: Joint problem solving among science, technology, and society.* Basel: Birkhäuser.

Klein, J. T. & Newell, W. H. (1997). Advancing interdisciplinary studies. In J. Gaff & J. Ratcliff (Eds.), *Handbook of the undergraduate curriculum: A comprehensive guide to purposes, structures, practices, and change* (pp. 393–415). San Francisco: Jossey-Bass.

McDonald, D., Bammer, G., & Deane, P. (2009). *Research integration using dialogue methods.* Canberra: Australian National University. Retrieved from http://epress.anu.edu.au/dialogue_methods_citation.html

Miller, R. (1982). Varieties of interdisciplinary approaches in the social sciences. *Issues in Integrative Studies, 1,* 1–37.

Newell, W. H. (2007). Decision making in interdisciplinary studies. In G. Morcol (Ed.), *Handbook of decision making* (pp. 245–264). New York: Marcel Dekker, CRC Press/Taylor & Francis.

O'Donnell, M. O., & Derry, S. (2005). Cognitive processes in interdisciplinary groups. In S. J. Derry, C. D. Schunn, & M. A. Gernsbacher (Eds.), *Interdisciplinary collaboration: An emerging cognitive science* (pp. 51–82). Mahwah, NJ: Erlbaum.

Organization for Economic Co-operation and Development. (1972). *Interdisciplinarity: Problems of teaching and research in universities.* Paris: Author.

Organization for Economic Co-operation and Development. (1982). *The university and the community: The problems of changing relationships.* Paris: CERI, Author.

Oxford English dictionary (Compact Ed.). (1971). Oxford, UK: Oxford University Press.

Pohl, C., & Hirsch Hadorn, G. (2007). *Principles for designing transdisciplinary research.* Munich: Oekom.

Pohl, C., van Kerkhoff, L., Hirsch Hadorn, G., & Bammer, G. (2008). Integration. In G. Hirsch Hadorn, et al. (Eds.), *Handbook of transdisciplinary research* (pp. 411–424). Berlin: Springer Verlag.

Repko, A. F. (2008). *Interdisciplinary research: Process and theory.* Thousand Oaks, CA: Sage.

Rosenfield, P. (1992). The potential of transdisciplinary research for sustaining and extending linkages between the health and social sciences. *Social Science and Medicine, 35*(11), 1343–1357.

Rossini, F. A., & Porter, A. L. (1979). Frameworks for integrating disciplinary research. *Research Policy, 8,* 70–79.

Sjolander, S. (1985). Long-term and short-term interdisciplinary work: Difficulties, pitfalls, and built-in failures. In L. Levin & I. Lind (Eds.), *Interdisciplinarity revisited: Reassessing the concept in the light of institutional experience* (pp. 85–92). Stockholm: OECD, Swedish National Board of Universities and Colleges, and Linköping University.

Stokols, D. B., Hall, K., Taylor, B. K., & Moser, R. P. (2008). The science of team science: Overview of the field and introduction to the supplement. *American Journal of Preventive Medicine, 35*(2S), S77–S89.

Szostak, R. (2002). How to do interdisciplinarity: Integrating the debate. *Issues in Integrative Studies, 20,* 103–122.

Taylor, A. (1969). Integrative principles and the educational process. *Main Currents in Modern Thought, 25,* 126–133.

Uli-Beer, S., Kaufmann-Hayoz, R., & Schwaninger, M. (2008). A transdisciplinary modelling approach for policy learning and analysis: Steps and concepts of a case study. In G. Hirsch Hadorn, et al. (Eds.), *Handbook of transdisciplinary research* (pp. 160–173). Berlin: Springer Verlag.

van Dusseldorp, D., & Wigboldus, S. (1994). Interdisciplinary research for integrated rural development in developing countries: The role of social sciences. *Issues in Integrative Studies, 12,* 93–138.

Vosskamp, W. (1994). Crossing of boundaries: Interdisciplinarity as an opportunity for universities in the 1980s? *Issues in Integrative Studies, 12,* 43–54.

Walter, A., Wiek, A., & Scholz, R. (2008). Implementing regional sustainable development: The transdisciplinary case study research approach. In G. Hirsch Hadorn et al. (Eds.), *Handbook of transdisciplinary research* (pp. 174–194). Berlin: Springer Verlag.

Wilson, E. O. (1999). *Consilience: The unity of knowledge.* New York: Vintage.

Conclusion _____

William H. Newell

_____ **Introduction**

When Allen, Rick, and I first conceived this book, we wanted to test whether the interdisciplinary process we had each been involved in developing under the aegis of the Association for Integrative Studies (AIS) is applicable to a wide range of topics drawing on diverse combinations of disciplines. We also wanted to learn how the process might be fruitfully adapted, if there were topics for which it was less useful. By both criteria, the book has been rewardingly successful. We now have a much clearer sense of when the process can be applied directly and readily, when it needs to be modestly reinterpreted, and just what that entails.

What I, at least, did not anticipate was how much we would learn about the implementation of each step in the process and how that implementation varies across the Academy. As a result, what I hoped would be a useful companion reader for Allen Repko's *Interdisciplinary Research: Process and Theory* turns out to constitute a major contribution in its own right to the professional literature on the interdisciplinary process. A book aimed at advanced undergraduates and graduate students has become of interest to interdisciplinary teachers and researchers as well. I hope the process on which it focuses will also become known to policy makers who are confronted with real-world complex problems.

Because I was the only co-editor who did not contribute a substantive chapter to the book, it has fallen to me to pull together the threads from disparate chapters into a coherent and synoptic overview of the lessons learned. I believe that task is best performed by playing the dual roles of cheerleader and critic. Consequently, this chapter is about what we still need to learn as well as what the book has to teach us. It is one person's candid assessment, albeit the assessment of someone who has been a student and teacher of interdisciplinary studies for more than 40 years.

Interdisciplinary Research Process Across the Academy

Whether the topic was macro level (economic growth) or micro level (action understanding), global (why we talk) or regional (Jewish marriage and Israeli identity) or local (metropolitan areas), horrific (school violence, suicide terrorism) or genteel (Parisian installation art), contributors employing the interdisciplinary research process ended up with novel insights from more comprehensive understandings than would have been possible using any one of the perspectives on which they drew. In their meta-discussions of interdisciplinary process, Klein and Szostak helped us understand why such an interdisciplinary research process might be fruitful. That said, it seemed to me that some contributors used the research process to guide their work (Repko, Szostak, Tayler, Van der Lecq), whereas others chose to adapt or expand it (Henry & Bracy, Keestra) or merely found parallels with (and validation of) their own interdisciplinary research process (Bal, Connor). All three approaches to the process provide useful alternative models to readers.

Likewise, the interdisciplinary process proved useful whether the researcher was drawing upon the social sciences (among the full range of disciplines), the humanities (mostly history and philosophy, but also religion and literature and, in Bal's case, most of the humanities and the fine and performing arts), or the biological sciences (especially evolution, neurophysiology, and biochemistry). It became abundantly clear, however, that the "disciplines" on which a majority of contributors drew included approaches that cross disciplinary lines (post-colonialism, feminism, constructivism, narrative studies, legal studies) or interdisciplines (cognitive science) as well as traditional academic disciplines.

That raised the question for me of how we ought to distinguish between the interdisciplinarity of one of the chapters in this book and the interdisciplinarity of, say, cognitive science on similar, if not the same, topics. This question came to a head in the chapter by Henry and Bracy on school violence, in which their challenge was to integrate a range of already-integrative theories. Part of the answer, it seems to me, lies in the distinction between being broader and being comprehensive. Interdisciplinary fields, like cognitive science and integrative theories in criminology, are broader than the disciplines in which they are grounded, but they do not aspire to be comprehensive. All our contributors strove to include every key relevant perspective, whereas the interdisciplinary fields and integrative theories on which they drew integrated a subset, but by no means all, of those perspectives. But another part of the answer lies in the insistence of the interdisciplinary process on including competing as well as complementary perspectives. Instead of developing a single but broader perspective, contributors to this volume set themselves the task of engaging all relevant perspectives, including those that clash. Hence, the broad interdisciplinarity attempted in this book is distinguished from the narrower interdisciplinarity of perspectives on which it drew by both its comprehensiveness and its diversity. As Keestra (Chapter 8) points out, following Klein, even the interdisciplines have their "own discipline-like contents, structures, and conventions."

Conceptions of Interdisciplinarity
Across the Academy

Underlying the common interdisciplinary process seemed to be a common overall conception of interdisciplinarity, what Klein has referred to as *instrumental interdisciplinarity*, irrespective of the topic or the perspectives from which insights were drawn. All chapters foregrounded the complexity of their topic and sought an interdisciplinary understanding that might aid in addressing what was seen as problematic about the topic.

Nonetheless, I was struck by the stark contrast between the *goal* for integration in chapters by contributors from the social and natural sciences and in the chapter by Bal (Chapter 4), who comes out of the humanities and fine and performing arts. She resisted the drive for a single best integration of disciplinary insights, preferring instead to lay out the range of possibilities for integration. Full integration is seldom wished for in the fine and performing arts, and by extension in the humanities disciplines wishing to respect the deliberate ambiguity inherent in the art objects they critically examine. Rather, the art object/text sets up integration and (usually implicitly) offers prompts that suggest some starting points for viewers to engage in integration themselves. Whereas interdisciplinarians in the natural and social sciences seek to integrate on behalf of others, presenting their new, more comprehensive understanding as a finished product, the fine and performing arts and the humanities studying them (and other aesthetic texts) seek to draw others (audiences, viewers, readers) into the integrative process and encourage them to participate in a shared integrative process.

The artwork generates emotional energy and provides alternative paths along which viewers can choose to expend that energy. Although scientific knowledge is disembodied and ideally purely cognitive, as is the integration of knowledge from different sciences by the interdisciplinarian, artistic expression is not only affective as well as (if not more so than) cognitive, but also potentially embodied, and so, too, can be its (partial) integration by the interdisciplinarian. It strikes me that the role of emotion in interdisciplinary integration, which Bal highlights, deserves more attention.

Bal's decision to focus on the installations by Ahtila permitted her to be faithful to the ethos of the humanities, yet responsive to the mission of the book. Ahtila sets up the integration by the audience of the challenges posed by the Algerian war, a real-world complex problem like those studied by interdisciplinary social scientists. But what of paintings, plays, novels, and operas that do not address complex problems or issues, or that do so only obliquely, or that create imaginative worlds, or that are deliberately much more ambiguous in focus? What of postmodernists who reject the very notion of a single best understanding (comprehensive or otherwise), who challenge the reality of the "real world," or who find the very notion of "problem" problematic? What's an interdisciplinary humanist to do then?

I see this issue of the role of the contemporary humanities in interdisciplinary studies as crucial not just for interdisciplinary studies but also for society and culture. Our contributors made some use of humanities disciplines, schools of thought, and interdisciplines, but not very much. That's not surprising, considering that most humanists adamantly resist addressing complex, real-world problems. If they insist they have nothing to contribute, or that the exercise is not worthy of their contribution, then interdisciplinarians may be inclined to ignore them. But I believe we need contributions from a wide range of humanists to make sure we are framing those problems well, asking the most important questions about them, and paying attention to the perspectives not just of disciplines but of people in different locations in society or in other affected societies.

The other challenge in this book to prevailing conceptions of interdisciplinarity has been raised by the very strategy employed by the editors. Contributors were asked to address at least briefly all steps in the interdisciplinary process but to feel free to focus on only one or two. It should come as little surprise, then, that contributors who focused on earlier steps did not complete later ones. Few tested their new interdisciplinary understanding, and some did not even attempt to carry out the integration of interdisciplinary insights. For me, this reintroduces an issue first raised by Don Richards (1996): Is research fully interdisciplinary if integration is not achieved (and tested)? One might sidestep this issue by correctly pointing out that the chapters in this book were intended to take a hybrid form—part interdisciplinary study, part commentary on that study and on interdisciplinarity itself. Nonetheless, it is clear to me that most contributors saw the research on which they reported and commented as a part of an ongoing, field-wide effort. Many made it evident that they were laying out a research agenda and reporting on work in progress. Several (Connor and Henry & Bracy, in particular) stated explicitly that they were pointing the way for others to follow.

Thus, by focusing on case studies of actual research instead of theorizing in general terms, this book suggests to me that we would do well to think about interdisciplinarity the way we think about science. Much as individual scientists and teams of scientists appropriately think of themselves as fully engaged in science when they are contributing to only one step in the scientific method, interdisciplinarians can appropriately think of themselves as engaged in fully interdisciplinary study when their research does not complete, or even attempt, all steps in the interdisciplinary process. Indeed, I would say that interdisciplinary researchers can be seen as engaged in fully interdisciplinary work even when they focus on a single step in that process, as long as they are contributing to an overall research effort that is fully interdisciplinary. Interdisciplinary research, like scientific research, transcends individuals.

What, then, of distinctions between interdisciplinary and multidisciplinary, or (one I have long advocated) between full and partial interdisciplinarity? As I look at these case studies of actual interdisciplinary research, I
realize that these distinctions should be seen as referring to intent, self-con-
ception, attitudes, practices, and values, not to achievements. Researchers
who are merely curious about connections between phenomena or comparisons between concepts, theories, or ideas; researchers who pursue the reductionist strategy of analyzing a complex phenomenon to its constituent parts
as opposed to the integrationist strategy of understanding it in its complexity;
researchers who are intent on promoting a particular perspective or ideology;
researchers who engage in either/or thinking to the exclusion of both/and
thinking—these people are not engaged in fully interdisciplinary studies even
when their research crosses disciplinary boundaries. Researchers who are
interested in ultimately understanding a complex phenomenon as a whole;
researchers who are drawn to an issue, problem, or question about that phenomenon; researchers who see connections or comparisons not as ends in
themselves but as means to illuminating different aspects of that phenomenon
or links between them; researchers who value and balance out competing perspectives; researchers who are inclined to holism as well as reductionism, con-
tinuums or spectrums as well as dualities; researchers whose impulse is to
include rather than exclude, who are drawn to diversity and who have
become leery of simplicity—these researchers are interdisciplinarians.

My suspicion is that the interdisciplinary studies profession, myself
included, has painted itself into a definitional corner wherein full interdisciplinarity meant completion of a process because most of us have been more
focused on teaching than research. Teachers of undergraduates, especially in
general education courses, tend to present our students with a post hoc, ide-
alized picture of interdisciplinary studies. Speaking for myself at least, even
when I teach advanced undergraduates to engage in interdisciplinary
research, I ask them to conduct separate research projects that seek to produce an interdisciplinary understanding. Consequently, they see themselves as
drawing on the work of previous scholars, but not as part of a collective,
ongoing effort. This book reminds us that is not how research is conducted
by professionals, however, and conceptions of interdisciplinarity grounded in
such undergraduate courses need to be rethought to make them appropriate
for professional research.

Modifications to the Interdisciplinary Process

Theoretical discussions of integration in the literature on interdisciplinarity
tend to focus on the strategies and challenges of integrating disciplinary
insights into the complex phenomena as a whole. A number of contributors
to this volume, however, find it useful to split the complex phenomenon of
interest to them into subsystems, aspects, or a linked sequence of phenomena, study them separately, and then bring together the integrated insights

into each one to achieve an interdisciplinary understanding of the complex phenomenon as a whole. Keestra decomposes action understanding into end-to-end (as Henry & Bracy put it) linked subphenomena (namely action recognition, intention understanding, and narrative understanding). Szostak divides economic growth into its widely recognized proximate causes: labor, capital, natural resources, and productivity. Van der Lecq splits her overall question about the evolutionary origin of language—What was the primary function for which language emerged?—into three sub-questions: Why did language evolve? Why only among humans? Why did language become so complex? Other contributors did not start out splitting up their complex phenomenon, but felt impelled to do so by the literature they reviewed. Repko eventually divides the phenomenon of suicide terror-ism into the causal factors of personality traits, power seeking, cultural identity, and sacred beliefs. And Tayler clusters insights according to the aspect of the complex question as a whole on which they focus. She ends up dividing insights into four categories: religious based, civil rights viola-tion, religious-political coercion, and freedom of and from religion. Thus, a majority of the contributors found it useful to tease apart their complex phenomenon and consequently disaggregate some, if not most, of the steps in the interdisciplinary process. It seems to me that abstract discussions of interdisciplinary process need to acknowledge this de facto modification and critically examine it.

Because the social and physical sciences rely on the development of theories to explain the phenomena they study, interdisciplinary integration in those areas has typically drawn on such theories to produce a more com-prehensive understanding of complex phenomena. The resulting interdisci-plinary understanding would ideally take the form of a single, more comprehensive theory, though it could be presented in the form of a system or conceptual framework. In a break with that approach, Keestra challenges the presumption that interdisciplinary integration involving both the social and natural sciences should focus on theories, especially for conceptually nebulous human phenomena such as *understanding*. Instead, he makes the case for what he calls mechanism-based explanation, which focuses on the micro-level physical and mental mechanisms underlying such phenomena. Essentially, he advocates adapting a research strategy from the natural sci-ences, specifically biology, to study characteristic subject matter of the social sciences. Shifting focus from theories to mechanisms, it turns out, changes how one operationalizes many, if not all, of the steps in interdisciplinary process.

I view such a shift more cautiously than my co-editors do, though it may be necessitated in some cases by the failure of the social sciences to sufficiently ground many of their theoretical abstractions in empirically accessible behavior. Even so, the mechanism-based approach strikes me as a welcome complement to the theory-based approach that dominates interdisciplinary social science, especially for the many human phenomena of interest to interdisciplinarians that, by virtue of their breadth, fall into the category of the conceptually nebulous, but also for human phenomena whose study is grounded in biology as well as the social sciences.

The concept of a mechanism-based explanation gets fuzzy for me, though not for my co-editors, when Keestra treats a particular *mechanism* at the one level as a *component* in (presumably) a cluster of mechanisms at the next higher level. Thus, as one ascends levels, a mechanism at a lower level can simultaneously be a component at the next higher level in a cluster of mechanisms (also called a mechanism), which in turn can be a component in a cluster of clusters of mechanisms (also called a mechanism) at the next higher level, and so on. When the very definition of "mechanism" is level-dependent, I fear that's a recipe for confusion, with scholars likely to find themselves talking past one another rather than communicating with each other.

Researchers employing the mechanism approach should not lose sight of the possibility of emergent properties: causal influences that operate only at more macro levels. As Szostak points out in Chapter 6, emergent properties are often harder to identify than individual relationships between variables. It would be unfortunate if a focus on mechanism-based explanation of the complex phenomena of interest to interdisciplinarians were to inadvertently reduce the phenomena to their complicated, or even simple, component parts and operations. After all, more macro-level human phenomena take on a life of their own, whether through the conscious efforts of human agents or through a process of emergence that characterizes complex systems. Thus, the connections between mechanisms within and between levels of phenomena become critical for understanding complex phenomena through this research strategy.

Keestra brings out quite clearly an analytical advantage to focusing on mechanisms: Scholars can engage in intervention, stimulation, or activation experiments with components or operations of individual mechanisms (as opposed to clusters of mechanisms, or clusters of clusters of mechanisms) and look for consequences on that level and other levels in a way they usually cannot when testing theories about humans. Keestra has performed an important service to interdisciplinarians by initiating discussion of this promising strategy.

_____ Operationalizing the Interdisciplinary Process

Even beyond the above contributions and issues, this volume turns out to be a rich source of insight into the nuts and bolts of how to conduct interdisciplinary research. These insights are reviewed here according to where they fall in the interdisciplinary process.

Readers interested in a single example of how to apply the interdisciplinary research process to a research problem might want to start with Chapter 2 by Marilyn Tayler. It offers the most explicit and thorough application of

Repko's steps in the book. As such, it stands as a model of how to use those steps to think through and carry out an interdisciplinary research project.

Connor (Chapter 3) sees an interdisciplinary process organized into steps as one way to achieve an "interdisciplinary synthesis for metropolitan studies," one that avoids the "episodic, ad hoc, and often contentious" nature of other ways that have been attempted. For him, the step of "identifying and evaluating conflicts" actually preceded Repko's Step 1 of problem definition. For me, that reinforces the interpretation of the interdisciplinary process as containing so many feedback loops that one can break into it at any point, even though one eventually ends up completing all the steps (and perhaps redoing those done out of sequence).

Students of IDS should take note that even though the "ultimate goal" of Connor's research may be to help metropolitan studies as a whole become more explicitly interdisciplinary, his strategy, like that of so many contributors to this volume, is to focus his research question so that it is narrowly delineated in time and space and let any larger implications emerge as they will. Interdisciplinarity is no enemy to specialization, and it is distinguished not by the breadth of its focus (though it can get very broad, indeed), nor by its depth (which can be as deep as the disciplinary insights on which it draws), but by the complexity of that focus. Put differently, interdisciplinary scholars can have a variety of different objectives that drive their work. Even though they are dealing with complex problems (and require an interdisciplinary approach to do so successfully), they do not all have the objective of trying to *solve* those problems. In Connor's case, his objective is to get other scholars to refocus where they *look* for problems by reexamining assumptions about the spatial locus of those problems, from urban areas to metropolitan areas, and then to demonstrate that they will understand metropolitan areas and their problems better if they take a more explicitly interdisciplinary approach.

In evaluating the appropriateness of an interdisciplinary approach, Van der Lecq shows that it can be useful even when all the theories are based in evolution. Henry and Bracy take the position that to qualify as appropriate for interdisciplinary analysis, a social problem should exhibit complexity, connectivity, polytely, opacity, and temporality.

Interspersed throughout the book are evaluative summaries of the potential contributions to interdisciplinary research of a large assortment of disciplines, subdisciplines, schools of thought, transdisciplinary approaches, interdisciplines, and even integrative theories. Each summary is tailored, of course, to the particular phenomenon or question, and the coverage is neither comprehensive nor systematic. Still, students and even faculty can gain much from mining these chapters for clues about which perspectives might be useful for their own interdisciplinary research project. Such knowledge is particularly useful to students who are not yet immersed in the complicated but important distinctions among fields and specialties. Tayler goes beyond most other contributors in adding some observations about differences between the humanities and social sciences as a whole.

Instead of asking (as Repko suggests) which disciplines have something to say about economic growth, Szostak asks which phenomena, theories, or methods are implicated in the issue and then which disciplines study or utilize them. Approaching interdisciplinary research that way, he finds that parts of all social science and some humanities are perceived as relevant. Unlike Van der Lecq or Keestra, Szostak finds himself drawing almost exclusively on disciplinary theories (instead of interdisciplines or narrow-gauge interdisciplinary studies), many of which do not discuss economic growth directly. That is probably because scholars from disciplines other than economics have not yet perceived that they can productively examine economic growth. (Referring to it as "economic" growth might have something to do with that perception.) In general, interdisciplinarians are probably well advised to let the majority of experts on which they draw determine whether they focus on theories, concepts, or assumptions.

A focus on mechanism-based explanations makes one appreciate the extent to which disciplines can talk past one another because they focus not just on different aspects of a complex issue but also on different levels of analysis. It helps clarify more precisely for interdisciplinarians at which level, as well as for which aspect, of the complex problem each discipline is developing its insights.

Tayler's strategy for creating common ground is not only to minimize the amount of change in a concept or assumption, but also to wield each technique for creating common ground in the way that is most responsive to, or best accommodates, the other aspects of the complex question as a whole. Thus, she steps back to see conflicting concepts or assumptions in the context of the overall phenomenon as well as focusing in on precise areas of overlap and non-overlap in their meaning.

Szostak's focus is on "achieving" common ground among conflicting theory-based insights. He differs from economics-based approaches to economic growth by foregrounding the cultural, social, and political contexts—what he calls "deeper causal influences"—shaping conventional economic variables (what Snowdon [2002] calls "proximate causes" of economic growth). He cautions that careful attention to the wording of the question asked about economic growth is required: If interdisciplinarians accept uncritically the wording of economists, the resulting research is likely to be less broadly interdisciplinary. He expands not only the variables of economists, but their assumptions about causal agents (methodological individualism expanded to include relationships and groups) and decision making (rationality expanded to include tradition, intuition, and rules of thumb; certainty expanded to include uncertainty).

Regarding common ground, Szostak (Chapter 6) emphasizes that disciplinary insights need to be critiqued when they are merely different as well as when they are conflicting. Differences in terminology may mean disciplines are talking about different causal processes, even if they appear at first blush to be talking about the same thing and disagreeing.

The easiest path to creating common ground involves relaxing the assumption made by each discipline that only its phenomena matter. . . . When different disciplines reach different conclusions regarding the same phenomena, the problem is often one of excessive generalization, and it can thus be solved by more carefully expressing the range of applicability of the theories involved.

As Henry and Bracy briefly discuss the creation of common ground via conceptual integration, they raise a question not previously discussed in the professional IDS literature, namely, the extent to which disciplinary perspectives need to be taken into account in the redefinition of concepts. They take the position that, much like the integration of insights, one test of appropriate redefinition is whether it is responsive to each discipline's perspective but dominated by none of them. Because I think it is rare for a disciplinary concept to be redefined to such an extent that its perspective no longer dominates the meaning of the concept, interdisciplinarians would do well to ponder whether they need to rethink how they go about redefinition, or whether this test is excessive. They also point out that there are as-yet-unexamined parallels between the interdisciplinary technique of redefinition and the "conceptual blending" that some cognitive psychologists assert occurs naturally.

Connor observes that

Differences in disciplinary terminology in this case cannot be resolved simply by identifying a common name for phenomena that crosses disciplinary boundaries. An adequate redefinition of terms must necessarily address the multiple parallel descriptors of metropolitan places; recognize that they refer to legal, political, cultural, and geographic qualities of places; and seek to substitute inclusive and expansive concepts for narrow and exclusive ones. (Chapter 3)

Keestra discusses in some detail how the challenge of creating common ground is quite different when the task facing the interdisciplinarian is to integrate components and operations into a mechanism instead of integrating concepts/variables into a theory. The "assumptions" that underlie components and operations (and the mechanism they constitute) are likewise quite different from those underlying concepts: Although both involve definitions, the former take the form of assumptions about how to decompose the phenomenon under study, which components and operations to include, how they are internally arranged, how they interact with their context or environment (including higher and lower levels), and how all this varies for different categories of people. For mechanisms comprising (lower-level) mechanisms, additional assumptions must be made about the interactions of those constituent mechanisms.

In evaluating theories, Van der Lecq demonstrates the usefulness of critical test analysis. She also evaluates theories by testing them against the pool of information to which research from all the perspectives contributed. And she reveals that complex systems theory can be useful in explaining otherwise inexplicable characteristics (e.g., tree structuring, excessive complexity and power of language) of the information base against which the competing theories are tested. Because interdisciplinary studies focuses on complex problems, issues, or questions, more interdisciplinarians should follow her lead and see how much of the pattern in the empirical evidence might be attributable to the nature of complexity itself. This would seem to be an appropriate early substep in the construction of a more comprehensive understanding.

It turns out that, well off the radar of most interdisciplinarians, a sizeable group of criminologists has developed the specialty of integrative criminology, in which they have addressed at great length and with impressive sophistication a literature on issues of theory integration that interdisciplinarians have only very recently started to consider. In their chapter on school violence, Henry and Bracy succinctly summarize and categorize the range of strategies and techniques they employ with reference to violent crime as a whole and then sketch out how they might be applied to school violence and what kinds of implications an interdisciplinary analysis based on them might have for policy. Although a number of other chapters engage in theory integration, readers seeking an overview of the range and kinds of strategies available for interdisciplinary theory integration might wish to start with Chapter 9.

Henry and Bracy start their discussion of theory integration by identifying five motives for integrating that implicitly suggest slightly different ways of thinking about integration. They identify four different categories of responses in integrative criminology to the "What should be integrated?" question: concepts (in the creation of common ground), propositions, causes, and levels. Drawing on the work of Liska, Krohn, and Messner (1989), they identify three possible types of logical relationships between propositions requiring integration: end to end, side by side, and up and down. They use these categories repeatedly and to good effect; indeed, these categories seem to offer a useful way for interdisciplinarians to organize their thinking about which set of integrative strategies to choose from.

Henry and Bracy identify four types of causal relations—linear, multiple, interactive, and dialectic/reciprocal—that seem to be a useful place for interdisciplinarians to start thinking about how causes seem to be related overall in the particular complex problem under consideration. For me, the multiple category subsumes two quite different and highly significant possibilities— the causal factors are relatively independent (as assumed by most forms of multivariate statistical analysis), and the causal factors are relatively highly interdependent (as is likely to be the case in complex phenomena, which are the focus of interdisciplinary study). Following Muschert (2007), they acknowledge 13 categories of "causes" of school violence operating on the levels of individual, community, and social/cultural contexts; they report that some scholars see them as not only interacting but nested (though they appropriately challenge scholars to pay close attention to the nature and strength of the interlevel linkages).

In their emphasis throughout the chapter on the importance of levels of causation and the linkages among them, Henry and Bracy take the most explicitly complex systems-based approach to integration of any chapter. Even more than other authors in the book, they emphasize the need for multi-level integration—micro, meso, macro—that addresses people, organizations, and cultures.

Regarding theory development, Szostak (following Singleton & Strait, 1999) identifies "four criteria for identifying a causal relationship: establishing correlation, establishing temporality (the cause should generally appear before the effect), ruling out alternative explanations of the result, and showing how the causal relationship unfolds in practice (including identifying intermediate variables)." These criteria are presumably necessary but not sufficient for evaluating interdisciplinary theories as well. He thinks "examining different causal links in turn (but not losing sight of emergent properties of systems)" should be carried out in tandem with the approach of complexity theory: "allowing different causal forces to operate along different links, [without assuming] any particular organizing principle (such as equilibrium) at the outset."

In constructing her interdisciplinary model, Van der Lecq starts with a base theory already incorporating both/and thinking and theory extension (cultural niche construction), rather than creating a new theory out of pieces of existing theories. That theory takes well-known facts normally treated as exogenous to the theory (especially alteration of their environments by organisms) and makes them endogenous to the extended theory and mutually interactive within it. A second theory (grooming and gossip) connects to the base theory by helping to explain one of its key elements (niche construction). A third theory (relevance for status) helps explain how another key element (communication) of the base theory operates. A fourth theory explains a prediction of the base theory (that language becomes more complex over time). Tayler and Repko use similar strategies. Interdisciplinarians ought to start collecting examples of such base theories and comparing them because they potentially offer insights into how to initiate the construction of a more comprehensive understanding. This theory seems to use the strategy of identifying parallel interactive processes, what might be called the "co-"strategy.

Connor's integration takes two forms: *spatial* integration at the metropolitan or regional (as opposed to urban or suburban) scale and *analytical* integration through attention to the legal, political, and cultural dimensions of relationships between metropolitan places. Thus, he seeks "a theory capable of extending across disciplinary domains to address the spatial assumptions of each perspective." He selects Lefebvre's (1991) "theory of the social production of space" in spite of what he sees as its shortcomings because it "supports a more integrated form of metropolitan study." To carry out his research based on that theory, he finds that he needs to strategically alter the traditional case study method of history because of its limiting spatial assumptions.

He reminds us (following Charles Tilly, 1996) that when dealing with complex systems (as all IDS do), time's arrow is not reversible. One of the tests he uses for the appropriateness of a theory is that it recognizes (or is compatible with) "historical contingency": The way things happen to play out constrains and shapes what is possible (or at least likely) thereafter. In more technical terms, complex processes are "path dependent."

Repko identifies two strategies for constructing a more comprehensive, interdisciplinary theory: Use both/and thinking to combine the good parts of theories, and expand one theory by adding elements (especially variables) from other theories. He advocates the former unless a (more narrowly) inter-disciplinary theory is available for expansion, as is the case with suicide ter-rorism. That theory, Monroe and Kreidie's (1997) identity theory, already addresses three of the four causal factors identified in the literature, and the fourth can be included with the least "stretching and pulling." He focuses on the goals of terrorists themselves as he reconciles theories, evaluates their strengths and weaknesses, and ends up using both/and thinking to extend the concept of rationality to include moral and religious beliefs. He makes use of factors at both individual and societal levels.

Integration of "insights" again takes on a somewhat different meaning when the interdisciplinarian is using mechanisms, not theories, to explain a complex phenomenon. As Keestra conceives it, the process involves using insights from another discipline to refine or extend the mechanism chosen to serve as common ground (remembering, of course, that a mechanism may be a cluster of mechanisms or even a cluster of clusters of mechanisms). He points out that the interactions between component mechanisms within a cluster of mechanisms need to be reexamined whenever the overall mecha-nism is refined or extended because the operation and internal organization of other components can be altered as a result.

Szostak points out that methods tend to complement some types of theories better than others. Thus, one might infer that when interdisciplinary theories are developed, the methods used to test them will probably need to be modified accordingly. (Connor makes this point regarding metropolitan studies specifically.) Szostak recommends comparative case studies as a com-plement to standard multivariate statistical analysis. He suggests that when testing an interdisciplinary understanding of economic growth, the researcher should focus not only on the interdisciplinary theory as a whole, but empirically test the causal links separately, using multiple methods.

Meta-Discussions of Interdisciplinary Research Process

For readers skeptical in any way about the feasibility, or even the desirability, of an interdisciplinary research process, Szostak's chapter on the interdiscipli-nary research process (Chapter 1) examines the issues probably underlying that skepticism and addresses them head on. Szostak also looks at a range of prominent alternative understandings of inter- and transdisciplinarity research for the ways in which they are compatible with an IDS research process.

His chapter suggests to me that there is enormous latitude within the interdisciplinary research process as currently conceived, such that fears of constrained freedom are unnecessary. Indeed, in some ways structure can be freeing: One can avoid reinventing wheels (or worse, failing to reinvent them) to permit a focus on those distinctive challenges of the particular research topic at hand. Beyond that, Szostak sees advantages to a shared interdisciplinary methodology. More important, following Augsburg and Henry (2009), he points out that interdisciplinarians need to be able to demonstrate to skeptics the standards that distinguish rigorous from superficial interdisciplinary work. As he implies, the age of the amateur interdisciplinarian is (hopefully) drawing to a close.

Szostak makes the argument that interdisciplinarians need to be able to engage in what Kuhn called *normal science* because a standard of revolutionary science would exclude most interdisciplinarians. Although I agree (as my comments on the distinction between fully and partially interdisciplinary research suggest), I do think that there is some potential, at least, for revolutionary science in almost any research that completes all the steps in the interdisciplinary process.

I find appealing his distinction between disciplinary and specialized research. One can reject disciplinarity (though I do not) and still accept the need for specialization in research. As with amateurs in interdisciplinarity teaching, I would argue that the age of the amateur interdisciplinary researcher must come to an end as well.

Perhaps the key point Szostak makes in his review of a number of recently published overviews of interdisciplinary research is that most of the literature on interdisciplinary team research fails to make the distinction between the cognitive and social challenges of interdisciplinarity. Clearly, the interdisciplinary research process exemplified by the chapters in this book focuses exclusively on the cognitive challenges of doing interdisciplinary work and ignores the social (and one might add intersectoral, political, gendered, and cultural) challenges. In some ways, that is a good thing. As those chapters make abundantly clear, those cognitive challenges are considerable. Moreover, they can too easily be overlooked, and often are, in discussions of team interdisciplinary research and transdisciplinary research. On the other hand, it is easy for those of us caught up in trying to understand interdisciplinary research cognitively to overlook these other real-world challenges.

Klein's history of the concept of integration identifies for scholars of interdisciplinarity the various professional literatures from which insights might be sought and adapted to current understandings of interdisciplinary integration. To those understandings, transdisciplinarity in its most recent form adds the interests of stakeholders in the perspectives of disciplines (broadly conceived) as sources of insight as well as barriers to overcome in achieving integration. Because those stakeholders can be located in different institutions, sectors, and strata of society, interdisciplinarity takes on the added dimension of intersectoral/interinstitutional political integration.

Klein responds to Repko's observation that interdisciplinarians need to reconcile different disciplinary denotations and connotations of a term by offering metaphors from linguistics (e.g., pidgin, Creole), strategic use of everyday language, and "bridging concepts" as strategies for coming up with common definitions of terms.

Klein identifies a wide range of methods that can be used to construct a more comprehensive understanding:

> systems theory and modeling, integrated environmental assessment and risk management, Delphi and scenario building, simulation, concept mapping, and computer synthesis of data and information flow. Other proven methods facilitate communication and common understanding, including mental mapping of stakeholder views, consensus conferences, collaborative learning, and collaborative workspaces. (Chapter 10)

She highlights the TIPS approach developed at the Swiss Federal Institute of Technology—"standing for Transdisciplinary Integrated Planning and Synthesis, TIPS embeds formal, scientific, integrated planning in a real-world setting"—and frameworks—"'idea tanks' that help to integrate different disciplinary perspectives and organizing blocks of insights while structuring the core issue of a project or program in a systematic process." And she discusses at length how to deal with the added interpersonal dimension when integration is carried out by a team instead of a solo interdisciplinarian.

Klein identifies several strategies—moving back and forth, bootstrapping, triangulation, and reflective balancing and weaving—that seem especially promising when adapted for the construction of a more comprehensive understanding. She also points to "comparing and contrasting multiple resources, discovering patterns, and making connections."

Conclusion

As noted above, interdisciplinary research should be conceived as a cumulative process in which interdisciplinarians build upon the work of both specialized researchers and other interdisciplinarians. The question of how to best perform (and teach others to perform) interdisciplinary research is itself a complex question worthy of cumulative interdisciplinary investigation. This book advances our understanding of the interdisciplinary research process while also suggesting avenues for further research. I and my co-editors look forward to continuing the conversation, and we thank all the contributors for their diligence and insights.

References

Augsburg, T., & Henry, S. (Eds.). (2009). *The politics of interdisciplinary studies: Interdisciplinary transformation in undergraduate American higher education.* Jefferson, NC: McFarland.

Lefebvre, H. (1991). *The production of space.* Oxford and Cambridge: Blackwell.

Liska, A. E., Krohn, M. D., & Messner, S. F. (1989). Strategies and requisites for theoretical integration in the study of deviance and crime. In S. F. Messner, M. D. Krohn, & A. E. Liska (Eds.), *Theoretical integration in the study of deviance and crime* (pp. 1–19). Albany: State University of New York Press.

Monroe, K. R., & Kreidie, L. H. (1997). The perspective of Islamic fundamentalisms and the limits of rational choice theory. *Political Psychology, 18*(1), 19–43.

Muschert, G. W. (2007). Research in school shootings. *Sociology Compass, 1*(1), 60–80.

Richards, D. (1996). The meaning and relevance of "synthesis" in interdisciplinary studies. *The Journal of General Education, 45*(2), 114–128.

Singleton, R. A., Jr., & Strait, B. C. (1999). *Approaches to social research* (3rd ed.). New York: Oxford University Press.

Snowdon, B. (2002). *Conversations on growth, stability, and trade: A historical perspective.* Cheltenham: Edward Elgar.

Tilly, C. (1996). What good is urban history? *Journal of Urban History, 22*(6), 702–719. doi:10.1177/009614429602200603

Author Index _____

Greene, J. R., 274
Greif, A., 176, 179
Grossenbacher-Mansuy, W., 15, 16,
    17, 18, 287
Grossman, J. R., 58

Haas, P., 259, 260
Habermas, J., 295
Hacking, I., 230
Hagan, J., 261
Hage, J., 174
Hall, K., 287, 288, 294
Hall, K. L., 11, 13, 14, 15
Han, S. H., 227, 250
Hard, B. M., 241
Harding, D. J., 271, 274, 275
Harris, R., 56
Harvey, D., 57
Hauser, M. D., 197
Hawkins, J. D., 261
Hayden, D., 56, 78
Haynes, C., 139, 250
Henry, S., 5, 8, 260, 261, 262, 263,
    265, 267, 269, 270, 272, 273,
    274, 275, 276, 277, 278, 312
Hirsch Hadorn, G., 6, 15, 16, 17, 18,
    283, 287, 288, 289, 290, 291
Hirschi, T., 261, 266
Hise, G., 78
Hobbs, F., 53
Hoch, C. M., 55, 75, 78
Hoffmann-Riem, H., 15, 16, 17,
    18, 287
Hollis, M., 245
Horowitz, D., 15, 34
HoSang, D. W., 78
Hotaling, G. T., 275
Hronick, M. S., 125
Huber, M. T., 286
Hudson, R. A., 130, 134, 143
Hunter, R. D., 273
Hurford, J. R., 208
Hurley, S., 239, 249
Hursh, B., 259, 260
Hutchings, P., 286
Hutto, D. D., 243

Iacoboni, M., 245

Jackson, K. T., 60, 78
Jacobsohn, G. J., 34
Jahn, T., 15, 16, 17, 292, 294
Jenkins, P. H., 274

Joerin, F., 16, 295
Johnson, M., 231
Johnson, R. E., 261
Joye, D., 15, 16, 17, 18, 287

Katz, S. N., 58
Kaufmann-Hayoz, R., 290
Keating, A. D., 59
Keestra, M., 247, 252
Kelley, A., 275
Kelly, J., 294
Kennedy, H., 78, 79
Kirlin, J., 75
Kitchen, J., 63
Klein, J. T., xv, xvii, 9, 14, 15, 18, 26,
    27, 95, 128, 233, 259, 283, 285,
    286, 287, 288, 289, 295
Knight, C., 208
Knowlton, B. J., 230
Ko, S. J., 275
Kohli, A., 175
Korazim-Körösy, Y., 183
Kreidie, L. H., 48, 133, 134, 138, 140,
    141, 151, 152, 154, 311
Krohn, M. D., 259, 261, 266, 269, 309
Kruglanski, A. W., 246
Kruse, K. M., 56, 61, 62
Kuhn, T., 5
Kumar, S., 241

Lakoff, G., 231
Lal, D., 175
Laland, K. N., 203, 204, 205, 206,
    207, 208, 221
Lane, L., 82
Lanier, M. M., 260, 262, 265, 270, 273
Lassiter, M. D., 61
Laub, J., 274
Lefebvre, H., 57, 58, 73, 310
Lewis, B., 135, 138, 140, 143, 151, 152
Lewis, R., 56
Lincoln, A. J., 275
Linkon, S., xix
Lipsitz, G., 60, 78
Liska, A. E., 259, 261, 266, 269, 309
Lissak, M., 34, 35
Lockwood, D., 275
Loeber, R., 275
Lorberbaum, M., 45, 46
Lozano, S. C., 241

Machamer, P., 240
MacNeilage, P. F., 197

Subject Index _____

SAGE Research Methods Online

The essential tool for researchers

Sign up now at www.sagepub.com/srmo for more information.

An expert research tool

- An **expertly designed taxonomy** with more than 1,400 unique terms for social and behavioral science research methods

- **Visual and hierarchical search tools** to help you discover material and link to related methods

- Easy-to-use navigation tools
- Content organized by complexity
- Tools for citing, printing, and downloading content with ease
- Regularly updated content and features

A wealth of essential content

- The most comprehensive picture of quantitative, qualitative, and mixed methods available today

- More than **100,000 pages of SAGE book and reference material** on research methods as well as editorially selected material from SAGE journals

- More than **600 books** available in their entirety online

Launching 2011!

$SAGE research methods online

Manufactured by Amazon.ca
Acheson, AB

12227856R00201